Explorations in Theology and Film

When I was a little younger ... I wanted to be a priest. However, I soon realised that my real vocation, my real calling, was the movies. I don't really see a conflict between the church and the movies, the sacred and the profane. Obviously, there are major differences. But I can also see great similarities between a church and a movie-house. Both are places for people to come together and share a common experience.

And I believe there's a spirituality in films, even if it's not one which can supplant faith. I find that over the years many films address themselves to the spiritual side of human nature. From Griffith's Intolerance *to John Ford's* The Grapes of Wrath, *to Hitchcock's* Vertigo, *to Kubrick's* 2001, *and so many more. It's as if movies answer an ancient quest for the common unconscious. They fulfil a spiritual need that people have: to share a common memory.*

Martin Scorsese *The Century of Cinema: A Personal Journey* **(1996)**

Explorations in Theology and Film

Movies and Meaning

Edited by Clive Marsh and Gaye Ortiz

BLACKWELL
Publishers

Copyright © Blackwell Publishers Ltd, 1997

First published 1997
Reprinted 1998, 1999, 2000
Copyright © Blackwell Publishers Ltd,

Blackwell Publishers Ltd
108 Cowley Road
Oxford OX4 1JF, UK

Blackwell Publishers Inc.
350 Main Street
Malden, Massachusetts 02148,
USA

British Library Cataloguing in Publication Data
A CIP catalogue record for this book is available from the British Library.

Library of Congress Cataloging in Publication Data

Explorations in theology and film : movies and meaning / edited by
    Clive Marsh and Gaye Ortiz.
        p.   cm.
    Includes bibliographical references and index.
    ISBN 0–631–20355–9 (alk. paper). — ISBN 0–631–20356–7 (pbk. :
alk. paper)
    1. Motion pictures—Religious aspects. I. Marsh, Clive.
II. Ortiz, Gaye.
    PN1995.5.E96   1997
791.43'682—dc21   97–10393
                                                              CIP

Typeset in 10 on 12pt Ehrhardt
by SetSystem Ltd, Saffron Walden, Essex
Printed in Great Britain by Athenaeum Press Ltd, Gateshead, Tyne & Wear

This book is printed on acid-free paper.

Contents

Contributors

ROBERT BANKS is Professor of the Ministry of the Laity at Fuller Theological Seminary, Pasadena, and Executive Director of the De Pree Center for Leadership there. He is also Chair of the Planning Committee for the annual City of Angels Film Festival in Los Angeles and has written books on early and contemporary Christian ideas of community, as well as on the theology and ethics of everyday life.

STEPHEN BRIE is a lecturer in Literature and Screen Studies at Liverpool Hope University College. He is also a freelance television director and is currently undertaking research into the television dramatist Dennis Potter.

STEPHEN BROWN is priest-in-charge in the parish of Ripley with Burnt Yates, and Officer for Local Ministry in the Anglican Diocese of Ripon, England. He has been Anglican Chaplain to Yorkshire Television since 1989, and involved with the relationship between theology and film for two decades. He has worked with Interfilm on European film festival juries and co-ordinated, with Gaye Ortiz, a fringe event *Faith and Film* for the 1993 Leeds International Film Festival. This became a part of the official festival in 1996.

DAVID BROWNE is Principal Lecturer in Theatre, Film and Television Studies at the University College of Ripon and York St John. His particular academic interest is British cinema. His professional career has included work in broadcasting, theatre, and regional arts. He has published a book, *That's the Way* (1982), to accompany a Yorkshire Television series, and is currently a subject specialist assessor for media and communications for the Higher Education Funding Council for England.

DAVID JOHN GRAHAM lectures in New Testament both at the Glasgow Bible College and in the Faculty of Divinity of the University of Glasgow, Scotland. He is a specialist in the Gospel of Matthew. His *Matthew* appears in the Routledge "New Testament Readings" series, and he is working on a commentary on the Gospel for the publisher Eerdmans. Originally a geologist, he keeps alive his interest in science and religion through Open University tutoring in Earth Science, and through a course at the University of Glasgow on "Science and Belief."

DAVID JASPER is a Reader in the Faculty of Divinity at the University of Glasgow, and Director of the Centre for the Study of Literature and Theology. A prolific writer, his recent publications include *The Study of Literature and Religion* (2nd edn Macmillan 1992), *Rhetoric, Power and Community: An Exercise in Reserve* (Macmillan 1993), and *Readings in the Canon of Scripture* (Macmillan 1995)

ROBERT JEWETT is the Harry R. Kendall Senior Professor of New Testament Interpretation at Garrett-Evangelical Theological Seminary in Evanston, Illinois, USA. A specialist in the writings and theology of the Apostle Paul, his recent work includes: *St. Paul at the Movies* (Westminster/John Knox 1993) and *Paul the Apostle to America: Cultural Trends and Pauline Scholarship* (Westminster/John Knox 1994). He is currently working on a commentary on Paul's Letter to the Romans.

IAN MAHER is an evangelist in the Church Army (UK). He has worked in an inner-London parish, co-ordinated The Certificate in Evangelism Studies, an ecumenical course, and is now tutor in ethics and world religions at the Wilson Carlile College of Evangelism, Sheffield.

PETER MALONE is an Australian Roman Catholic priest who lectures and writes on film. His books include *Cinema Down Under, Worth Watching: 30 Film Reviewers on Review* and *Movie Christs and Anti-Christs.* He is President of the Pacific Region of OCIC (the International Catholic Organization for Cinema), and is in charge of the Film Office of the Australian Bishops' Conference.

CLIVE MARSH lectures in theology, religious and cultural studies at the University College of Ripon and York St John, England, and in the Biblical Studies Department of the University of Sheffield. His interests include the history of quests of the historical Jesus, and modern and contemporary systematic theology. He is currently working on a book on Christology, using art and film as resource material.

GAYE ORTIZ lectures in theology, religious and cultural studies at the University College of Ripon and York St John, England, and is a media writer and broadcaster, specializing in theology and the media. She is a member of the Catholic Theological Association of Great Britain and a founder member of the Leeds Diocesan Media Commission. As a member of OCIC (the International Catholic Organization for Cinema) she has served on international film festival juries, twice as jury president. Together with Stephen Brown she has co-ordinated *Faith and Film* for the Leeds International Film Festival.

DAVID RHOADS is Professor of New Testament at the Lutheran School of Theology at Chicago, Illinois. His 1982 work *Mark as Story* (written with

D. Michie) has been highly influential, as has his essay of the same year "Narrative Criticism and the Gospel of Mark." He continues to be interested in literary and social scientific approaches to the Gospels but in recent years has also been undertaking dramatic performances of New Testament texts, including the Gospel of Mark, the book of Revelation, the Letter to the Galatians and the Sermon on the Mount. He has just published *The Challenge of Diversity: The Witness of Paul and the Gospels* (Fortress 1996).

SANDRA ROBERTS is ordained in the Lutheran church in the USA and is chaplain of the county jail in Kenosha, Wisconsin. She is a certified Pastoral Counsellor with the American Association of Marriage and Family Therapy.

VAUGHAN ROBERTS is Diocesan Vocations Advisor and vicar of three rural parishes in the Anglican Diocese of Bath and Wells, in the West of England. Until recently he was Anglican Chaplain to the University of Bath, where he also taught in the School of Education and in the Centre for Continuing Education.

MAGGIE ROUX is Senior Lecturer in the School of Media at Trinity and All Saints University College, Leeds, England. She is a member of the Central Religious Advisory Committee to the BBC and ITC, a founder member of the Leeds Diocesan Media Commission, and a member of OCIC (the International Catholic Organization for Cinema). She is a regular broadcaster on media, film and religious issues.

WILLIAM R. TELFORD lectures in Christian Origins and the New Testament in the Department of Religious Studies at the University of Newcastle, England. A specialist in the Gospel of Mark, he has recently published a revised edition of *The Interpretation of Mark* (T & T Clark 1995), *Mark* (Sheffield Academic Press 1995), and is shortly to complete *The Theology of the Gospel of Mark* (Cambridge University Press). He has taught a Bible and Literature course (including film) in Newcastle for a number of years, and is Degree Programme Co-Director for the MA in Religion and Literature.

DAVID TOREVELL is a Senior Lecturer in the Department of Theology and Religious Studies at Liverpool Hope University College. His main research at present is ritual studies, though he is also interested in Christian-Buddhist dialogue and contemporary Christian worship. With Stephen Brie, he runs a highly popular and successful undergraduate course on Theology Through Film.

Plates

Introduction

Clive Marsh and Gaye Ortiz

For one of the contributors to this book, the project began life with an
overheard conversation in a pizza parlour on a Saturday evening in North
London, England, in the late 1980s. Most of those who had queued for tables
had just spilled out from a nearby cinema; the place was packed out; the
discussion was lively. There was a heated discussion going on around at least
one table. An informal theology seminar was in progress. Of course, the
participants in that discussion may well have been regular churchgoers who
would dutifully turn up at mass/communion/morning service on the following day. It is, however, unlikely that either on that day, or on many others
in the life of local churches, such an involved theological discussion, directly
relating to affairs in the world, would have occured. This is sad, but it is
true. Theological debate happens in the church. But there it is conducted
more often than not by recognized theologians. It sometimes happens outside
the church – with Christians involved, but many others too (of explicit
religious affiliation, or not) – though it often takes shape there in a rather
different way. As we have seen in recent times, sometimes the media seize
upon a religious scandal, provoking public debate in the press and over the
airwaves. Sometimes, all manner of people argue publicly about religious and
theological matters with a passion which often puts regular churchgoers to
shame.

There has been for some time, however, a concern throughout Christian
churches in the West to foster lay training, adult theological education, and to
stimulate theological debate. Yet the concern to ensure that such training,
education or discussion is "informed" often means in practice that it is less
creative or exploratory than it might be. For "informed" often means, in
practice, that it "conforms." Christian orthodoxy is then not expanded,
reinterpreted or rediscovered. It is not introduced as a vital resource into a
lively debate about human life, and the ground of human life, but functions
simply as a means of assessing whether or not something is really Christian or

not (as if Christianity itself, and the God whom Christians worship, were clear-cut, fully known, with no element of mystery about them).

Meanwhile, millions of people watch films. Christians are among them. The thinking of Christians (their theology) is thus in part informed by their cinemagoing and video-viewing. And the theological/religious/ideological viewpoints of those who would not wish to call themselves Christian are likewise in part influenced by movie-watching. Theological discussion is therefore stimulated by this worldly activity whether churches like it or not. Christians are contributors to this discussion, learning from others in the process. That such activity goes on has consequences for the way the very task of theology is understood to work. This dynamic is a feature of this book, though not the main focus. Our concern in this book is to pass on some of the results of conversations in which most of us have ourselves been involved, and to push these discussions further. Most, but not all, of the contributors write explicitly from a Christian perspective: they are seeking to undertake creative Christian theology in conversation with films, knowing that films provide so much of the "cultural currency" in which discussion about life and death (and life and depth) issues are conducted. Most of the contributors are teachers or tutors of one form or another; most are teachers or tutors of a branch of theology.

With this book, we are adding to a genre of literature which has existed for nearly three decades. In our view, though, much of the "theology and film" debate has been too general to be helpful to those who stand within particular religious traditions and who want to engage with the questions (and sometimes answers) which films offer, sometimes tentatively and elusively, to situations in human life. We have tried to begin to suggest how theology (as opposed to religion) can work with film in a creative way, acknowledging that baggage – in the way of attitudes, beliefs and values – is being brought to a film. Baggage is brought by all interpreters to any work of art in order to undertake interpretation at all. It has to be. In our case, the issue is whether that baggage is going to help justice to be done to the subject-matter of a particular film, and to provide insight into life/reality as a result of the conversation. In the process, the adequacy, and potential modification, of any (Christian theological) baggage brought will be being tested. If the conversation proves fruitful, then all sorts of possibilities open up. Movies offer resource material for theologians to expand their understanding and/or check out the contemporary adequacy of an aspect of Christian theology. Students of film are presented with a possible conversation partner in the task of interpretation before them. Christian workers and ministers whose task is to explicate Christian faith, or support people in their discovery of the value (or not) of Christian faith in today's world, are provided with a way of integrating a potentially valuable resource into their work without disrespecting the integrity of the art-medium being used.

It is, however, both the right and wrong time to be publishing this book. It is a timely book in so far as it acknowledges that students of theology very often bring little basic knowledge of biblical narratives, religious traditions, or Western literature and culture to their study. Bernard Brandon Scott begins his book on film and biblical study with an account of his own realization that he needed to undergo a conversion experience, given the screen literacy of his students (Scott 1994: ix). Similarly, in film and media studies, though screen literacy may often be very high indeed, attentiveness to religious symbolism and theological tradition – both implicit and explicit in so many Western films – may not. Christian theology's influence upon Western art, from ancient to contemporary, is frequently overlooked, if not ignored. In both disciplines, then, this book is sorely needed.

In another sense, the book comes at a bad time. Christian theology itself is changing. Under the influence of contemporary currents in Western cultures – often brought together under the single heading of "postmodernism" – Christian theology in the West is poised to develop in a number of different directions. In some quarters it is welcoming the seemingly liberating influence of the openness of postmodernism in its most extreme version. Under the impact of a realization that "all is text" (and that God is a necessary fiction), it would be feasible for theology to accept that it is one ideology amongst many, the truth of which cannot be established but must be asserted as one consensus amongst many. Films, as works of art (some of which attain "classic status"), resist closure, i.e. it cannot be said of a film that it has a single, definitive meaning. In the contemporary climate, then, film analysis and theological construction may well be able to join forces. But if so, film is unlikely to engage in easy conversation with a defined theological tradition labelled "Christian theology." Postmodern religion (and theology) must by definition be less systematic than any particular religion would like it to be. Postmodernism entails eclecticism, selectivity and leads inevitably in the end to the triumph of the individual. Diversity of interpretation brings with it radical diversity of belief. Whilst many forms of postmodernism seem to recommend a limitlessness to such interpretative freedom, theology is unlikely to be able to go so far. It is thus not in the least surprising that this possible direction of Christian theology in a postmodern climate is not one shared by all. This issue is one to which we shall need to return (in Part Three).

This book is best seen, though, as a contribution to the ongoing debate, one which takes seriously the challenge offered to the way in which "theology and film" discussions have often been conducted, yet one which takes issue with the relative neglect of film in the work of Christian theologians. The neglect may be attributable to cultural snobbishness or suspicion, a desire for doctrinal purity, a concern that theology be prevented from becoming too worldly, or a simple belief that the conversation is not very fruitful (no matter how good films may be). On the other hand, zealous evangelists may see film only as a proselytizing tool, to be used in a prescribed manner for showcasing a particular type of Christian message. Be that as it may, if Christian theology is not now to become a discussion between fewer and fewer people (i.e. if it is to acknowledge its public role and responsibility not merely in an arrogant, declamatory fashion), then the central question is not *whether* Christian theology converses with film, but *how*. This collection of studies addresses this question.

Part One of the book is scene-setting. The first two chapters try to introduce the respective disciplines on which the work draws – film studies and theology – to readers from both sides. Readers might find a whole chapter on each of those tough going, but should find one or other to be a summary of material with which they are already familiar. The third chapter begins to consider what happens when you put bring two sides together.

The essays on particular films, or groups of films, which form Part Two of the work, range widely in the genres of film and in their style of approach. Some are written by biblical scholars (e.g. Jewett, Telford). Others draw on the experience of practical Christian ministry and mission in the contemporary UK and the USA (e.g. Brown, Maher, Roberts, Rhoads and Roberts). All chapters make an attempt to hear the films in their own right, in the course of conducting a conversation with them. The films discussed were not directly chosen in order to address all the sub-themes of Christian theology (e.g. the doctrine of the trinity, human being, Jesus Christ, Holy Spirit, church, sacraments, eschatology); the selections were largely based on films that writers knew well and had worked with a number of times. Almost all contributors have shown the films selected, and led discussions on them, in a variety of settings, in contexts of formal and informal theological education. The studies offered here thus reflect the results of group interaction with film-watchers, Christian and otherwise, across three continents. Out of the many films that could have been chosen, however, the reader will note that a variety of themes from Christian theology are, in fact, addressed. We draw attention to this now, and shall return to the point in Part Three.

Aspects of Christian understanding of *what it means to be human*, and how human beings are to act, are taken up in the chapters on *Dead Poets Society*, *Groundhog Day*, and the *Terminator* films. The *corporate dimension to being human*, and the inevitable institutional elements and power issues which require examination (including those in the church) are considered in Vaughan Roberts' chapter. *Christology and salvation* are handled in a variety of different ways in the chapters by Peter Malone, William Telford, David Rhoads and Sandra Roberts, Robert Banks, Ian Maher and David Graham. A recurring theme throughout the book – receiving different answers from different contributors – is the extent to which it is possible or advisable to spend time hunting, or identifying, "Christ-figures" in film. The chapter by Malone offers an extended worked example of a Christ-figure, and Telford's chapter is a comprehensive survey of the way in which what may be termed the archetypal Christ-figure, Jesus, has been portrayed in the cinema. Telford also draws on some Christ types in his study. *Shirley Valentine* provides an opportunity to consider Christian *understandings of spirit/holy spirit*, and *Babette's Feast*, it is argued, requires attention through Christian reflection on *sacramental theology and practice* in order adequately to be engaged with as a film. Finally, Stephen Brown's chapter compares and contrasts a range of "feelgood movies" in relation to the Christian *theme of hope*.

This range of essays in no way provides a Christian systematic theology; they do not deal with all theological topics which one might expect to see addressed. Nor do they offer a systematic theology of film, in the sense that they treat all the topics which it may be felt that film (or even just the specific films considered) can handle theologically. For example, arguably any "human relationships" film provides material through which the doctrine of the trinity could, by analogy, be explored. Nor, again, does the collection of essays in Part Two pretend to be identifying *the* (only) way in which the films considered can be explored theologically. Our procedure for each chapter was simply to restrict the focus to a single film or small group of films, and to undertake some creative theological work in dialogue with the film/s in a limited way. The resulting theological reflection in each case is not intended to be exhaustive in its conclusions. Much more, theologically, needs to be said. The hope is merely that in a variety of ways this collection provides the stimulus for theological thinking and raises some legitimate, provocative (and not merely illustrative) points.

In Part Three, David Jasper offers a critical response to the material presented in Part Two. This in turn provides the opportunity for us as editors to have a "last word," using Jasper's insightful critique as a springboard for a proposal of where theology and film discussions should head next. The book closes with an annotated bibliography, which itself constitutes a useful resource list for those interested in taking further the links between theology and film, and a range of indices. There is a biblical index drawing together all the references to the Christian Bible used throughout the work, no matter which version is quoted (no attempt has been made to draw all the biblical quotations used from a single translation). Different authors have used different versions, including the Revised Standard Version, the New Revised Standard Version, the New International Version, the New Jerusalem Bible and the Revised English Bible.

This book has been long in the making and has found us working as a dispersed team across three continents. There have been groupings of contributors, and most of the British contributors managed to meet residentially twice to hone the project into precise shape. As editors we are most grateful to all the contributors for producing their material, and even for responding well when a bit of editorial bullying proved necessary in the final stages! Steve Nolan, Robert Jewett and David Rhoads provided particular help with bibliographical material. We record special thanks to Church Army (UK) for hosting the residential meetings of the British group. This project is seemingly far removed from so much of Church Army's work, yet is arguably related to its work at the sharpest of edges – how is the understanding and recommendation of a Christian perspective on human life at all possible today? – (thus: "to those who have ears . . ."). We are grateful to Martin Scorsese for showing early interest in this project; he has been pointing out for years the theological significance of movies in contemporary Western culture. In many ways, this book is an attempt to assess, from a different perspective from his own, how that significance takes practical shape. As moviegoers, we greatly respect his work and are delighted by his interest in our academic efforts. We also thank the British Film Institute for making available the stills used in this book. Finally, we express thanks to Alison Mudditt for taking the project on, and to the team at Blackwell for seeing it through.

Part One

Part One

1

Film, Movies, Meanings

David Browne

Cinema has just celebrated its centenary; one of the "youngest" arts, it rapidly became one of the most pervasive and powerful. The domination of particular centers of production (Hollywood, Bombay, Hong Kong) and the increasing technical ease of distribution and exhibition (satellite and cable transmission, distribution via videotape) gives film a truly global profile. Arnold Schwarzenegger and River Phoenix join John Wayne, Marilyn Monroe and others before them as "cultural icons." Film is massively popular; cinema attendance in the UK continues the upward trend of the past ten years to reach comfortably over 120 million annual admissions in 1995. Equally, the number of cinema screens in the UK continues to grow, and around 2,000 screens are predicted by the end of the century, including a number of 20/24 screen "multiplex" sites. Even feature film production in the UK, that much-abused Cinderella, currently enjoys yet another "renaissance." In 1989, 27 British films were in production; during 1995 there were 73. Cinema-going as a social activity, however, has a more specific profile. Social trends surveys tell us that regular cinema attendance is most clearly marked in the 16–25 age group as part of the "evening economy" of young peoples' lives. In the UK, as elsewhere, multiplex cinemas capitalize on the commercial opportunities afforded by this audience group, in the form of fast food, soft drinks, and tie-in merchandising. Cinema is increasingly part of a global leisure industry with a billion dollar turnover and exploitative connections across a complex range of "lifestyle" industry conglomerates. The latest "blockbuster" now competes for a global marketing share alongside soft drinks, sportswear and popular music, often as components within the same multinational enterprise. To most people "cinema" is thus identified and defined. It often stands accused of being vulgar, of trivializing or taking a tabloid approach to the stories it tells. It is accused of corrupting the young, debasing moral standards, being part of the fabric of social decline, promoting "mindless" entertainment. And yet, in its brief century it has produced sublime works of art which touch on the "human condition" with the compassion, grace, and skill of masterworks in other art-forms. Even at its most "commercial" one must not dismiss, to misquote Noël Coward, "the potency of cheap movies." As with the other arts, then, assertions can be treacherous. This chapter offers an overview of the "art" of film, and suggests other avenues of enquiry to the reader. It is not exhaustive, and not even comprehensive, but it does attempt to provide signposts for theologians who do not intend to become film theorists.

Film, alongside other creative and performing arts, is a hybrid. It may be helpful to regard it as being embedded in a matrix whose vertical axis signifies "realism" at one extremity and "fantasy" at the other, and a horizontal axis which polarizes "art" and "entertainment." Thus, in a crude graphical way, it is possible to "plot" individual films or film genres within this matrix. Thus the *Terminator* films lie somewhere within the "entertainment/fantasy" quadrant, whilst the films of British directors such as Ken Loach and Mike Leigh would be located within the "realism/art" quadrant. Plotting films within this matrix, whilst rather reductionist, allows the plotter to identify clusters of films/film groups within the cultural and technological territory that cinema occupies. This exercise would almost certainly produce two broad polarizations between "art" and "entertainment," and therein lies a minefield. The words we use to identify and describe cinema are prone to value judgment; the use of "film" indicates a product (text) which is to be taken seriously (witness the rather portentous label of "regional film theatre" to the British Film Institute-supported regional cinemas) whereas "movies" resonates with the hedonistic pleasures associated with Hollywood and the multiplex cinema chains. Likewise those who write about cinema professionally are "critics" (in the broadsheet press and second/fourth UK terrestrial television channels) or "reviewers" in the tabloids, first/third TV channels and popular magazines. How, then, do we make sense of the cinema of "film" and the cinema of "movies"?

Culture and Ideology

Cinema was born out of a desire to reproduce images which represent the world in which we live (or, rather, *re-present* the world through the eyes and ears of its makers); to capture life and "freeze" it for posterity. Equally, cinema affords the opportunity through its technology to work within the realms of the imagination; to delight, to astonish, to elicit the gasp of wonder from the child within all of us. Cinema itself is an illusion, relying as it does on the persistence of vision within our eye/brain sensory system and the consequent illusion that we are witnessing lifelike movement on the screen rather than 24 still images projected every second. The central antinomy of

film is thus its photo-mechanical reproduction of "real-ness" (used as we are
– and early audiences were – to the still photographic image) alongside film's
ability to deal in illusion, trickery, artifice. The very first films projected in
public in Europe demonstrated this in the work of the brothers Auguste and
Louis Lumière with their beautiful one-minute "actualities" (attendant with
the apocryphal story that audiences felt the films so "lifelike" that they fled
from the cinema when a train approached them on screen!). Concurrent with
the Lumière's traveling shows Georges Méliès was producing astonishing
"trick" films from a makeshift studio in his house in Paris. Film as a cultural
commodity is also identified by another shifting antinomy; on the one hand it
is the "seventh art" (a term used by early theorists to locate and justify its
relationship to the other six) used by twentieth century *auteurs* to make
profoundly personal statements (primarily, but not exclusively, within West-
ern-European cultures), and on the other a mass form of cheap entertainment
and diversion; in short the cultural industry most usually personified by
Hollywood.

Central to our understanding of cinema is the fact that film is located within
culture, and culture within ideology. Film's determinants are cultural/
ideological, in the West as much as the East. Thus, in relation to audience,
the central dynamic is the relationship of film to culture; or more specifically
between cinema and audience/reader and text. Film, like its sister arts,
"exists" and has meaning only when it is in dialog with a "reader", individually
or collectively as an audience. The cans of film and cassettes of videotape on
the shelves of my study lie inert until I allow them to "speak" to me. There is
thus a dynamic between text (the film) and reader (the audience) and the
central characteristics of the way that relationship functions must be recognized and understood. Film is most truly "cinematic" when it is in dialog with
a cinema audience (videotape is a very poor, but understandably easy and
accessible, substitute). The relationship between audience and film is dynamic
(witness an audience of children watching *Raiders of the Lost Ark*!) as is the
relationship between an individual and a film: the film may connect directly
with the "meaning making webs" we construct as individuals.

Theorists such as Christian Metz have identified some of the characteristics
of film audiences, and writers such as John Ellis provide an accessible overview
of the audience as "spectators" (Metz 1982; Ellis 1992). The intellectual and
professional precepts of psychoanalysis, predominantly (but certainly not
exclusively) around the issue of cinema mimicking the state of "dreaming"
and issues of, for example, identification, narcissism, wish-fulfillment and
voyeurism, have enabled theorists to conceptualize this relationship between
individual, audience and text. The cinema screen is generally letterbox-shaped
and we, the audience, occupy a darkened space to witness the "world" within
the cinema frame with the characters within that world not (unless the film is

postmodern) being aware of or acknowledging our presence. The astonishing "picture palaces" of the 1930s, with their promise of warmth, luxury and pleasure, give testimony to this view of cinema as "dream factory." Many British cinemagoers during this period would have been unfamiliar with "central heating" or the luxury of carpeting in their own homes, quite apart from the opportunity cinema afforded to indulge fantasy and "escape" (for the price of an admission ticket) from their lived experience. Perhaps the most direct form of identification is the phenomenon of "stars," predominantly within the Hollywood firmament, with its attendant "fandom."

Cinema cannot thus disconnect from culture as a component within ideology. During the past twenty years or so film theorists within the Western capitalist economies have interrogated the relationship of film to capitalist ideology. Writers such as Louis Althusser promote a view of cinema as an ideological state apparatus; as a technology and methodology of containment and concealment. Marxism affords a detached and rich seam of enquiry into the relationship between cinema and society, and whilst the theoretical treatises sometimes suffer from inaccessibility their perception is illuminating.

The Language of Cinema

One can "read" a film only if one is familiar with its "language." Whilst film is not a language in itself it generates its meanings through systems which work as languages in relation to the film text. Moreover, film is layered with meanings; they may be likened to the many layers of a large onion; there is intellectual and emotional pleasure to be had in peeling away the layers. At face value it is claimed that anyone can "read" a film. One of the many sins laid upon cinema is that it is undemanding and – like its younger sibling television – the source of banality and trivialization. Most of us within Western societies are so familiar with the language of film it (literally) becomes invisible. Rather than turn to the constituents of that language most cinemagoers frame their experience of a film through value judgment ("Did you like it?," "Was it a 'good' film"?) Discussion of cinema framed in this way is always superficial, often relies on emotional response, and is ultimately sterile. More worryingly, this approach tends to construct a hierarchy of "good" and "bad" films, consigning the latter to oblivion. It has even been claimed that analysis of a film (through repeated viewings, for example) "spoils" it for the viewer! A far more illuminating (and enjoyable) approach to film is to uncover the language of a film, and through that language to understand its meaning(s).

Film should be primarily regarded as a system of signification, and those systems of signification produce "meanings" for the reader. The theoretical and intellectual framework for this approach derives from semiotics, and primarily from the work of Ferdinand de Saussure. Semiotics allows us to understand the relationship between signs and their social meaning; "signs" being words, a visual image, a sound or any of the components of "the world within the frame." Thus film is an interconnected series of signifying systems, unlike the unitary signifying system of writing. As a consequence, the understanding of film language can be very much more complex. Moreover, unlike language, film does not have a discrete syntax. Whilst it is tempting to talk about the "grammar" of film, attempting to identify its syntax would lead to a catalog of qualification. It is more constructive to think of film's language in terms of a taxonomy. I outline below some of the constituents of the film's world, or in the more generally used term, its *mise-en-scène*.

Framing the world

Like the human eye and the cinema's projection system, the film camera isolates and frames. The camera framing can be haphazard (as any viewer of amateur video footage can testify) but is generally predetermined. It includes all those constituents that the director (or perhaps the director of photography) intend, and excludes anything considered extraneous. The camera can either show us something (i.e. provide an objective viewpoint) or can place us within the world of the film by the use of point-of-view shots where we are looking, as it were, through the eyes of a character in the film. The former allows the story of a narrative film to unfold as we observe; the latter – used often in the horror/thriller genre – implicates us in the plot action. The screen image can comprise a panorama (a key visual device in "road movies" or Hollywood biblical epics) or an extreme close-up, generally to heighten screen emotion. The camera can frame in a precise, almost proscenium arch or painterly, way (witness the work of the British director Peter Greenaway) or can frame with fluidity to suggest a world outside the frame (the work of the Italian "neo-realists" or of directors such as Jean Renoir and Federico Fellini). The camera can be still and frame the action from a fixed viewpoint (often accompanied by long camera takes, for example in the films of the Japanese director Ozu Yazujiro) or can move with astonishing fluidity, as for example in Busby Berkeley's 1930s Hollywood musicals (nowadays with the benefit of advanced crane technology and the use of "steadicam" apparatus). This fluid camera movement, exploited by documentary makers following the development of lightweight camera technology, features often in contemporary Hollywood releases and gives "pace" and "speed" to many an action movie. Virtuoso camera work, however, can often disadvantage the film by its prominence, unless used with the skill and flair of directors such as Martin Scorsese or Orson Welles. Welles's 1951 film *Touch of Evil* begins with a five-minute sequence shot in one continuous take, which is all the more astonishing as most audiences would not be aware of it! Advances in camera lens technology now mean that the ability to show scenes in "deep focus" (giving a greater illusion of three-dimensionality) are nowadays more commonplace than the celebrated scenes photographed by Gregg Toland in Orson Welles's masterwork *Citizen Kane*. In films such as *Thelma and Louise* or *My Own Private Idaho* deep-focus photography allows audiences to really feel the vastness of American landscapes. Even the height of the camera in relation to its subject can be significant; whilst most feature films are shot at "eyeline match" (i.e. at the height of the adult character's eyes) placing the camera at low or high angles alters audience perception of both the characters and their world. The agreed convention is that a low viewpoint suggests "power" or "authority" by looking up at the subject, whilst a high angle suggests "weakness" by looking down.

Whilst the camera records all the visual components of the film (and allows for interesting theoretical work in relation to iconography) it is aided by other systems of signification, which are all additional components of *mise-en-scène* – the world within the frame. The visual world of the film – its setting – can frame "reality" through the use of location photography, and utilize many of the devices of the documentary filmmaker. This verisimilitude can thus blur boundaries of "fiction" and "fact": the work of the British writer/director Mike Leigh provides good examples, and – from an earlier period of British Cinema – 1960s "new wave" films such as *Saturday Night and Sunday Morning* or *The Loneliness of the Long Distance Runner*. Equally, the use of "sound stages" (indoor studios) allows artifice full reign, for example in the "fantasy" theatrical worlds of musicals or spectacular set-pieces in James Bond movies. Nowadays the artifice is often digitally generated and the "worlds" are virtual. Computer technology, like cel animation before it, can "free" cinema from its photographic heritage, and it remains to be seen whether audiences rate "spectacle" above "reality." Lighting is another signifier, although perhaps less obvious. Developments in film stock now allow directors to film a scene in "low key" (in conditions of very low light, including candlelight) or conversely "high key" (full use of studio or location lighting). Perhaps the most consistently "dramatic" use of lighting for film was that originated by the German Expressionists and adopted by Hollywood in their 1930s and 1940s "film noir." Films such as *Mildred Pierce* and the aforementioned *Touch of Evil* exemplify the skillful play of light and shade that "expressionistic" lighting can provide. The use of color or monochrome film stock (occasionally the use of both in the same film, for example in Lindsay Anderson's film *If...*) or the use of still images/freeze frame and fade in/out are equally important signifiers. A recent vogue for ending a feature film on a "freeze frame" literally "freezes" the plot and disrupts narrative closure, a convention now well understood by cinema audiences. Interfering with the normal running speed of feature films (24 frames per second) to give slow motion ("overcranking" – a term derived from the very earliest days of cinema, and utilized with powerful effect in the opening "burning playground" shots in James Cameron's film *Terminator 2*) or fast motion ("undercranking"- less used to create mood because of its "comic" overtones), and the use of graphical and computer-generated digital effects (again utilized in the *Terminator 2* opening sequence) can be equally powerful constituents of the "world" of the film. Likewise, the importance of sound to the film's diegesis must not be underestimated. The development of "talkies" had a profound impact on cinema; once silent film became language-specific (in the form of spoken dialog) its capacity for universality was forever gone, and nowadays silent film with musical accompaniment often seems "quaint." Unluckily for British cinema the "universal language" of talkies was, and remains, English, due to the dominance of Hollywood film production. Language as a component of culture thus plays a pivotal role in the signification of film and sound – also in the form of music – and is often part of our "mental map" of films recalled from memory. All of the above, alongside performance and characterization by the actors on screen, constitute the film's "diegesis" or story-world. There are non-diegetic elements, for example title sequences, increasingly lengthy credits, and the use of music to heighten audience emotion, but all combine to create an overall "diegetic effect" or, in simpler terms, the emotional and intellectual impact of the film on an audience. The relationship of a film to a viewer is singular, yet the diegesis can be more powerful when collective; witness the impact of a film such as Steven Spielberg's *Schindler's List* on a cinema audience.

Joining the shots

Editing is the process in film and video whereby shots are joined, at specific junctions or "cutting points," to construct narrative meaning in a movie. It is a complex and highly creative process, which allows the filmmaker control over the graphic, rhythmic, temporal and spacial relationships between individual shots in the film. Given that "realism" was and is the most dominant mode of feature film production the form most familiar to filmgoers is "continuity editing," whereby the plot action between shots and scenes appears continuous and the space/time relationship is coherent. This is not to discount the use of "flashback" and "flashforward" as narrative devices, or the use of "parallel cutting" to portray simultaneous segments of the plot, but its overall aim is verisimilitude. Non-narrative cinema provides a host of alternative editing styles, breaking temporal and spatial continuity. The films of Busby Berkeley and Ozu Yasujiro, mentioned earlier, provide examples. The process of (literally) joining the shots brings yet other processes of signification; meaning is created by the juxtaposition of shots and the impact upon audiences is demonstrable (most famously outlined in the "montage" experiments of Lev Kuleshov and the Russian formalists).

Narrative

Narrative serves an essential social and cultural function; it is partly through stories that we make sense of our world. Narrative (i.e. "feature") film is the subject of this book and, as such, an understanding of film narrativity is central to an understanding of the relationship of film to theology. Narratology is a complex theoretical arena, drawing from anthropology, linguistics, semiotics and cultural studies (Barthes 1972; Propp 1975; and the work of Claude Lévi-Strauss). This work has informed our understanding of film narrativity, particularly in relationship to "popular cinema" and, as a formal system (especially in what is often described as "classical narrative – Hollywood – cinema"), provides a framework for analysis. Bordwell and Thompson's book *Film Art* (4th edn 1993) provides an excellent exposition around their definition "a narrative is a chain of events in cause–effect relationship occurring in time and space." Principles of narrative construction allow us to understand the relationship of story to plot, the importance of causality, time and space, the range and flow of story information (particularly in its dynamic relationship with audience), narrative conventions (especially in relation to the notion of film genre), the construction of character, the relationship of narrative to the film's diegesis. Unlike a book, a feature film exists within a given time frame; it controls what we see (and hear) and when. Videotape allows us to rewind, replay, freeze-frame or fast-forward a film, but to do so is to destroy the film's continuity and diegesis. Film literally "takes us on a journey" from opening titles to final credits, and narrativity is the "engine" which drives us. The journey need not necessarily be ordered chronologically; films often deploy "flashbacks" or "flashforwards" or the plot can tell the whole story backwards; a typical device in films with a biographical theme (or "biopics"). The plot can tell the same story from a number of viewpoints (Welles's *Citizen Kane* is the most oft-quoted example), or can tease the audience by withholding story information (a central device in suspense/thriller movies, and elegantly used by Alfred Hitchcock in many of his films). "Popular cinema" is perhaps most clearly defined by the limited range of "stories" it tells; the more "simple" the story the more chance of successful theatrical release worldwide. Thus there is a "folk tale" or even "fairy tale" dimension to popular cinema; a cinema of heroes and villains, good versus evil, the known versus the unknown. Equally, in the case of film genre (e.g. the Western) the same stories are told over and over again. Issues of ideology and mythology lie beneath the surface of the "good story," and whilst they are sometimes evident (for example in the film *Independence Day*), they more usually need uncovering. The theoretical work of Theodor Todorov and Vladimir Propp provide useful baselines for an understanding of narrativity, which is perhaps most central to the issue of film as a component of culture and ideology.

"Reading a Film"

Film scholarship in the UK and elsewhere over the past 30 or so years has resulted in a cluster of approaches to film theory and analysis. What follows is an over-simplistic catalog of these approaches, which does not do justice to that scholarship but may assist the budding film-scholar through the growing range of published material. The brevity of this account prevents any acknowledgment of the influence of the Russian formalists, the work of Rudolf Arnheim and the "realist" film theories of Siegfried Kracauer and André Bazin, or the work of writers and theorists on the relationship of film to the other arts, although this work is signaled in the Annotated Bibliography at the end of the book.

"Leavisite"

Adopted by a group of British writers, teachers and critics in the 1960s, this approach to film took its central tenets from the work of the influential Cambridge Professor of English, F. R. Leavis. Leavis's intellectual energies were focused on the novel, not cinema, but his approaches to European literature were readily adaptable to film. His form of "literary criticism," subsequently adopted by many English Literature teachers, helped fuel the fledgling growth of "film studies" in the British university sector. Amongst the most active at that time were the group of writers and teachers contributing to the occasional journal *Movie*, and perhaps the most distinguished (and prolific) writer was Robin Wood. Although Wood in his later book *Personal Views* disassociates himself from the "Leavisite" position, his work both then and now displays both the intellectual rigor and profound "humanity" of Leavis's teachings.

Semiotics

It was not surprising that France should become the focal point of a new direction in film theory, given the work of André Bazin and the development of a rigorous "film culture" through the Cinémathèque Français, film clubs and the influential film journal *Cahiers du Cinéma*. Arising from a desire to order a more structured and "scientific" approach to film analysis, French theorists (notably Christian Metz) borrowed and adapted from the tenets of structural linguistics, notably those of the Swiss linguist Ferdinand de Saussure and the American philosopher Charles Saunders Pierce. Semiotics is, crudely, the "science of signs" and provides a structured approach to interrogating meaning in texts ("texts" being films, TV programs, photographs, advertisements etc., as well as printed material). This approach is exemplified in the work of the contemporary French writer Roland Barthes and the Italian writer Umberto Eco, and found its focus in Britain in the journal *Screen*. Often classified as "difficult," this theoretical methodology provides us with precise tools to "unlock" meanings in texts, and its application can be rewarding.

Marxism

France also helped nurture an avowedly political theory of film, which located cinema as a component within capitalist ideology. This view sees cinema not just as an industry but as mental machinery, wherein the audience consume ideology through their spectatorship. The key concepts of Marxist thought (alienation, materialism, class conflict, hegemony) can be brought to bear on cinema, and provide illuminating insights into the appeal of "popular" cinema, "stars" and "heroes." Notable writers in this field are the French philosopher Louis Althusser (whose 1970 essay on "Ideology and Ideological State Apparatuses" defines "the media" as such a state apparatus) and the British writers Raymond Williams, Stephen Heath, and Colin McCabe.

Psychoanalysis

From the 1980s to the present day in Britain, analytical focus on film moved to issues of gender, sexuality and the "pleasures" (visual and otherwise) to be gained in the audiences" experience of cinema. Adopting the tenets of psychoanalytic criticism, primarily through the work of Sigmund Freud, it is possible to locate cinema's relationship to the unconscious, the Oedipus complex and other neuroses, dreams, voyeurism and scopophilia, fetishism, aggression and guilt. Concerned as it is with the "nature" of human beings and their non-rational forces, this is a complex and potentially difficult arena, with the danger of over-simplification and reductionism, but it does illuminate the fascinating relationship between audience and film. Key writers include Bruno Bettelheim (notably *The Uses of Enchantment: The Meaning and*

Importance of Fairy Tales), Carl Jung, E. Ann Kaplan, Elizabeth Cowie, and Laura Mulvey.

Sociology and ethnography

Primarily focused around US scholarship, this approach borrows from the fields of social science to examine the "effects" of cinema, the issues of gender and ethnicity, deviance, "uses and gratifications" and from ethnography to examine the constitution of cinema audiences. Key writers include Arthur Asa Berger, Marshall McLuhan and the raft of writers and researchers dealing (generally through the use of empirical research) with media effects.

Rereadings

A current stream of critical work in the 1990s is focused upon "reclaiming" or "rereading" film for audiences who have not until recently felt they have had a voice. Concurrent with the feminist movement, and the work of – primarily – British and American feminist writers, this provides new and illuminating perspectives on mainstream cinema. Equally, the striving for racial equality has allowed the "reclaiming" of films for black audiences and raised issues of black consciousness. Latterly issues of sexual identity have become prominent, notably in the rise of "new queer cinema" and the rereading of films by lesbian and gay writers. Key writers in these fields are Charlotte Brunsden, Tessa de Laurentis, Christine Gledhill, Annette Kuhn, the films and writings of Spike Lee (USA) and Isaac Julien (Britain), Richard Dyer, Mandy Merck, Amy Taubin, and Andy Medhurst.

Conclusion

Knowing about the conventions of film makes the viewer aware of the way in which technical elements of filmmaking are so powerful as signifying systems of meaning. If, as Marshall McLuhan famously said, the medium is the message, then it is not difficult to develop a respectful approach to the skill and artistry of filmmaking. Film shows us ourselves, and is a mirror both of our achievements and of our strivings; we make meaning in all we do, whether this is done in order to illuminate our path or to search for the infinite. In learning to read a film, we become fluent in interpreting the language of life.

2

Film and Theologies of Culture

Clive Marsh

This chapter will complement the previous chapter – which began from the perspective of film criticism – by approaching film from the perspective of Christian theology. It will discuss ways in which Christian theology must be understood if it is to make creative use of the medium of film.

Film and Theology: the Nature of the Challenge

In the early stages of the production of this book, I was questioned by a (male) British, ordained Methodist minister about the undertaking. We were talking specifically about the film *Shirley Valentine* (see chapter 14). The minister's reservations about the whole project, and the use of that film in particular, were contained in his expressed disbelief that anything good, let alone Christian, could be drawn from a film in which an adulterous act is apparently not condemned. Indeed, the act may even be implicitly condoned in that there is the possibility (the film's ending is ambiguous) that good may result from it.

That personal encounter may, of course, only indicate something about that particular minister's theology, or his keenness to present a distinct and clear Christian approach to sexual morality (an approach which, in his view, was unambiguous and thus not open to question). However, the exchange of views can be understood more broadly. It certainly says something about how the Church and/or Christian theology has dealt with matters sexual (often badly). But it also stands as an example of clashing theologies of culture, i.e. of how issues or questions which are thrown up by life are to be handled by Christian theology.

To take this concrete encounter a stage further: sex – something in which "the world at large" also seems very interested, though frequently reaching conclusions rather different from the Christian Church – is a good example of an area of life about which every human being must make some decisions and adopt convictions. It is one of many "life issues" which can easily become starting-points for theological discussion. From a Christian perspective (of whatever Christian persuasion) it is likely that all such "life issues" – law and order, fair world trade, war, care of the earth, healthcare, education are other topical examples – will be deemed to be only adequately dealt with when considered theologically. In other words, they will only be appropriately addressed when a Christian understanding of God is brought alongside the issue in question and used in some way to inform an individual's handling of the issue. The question, of course, is how that phrase "in some way" is to be understood. In my discussion with the Methodist minister, we were each bringing our Christian understandings of God to bear on our readings of the film, and the issue, in question. We were disagreeing as to how those understandings informed our readings, and thus the results of the interaction. We were, in short, representing two different ways of understanding theology's critical interaction with culture.

In this chapter, I shall offer a number of models by which the interrelationship of theology and culture can be understood. I shall ultimately defend one of those understandings, one which distances itself from that view held by the questioning Methodist minister. In effect, the view I defend offers one possible rationale from the perspective of Christian theology for much of what is undertaken in part two of this book. It would be quite wrong to suggest that all contributors to that section do so in direct agreement with the mapping exercise I undertake here. In drawing attention to other possible models, therefore, I am stressing that whilst the model I opt for may be deemed, from my own point of view, the most *obvious* theological framework within which part two of this work is to be understood, it is certainly not the only one.

Students of film and theology are thus offered in this chapter different construals of "the way theology works", and one of those possible construals is then recommended both as a basis upon which to understand the separate chapters in part two, and, in my own view, as the best way to do Christian theology. As a theological method, the recommended proposal is thus using film as an example of the way in which any aspect of culture can become a critically received theological resource.

Some Working Definitions

"Theology" is "God-talk." The simplest and most important distinction to be made in order to grasp how theology works is that between theology as talk *about* God and talk *from* God. All theology is talk about God. "God" is a word, or concept, used to refer to ultimate reality, the source of all being, in whatever way ultimate reality or being are understood. Those who engage in theology thus stand within a particular theological tradition (Muslim, Christian, Jewish, or whatever) and rework the understanding of God in relation to that tradition, usually as believers within that tradition themselves. Be they committed to a particular tradition or not, they will, however, seek to relate the understanding of God with which they work to the living experience of God claimed within that tradition, as expressed preeminently in worship and ethical practice.

From the perspective of religious belief, then, theology also entails handling talk "from God." Though metaphorical to the extent that most religious believers do not claim to literally "hear" the voice of God, the notion of theology as *from* God seeks to do justice to the conviction that what people say about God is not simply a human work. Because human beings do not invent God, and because God is held to be a reality independent of human experience, then theology cannot comprise merely human conceptualizing. The borderline between talk about and from God can, however, at best be fuzzy. Frequently it cannot be determined at all. Being human and having our own freedom and responsibilities also entails considerable unclarity about God's being and action. Those who speak about God thus need to remain in constant conversation with others inside and outside their tradition in order to examine and reexamine their understandings of God. God is the property of none, though available to all. That insight is reflected in the way theology understands itself and functions as a human discipline of study.

Most religious people whose belief system employs the word "God" are, in practice, "realists." They believe that when they use the word "God," that word actually refers to a reality which "exists." They usually do not mean that God "exists" as an empirical, objective reality in the same way that a chair, table, or tree "exists." But they want to stress, by their realism, that God really "is," and is not simply a concept or word. God is not merely the result of human myth-making or a figment of people's imagination, even if religion and theology undoubtedly entail the use of myth and imagination. Story, myth, image, symbol, imagination, poetic language, metaphor are all brought to bear in religion and theology. But they are employed in order faintly to grasp a reality which is believed to be "really there." Theology thus usually operates on the assumption that God is, even if the way that God is, and who God is, may be differently understood within and across religious traditions.

Christian theology is thus, specifically, talk about God and from God as understood within the Christian tradition in all its diversity. The prior judgment cannot be made that God be held to "speak" only within the Christian tradition. Nor can it be assumed that Christians alone have grasped who God is. Beginning theological reflection from within the Christian tradition/s simply means that theology is undertaken with respect to Christian tradition/s, on the conviction that Christians, by and large, believe that they really do encounter God as (an) independent reality and that God really does "speak" to Christians.

"Culture," in the sense to be used throughout this book, is, by contrast to theology, a wholly human construct. In its most general sense it means the whole web of interpretative strategies by which human beings make sense of their experience. Religions are thus part of "culture" in the sense that they contribute to the meaning-making webs of interpretation which humans construct. At some points that "meaning-making" is more explicit than at others. Religions and certain forms of art, e.g. iconography, seem more interested in meaning than some soap operas or other forms of art, e.g. pop art. But much of the contemporary discussion surrounding the place of "popular culture" in society and academy (e.g. Ross 1989, Fiske 1989, Strinarti 1995) raises the question whether the lines are drawn too clearly and too early between particular art forms. Notions of what constitutes "fine art" or "high culture" have long been around. It is right that some of the canons of culture be questioned – religious canons included. But one need not then go to the opposite extreme and conclude that all culture is equally valuable or useful, or all art equally esthetically satisfying or important in order to be able to state that many more aspects of culture do, in practice, contribute to the making of meaning than have often been realized.

Culture, even when defined as the whole web of interpretative strategies which human beings use to make meaning, may thus include forms of entertainment and leisure. Some forms of meaning-making entail escapism. Not all entertainment entails escapism. Culture is thus a complex field of enquiry, because it potentially includes all forms of human creativity – whether consciously meaning-making or not: art, music, TV, film, poetry, fiction, drama, sculpture, sport, religion, gambling. How theology might relate to this vast world of meaning we must now consider.

Models of Theology and Culture

There are three main ways in which the relationship between theology and culture can be understood. These relate directly to the five possible understandings presented by H. Richard Niebuhr of the way in which Christ and culture can be said to relate to each other (Niebuhr 1951, esp. here 39–44; summarized in Jenkins 1983; discussed briefly e.g. in Carr 1990: 138–41, McGrath 1993, and extensively in Stassen et al. 1996). Niebuhr's five construals see Christ in opposition to culture ("Christ Against Culture"), in fundamental agreement with culture ("Christ of Culture"), or in one of three possible dialogical or dialectical relationships with culture, i.e. in which a distinction and a unity is simultaneously maintained in some way ("Christ

Above Culture", "Christ and Culture in Paradox," and "Christ the Trans-former of Culture"). Each of these three basic approaches will be considered in turn in relation to our immediate interest: the way in which the study of film may or may not contribute to Christian theology's constructive task.

First, theology and culture can be seen as standing in stark opposition to each other. Theology thus consistently critiques culture. There is no way in which culture, or a consideration of any aspect of culture, could deliver theology its subject-matter. It would not be possible to conclude that talk from God is contained within any words about God which are gleaned from human culture. In Christian theology in this century, this approach has been exemplified in the work of Karl Barth. Barth was far from "uncultured", in the popular sense of the term. He enjoyed listening to Mozart (and expected, or at least hoped, Mozart's music to be playing in the forecourts of heaven!). But any sense of God which could result from Barth's hearing of Mozart could only be secondary to Barth having first grasped something of God through revelation. As Barth insisted throughout his work, "God is known only by God" (Barth 1957: 179). In other words, only God can reveal God, and nothing which human beings fashion can enable revelation to happen. People come to know God through God alone, not on the basis of human activity. On this understanding, culture could merely confirm what was known on other grounds. Film could thus but illustrate a theology derived from elsewhere (i.e. through revelation). In a telling passage, Barth speaks of the limitation of using literature and art to try and stimulate appreciation of Jesus as the Christ. He writes:

> The attempt to represent Him can be undertaken and executed only in abstraction from this peculiarity of His being (i.e. in relating divinity and humanity), and at bottom the result, either in literary or pictorial art, can only be a catastrophe . . . the history of the plastic representation of Christ is that of an attempt on the most intractable subject imaginable . . . from the point of view of Christology there can be no question of using the picture of Christ as a means of instruction
>
> *(Barth 1958: 103)*

One can only assume that Barth would reach exactly the same conclusion about film.

The second model deems theology to be derived from culture in such a way that distinctions between religions or the particularity of any particular faith (or, in Christian terms, the particularity of the Church) do not carry much weight. God-talk is thus extracted from culture on the understanding that God is to be discerned equally in and outside religious traditions. "Natural theology" – an approach to theology which does not privilege particular religious traditions but draws theological conclusions from experience available to all human beings – is thus emphasized. This understanding of theology's relation to culture fits comfortably with an understanding of God which sees all major religions of the world as embodying equally valid paths to the one God (Ultimate Reality), who/which lies behind or beyond all traditions. Culture thus includes all religions and much more, and God can be discerned at any point.

Adopting this stance in the present entails extending Niebuhr's reading of the "Christ of culture" to its postmodern limits. Accordingly, no obviously privileged position can be granted to any particular, including Christian, insight. "Christian theology" is therefore effectively a set of intertextual preferences, opted for in continuity with what can be seen to have been labelled "Christian" historically. Christianity and Christian theology thus become (because they have always been, even when this was never realized) cultural constructs from out of the vast array of source material available about human life. What makes a certain set of preferences "Christian" is the fact that the Christian story/tradition is the primary "text" being worked with. Furthermore, on this model of the relationship between culture and theology, "God" may be understood to be either a reality or a fictional figure. For when theology becomes a discipline dealing solely with theological "texts" (i.e. cultural products), then "God" can be seen as a character in a story, but need not be held to have any independent existence.

It is questionable whether any Christian theologian has really held this second position in the sense just described and remained identifiably Christian. Paul Tillich is often cited, rightly, as a "theologian of culture." But Tillich's understanding of the relationship between theology and culture, as we shall see shortly, is much more nuanced than this second model proposes. John Hick offers a pluralist understanding of religions, according to which the privileged position of Christianity is taken away (e.g. Hick 1983, 1989). He thus favors a natural theology more strongly than most Christian theologians. But he still believes that religions are significant for theology in a way that other aspects of culture may not be. And he believes that the Real really is! In *Christ and Culture* Niebuhr suggests that nineteenth-century Liberal Protestantism followed this line (Niebuhr 1951: 91–101). This is, however, open to serious challenge given a century of hindsight. For Liberal Protestantism has by no means automatically led to the potentially non-realist, postmodern position I have described. This suggests that Liberal Protestantism's approach to the relationship between theology and culture was more dialectical than is often supposed.

The submergence of Christian theology into culture means, for film, that any use of Christian imagery, however ironic, indifferent, or inconsistent, would count as a contribution to Christian theology. The basis for a dialog between theology and film would be hard to locate, for Christian theology itself has become a collection of textual references without a dialectical (and thus prophetic) edge. It would thus raise the question whether the "theology" which was being constructed could retain, in the long term, its adjectival prefix "Christian." To be a *particular* theology – which any theology has to be to function religiously – there has to be some link with a particular community/set of communities and an identifiable tradition of theological discourse.

A third approach to the relationship between theology and culture must thus be found if film is to have a constructive role to play (thus opposing the first model) without itself being considered uncritically (thus opposing the second). On this third understanding, film is allowed to contribute with its own integrity to Christian theology, but Christian theology brings its own agenda. Christian theology cannot, however, simply quarry film for good illustrative material. It looks for confirmations of its own content, but also expects to be challenged and even radically questioned in the process. For this to happen, theology and culture must be understood as in dialog: existing in a critical, dialectical relationship. Any aspect of human culture – including film – which explores in however slight a fashion such themes as "the human condition," the nature of reality, or how people should live is addressing subject-matter of concern to Christian theology, and about which Christian theology has things to say. Christian theology overreaches itself when it simply offers an "answer" to any question which culture poses. For culture is, in any case, diverse and complex. Films, books, fine art offer a range of ways of formulating such life-questions and their answers. But Christian theology undersells itself when it simply welcomes uncritically all that culture offers. A mutually critical dialog has to occur (and of the three positions which Niebuhr identifies as dialogical, this comes closest to his "Christ and Culture in Paradox").

The rules of such dialog are now becoming well established. Much ground has been covered in this area by those engaged in interfaith dialog (Swidler et al. 1990: esp. 1–18). How do you genuinely hold a dialog with someone when you really believe you're right, but when, at the same time, you want to respect fully your dialog-partner in his/her otherness? As far as theology's dialog with culture is concerned, Christian theology will bring its grasp of truth and be reluctant to give ground when, for example, the content of a film presents a challenge to it. But if it is unwilling to be questioned, and reluctant to consider the possibility of change, then it has ceased to live as theology.

The significance of the fact that Christian theology struggles to be an "it" at all must, of course, be stressed. Christian theology is itself a concept which unifies a number of diverse strands of Christian traditions and understandings. Christian theology is, in practice, a collection of identifiably similar theologies,

some of which may, however, be markedly different from each other. In this
third model, then, the relationship between theology and culture should
perhaps best be seen as a discussion around a (rather large) round table, than
a dialog between two people (a theologian and a filmmaker, for example). For
just as there is no single "meaning" of a film (but the range of interpretations
is nevertheless constrained by the film's own integrity), so also there is no
single Christian theology (even though questions must always be asked about
what the borders of the identifiably Christian are).

In the process of that round table discussion, therefore, Christianity
struggles to identify what it must retain and what it may, or should, lose as it
develops. Being itself pluriform, defining its "essence" has always proved
problematic. Christianity seems to be "an essentially contested concept"
(Gallie's term, adopted and developed in relation to Christianity by Sykes
1984: 251–6). But despite problems of definition, Christianity has retained an
identity nevertheless – around creeds, however diversely interpreted, and
around religious practice, however different forms of Christian worship might
be. The "family resemblance" across diverse forms of Christian belief and
practice has kept them together.

There are, then, three models for understanding the relationship between
Christian theology and culture:

- theology against culture
- theology immersed in culture
- theology in critical dialog with culture.

It is in relation to the third possible construal that the work undertaken by
contributors to this book is, in my view, best understood.

It is, of course, true, that for this third model to operate, then it must
acknowledge that it incorporates elements of the first two models within it.
Christian theology has no choice but to be part of culture (as in the second
model). And as it struggles to define itself and make a contribution to the
betterment of human beings and the world, it must have a prophetic edge (as
in the first model). The third model, however, accepts the difficulty as well as
the necessity for Christian theology to be prophetic, thus observing the limits
to the first model. And in opposition to the second model, it accepts the
necessity as well as the difficulty for Christian theology to be distinctive.

The Theological Basis of Theology's Critical Dialog with Culture

There is not the space in this chapter to offer a full theological discussion of the three possible models for understanding the relationship between theology and culture. It is, however, important to note some specific theological commitments which lead to a recommendation of the third model. It is also important to offer a brief discussion of the particular theological tradition out of which such a stance emerges in the recent history of Christian theology, if for no other reason than to demonstrate how criticisms of that approach are to be met. In this section, therefore, the Christian theological credentials will be presented on these two fronts.

The third model is based upon a strong conviction of the presence and action of God in creation. In contrast to the first model, the third model wishes to emphasize the presence and action of God in the world beyond the church. The particularity of the church is, however, far from lost. The need to question constantly the nature of the "distinctively Christian" in the midst of the film/theology dialog that the third model proposes retains a clear imperative for the church. But the reality of the dialog precludes the church from claiming too much for itself and for its role in being a medium for clarifying the revelation it believes it has received from God.

The stress upon the presence of God in creation extends to the more positive approach to human creativity adopted by the third model in comparison with the first. Human beings are made in the image of God. They are far from perfect and no understanding of the human being which did not also stress human frailty, limitation and evil ("sin") would be both inadequate and not Christian. But *because* human beings are believed by Christians to be made in God's image, then they are shown to be capable of being co-creators with God of what God wants the world to be and be like. Artists are, then, potential co-creators, whether conscious of this function or not. In the creative process, as they "read" and interpret the world around them, they can reflect their being made in God's image. Furthermore, they participate in the creative energy of the spirit of God as they undertake their work. From a Christian perspective God – as spirit – is seen to enliven and inspire all human creativity (Doctrine Commission 1991: ch. 7).

Films are, however, often about very ordinary, day-to-day subjects. They also often take the temperature of society through examination of its underside. The chapter by David John Graham on the films of Martin Scorsese highlights this point. Is there a theological rationale for this? There is in the attention which Christian theology's "christological concentration" (the term is Hans Küng's) suggests should be paid to the very concrete aspects of human life.

Precisely because Christianity puts the figure of Jesus the Christ at its center, Christian theology cannot therefore but attend to life in its ordinary messiness. Not for nothing has Christianity been called "the most materialist of religions" (William Temple).

Five theological commitments thus result from our exploration of the third model of the relationship between Christian theology and culture:

- God present and active in creation, in the world beyond the church
- the importance of the church
- human beings made in the image of God
- the creativity of God's spirit
- the concreteness of Christianity caused by Christianity's christological concentration.

These five hallmarks of the third model do not exhaust the theological dynamics at work within the model. But they do offer a basic defence of the theological credibility of the model. They also do not prevent the notion of "only God revealing God" still being tenable. What they do is qualify the extent to which that conviction can detach itself from the cultural currency within which Christian theology must trade. In other words, though a distinct Christian voice will be sounded somewhere – and the church has a role to play in enabling that voice to be sounded – it will be one voice amongst many. It will also be a voice which clashes with other voices, and harmonizes with others. Harmony and discord may not always, however, be easy to hear.

Not surprisingly, such theological commitments should be able to be found in any recent theologian who to a large degree represents the third model suggested in this chapter. Paul Tillich (1896–1965) is perhaps known as the preeminent "theologian of culture" in this century. At its simplest, Tillich's whole theological system (Tillich 1951, 1957, 1963) can be regarded as a work of Christian apologetics. Tillich sought to "read" Western culture in order to identify its key concerns, in relation to which he could then present Christian responses appropriate for the present. His was a "theology of correlation" which brought together contemporary cultural concerns and Christian theology so that Christian theology could be allowed to address actual questions (Clayton 1980, Leibrecht 1984, Berkhof 1989: 287–98; Kelsey 1989).

Such a method was naturally theologically able to find a place for the arts. Tillich could build into his system reflections upon the arts (e.g. Tillich 1963: 196–201), and wrote extensively on art and architecture (Tillich 1989). Tillich's theology has, however, not been without its critics, even amongst those sympathetic to his use of the arts in theology. There is not space to offer a full defence of Tillich's approach. Nor would it strictly be necessary, for we are not simply adopting Tillich's theology of correlation uncritically. Whilst acknowledging the similarity of his approach to what is offered in this chapter as the third model for understanding the relationship between theology and culture, we must, however, take note of the ways in which Tillich's approach must be modified to be usable today.

Tillich's theology of correlation needs three significant modifications. First, as John Dillenberger has noted, Tillich's *theological* use of art is "not sufficiently grounded in the arts themselves" (Dillenberger 1987: 221). In other words, Tillich's approach to the arts was too heavily controlled by theological needs to allow the works of arts he considered to speak with their own integrity. His approach must thus be adjusted to ensure that in our contemporary use of film in theology we do allow the films to "speak" in a way that is true to their own integrity. They may well not deliver what theologians want to hear. The "common ground" may often be subject-matter more than precise message. But important films which address the themes which Christian theology has also addressed cannot but be contemporary material for theological consideration. In dialog with such films, Christian theology cannot simply call the shots. Films can thus not simply be expected to *illustrate* theology. They may well offer a real *contribution* to Christian theology. But this will only be satisfying and authentic as dialog if the film retains its integrity and the dialog is genuine between the two disciplines.

The second modification to Tillich's approach relates to his tendency to read culture in too uniform a fashion. Admittedly, Tillich's system was primarily worked out in relation to Western culture. In that sense he acknowledged he was constructing a system for a specific (Western) context. But even writing for a "Western context" must now be regarded as not being specific enough. It is no longer possible to claim that "Western culture" can be read in its entirety and that such a reading easily delivers a set of concerns or issues which need addressing. Somewhat ironically, the globalization of communication networks has been accompanied by a greater attention to particularity and the local. The diversity of human culture will not, then, permit the theological use of film to deliver up ready-made residual Christian values or implicit Christian messages. Whilst implicit Christianity may still be there to be worked with in Western culture, even if only in the way in which questions are posed, the dialog is likely to prove quite complex.

Third, it is clear that Tillich was simply too highbrow in his approach to culture. As Kelton Cobb has recently shown (Cobb 1995), Tillich did not really find a place for popular culture in his theological method. This weakens his achievement. Using Cobb's analysis, we can see that Tillich's theology was not apologetic enough in the sense that it related only to one segment of Western society in practice (a cultural elite), whatever the *potential* of his theological method to be taken further. Our adaptation of Tillich's approach thus takes that further step. Rather than follow Tillich's approach and consider only "art-house" films, we have taken pains to explore a number of films which have been major box-office successes and are likely to be readily available on video. They thus function culturally (admittedly especially, although by no means exclusively, in the West) like works of literature which seem to be classifiable as both "high culture" and "popular fiction," e.g. the paperback editions of Jane Austen, the Brontë sisters, Charles Dickens, John Fowles, D. H. Lawrence, and David Lodge, the contemporary English, comic novelist. In taking this step, we acknowledge that we run the risk of being accused of trivializing theology. In response, we need only say that it is a risk worth taking in order to stimulate theological discussion as widely and as publicly as possible.

Taking the three modifications of Tillich's approach to theology's interaction with culture, then, entails our using film in a way which is willing to make no initial distinction between what is useful or not on the grounds of a film's artistic merit as defined by an artistic elite. The popularity of a film may, indeed, be an indication of its importance. Having said this, attention to the first modification reminds us that a film needs considering in terms of its own integrity, and this will entail attending to issues such as whether a film is well made. We would be unwise to try and conduct a theological conversation, however useful its subject-matter may be, with a "bad film:" a film which people simply would not want to watch. Films cannot merely be fodder for a good sermon. Nor would it be true that any film will do. And within this dialog, we shall expect a complex conversation to be taking place, whereby Christian theology finds its own feet in the midst of many diverse conversations within a pluriform culture.

Some Consequences of Theology's Interaction with Film

I have suggested elsewhere what the adoption of this third model, in a form which revises Tillich's own theology of culture, means for theology itself (Marsh 1997). Here I shall simply summarize the four conclusions drawn there, adding a fifth as I do so. What does film "do" for theology, if this revised Tillichean theology of culture is adopted?

First, using film in theology is a key way in which Christian theology can work out what it is going to be possible to say in our contemporary climate about any of theology's major themes. Taking this too far would mean, of course, allowing contemporary relevance wholly to shape the content of Christian theology today. This is not my intention. Attention to film does, however, remind us firmly that Christian theology's content is only in part to be related to the context of the church. Second, using film in theology reminds us of the importance of the public dimension of any Christian theology. In the same way as Tillich's theology can be viewed as apologetics, so also a theology of culture unavoidably enters the realm of missiology. In other words, attending to material of theological significance which does not derive directly from the Christian church, yet which may nevertheless relate to Christian theology's task, cannot but bring a theological interpreter face to face with the question of how "church" and "world" interrelate (on which, in relation to biblical studies, see e.g. Watson 1994, Davies 1995, Marsh 1996; and see further below, ch. 18). Third, films enable Christian theology to be reminded that it is a discipline which seeks to do justice to the emotional and esthetic aspects of human life, as it deals with life's issues. Precisely because film as a medium works through the creation of an *emotional* response first and foremost, as a reaction to the visual image presented, film invites theological reflection to begin through an emotional channel. Fourth, films are vulgar in the sense of being "of/for the people," i.e. they constitute arguably one of the most influential cultural media at the moment in the West today (television alone being perhaps more influential) (Jowett and Linton 1980). They are accessible, can be watched by people without necessarily being understood, in a way in which books cannot be read (you can simply sit through a film and let it wash over you; you cannot get through a book as easily if you do not understand it). Video makes film yet more accessible, even if the medium of video creates a different experience from that of the cinema. What the vulgarity of film entails, however, is the potential raising of theological questions (and even at times the provision of some suggested answers) well beyond the reach of the house of authority (the church). This is why the third modification to Tillich's approach is so necessary. Fifth, and finally, theology comes much closer to journalism than it may ever care to admit. Theology which takes film seriously reminds itself of its own ephemeral character. We have already noted a word of caution about theology simply desiring to be relevant. But attending to that caution does not mean – as has happened so often in the history of Christian theology – seeking to say a word which is valid for all time. Tillich's own "system" belies its own ephemeral nature here. As John Clayton states: "By incorporating the present cultural situation into his methodology, Tillich gave to his theology a planned obsolescence which precludes his system's having direct relevance for any but the cultural context in which and for which it was constructed" (Clayton 1980: 5). Attending to film will remind us more that all attempts at Christian theology need to plan their own obsolescence if they are to continue to be useful.

My proposal – a revised Tillichean theology of culture, developing the third of the three models outlined at the start of this chapter – thus amounts to a kind of "theology by negotiation" rather than correlation. It has affinities with what Browning has undertaken with respect to psychology with his "revised critical correlational approach to the theology of culture" (Browning 1987: 15–17). With a proper critical dialog existing between the world of film and Christian theology, then perhaps theology can at least go some way towards speaking appropriately in the West today. Rather than constituting a call for mere "relevance," it is envisaged as part of the quest for truth, and truth will always be relevant. It is because of that quest that I assume anyone takes an interest in theology. It is often, though by no means always, the reason why people take an interest in the arts. Such an interdisciplinary dialog, engaged in such a quest, undertaken with a more critical edge that he employed, would delight Tillich.

3

The Uses of Film in Theology

David John Graham

The Use of Film as a Medium in Theology

The bringing together of the words "film" and "theology," either in the title of this book (and chapter), or in conferences and discussions with colleagues which I have had over the last few years, has elicited very different reactions. In many cases, there has been a response of incredulity. Film is often associated with popular culture, and as a medium is seen to be far removed from the religious formulations which the word "theology" brings to mind.[1] Other people are, however, more enlightened! In this chapter, I want to show in general terms the ways in which film can be used – indeed, can be a stimulating source of theological ideas and reflection. This will preface the more specific studies of films in the later chapters of this book.

Film is a medium. It is a relatively modern one, although at now over a century old it should be given more recognition than it often is.[2] It is a medium nevertheless, and it is also a type of text. Media and texts are both defined by their function in communicating: that is, they convey information, from a source (in this case the film itself) to a receiver (the viewer). But in the process, as with any other example of communication, that information has to be interpreted. It is the interpretative process which results in what one "hears" or "sees," which is why there can be so many different interpretations or "readings" of any texts, including film. This process of interpretation, or reading, is not totally uncontrolled, however. There are constraints which are put upon the interpreter by various factors. These, to express the matter at its simplest, are an interplay of the information being transmitted and the reader, i.e. reading or interpretation comes about as a dynamic relationship between the film and the viewer.

Experiencing the Religious through Media

I now want to look at ways in which this process can operate in the context of the exploration and interpretation of religious and theological ideas. Like other media, film can stimulate or communicate theological reflection in the reader of the film. That can be evoked by the often powerful effect which film has as we watch it and later reflect on that experience. By the very nature of the experience of watching it, film tends to be all-absorbing, especially when in the cinema. Even film on television can exercise a similar demand for total commitment from us, even if interruptions are more likely. The experiential dimension of watching a film, which can be close to being an existential experience, can mimic or stimulate the existential dimension of religious experience. Let me give two examples. I will never forget seeing *Schindler's List* for the first time. After three hours of quite harrowing viewing, I walked out of the cinema with the two friends I had gone with. There was complete silence between us, almost all the way as we drove home. The experience had been like being in the presence of something awesome. Like Isaiah in the temple, we felt the overpowering sense of the numinous, and after that experience words were inadequate.[3] I recall something similar after seeing *Cry Freedom*, as the final credits showed a long list of black South Africans who had met untimely deaths under the apartheid regime. Now it might be argued that this was not a specifically religious experience, and added little to theological reflection. However, in both of these cases the effect of the film was to make us think very profoundly about issues of religion, ethics, and human rights. Watching a film about the Holocaust has resulted in deep theological thinking and questioning, as of course the original experience of the Holocaust has done within Judaism itself. Likewise for the church in South Africa after apartheid: were not many of the sermons, theological ideas, and ethical principles forged in the heat of oppression? Although the film medium is only a representation of the events, and also an interpretation of them – since every representation must necessarily be selective – it can nevertheless have a similar effect.

The Sacred through the Secular

In other ways, more cerebral than emotive, film can also be an important medium for shaping or questioning theology.[4] The rationale for this book, for example, is to use the motifs and messages in film as a source of theological reflection. On this level, that of the printed word and the discussion of film rather than the immediate viewing of it, the messages encoded within this medium can be disclosed, taken up and interpreted within a theological framework. Once again, interpretation is important. The science of interpreting texts, the technical term for which is hermeneutics, applies not just to the written word, and certainly not only to ancient texts such as the Bible, but also to other text forms such as film.

Let us return for a moment to the first point made above, the emotive or affective influence of film as it is actually viewed. A number of writers have argued that the religious dimension in life can and should be seen, not only in the symbols which we usually label as "religious," but also in the other symbols around us in the world. In other words, the popular distinction between religious and secular, or sacred and profane, does not hold. Religious encounter, then, will not be limited to sacred buildings, religious symbols or architecture, or even writings which are religious or theological in character. The notion of "God-in-everything" (however God may be conceived) then operates. This view cuts away the dualism (i.e. the view that sacred and secular are polar opposites) that is often found in religious thinking, and replaces it with a more holistic view of life. What we are discussing here is not the view that God is to be found in everything (sometimes called pantheism), but the idea that the experience of God can be transmitted through anything.

Mircea Eliade is one writer who addresses this theme. In words which echo the earlier writings of Rudolf Otto, he has made us aware of the ways in which an experience of the sacred can be manifested through some other thing or person. This is sometimes referred to as a hierophany, the manifestation of the sacred (Eliade 1961; see also, in relation to film, May and Bird 1982). This might be compared with the experience of a manifestation of God, a theophany, which is usually how the religious experiences of the patriarchs of the Hebrew Bible are understood. God (sometimes under different names: Yahweh, Lord, God Almighty, and so forth) is experienced by Abraham, Hagar, and the others. But this often happens at particular places, such as wells, springs, hilltops, or trees. These may previously have been cultic sites, we do not know, but they certainly became sacred shrines later, often renamed to identify what had happened there (e.g. Jacob at "Beth-El," Gen. 28:10–22). It seems that in a number of such examples, the place of the encounter was important, and the possibility of experiencing God in and through natural symbols should not be discounted. Indeed, the burning bush of Moses has also been explained as a natural desert phenomenon, which mediated a sense of the divine presence to him (Exod. 3:2).

What has this to do with film? Culture, media, and technology can all be potent sources which provoke religious experience and theological reflection. In the words of Paul Tillich: "everything that expresses ultimate reality expresses God whether it intends to do so or not" (in Apostolos-Cappadona

1984: 220, where he gives a useful fivefold categorization of religious experience and the art forms associated with each). It is important to say that this need should in no way be seen as undermining the unique place that scripture has always had, certainly within the Christian faith, as the fundamental revelation of God. Nor are we advocating a sort of pantheism. Rather, what this book attempts is at another level, the reflective and discursive. The use of the film medium in religious discussion may make us reflect upon our theological ideas or religious praxis. Larry Kreitzer calls it "reversing the hermeneutical flow" (Kreitzer 1993 and 1994). It can, and should, throw us back to our ideas and practices, and rethink them in the light of the impact of the medium.

The Primacy of the Visual

Cinema is a powerful affective medium. That is, it engages us at the level of the feelings and emotions. And it is much more immediately affective than it is cognitive, engaging our feelings before it does our logic and rationality. The "willing suspension of disbelief" is the phrase sometimes used for this: watching a film does not involve simply being duped, but it does involve being drawn into the world created by the film. John May (in a discussion of this in which he refers to the work of T. S. Eliot) paraphrases a statement of Roger Angell, thus: "Movies are felt by the audience long before they are 'understood' *if indeed they are ever fully understood*" (May 1992: 3; May's emphasis). We cannot therefore underestimate the power of film to stimulate, convince, and affect the viewer. While much of the discussion of postmodern texts and interpretation, especially in the work of Jacques Derrida, has centered round the competing claims of the written or the spoken word (so-called logocentrism or phonocentrism), it could also be argued that seeing – the visual medium – takes precedence over both (perhaps we could coin this as "optocentrism," the priority of the visual). "The primacy of sight is undeniable. Seeing is that human experience which precedes speech" (Apostolos-Cappadona, in May 1992: 104). Mark C. Taylor describes what he calls the "post-print culture," in which "the word is never simply a word but is always also an image . . . Since image has displaced print as the primary medium for discourse, the public use of reason can no longer be limited to print culture" (Taylor and Saarinen 1994: 4). Taylor asks: "Where would Socrates hold his dialogues today? In the media and on the net" (ibid.: 3). Indeed, much of the book from which these quotes are taken consists of a dialog between its authors (between the USA and Finland) on the Internet. But even with the older technology of the screen, the case for the dominance of visual imagery scarcely needs to be argued: in holiday campsites in rural Europe, almost everyone watches television in the evenings, and in the poverty-stricken slums of Pakistan, people will crowd round a video to watch films.

Film as a Stimulus for Theology

Film is one means of presenting themes of religious importance in a striking visual medium. As discussed above, these need not be restricted to what has traditionally been labelled as "religious," but include all the questions which pertain to human experience and destiny. And this medium can have powerful influences on the viewer's emotions and reactions. One way in which this can be described is to compare the film to a parable. John Dominic Crossan distinguishes between parables and myths by suggesting that "Myth establishes the world, parable subverts it" (Crossan 1975, cited in May and Bird 1982: 32). In other words, the effect of the mythical as a vehicle is not to challenge or stimulate us to rethink our views, but only to confirm that we are already right. Thus, myths (ancient or modern) serve to explain the status quo, to give some sort of rationale or etiology for why things happen as they do. Parable, on the other hand, is subversive. It undermines and questions the very ground on which we stand. If we think, for example, of the parables of Jesus (perhaps the best known among the genre of parable), we see that they challenged the religious and ethical practices and attitudes of the hearers: for example why Samaritans and tax collectors were considered unclean, whether ethnic identity was important in God's kingdom, and the meaning of the unconditional love of God. Most of them were effective because they turned prevailing attitudes on their head, often with a "punch-line." The parable makes the hearer go and think again.

Films may function in either of these two ways, as myth or as parable. They may therefore either establish our worldview, scarcely altering or challenging our horizons of expectation, or they can also do the opposite, either by subverting a familiar genre or presenting us with a new one. They expand and broaden our understanding of the world by questioning our world-view. I would argue that, for film to be effective, indeed for it to say anything at all, it must function as "parable" rather than "myth," according to Crossan's definition and distinctions. If the effect of a film is only to make us come out feeling nice and agreeing with what we have seen, then our horizons have not been expanded. The literary critic of the Konstanz school of "reception esthetics," Hans Robert Jauss, has argued that texts function by expanding our horizons. Indeed, he argues that it is this very aspect of a text which distinguishes "domestic" texts (or "culinary," as his translator puts it) from classics. The classic will expand our horizons of expectation by just the right amount for the text to move our expectations and worldview, whereas the text which does not do so (or attempts to do it too much, and is unconvincing and therefore fails) will not "say" anything, and soon be forgotten (Jauss 1970). Pulp fiction (i.e. paperback novels, not the film!) is like that: it entertains but either leaves the reader unchanged by the experience or, like Crossan's "myths," confirms their outlook on life. In contrast, innovative and stimulating texts will result in the fusion of the horizons of the reader and the text (Jauss's language echoes that of Gadamer 1979 and, more recently, Thiselton 1992), producing new ideas, beliefs and behavior.

What Jauss describes in terms of written texts also applies to visual ones. Innovative film can interact with our religious expectations, resulting in a hierophany, different views and ethical behavior. Langdon Gilkey describes this as a "prophetic" role of art, when art becomes a critic of culture (in Apostolos-Cappadona 1984: 190). Art can thus enhance our experience, and when it does so, "Art opens up the truth hidden behind and within the ordinary ... the transcendent appears through art, and art and religion approach one another" (ibid.: 189).

The Religious in Film

One of the few explorations of film as a medium for conveying the religious was written by Paul Schrader, who later himself became an influential Hollywood screenwriter. He discusses what he refers to as "transcendental style" in film. While stating that there is little agreement on what actually constitutes transcendence, Schrader himself defines it as referring to that which is "beyond normal sense experience, and ... by definition, the immanent" (Schrader 1972: 5). This discussion of Schrader's originated as his university thesis, before he became well known in the film world. His discussion of transcendence in film was limited to the work of three particular directors. Arguably, he himself later became the leading exponent of what he describes, especially in his long association with Martin Scorsese. Although Schrader's own views have changed with the years, this early discussion of his still has much to say. He applies to the medium of film the sorts of views held by writers like Eliade, which we discussed earlier in this chapter. Whether or not one thinks, as some writers on this subject do, that the traditional language and symbols of religion are *passé*, the power and influence of the new media to express religious phenomena can hardly be denied. Eliade, after discussing the "death of God," in Nietzsche, and the "eclipse of God" in Buber, says that the "death of God" concept "signifies above all the impossibility of expressing a religious experience in traditional religious language" (in Apostolos-Cappadona 1984: 179). Thus, we have to find ways of expressing the religious (Schrader's "transcendent") in non-traditional forms. Even in cultures where

God is regarded as dead (i.e. irrelevant and therefore invisible) art, suggests Eliade, shows that the religious dimension survives in the human unconscious, despite all protestations by people or societies to be areligious.

But can the religious dimension, the concept of "the holy" in film, be explored further? Indeed, is it a valid concept at all? Schrader tries to see the "spiritual universality" of a film: something, he believes, which can only be demonstrated by critics, even though it may be interpreted variously by theologians, estheticians, and psychologists (Schrader 1972: 3). This is not the same, he contends, as a "religious" film. He explores the (rather limited) concept of transcendentalism, stating that: "The proper function of transcendental art is, therefore, to express the Holy itself (the Transcendent), and not to express or illustrate holy feelings" (ibid.: 7). This is a rather limited remit for the function of art in the expression of the religious, and may conflict with the views of May who, as we have seen, believes that the emotional precedes the cognitive when film is viewed. Schrader may be speaking as a screenwriter (albeit at the beginning of his professional career when he wrote this). May writes from the perspective of someone viewing and analyzing films, Schrader from that of someone intimately involved in their production. Schrader's work consists mainly of a detailed study of three directors (Yasujiro Ozu, Robert Bresson, and Carl Dreyer), with some references to others. For that reason, it is a useful and pioneering study, but of necessity limited in scope. It is also a study of style, and therefore restricted to "general representative form" (ibid.: 8).[5] Those caveats must therefore be borne in mind when looking at Schrader's ideas, and the work of other writers, such as Eliade, may be used to complement Schrader's study. But before we proceed, let us allow him to conclude in his own words:

> Transcendental style can take a viewer through the trials of experience to the expression of the Transcendent; it can return him (sic!) to experience from a calm region untouched by the vagaries of emotion or personality. Transcendental style can bring us nearer to that silence, that invisible image, in which the parallel lines of religion and art meet and interpenetrate.
>
> *(ibid.: 169)*

Using Film in Theology

Thus far, we have largely discussed the ways in which film as a medium can provoke religious experience. But that is primarily on the personal, existential level. As we have already mentioned, however, that is just one aspect of the equation. There is also the value of using a medium like film in critical analysis of theological ideas. In particular, it can be used in ways which challenge the received wisdom of religious traditions. The work of some other scholars has been useful in analyzing the religious dimension and uses of film in this way. Diane Apostolos-Cappadona and others, for example, have used insights from Eliade to explore the interconnectivity of art and religion in general, and their insights are useful for film as well as for other forms of art (Apostolos-Cappadona 1984; Adams and Apostolos-Cappadona 1987). This need not be confined to "theology" in the traditional sense of doctrinal ideas alone. As will be seen from the later chapters in this volume, there is also of necessity a strong narrative function in this. Films tell a story, and religion also has its own narratives to convey its ideas. The narrative of film can function either as a subversive story which rethinks the religious tradition (like the parables, as discussed above), or it can even become an alternative religious narrative which reinterprets reality in a new way. The phrase "cult movie" then takes on a whole new meaning.

But in case readers are concerned that film will only shake their religious views by challenging them, and not reaffirm them, it must also be said that movies can make a very positive contribution to theology. But they do that, surely, only if they say something new. For unless theology can say things in new ways, and unless it can say new things, it will cease to be interesting, and – perhaps worst of all – cease to be relevant.

Conclusion

Film is a very popular and pervasive medium, and its influence can be compared to that of the traditional religions. For example, there is a web page and network news group on the internet devoted to the work of the film actor-director Quentin Tarantino, with the provocative name "the Church of Tarantino."[6] Fibre-optic cable communications are bringing video on demand into many homes. Interactive CD and video will be the next technological step forward: the technology is already available, and becoming increasingly familiar in everyday use. John May says that "video tapes will . . . shortly become the principal texts that our children and grandchildren take home" (May 1992: 3).[7] This may be oversimplistic. Nevertheless, it is an interesting question whether and when the visual text will supersede the written text as a source of religious ideas. Written texts have dominated theological debate since writing was invented, and in ways previously unim-aginable after the printing press was invented. The advent of the online, electronic global village presents new challenges and opportunities to the religious groups in society. It is a fair criticism that many religions have traditionally clung on to the old ways of communicating, and have been reluctant to embrace the new technologies. We hope that part of the effect of this book will be to change that.

Notes

1 "Film" has been used in the main title of this book, and "movies" in the sub-title. Generally, "movies" tends to have a more American flavor. "Film" and "cinema" are perhaps more often used in Europe, sometimes for "art-house" cinema. The recent centenary of the Lumière brothers has been the centenary of cinema. "Theology" I use in the broadest sense, to describe any reflection on religion and the divine.

2 For example, Ian Christie, one of the great British writers and interpreters of cinema, recalls how difficult it was to put film on the agenda of Oxford University. He is now Oxford's first visiting lecturer in film.

3 Isaiah also realized the inadequacy of human speech as he cried out with "unclean lips" (Isa. 6:5).

4 In this sense, both hemispheres of the brain are involved. For an interesting exploration of this with respect to the study of the Bible, see Wink 1980.

5 He is quoting Heinrich Wolfflin here, and emphasizes this definition of style which is concerned with the universal rather than the particular. To be fair, he has since modified his own views, regarding his thesis as being unduly cautious; see Jackson 1992: xv.

6 The web page is http://www.aston.ac.uk/~smallmj, and the newsgroup is alt.fan.tarantino. A brief report on this can be found in the *Times Higher Education Supplement* May 26, 1995.

7 The technology of CD-ROMs may overtake the videocassette, but his point is still valid.

Part Two

Part Two

4

From Domination to Mutuality in
The Piano and in the Gospel of Mark

David Rhoads and Sandra Roberts

> *You know that those who rule the Gentile nations lord over them and those
> who are considered to be great among them exert authority over them, but it
> is not to be like this among you. Instead, whoever wants to be great among
> you is to be your servant and whoever wants to be most important among
> you is to be everyone's slave.*
>
> (Jesus, in the Gospel of Mark)

This chapter is an experiment in intertextuality, understood here as the
juxtaposing of two different works as a means to understand each work more
fully.[1] Although there is no reason to posit any connection between the
contemporary film *The Piano* and the first-century writing the Gospel of
Mark, both works manifest the common themes of domination and liberation.
The Piano is about the fate of three people caught in a triangle of love in the
forests of New Zealand in the nineteenth century. Mark is about a man on a
mission to usher in the kingdom of God in ancient Israel. Despite the great
differences between the two, the juxtaposition of the film and the Gospel is
illuminating of each. The dynamics of Mark's Gospel illuminates the transformation that takes place in the film, and the film portrays a concrete illustration
of the liberation from oppression called for in the Gospel. We would therefore
like to offer an analysis of *The Piano*, then give an interpretation of the
Gospel of Mark, and finally to share some reflections on the intertextual
comparison.

A Reading of *The Piano*

The Piano is a dark film about power – the power of the will against the power
of domination.[2] Jane Campion, writer and director of the film, won the award
for Best Director at the 1993 Cannes Film Festival for this haunting work of
art. Ada (Holly Hunter), a Scottish woman of uncommonly strong will, is
married off by her father to a stranger who lives in the wild and lush rain

forests of New Zealand. Ada stopped speaking at age six; "no one knows why, not even me," she says in a voiceover at the opening of the film. We know little of her childhood except that her father says her muteness is "a dark talent and the day I [Ada] take it into my head to stop breathing will be my last." Whatever the family dynamics behind this statement can only be guessed; but one suspects that Ada's range of possible responses to life are as confining as the Victorian corsets that she must wear. And so Ada ends up with no voice (literally) and a husband who lives halfway around the world, selected for her by her father.

Ada has, however, significant power in silence, which, as she says in the voiceover, "affects everyone in the end." She has an awesome gift of telepathy which frightened off her first lover. In her own muteness, she communicates to others by writing on a tablet and through her young daughter Flora (Anna Paquin), who has gone with Ada to New Zealand. Flora was born of that first affair, and in many ways she is a fused alter ego for her mother, bound to her in part through her role as interpreter of their own sign language. In addition to her daughter, Ada also has her piano, which is the medium through which she communicates her emotions and her passion, and which she loves beyond everything except Flora.

A struggle begins upon the first meeting of Ada and her new husband Stewart (Sam Neill), as he arrives on the windswept beach to pick her up. He is on first meeting disarming – shy and uncomfortable, hair slicked back for the meeting – but his inability to understand and accommodate Ada's need to have the piano portends an increasingly horrifying pattern of domination that will end in the most shocking and heinous abuse. Stewart is blind to Ada's needs and her feelings. The piano is left behind on the beach because there are too few to carry it; however, Stewart refuses even to make the attempt, and he offers no assurance that it can be retrieved later.

In subsequent days, as Ada pines for the piano, she elicits the help of Stewart's neighbor Baines (Harvey Keitel) to make the difficult trek back to the beach for a rapturous reunion with the piano. Later, Baines retrieves the piano from the beach. When Stewart agrees to let Baines have the piano in exchange for land and insists that Ada give Baines lessons, Stewart trades away the possibility of any real relationship with her.

Stewart is as trapped as Ada, it would seem, but in a different way. As a male colonist from Europe, he is caught in the powerful social assumption that he possesses the right to have control over all that he owns, including his wife. Campion's portrait is the more chilling because Stewart's assumptions and behavior are out of the range of his own awareness. He is as blind in his way as Ada is mute. He can see only what he expects to see as one trained and taught by his society as a dominant European male landowner. He clearly wants to be loved in a most desperate way, but he cannot leap across his role to enter into the soul of his wife and give to her what she needs.

This same pattern of domination can be seen in Stewart's relationship to the land. The land around his house has been clear-cut and burned; in stark contrast to the lush forest, it is black and bare. He cannot understand why the local Maori will not sell their land for blankets and guns. "What do they want it for?" he asks Baines. "They don't cultivate it, burn it back, anything. How do they even know it's theirs . . .?" His possession of the land and the consequent mutilation of it parallels his possession of Ada and his mutilation of her. In this respect, the film is a striking illustration of the parallels in patriarchal systems between the treatment of women and the treatment of nature (see e.g. Gray 1981 and Ruether 1992).

Stewart's relationship with the Maori people underlines the same pattern once again. He has not bothered to learn their language. He insults them with payments of buttons when they bring the piano to his house. He insults them more deeply when he fails to understand their reverence for their land. Fortunately, they are keen critics and are not about to be dominated. They call him "dry balls" and spit at his insulting offers.

Stewart's struggle for control of Ada becomes increasingly overt as the relationship continues. At first he is patient about Ada's lack of affection toward him and does not push himself on her. When he sees, however, that she is passionate toward Baines, his veneer of forbearance quickly turns to rage and he attempts to rape her. He then boards her into the house much as he had fenced in his land (both are, after all, his possessions). Then, when Ada attempts to send word of her love to Baines, Stewart's rage reaches its climax: he chops off her finger, and sends it to her lover, threatening to take off another and another if Baines sees her again. Later, as she lies feverish, he attempts to minimize (!) his crime, telling her "I clipped your wing, that is all." Aroused at the sight of her, he would mount and rape her comatose body except that she awakens and burns her thoughts into his mind. In the end, he relinquishes her (to Baines), saying "I want myself back; the one I knew." One suspects that this is precisely what he will get; not a transformation of self but a return to his old self, safe from passion or rage.

Baines is the character in the movie who chooses to let go of his power to control and who thereby saves himself and Ada. Baines is a liminal figure, a Scotsman gone half native. Unlike Stewart, he has learned the Maori language, has tattooed his face, made friendships with the Maori, and seems to have adopted many of their values. In the end, he abandons completely the Western colonial mentality of Stewart, relinquishing all of his land and possessions.

From the beginning of the film, we see signs of the capacity for empathy in Baines. He notices that Ada looks tired when she arrives. He gives in to Ada's request to make the trek back to the beach. Following that visit, Baines is smitten with Ada, and he contrives a plot to trade his land to Stewart for her piano. He then strikes a bargain with her that she can earn back her piano by allowing him voyeuristic sexual favors, one visit for each black key. This arrangement is crassly manipulative and intensely disturbing; yet it is different from Stewart's relationship with Ada in that Baines has the ability to see what he is doing to Ada and to discern the difference between domination and a true relationship. After a number of these encounters, he can no longer live with himself: "The arrangement is making you a whore and me wretched," he tells her. He gives her back the piano and, though obsessed with love, releases her. If the love is not mutual, he does not want her.

Ada is now for the first time set free. The result is that she is able to love, a love that was not remotely possible in her previous relationships with either Stewart or Baines. She is now safe enough with Baines to express her pent-up fury at his perverse control over her. Once this anger is expressed, a mutual relationship becomes possible, and passion follows.

Ada's passion, once released, overflows the banks of reason and caution in erotic expression. She goes to Baines, in spite of the obvious distress of her daughter, to consummate the relationship. Stewart follows and spies upon the lovers. When she is subsequently imprisoned by Stewart and forbidden from seeing Baines, she turns the tables on Stewart and tries to use him for the gratification of her passion, just as Baines had earlier used her. Stewart knows, however, just as she knew, that he is being used.

Upon learning that Baines will be leaving the territory, she pulls a key from her piano and writes "You have my heart," signing her unmarried name (the marriage had never been consummated). She forces her daughter to carry the key to Baines. Flora, perhaps jealous of her mother's attachment to Baines or desperate to keep the only father she has ever had, takes the piano key instead to Stewart, and the horrible scene of Stewart's mutilation of Ada's finger ensues.

It is Baines who takes Ada and Flora away. However, in a surprising twist of plot with a haunting ring of truth, it becomes clear that a man's love alone cannot save Ada. As they leave in the boat, she insists that the piano be thrown overboard because "it is spoiled" – perhaps because one of its keys is now missing or because of the tragedy that has surrounded it. And Ada deliberately catches her foot in the rope attached to the piano and goes down into the ocean with it. Presumably she likewise is "spoiled" now that she has no finger with which to play.

However, in the moment of death she chooses life. She pulls herself free of the rope and thereby separates herself from her piano (literally and psychologically) and struggles to resurrect herself from the watery grave. As she moves upward through the water, we hear her thoughts: "What a death! What a chance! What a surprise! My will has chosen life!" In this, her own will's choice, she begins her new life with Baines.

Campion's story is all the more compelling because of the complexity and contradictions in the characters. There are times when the viewer is drawn into sympathy with Stewart, trying so hard to woo this strong-willed wife, exposing his intense vulnerability in spite of himself. It would be easier to watch a two-dimensional figure like Bluebeard, depicted in the little play that prefigures Stewart's act of violence. Nor is Ada the typical Victorian heroine. Her behavior can at times be shocking and self-absorbed. Campion has a true gift for capturing most realistically the complex nature of human beings.

The film is further enhanced by the most memorable visual images. Several scenes become etched on the memory: the piano on the vast beach; Ada floating above the piano in the ocean depths; the beauty of the rain forests of New Zealand that conjure up images of Eden. Here we see in the intense relationships between three people isolated in the primeval forest what went wrong in paradise and how people might recover a piece of it in the midst of domination and destruction.

A Reading of the Gospel of Mark

The theme of domination is also illuminated with particular brilliance in the Gospel of Mark, a first century story about the efforts of Jesus of Nazareth to challenge the systems of domination in his nation Israel. Mark was probably written during or just after the Roman-Judean War of 66 to 70 CE.[3] In that war of Israel's revolt against Roman domination, the Romans defeated the Judeans, conquered Jerusalem, and destroyed its Temple. Some 40 years after Jesus' death, the author shaped his version of the story about Jesus, in part, in order to show that any attempt to dominate others with force – by nations or by individuals – was contrary to the way God intended for human beings to relate to each other.

Mark is not, therefore, addressing issues about the legitimate use of power to maintain social order but the illegitimate use of such power over people by leaders in order to retain their own power and control over others. The historical authorities in Israel (in contrast to the authorities as Mark portrays them) might have argued that they were only keeping order. Mark, however, was written from the peasant perspective which experienced this patriarchal order as exploitative. Hence, Mark presents a contrast between those with authority who dominate others and aggrandize themselves and those who benefit others by their refusal to use power over others and by their use of power in service to others (see further Myers 1988 and 1996).

Throughout Mark's portrayal of Jesus' activity in Israel we see the constant struggle between two contrasting ways of life: on the one hand, the way of human domination over others – the acquisition of wealth, status, and power obtained and maintained at the expense of others; on the other hand, the way of mutual service in God's rule – the relinquishment of wealth, status, and power to serve others.

The Gospel of Mark begins with the adult Jesus being baptized by John the Baptist. After he receives the anointing of the Spirit, he announces that the realm of God is at hand. The events then proceed at a dizzying pace, with Jesus proceeding to use his power to heal the sick, cleanse lepers, and drive demons from the possessed. Furthermore, he pardons sinners, eats with the hated tax collectors, and welcomes the poor and the unclean. He travels throughout the countryside of Galilee and even into surrounding Gentile territory, teaching through stories and parables what this arriving realm of God is about. At one point Jesus clarifies the ethical basis for everything he teaches and exemplifies, as contained in the two great commandments from the Judean law – that people are to love God and to love their neighbors as themselves. The practical application of these commands to life is illustrated over and over in the story and includes in many instances the willingness to give up domination over others and instead to become servants.

In the course of these actions, Jesus quickly begins to draw opposition from those who have power in the society. Because this rulership of God in the world challenges every other claim to power, there is resistance from those who do not want to relinquish their power but who instead use their power over others as a means to aggrandize themselves.

In Mark, the authorities outside and inside Israel exert such human domination. Externally, Israel is dominated by the Roman Empire, represented by Herod, the procurator, and the high priest who serves at Rome's pleasure. In turn, the people within Israel are dominated by the authorities in Judean society, the wealthy and powerful high priests and elders, along with the scribes and the Pharisees. In the depictions in Mark, the authorities seek to guard a system that maintains their status and power. They are motivated by fear – fear of Jesus, fear of the crowds who follow him, fear of loss of face with the populace, fear of riots, and ultimately fear that they will lose their power. They use laws and purity traditions to control the people's behavior. In response to someone who resists or whose presence threatens their control, the authorities reveal their worst traits. Threatened by Jesus and his popular following, the Judean and Roman authorities seek to destroy him by trickery, betrayal, and false testimony, followed by beatings, ridicule, and execution. Jesus' challenge to their systems of domination creates a struggle that escalates until finally he is captured and killed.

The way of domination is not solely the purview of the powerful, however. It is at heart a human sin. This is nowhere more poignantly portrayed than in the character of the disciples, who have themselves been chosen from those of modest means and marginalized positions and have traveled with Jesus. As the story unfolds, it becomes clear that the disciples themselves are steeped in the way of domination. To be sure, they have followed Jesus in part out of faith and fascination. Yet they also hope to get from him what the authorities already have – wealth, status, and power over others. So Jesus contends with the disciples to get them to understand the contrasting rule of God in the world and to follow him in exercising God's power in the service of others.

Midway through the Gospel Jesus and his disciples begin a journey to Jerusalem for Passover. Here we see the struggle between Jesus and his disciples portrayed most forcefully. At the beginning of the pilgrimage, Jesus predicts to the disciples his impending persecution and death. Peter cannot listen to this, and he takes Jesus to task. Jesus in turn rebukes Peter and then explains the courage and sacrifice necessary to live by the values of the rule of God: "If any want to come after me, let them deny themselves and take up their cross and follow after me. For those who want to save their lives will lose them, but those who will lose their lives for me and the good news will save them" (Mk 8:34–35).

A short while later, Jesus predicts his death a second time. Shockingly, even as Jesus is teaching about his coming death, the disciples are arguing about which of them is most important. In response, Jesus' teaching focuses this time not on the willingness to die but on the willingness to live as a disciple: "If any want to be most important, they must be least of all and servant of all" (Mk 9:35). He dramatizes this teaching by taking a child – symbolizing those with the least status and power in society – and he elevates the welcoming of the child to the same importance as welcoming Jesus himself. In short, it is the position of serving those with less power, such as caring for a child, and not the position of domination, such as being the most important disciple of a popular rabbi or gaining power from being a follower of The Christ (i.e. the Messiah), that makes one a follower of the rule of God. Sadly, the disciples are very soon thereafter found pushing little children aside, presumably in order to get on with their "important" work.

As if this episode were not enough, the scene is repeated once again. Jesus and the disciples are nearing Jerusalem and the reality of Jesus' prediction must be sinking in, because the disciples are afraid. For a third time, Jesus predicts to them what will happen to him: he will be handed over, tortured, killed, and rise again. Astoundingly, James and John respond by asking if they can sit on Jesus' right and left hand in his glory! This precipitates a fight among the disciples. So once again Jesus teaches them, as clearly and pointedly as possible, what God's rule is about: "You know that those who rule the Gentile nations lord over them and those who are considered to be great among them exert authority over them, but it is not to be like this among you;

instead, whoever wants to become great among you is to be your servant, and whoever wants to be most important among you is to be slave of all" (Mk 10:42–4). This statement does not refer to coerced servitude to those with greater power, the kind that has been forced upon women and slaves in many societies. In Mark's portrayal, Jesus' whole life and teaching have stood in opposition to such servitude. Rather, Jesus teaches voluntary service on behalf of those with less power and the refusal to use power over others.

Rather than relationships based on domination, Jesus seeks to establish relationships of mutual love and responsibility. Such relationships have been called the "discipleship of equals" (see Fiorenza 1983; Dewey 1994). We see this mutual service in the minor characters who serve God and others at great risk and at great cost: those who bring friends or relatives for healing, the woman who anoints Jesus ahead for his burial, Joseph of Arimathea who risks his reputation to bury Jesus, the frightened women at the grave ready to anoint Jesus' body, and the models of servants and slaves that Jesus refers to in his teaching.

We clearly see the emphasis on mutuality in Jesus' teaching about marriage and divorce. In Jewish practice at this time, only a man could initiate divorce, and it could be done for rather insignificant reasons. This left the woman not only alone but also in a very precarious position in the society, without means or status. In Mark, Jesus reframes the entire issue in light of God's intention for mutuality in marriage, expressed in scripture, that the two become one flesh. Therefore, either husband or wife will be guilty of adultery if he or she divorces and marries another. The wife is not property to be discarded, but she is also equally responsible to make the marriage work as God intended.[4]

The summation of Jesus' teaching on power and domination are the commandments from the law to love God with all one's heart, life, mind, and strength and to love one's neighbor as oneself. This love of other as self is the consummate expression of the nature of God's realm – in contrast to the systems of domination that result from fearful people controlling and maintaining power over others to secure their own positions and to aggrandize themselves. Jesus manifests God's rule in his willingness to live in service and even to die rather than to lord over others. His example encourages others to be committed to the same life of service.

Once in Jerusalem, the forces against Jesus build quickly. After he upends the tables of the money changers in the Temple, his execution is inevitable. In his prayer in the garden before his death, Jesus is clearly afraid to die. His will is choosing life. Yet he is able to say to God, "not what I will but what you will" (Mk 14:36). Though Jesus, like Ada, would choose life for himself, yet he is in a different position: he is risking death in the course of serving others in the reign of God. In this context, he is willing to submit even his death to God, and in so doing he gives up control of others – triumph over his enemies or the possible success or failure of his movement. He has been able to live without dominating and without controlling. He will die opposing oppression without becoming an oppressor himself.

In the end, Jesus is put to death just as violently and gruesomely as he had predicted. Mark, more than any other gospel, portrays the horror and the suffering on the cross. Jesus' death shows most clearly that this was a life lived for others in spite of the cost. At the end of the story, the resurrection of Jesus, made known by the announcement of the young man at the empty grave, puts God's ultimate affirmation on Jesus' life and teaching.

Experimenting in Intertextuality

When we put the Gospel and the film *The Piano* next to each other, we can see that Campion's story presents us with a compelling illustration of the human condition when people "lord it over" other people. In the Gospel of Mark, Jesus always points to examples that are not explicitly religious in order to illustrate his teaching: a woman who patches clothes, a farmer sowing seeds, a kingdom divided against itself, or a landowner dealing with violent tenants. In a similar way, the film provides a modern, extended illustration of the dynamics of the rule of God as applied to individuals: the transforming power of mutual service in contrast to the futility of coercive domination.

Thus, looking at *The Piano* through the framework of Mark enables us to see more clearly the dynamics of power in the film. For example, we see more clearly the tragedy of Stewart's attempt at domination. It could have been different had he had a framework for his life other than "the rulebook that stringently tutors him on patriarchal duty, feminine docility, the white man's imperial burden" (Greenberg 1994: 46). Stewart is blind precisely in the way the authorities in the Gospel are blind: from their point of view, they believe they are doing right, just as Stewart does. He thinks he is upholding society and world order according to the expected/accepted social-religious norms, and he cannot see how it leaves him unable to love, unable to experience mutual service in a relationship of equals. People in positions of power are certain that they are right because the core values of the culture – in this case, the quest for wealth, power, and status – support them.

Like the leaders in the Gospel who have power, Stewart must stay in control of his domain. Mark makes it clear that fear underlies the human need to control. Just so, as Stewart begins to lose control, he becomes increasingly fearful and rageful. Although one might interpret his jealous rage as unrequited love, it is clear that he never loves Ada in the mutual way that is set out by Jesus ("love your neighbor as yourself"; "the two become one"). Had he been able to trade the framework set out by Jesus for his own, he might have learned to serve Ada's needs and to let go of his need to control her – whether she chose to love him or not.

It is likewise with Ada's will. We are tempted to find Ada's strong will heroic when we imagine what would have been the extent of her victimization without it. But Campion does not glorify Ada's will. While it has perhaps been her only weapon in the twisted power relationships of her culture, it has cost her a lot. She lives mute, has supplanted most human relationships with her love of the piano, chooses virtually to prostitute herself to keep it, has a daughter born out of wedlock who yearns for a father, puts her daughter in great emotional peril to consummate her passion with Baines, and predicts to Stewart (through her burning thoughts) even more devastating consequences from her will if Stewart does not release her.

It is interesting to watch what happens when Ada emerges from this relationship of domination and is able to experience a chosen, mutual love. She is able to let go of those things to which her will is so attached, and we watch the unknotting of all that has been so twisted up. Her will chooses life; she is able to separate herself from the piano and leave it behind in its watery grave; she is resurrected to a new life, and she even begins to learn to speak. To be sure, she says in a voiceover at the end of the film that death continues to pull on her; nevertheless, she is sustained by her will to live. This is an illuminating example of what can happen when one experiences mutual love similar to that which Jesus teaches and lives out in the Gospel of Mark. There is no longer the need to control, either in aggressive or passive-aggressive ways.

In letting go of Ada and his consuming desire for her, Baines stops "lording it over" her and offers her a relationship of mutual love. He is willing to risk losing what is most important to him in order to have a relationship that is non-coercive and reciprocal. Their lovemaking, as they face each other side by side, becomes a symbol of this new relationship. He then becomes her "servant," taking her from Stewart, insisting that her piano be transported with her in spite of the danger, making a metal finger for her so she can play the piano again. Though the seeds of compassion were evident in his character from the beginning, so was the power of domination. It was his choice to relinquish his will to dominate that turns his love into a redemptive force. Thus, with all his flaws and humanness, he is a compelling example of Jesus' teaching on choosing mutuality and servanthood.

Once we have seen the dynamics of power in *The Piano* in light of Mark, we are in a better position to see Mark in light of *The Piano*. By comparison with the film, the Gospel extends the dynamics of power beyond the personal to the societal and the political (on this, see Nelson-Pallmeyer 1992: esp. ch. 8).[5] It is precisely the power of *The Piano* that it focuses so intensely on the personal, with sparse commentary, leaving the viewer spying in upon this tangle of very human, contradictory relationships. However, the film does not draw implications for society, even though the whole of Western society is implicated in what happens in this remote spot in New Zealand. The Gospel of Mark, however, provides us with a vision of how the transformation from domination to mutuality in *The Piano* might be attempted as a renewal of the political and social order as a whole.

Furthermore, whereas *The Piano* does not foreground the spiritual dimensions of life, the source and impetus for the restoration of mutual love in Mark is the power of God in service to humanity. In the film, the theme of God's restoration of creation is only glimpsed ephemerally in the most contradictory symbols – Eden spoiled by mud, the clergyman staging a play about Bluebeard, Flora's angel wings full of dirt. *The Piano* is essentially a story of redemption through human love. Yet, when the film is placed next to Mark, we can see that this love mirrors the redemptive love of God. The Gospel of Mark displays a love that is larger than the love between a man and a woman. It is about a love at the source of life, which both empowers human love and allows humans to love the divine in return. In the view of Mark, this love of God can be a source both for the redeeming of personal relationships and for the renewing of society.

Finally, while the film leads viewers to discern the dynamics of domination and mutuality, the rhetoric of the Gospel of Mark goes further by urging readers to embrace its story as their way of life. The portrayal of the ultimate self-giving of Jesus is meant to inspire readers to give up their tenacious self-centeredness and be like him. The abrupt ending, with the women fleeing the tomb afraid and failing to say anything, propels readers to take up the story themselves and to be courageous in spite of the risks. And seeing the nature of God's rule and the alternative it offers to wealth, power, and domination empowers readers to choose a new realm of life comprised of relationships of mutual service.

Notes

1 For other such dialogues between biblical works and contemporary films, see Jewett 1993, and Scott 1994.
2 On strategies for reading film, see e.g. Bordwell 1989; Giannetti 1990, and Monaco 1981.
3 We are treating the Gospel of Mark as a narrative version of the historical figure of Jesus. It is surely important to affirm that Mark's story is based on history, yet we are here focusing on the distinctive features of Mark's portrayal of that history. For analyses of Mark's Gospel as a narrative, see Rhoads and Michie 1982, and Beck 1996. On modern methods of biblical criticism, including narrative criticism, see Anderson and Moore 1992.

4 Given the opposition to domination in Mark, we can infer that Mark presents Jesus' prohibition of divorce as the most humane course for marriage in his cultural context.
5 For an analysis of modern culture similar to Mark's portrayal of ancient culture, see the works of Becker (1975 and 1985).

5

The Drama of Salvation in George Stevens's *Shane*

Robert Banks

By almost universal consent *Shane* (1952) is one of the truly great Westerns, in my opinion the best and most durable of them all. This is partly because it is a cinematic *tour de force*, and partly because of the purity of its mythical vision. The film represents the high peak of the genre, both from a popular and critical point of view, before it began to go out of fashion. Though some fine Westerns were made periodically between the mid-1950s and mid-1980s, only in the last few years has the genre experienced something of a renaissance (Smith 1993: 45–9). The centrality of the Western to American cinema, and the firm place occupied by *Shane* within its canon, makes it worthy of close attention, especially given the way the genre has explored and even exploded the basic American myth.

During the last few decades, it is Clint Eastwood who has done most to keep the Western alive. Since his film *Pale Rider* (1985) – in which he both starred and directed – was largely a reworking of *Shane*, it is fitting to include a comparison between the two. *Pale Rider* is not his best Western – that, depending on taste, is either *The Outlaw Josey Wales* (1976) or his Oscar-winning *Unforgiven* (1992). *Pale Rider* falls midway between these two films in terms of his development of the genre.

The Savior in the Saddle: Rescuing the Community by Restoring Justice

Shane was based on the best-selling first novel of the same title by Jack Schaefer that appeared in 1949 (Work 1984). Its spare yet eloquent prose, basic yet elemental story, and everyday yet heroic ethos, made it enormously popular. The book came to the attention of George Stevens, then at the height of his filmmaking powers and public success. In the story Stevens saw the opportunity to make a different kind of Western. Though the form was riding high in the wake of *High Noon* – the most lauded of the new breed of psychologically oriented Westerns – Stevens wanted to go further. He sought to distill the essence of the Western and at the same time critique its celebration of violence. This was a tall order, for on the one hand it meant heightening the mythical character of the Western and on the other documenting the way violence exacted such a terrible toll.

The story of *Shane* is well known so I will not repeat it here. Almost all the classical elements of the Western can be found in it:

1   the main character enters a community;
2   he comes as a stranger;
3   his exceptional ability becomes apparent;
4   he is accorded a special status;
5   the community does not fully accept him;
6   there is conflict between villains and the community;
7   the community is weaker than these antagonists;
8   the latter threaten the society;
9   the hero tries to avoid involvement in the conflict;
10   the opponents endanger someone he has befriended;
11   the hero fights the villains;
12   in the process he defeats them;
13   the community is now safe;
14   the hero moves on.

(W. Wright 1975: 48–9)

The power of the film does not lie only or mainly in its embodiment of so many formal elements of the classic Western. It is due to the special vision that informs the work of Schaefer and Stevens, and to their detailed and distinctive realizations of that. The result is a story that lives and breathes in its own right, not just as the embodiment of a myth.

As with all his films, Stevens took great pains and considerable risks to achieve his goal. He chose carefully in all the main departments – screenwriter, cast, cinematographer, composer – and set his story against the backdrop of Wyoming's majestic Grand Teton range. Although *Shane* is one of the most faithful adaptations of a novel in cinema, Stevens made a number of other small but significant changes. Some stemmed mainly from the difference between writing a book and making a film, some were introduced to heighten the dramatic impact of certain elements in the story, and some give the story a stronger religious dimension.

Among the changes that were dictated by the change from a written to a visual medium were Stevens' replacement of an older Joey's reminiscing in later life about Shane to seeing Shane through young Joey's innocent and idealistic eyes, his signaling the conflict between the cattle barons and homesteaders much earlier in the film than in the book, his visualizing Shane less through one person's impressions than through his relationships with others, his describing Shane less in metaphorical and symbolic ways in favor of a more straightforwardly physical portrayal of both, and his giving prominence to Shane's main opponent, Wilson (Folsom 1970: 380–2).

However, I want to concentrate on the changes Stevens introduced that give the story a stronger religious dimension, especially on the way Shane is represented in some measure as a savior figure. According to Schaefer, the figure of the book was modeled primarily on his father, a Cleveland lawyer, though he also sought to embody in Shane the best of the human spirit as it came to expression in the American West. There are a few Christian echoes in the book. For example, the main couple are called Marian and Joe, who like the parents of Jesus are raising a young boy upon whom, with others his age, the future of the valley ultimately rests. Though he comes from outside their world, Shane joins and identifies with the farmers by living and working with Joe and Marian and wearing typical farmer's clothes. On occasions he allows his violent, repressed side to appear, as in an unprovoked fight, leading others to comment on his seeming "tireless and indestructible" whom "no bullet can kill." In the final confrontation he is wounded and then leaves the community behind. In words reminiscent of Tom Joad's at the end of *The Grapes of Wrath*, Marian says of Shane: "He's not gone. He's here, in this place. . . . He's all around us and in us and always will be."

In spite of these echoes, Schaefer himself commented:

I doubt if there is much Christian influence in my book, even sneaking in out of the cellar of my mind. My Shane may qualify as a "savior," but not as a Christian one – much more, and this deliberately, as a universal, a human, an all-mankind one. . . . There is a sound and more authentic background for what Shane did in the biological background of *homo sapiens* than there is in any religious tradition. He is more an alpha primate male fulfilling his genetically ingrained obligation to his kind than he is a repetition of a Christ-tradition.
(Letter by Schafer, April 8, 1974, cited in Marsden 1977–8)

The film critic Robert Warshow says of the portrayal of Shane:

The hero is hardly a man at all, but something like the Spirit of the West, beautiful in fringed buckskins. He emerges mysteriously from the plains, breathing sweetness and a melancholy which is no longer simply the Westerner's natural response to experience but has taken on spirituality. . . . The choice of Alan Ladd to play the leading role is

alone an indication of this film's tendency.... Ladd is a[n] ...
"aesthetic" object, with some of the "universality" of a piece of sculpture.

(Warshow 1974)

Whether drawing on his own religious convictions or on Christian motifs
present in the wider culture, Stevens and his colleagues gave the film a greater
biblical resonance.[2] A comparison between the film and the novel brings this
out in five interesting ways:

1 The opening and closing frame of reference is altered. In the book Shane
is first spotted by young Bob along the road in the distance: in the film (where
the name Bob is changed to Joey) we first see Shane riding down from the
high mountains into the valley. In the book his riding out of the valley along
the road is not the final scene: the film concludes with Shane riding not only
out of the valley but back up into the mountains. The motif of decent and
ascent could not be clearer, though Shane comes down from and returns to a
kind of Western Olympus rather than a Christian Heaven.

2 In the book the boy's first sighting of Shane is from a corral near the
house; in the film he is in an idyllic setting nearby, looking across a beautiful
pond, where a deer is gracefully drinking, framed by the awesome beauty of
the snow-capped mountains. Later the camera dwells on a garden in front of
the house which Marian has carefully cultivated, a detail never mentioned in
the book. Into this Eden-like setting evil intrudes, first in the shape of Joey's
gun aiming at the deer (which turns out be a toy but portends the violence to
come), and second, in the form of the rancher's men (riding their horses
roughshod over the garden as they approach) who have come to threaten
Joey's parents who are creating a new world in the West.

3 The clothes worn by the main protagonists differ. In the book Shane
wears darker, dust-covered clothes and Wilson the gunfighter appears in a city
outfit. In the film Shane wears buckskin that bears no trace of his journey,
underlining his mountain origins but intimating his un-ordinary character. In
contrast, Wilson is fully clothed in black, a statement – perhaps overstatement
– of his connection with evil. Though eventually, and reluctantly, he straps on
his gun, in the film Shane initially puts it away, thereby divesting himself of
his extraordinary ability.

4 The film introduces a Fourth of July celebration as a pivotal scene.
Though this is as much a celebration of the family, community, and nation as
a religious occasion – or, to put it differently, an exercise in civic religion – it
is Shane who (on the knoll where the cemetery is located) preaches a kind of
sermon on the mount reminding the farmers of what is at stake in their
struggle. On his final ride into the town to confront the hired gunfighter, there
is a most remarkable piece of editing by which his Christ-like role is visually
underlined. He passes again through the cemetery and instead of a cut to the

next scene where he is silhouetted alone against the sky Stevens dissolves into it in such a way that one of the graveyard crosses appears for a time to follow along behind him as he rides.[3]

5 In the final scenes, Stevens adds two significant touches. After the gunfight, in which Shane is wounded in the chest, he and Joey have one last conversation. A hand that, in the novel, a saddlebound Shane extends to but never touches Joey with becomes, in the film, a kind of laying on of hands: it is as if Shane were consecrating the boy for his future task of building on the example he had set for him prior to the final confrontation. And instead of just watching Shane ride out of the valley, the film has Joey chasing after him, calling out at the top of his voice, "Come back, Shane! Come back!"

In these ways the plot of the film reflects more of the biblical drama of salvation than the book on which it is based. It is always possible to overdo these similarities. One example of this is comparing the massive tree trunk Joe and Shane combine to uproot early in the story with the tree of paradise in the Garden of Eden (Scott 1994). And there are also clear limits to the comparison with Christ. Though he is clearly someone out-of-the-ordinary and even a projection of the ideal Westerner, there is no suggestion, in either novel or film, that he is a supernatural figure. Though he is able to help knit the community together, he has no special power to heal or forgive and, even with respect to Joey, forms no band of followers. Though he is reluctant to use violence, is willing to risk death on behalf of the people, indeed is himself wounded, ultimately restoration comes out of the barrel of his gun not the laying down of his life.

Shane is therefore a variation on the Christ-figure. Stevens once said that he sought to enlarge the Western legend by depicting the American pioneers as filling a similar role to the knights of the medieval legends. From this standpoint Shane is the knight *par excellence*, and he has more than once been compared to such a figure (Schein 1984). The medieval knight, however, is already in part a Christ-figure, so speaking of Shane this way still leaves us with the question of whether he is a compromised Christ-figure or a rather a legitimate blend of types appropriate to his context. Another set of figures with whom Shane has been compared is the Old Testament judges. In their time the law was in some disarray, and from time to time individuals arose who drew the people together and helped save them from a common enemy. They had to use force to do this, though generally they were outnumbered and it was through God's power that victory came. Shane could be viewed as representative of this Old Testament tradition, infused by certain motifs from the later Gospel story (Marsden 1984b: 395).

How, then, are we to evaluate Shane from a theological point of view? He could simply be regarded as a cultural distortion of the savior figure, one who fits the American myth that justifies violence but not the Christian way of operating. This is the view of Bernard Brandon Scott, who argues that:

> with Jesus as movie producer, when Shane entered the saloon, instead of destroying his enemies, they would have put him to death, and that would not have been a tragedy but a moment of conversation that leads to a new vision of God.
>
> *(Scott 1994: 66)*

If a conversation had been held after such an event, whether in real life or the film, I doubt whether it would have led to a new vision of God! Simply a recognition that evil had once again triumphed and that it was time to get out of there! But the larger question is whether, no matter what the outcome, Shane should have acted as Scott suggests. And to answer this question we have to ask another. Given the circumstances in the film, what was Shane's vocation? Was it to be a suffering servant, laying down his life as Jesus did, as a kind of messianic figure? This could be the role that a pastor or pacifist, called to model a non-violent way of life would have, but is this appropriate to Shane? Alternatively was his vocation to stand in for the law that is absent, as a kind of unofficial sheriff, and restore order to its rightful place? If that was his task, and this seems to be the way he at least perceived it, is there any other way he could have acted than he did? If he had first sought to arrest the antagonists, even though he had no authority to do that, or instead ordered them to leave town, would things have ended any differently?

If Scott's suggestion is to have force it must be placed in the kind of framework provided by the Mennonite tradition, which forbids the use of force by anyone under any circumstances. This was done in another fine Western, William Wyler's *Friendly Persuasion* (1956), and would provide a criterion for judging the legitimacy or otherwise of Shane's action. But one could also evaluate Shane in the light of Reformed theology as taking on the role of the representative of the law or even engaging in a limited version of a just war for peaceful ends. Such an interpretation could build on the biblical base provided by the judge-redeemers in Israel. His use of violence is after all only as a last resort, fitted to the need, and terminated as soon as the crisis is over. Questions could still be asked about certain differences between these stories and *Shane*. The judges called for and relied on divine aid to give them victory and mostly called on a remnant of the people to help with the struggle. Shane relies on his technical expertise with the gun and does it alone. We could also ask whether the specific Christian motifs in the film clarify or confuse his identity and role.

A third way of approaching the film is suggested by the Catholic writer and film critic, Peter Malone (a contributor to this volume), who draws on Jungian categories. He regards Shane as a mysterious figure who, like Christ, is a "sign of contradiction" containing both a light and shadow side (Malone 1990). He comes as the healer and the judge, and there is a place for both dimensions in his life and work. Such an interpretation raises questions about the status and nature of evil, and not all would feel at ease with this particular psychological framework. Other issues would also have to be discussed, such as the difference between the ways Shane and Christ use their shadow side for good.

This is the kind of theological debate the film engenders. But such a discussion would only be fully fruitful if the content of the American myth was also scrutinized, and not just the circumstances of the story.[4] John Wiley Nelson sums up the content of the American dream as: evil intrudes from outside the essentially good society: people are basically good not evil, but some have yielded to their baser instincts; this breaks social relations and threatens social institutions, such as the family, community or nation; the source of deliverance is also external: it comes through a mysterious, celibate individual with special powers; the outcome is preservation of the family-community-nation, and the future guarantee of schools, churches, law and order (Nelson 1976). There are strong echoes of this myth in *Shane*; though evil is present and people are weak, most are regarded as basically good; despite the presence of community, there is a reliance on a strong individual and upon an idealized humanity; and religion acts more as a support for familial, moral and civic values than as having some further transcendent goal.

Aspects of this myth are questionable. Challenging it would force us to consider more than how Shane should have acted. It raises more general questions about the basic structure of the plot. This is not to suggest that the story should have had a more overtly "religious" flavor – after all, Jesus' parables are quite "secular" in character. They rarely refer to anything formally religious and do not introduce God as one of the agents in the story. Indeed, apart from the opening reference to the kingdom of God, there is no reference to God at all. Changes in the structure of the plot, however, would move the story away from its classical form. It is interesting to contemplate the different elements in Akira Kurosawa's great "Eastern" *The Seven Samurai* (1953), which came out a year after *Shane*, where rescue comes from a group not an individual and with the help of the people. This film affected the form of the Western, which in other ways underwent change from the late 1950s. Though harking back to *Shane*, *Pale Rider* reflects other changes, and it would now be helpful to compare the two.

The Avenger in the Saddle: Executing Retribution and Saving the Community

Pale Rider was released a little over 30 years after *Shane*. Despite the disclaimers of Dennis Shyack, one of the screenwriters (*New York Times*, July 21, 1985), perhaps on professional grounds, Eastwood has acknowledged its dependence upon Stevens' film. It was both a homage to it and a revision of it. Though it is generally well-made, and has some singular scenes, *Pale Rider* is not in the same class as *Shane*. The earlier film reflects a greater vision, is technically superior, and has a stronger cast and script. The similarities between the two are obvious to anyone who has seen both films and there is no need for me to dwell on them here. It is the differences that are more interesting.

Eastwood's film is set a generation earlier than *Shane*, in California not Wyoming, and portrays the conflict between an environmentally rapacious mining baron and a group of poor, more earth-friendly, gold prospectors. It begins with the villains swirling down from the foothills into a quiet settlement, which they largely destroy. Megan, the 15 year-old female counterpart to Joey who lives with Sarah, her widowed mother, prays over her dead dog. The girl recites the words of the Twenty Third psalm, inserting some skeptical comments, but also asking for a miracle to demonstrate God's existence. There is a cut to a grizzled stranger appearing out of nowhere, who is wearing a strange mixture of clothes. He is mostly referred to as "Preacher" on account of his unexpectedly turning up wearing a clerical collar during a fight, in which however he bludgeons some of the villains. A male figure called Barrett (compare Starrett in *Shane*) is engaged to Sarah, though she is reluctant to fully commit herself to him.

Later, we see the young girl reading about the fourth seal in the book of Revelation. As she talks about a rider, Death, seated on a pale horse, and Hell following with him (Rev. 6:7–8), she sights the stranger who then visits her home. Megan falls in love with the stranger and later asks him to make love to her. Her mother, like Marian in *Shane*, is not only attracted to him but declares her love for him and, after initially resisting, yields to his sexual overtures. "The preacher" and Barrett then succeed in blowing up the mining baron's operation. The final confrontation is with a corrupt marshal rather than, as in *Shane*, with a hired gunslinger, one with whom "the preacher" has a personal score to settle. But first he has to dispatch 11 others (only three in *Shane*), which he does with uncanny skill and timing. Then he rides back out of town.

In focusing on the differences between the two films in the way they present their "drama of salvation," a further comparison of the way the two directors have modified their sources is in order. The best way to look at the changes rung in Eastwood's film, is to compare those rung by *Pale Rider* in this area with the ones Stevens introduced into his film of *Shane*.

1 In *Pale Rider* there is no opening descent of the hero at the beginning of the film, but rather a sudden later appearance. Though he rides out towards the hills at the end it is more an exit than an ascent. Instead his mysterious appearances and disappearances at critical moments in the story, and his complete silence on where he comes from, suggests a more supernatural figure who once lived but was fatally shot and adjudged dead. Interesting are the expressions "God damn" when he defeats the villains, or of "Jesus" when he comes out unscathed from a gunfight with five men, for these appear to be as much identifications of who is at work in him as profane exclamations. While he may not, as the reviewer Vincent Canby noted, be exactly a "god of some sort" (*New York Times*, June 28, 1985), he does have the character of an avenging angel more than a Christ-figure.

2 Though it is clear the prospectors are basically good people who do not exploit the environment in the way the miners do, there are no echoes of their forming a little Eden through their settlement of the valley, only hints of some future civilization. To a point, they are in the same business as those who wish to get rid of them: they just undertake it more responsibly and are more open to considering a long-range stay. In *Pale Rider* there is no portrait of a stable family or of traditional family values. The central "couple" are living in a de facto relationship, and the widow, generally a fine person, nevertheless has sex with "the preacher." The mysterious stranger is single but not a celibate, and though he rescues damsels in distress he is not quite the chivalrous knight. On the other hand, the evil nature of the villains is dramatized in the opening frames of the film and heightened consistently throughout. This gives the whole film a more apocalyptic tone, one supported by the reference to the book of Revelation early in the story.

3 "The preacher" does not change his garb and identify with the prospectors by living among them. Instead he remains aloof, his comings and goings largely dependent on their need for help. Though he only puts on his gun towards the end of the film – which is also the point at which he takes off his clerical collar – he never appears reluctant to use force. In comparison with *Shane*, the violence "the preacher" resorts to takes place earlier, is more drastic, occurs with greater frequency, and is exercised on more people.

4 The pivotal Fourth of July celebration scene in *Shane*, with the stranger's sermon about founding a genuine community in the valley, is omitted. If this is replaced by anything it is Megan's attempted rape by some of the mining baron's employees, and the consequent destruction of their camp and equipment. There is no hint of a connection between the Cross and the stranger, only the language of divine intervention to describe his appearance.

Since, in the figure of the marshal, the law plays a more ambiguous role in *Pale Rider* and, in the motivation of "the preacher" there is a score to settle with this old adversary, the figure played by Eastwood is less the upholder of law and order than an agent of excessive vengeance.

5 There is no final contact with, or "consecration," of Megan after the final gun battle. She arrives too late for both the fight and a farewell. As he rides on into the distance, however, she does, like Joey, call out, but it is to repeat her declaration of love rather than cry for the stranger to "come back."

Throughout *Pale Rider* there is more overt religious, indeed scriptural, language than in *Shane*. Witness Megan's comment about miracles: "the book says they happen"; the people's description of the stranger as "the preacher"; the mining baron's anxiety on first hearing about the stranger: "he could give them faith"; Eastwood's comment after beating one of the villains with a sledge-hammer: "well, the Lord does certainly work in mysterious ways"; also his response when faced with the temptation to shift his ministry to the town in a church that the mining baron offers to build: "you can't serve God and mammon." Even the corrupt marshal's name, Stockburn, evokes associations with hell. With respect to his own role in the film, Eastwood has acknowledged that "to develop the biblical parallels I ended up accenting the supernatural aspect a bit" (Guerif 1986: 186).

In spite of this the film has little of a religious feel to it. The spiritual references and framework are more of a dramatic device than, as in *Shane*, a shaping presence. The overall effect is more of a baroque allegory than a genuinely spiritual struggle. The religious lobby group which praised the film on its appearance for its "positive Christian values" failed to recognize this (Kraps 1985: 740).

Robert Jewett's instincts are therefore correct in bringing *Pale Rider* into dialog with Paul's teaching on divine retribution (Rom. 12:19–21) and in critiquing the film for its confusion of personal vengeance with the bringing of justice (Jewett 1993: 118–33). We can compare the film with the elements Wright identifies as present in the "vengeance variation" on the classical Western (W. Wright 1975: 69). Eastwood's film may not have the hero emerging out of the community to exact vengeance, later giving this up, and finally returning to the community. But the hero has in the past been a victim, does decide to seek vengeance, and is asked to desist from this by those he has befriended. What is a possible interpretation of *Shane*, namely the legitimacy of upholding the law by force as a last resort, is somewhat obscured. Though "the preacher's" action could be regarded as executing divine wrath, especially in view of his apparently supernatural character, the presence of mixed motives and his excessive use of force work against this.

More substantially than Scott, Jewett raises the important question: what to do as an alternative to the use of force when unjust violence occurs or threatens? He refers to Paul's injunctions to leave judgment to God, do good to one's enemy, and obey lawful authority. The first rules out vigilantism, which is presumptuous; the second seeks to break the cycle of violence, the third waits on properly appointed people to do their work. The difficulty in *Pale Rider* is that, unlike the relatively positive exercise of Roman authority when Paul gave this advice, rightful authority has been preempted by corrupt officials who perpetuate evil rather than resist it. What choice is there but to confront a Stockburn and his men with force? The problem lies, says Jewett, with the American myth's defective view of lawful authority as executing God's wrath: it is this that has necessitated the compensatory invention of individual instruments of providence to make up the lack (Jewett 1993: 130).

This, I think, takes the issue back to where it belongs, raising a similar kind of question to the one I posed in connection with *Shane*. The difference between the two films is that even as the story stands in *Pale Rider*, the stranger could and should have purged his personal motives (in relation to Sarah as much as Stockburn), and sought to kill Stockburn first rather than last (thereby scaring off the miner's, and perhaps even the remainder of Stockburn's, men). That he was capable of these is clear from other responses he makes in the film. If he had done these two things he would have at least brought himself into line with Shane, whose response to Marian and challenging of Wilson alone fits the pattern I am suggesting.

Where does this leave us with respect to our understanding of salvation? It could be argued that, for all their differences, the films have more in common than not at this point. After all, in both it is only through the use of violence that the beleaguered community is rescued. It is by the taking away, not giving up, of life, that rescuing of the oppressed comes. It is a matter of force not faith. Whether this is undertaken reluctantly (as in *Shane*) or aggressively (as in *Pale Rider*) is ultimately beside the point. The answer to the question of the implications of this for our understanding of salvation depends on correctly perceiving the filmmakers' intentions. It is important here to avoid an inappropriate heteronomous evaluation of the film without properly taking into account its own autonomous integrity (see further May and Bird 1982: 23–43). How far were Stevens and Eastwood trying to depict *the basic human condition*, its flaws and repercussions, and how these can be overcome, or to portray simply *one area of human conflict* that is recurrently problematic? In other words, are these films parables of individual and corporate salvation or of liberation from concrete injustice and oppression?

If it is the former, they challenge the classical approaches to the atonement, arguing (as on different grounds does some feminist and Liberation Theology) that the act of salvation includes a legitimate place for violence. If, however, we view the films as mainly raising questions about injustice and oppression, they challenge only a non-violent approach to the social dimensions of the Gospel as represented in the peace churches and their theological traditions. Clearly the films reject an individualistic or privatized understanding of salvation. Whether they only express a form of the "social gospel" cannot be deduced from these films alone. One would have to look at the wider body of work from both directors to see if they displayed such an interest. In Stevens's case, given his subsequent making of *The Greatest Story Ever Told* (1965), we would, I think, have to answer no. What neither does, however, even within the confines of their own stories, is reach as deep into the ambiguity and fallen state of the human heart and soul as do classic Christian approaches to salvation – viewed from the personal or corporate side.

There are many other motifs for investigation in these two films that have theological significance – their depiction of gender roles, and the family, the opposition between nature and civilization, country and town, small and large operators, the role of law and order – as well as the interesting question of how much these films are a cultural product of their times. By focusing on their reflection of the drama of salvation I have sought to clarify the extent to which they present a mixture of Penteteuchal (*Shane*) or Apocalyptic (*Pale Rider*) and Gospel elements. In this way Shane portrays a man who reflects characteristics of the judges in the Old Testament within a framework partly suggestive of Christ in the New Testament. For its part, *Pale Rider* presents a figure who appears more in the guise of an apocalyptic messenger with echoes of elements in the Jesus story. If the first draws consciously on the two Testaments, the second combines biblical and intertestamental ingredients. This is why for me, at least, *Shane* resonates more fully with Christian instincts. On the other hand, both films contain features suggesting that the influence of Christianity upon American culture has resulted in not only an interesting fusion and development of biblical motifs, but also a questionable confusion of them. One can cite here a more individualistic streak, religion as a support of moral and social values rather than a catalyst of creative ways of furthering them, a less profound understanding of the roots of good and evil in the human psyche. It is the clearer and purer portrayal of these in *Shane*, together with its more impressive literary and cinematic credentials, that makes it the more significant achievement.

Notes

1 The only two elements not fully present in *Shane* are: a strong friendship or respect between the hero and the villain, and the community's acceptance of the hero. There is certainly a respect for Stark's prowess with a gun but not for Stark himself, and while the community accepts Shane to a degree a certain wariness remains.

2 I am following here the hermeneutical procedure set out in relation to other films based on books, discussed by Kreitzer 1993.

3 I am grateful to my good friend, fellow biblical scholar and film buff Lincoln Hurst for this observation. He is presently completing a book on "Christ and Hollywood" that contains additional revealing insights into the film.

4 This is seen but not quite accurately formulated in the suggestive article by Michael T. Marsden (Marsden 1984b). He argues that: "Shane brings with him all the trappings of a wrathful God out of the Old Testament – omniscience, swift judgment or justice, and an anger born of 'injustice'"(p. 399). There is a false dichotomy here between the God of the Old and of the New Testament, and a depiction of Shane as a supernatural figure rather than as an agent of divine justice and vindication. The author is right, however, to stress the way the American imagination views both Christlike love and mercy and the contemporary judicial system as inadequate to the past or present problems of the country, and its preference for a superhuman figure to intervene and resolve pressing social and political problems.

6

Edward Scissorhands: Christology from a Suburban Fairy-tale

Peter Malone

The movie magazine gossip in early 1990 was agog with the news that heartthrob, Johnny Depp, best known for the American TV cop show, *21 Jump Street*, and John Waters's parody of a teen idol, *Cry Baby*, was spending hours in make-up to be transformed into a grotesque creature and that he was practising arm movements in order to wield garden shears in place of hands. This was odd enough, but the gossip also noted that Tim Burton who had been responsible for such "weird" movies as *Pee Wee's Big Adventure*, *Beetlejuice*, and *Batman* was directing him. This made it sound even odder.

Eventually, the film was released, not with a great deal of fanfare, but it turned out to be one of the most imaginative and gentle films of the early 1990s, a modern fable that appealed to adults and adolescents alike, *Edward Scissorhands*. It seemed to incorporate elements of myths, of fairy-tales and, many audiences noted, gospel parallels. Almost immediately, *Edward Scissorhands* was being given religious interpretations. The film is being analyzed in this chapter in order to offer an approach to contemporary insights into Christology.

The Fable of *Edward Scissorhands*

A brief plot outline will highlight the Jesus parallels. A master inventor, played by Vincent Price, creates from various parts, both human and mechanical, what is intended to be a good young man. Already we have a benign variation on the Frankenstein myth. The inventor is old and has had to work long and hard to perfect the young man's hands. In the meantime, Edward has been using large scissor shears. As he is about to fit the hands, the inventor has a heart attack, collapses and dies, Edward piercing one of the hands that are never to be his. Edward grieves that he does not have hands. Perhaps "grieves" is too strong a word, for the other human organ that Edward lacks is a heart.

The inventor, however, had educated Edward well, infusing his mind with both the wonders of poetic and scientific nature. "Up there," in a castle on a hill, Edward lives alone until a sweet Avon lady, Dianne Wiest, invites him down into the world – a pastel "little boxes" American suburb – to live with her family. Edward, with his pasty complexion, his unruly black hair and his eccentric matching black clothes, appears too different from ordinary people. But he soon wins them over, especially with his tonsorial skills, wielding his scissors on shaggy dogs who then look like show champions, on shrubs and on bored housewives' hairdos. His designs for humans, animals, and plants alike are masterpieces.

The daughter of the house, Kim (Winona Ryder), befriends him and becomes lovingly devoted. Her macho boyfriend, Jim (Anthony Michael Hall), is jealous and traps Edward into participating in a robbery. Edward's days down in the suburbs are numbered.

Edward has tried to be a human amongst humans, bringing the best out of most of the people he encounters. But then they turn against him. Edward is saved by Kim but has to defend his life against the angry Jim who falls to his death. Kim leaves Edward alone, back in his castle heights. She sends the hostile crowd away telling them that Edward is dead. However, it is she, as an old woman, who is recounting his story to her granddaughter, keeping alive his memory and his spirit. In his castle, Edward continues to shape beautiful gardens and ice sculptures. Kim dances in her memories in falling snow.

Audiences responded well to the fable. In fact, many commentators saw the film as a contemporary fairytale, a contemporary suburban fairytale.

The Perspective of Director Tim Burton

The screenplay was written by Caroline Thompson who adapted Frances Hodgson Burnett's *The Secret Garden* for the screen and who wrote and directed a version of *Black Beauty*. Her imagination delights in fables that dramatize values and she responded to the basic plot outline given her by Tim Burton. Burton brings his combination of the fey and the sinister to make *Edward Scissorhands* a tantalizingly attractive film:

> The idea actually came from a drawing I did a long time ago. It was just an image that I liked. It came subconsciously and was linked to a character who wants to touch but can't, who was both creative and destructive – those [sic] sort of contradictions can create a kind of ambivalence. It was very much linked to a feeling. The manifestation of the image made itself apparent and probably came to the surface when I was a teenager, because it is a very teenage thing. It had to do with relationships. I just felt I couldn't communicate. It was the feeling that

your image and how people perceive you were at odds with what is
inside you, which is a fairly common feeling.

(Salisbury 1995: 87)

Edward's appearance is striking but strange, a combination of the creative and
the destructive that Burton refers to, an outer manifestation of human duality.
Commentators on the film refer to Edward as in some way a "monster." He is
the beast of the fairy-tale "Beauty and the Beast." But monsters are not
necessarily monstrosities. They can be both frightening and fascinating – which
is how the German philosopher, Rudolf Otto speaks about "the Holy."[1] Burton
himself says: "Every kid responds to some image, some fairy-tale image, and I
felt most monsters were basically misperceived, they usually had much more
heartfelt souls than the human characters around them" (Salisbury 1995: 3).

The appearance can be both a mask, concealing reality, or a way for an
individual to express the inner reality. Speaking about his *Batman* films,
Burton reflects:

Masks in this country symbolize hiding, but when I used to go to
Hallowe'en parties wearing a mask it was actually more of a doorway, a
way of expressing myself. There is something about being hidden that
in some weird way helps you to be more open because you feel freer.
People would open up much more. They were always a little bit wilder,
because something about wearing a mask protected them. It's something
I've noticed in our culture and have felt myself. When people are
covered, a certain weird freedom comes to the surface. It seems the
opposite should be true, but I've found that it isn't.

(ibid.: 106)

Some of the ideas expressed in these quotations will be helpful in the
Christological quest, through an examinination of *Edward Scissorhands*. This is
not to say, of course, that Burton himself had any explicit theological intentions
when he was directing the film. The quotations already cited indicate that he
wanted to work on the level of values. Values are universal but they must be
perceived and interpreted according to the concepts and language of particular
systems of values. This includes the Christian concepts and language we are
using in this chapter.[2]

Jesus-figures and Christ-figures

A fruitful use of stories for theological exploration is to identify and analyze
"Christ-figures" (Malone 1988 and 1996). One can make the distinction

between "Jesus-figures" and "Christ-figures." The basic distinction is between representations of Jesus himself (Jesus-figures) and characters in real life and in the arts who resemble Jesus (from his messianic title, Christ-figures). The resemblance needs to be significant and substantial, otherwise it is trivial. It also needs to be understood from the text and texture of the work of art, be it classical or popular, and not read into the text with Christian presuppositions.

There are many Jesus-figures, whether they be crucifixes, the Jesus of a Renaissance painting or of a nineteenth-century plaster statue. Most of the artists who have painted or sculpted Jesus-figures seem to have assumed that they were offering "realistic" figures, Jesus as he was. However, even the most "representational" paintings or statues, while they might have seemed real to people of the culture that produced the work of art, are not a representation of what Jesus himself was actually like. Rather, they have been "stylized," adapted to the conventions of the current culture.

This is also true of movies that portray Jesus (see chapter 9 by William Telford in this book). Filmmakers and audiences may have thought that *King of Kings* or *The Greatest Story Ever Told* are realistic, when they are, in fact, "Hollywood stylized." Even Pasolini's admired *The Gospel According to St Matthew* is Italianate. The screenplays of these films often take a very literal, even fundamentalist, approach to the Gospel texts which also undermines their attempts to be realistic. With the advent of *Jesus Christ Superstar* in the 1970s and its subsequent popularity, filmmakers have felt freer to follow the lead of the visual arts in offering stylized Jesus-figures.

Biblical Criteria for Christ-figures

Christ-figures in the movies should be interpreted through biblical criteria; they can be seen as redeemers, saviors, and liberators.

There is a long tradition in the Jewish scriptures of redeemers, those who suffer and die on behalf of others. The most impressive and profound example of this tradition is found in the Old Testament book of Isaiah, in the section usually called "The Servant Songs" (and usually regarded as compiled by the second "Isaiah" to be found writing within the book). Of the prophetic servant Second Isaiah writes:

> he was pierced through for our faults, crushed for our sins.
> On him lies a punishment that brings us peace,
> and through his wounds we are healed.
>
> *(Isa. 53:5)*

The gospel passion narratives rely on familiarity with the Servant Songs of Second Isaiah, often using detail from the songs as "short-hand" for describing Jesus' suffering. In Isa. 50:6, the servant is struck on the face, spat on, his beard pulled and his back beaten. In this same way, Jesus' torture is described in the Gospels (Mk 15:16–20). The First Letter of Peter (at 2:21–4) quotes Isah. 53 explicitly. In fact, the author uses the language of the Christ-figure to exhort readers to be Christ-figures themselves: after speaking of suffering (in a passage about slaves being punished justly and unjustly), he states that "Christ suffered for you and left an example for you to follow the way he took" (v. 21; on all this, see Malone 1988: ch. 10).

Another tradition from the Jewish scriptures is that of saviors, those who transform others' lives or lead them into a new life. They range from Abraham, the patriarch migrating with his clan, to Moses leading the descendants of Abraham out of oppression in Egypt towards the promised land. The climax is the vision in Daniel 7, where the Son of Man, representing the faithful people of Israel, comes on the clouds of heaven to receive the reward for those who had remained faithful to God's promises to Abraham, those who were faithful to the covenant between God and his people. This term, Son of Man, relates to Jesus' reference to Caiphas when Caiphas asks Jesus who he really is (Mt. 26:63–6). Jesus is the Son of Man who, after suffering like the servant, will be glorified by God and lead his faithful into the new, heavenly, risen life. Saviors empower others to a rising to new life (Malone 1988: ch.14).

In recent times, especially in the countries of Latin America and in the Philippines, theologians influenced by Liberation Theology have been considering Jesus as Liberator. The title combines the aspects of redemption (being saved from suffering) and salvation (being empowered to live a new kind of life) with the liberator, who initiates action for justice and frees people from oppression. Liberation theologians see Jesus as an outspoken activist (for instance, his denunciations of the abuses by the Pharisees in Mt. 23) and as a man whose compassion is especially given to the marginalized (like the outcast leper of Mk 1:40).

Christ-figures, men and women (and perhaps even creatures of fiction like Hobbits) are "analogies" of Jesus, images of Jesus, who can assist us in our attempts to give depth to some understanding of him.

Jesus of Faith and Jesus of Culture

It should be said that theologians who pursue this fruitful exploration of the mystery of Jesus are looking at the Jesus of Faith, the Jesus whom they follow in belief and in commitment. However, many storytellers (especially in cinema) are not believers or committed to Jesus. And yet, many of them use Christ-figures, consciously or unconsciously, in their work.

The way that they look at the Jesus of the Gospels is as a Jesus of culture. Whatever the facts about Jesus of Nazareth and his historical reality, Jesus Christ is admired and his words and actions interpreted by peoples of diverse cultures, inside and outside the Christian tradition. Diverse cultures around the world have absorbed the Gospels into their consciousness and into their imagination and language, enabling any artistically creative person to draw on the stories and the person of Jesus as a metaphor, as a symbol, as an image of values they are exploring. They are religious analogies in the broadest sense. They are not necessarily faith analogies.

The consequent theological insights can be intellectual, remaining at the intellectual level, offering greater understanding or deeper understanding of the truth of the mystery. But the insights are also symbolic, operating on an esthetic level of appreciation of the beauty of the mystery. Insights gained – though insight may not be the best term for this experience, of course – can be on the level of feeling; desire and feelings – an acknowledgment of the goodness of the mystery.

Theologian Anthony Kelly gathers these themes together:

> As expressed in his human existence, the Word has a history. Jesus is born, lives, suffers, dies, rises. As he enters into the heart and mind of man [sic], the Word becomes a story. As projected into the history of all men [sic], in all times, in all cultures, the Word becomes a story told and re-told. The occasions for such retellings are as frequent as the number of the life-stories of men and women who hope that their story is a good story. The Word becomes the way of telling our story, the way of accounting for how we belong together, from the beginning unto the end.
>
> *(Kelly 1974: 27)*

The Word becomes the story, the Gospel. Jesus does not become first of all doctrine or dogma or theology. Each of these is only part of his story. And so, it is essential to note the narrative of how the Word lives amongst us and invites us to listen (ibid.).

Christology

The use of stories, of analogies, means that the Christology we are exploring is "Low Christology," "Christology from Below." Theologians make the distinction between "High Christology" and "Low Christology." "High

Christology" takes as its starting point the divinity of Jesus. Jesus comes down to earth from "above," from "the right hand of the Father" and any theological reflection sees Jesus of Nazareth in this light. John's Gospel and the New Testament letters of the Apostle Paul offer "High Christology." "Low Christology," on the other hand, takes the human Jesus as its starting point, trying to understand how Jesus is fully human as well as fully divine. This is the Christology of Matthew, Mark and Luke – the Synoptic Gospels. "Christology from Below" has its focus on Jesus of Nazareth and his humanity rather than on Jesus as the Christ, the Risen Lord. While this does include Jesus' deep and close relationship with God, with "Abba," his father, and the intimations of divinity which are sprinkled through the narrative, the course of his public life shows a gradual revelation of his oneness with the Father and his disciples' realization that he is the Messiah. This climaxes in Jesus' death but, principally, when the Father, listening to the "yes" of Jesus given utterly on the cross, reaches out to embrace his dead son and loves him into new, risen, divine life.

This makes the study of Christ-figures more credible. They are not (usually) superhuman beings with whom we cannot identify; they are human beings like us who can reveal something of what the Incarnation is and is like. But the Christ-figure is also something more, someone who can reveal our potential to us. We can see the completion of their stories, their beginning, middle and end, and the directions in which our uncompleted stories might go.

Edward Scissorhands can be seen as a Christ-figure. He is, for some, a redeemer. He is also, for some, a savior. And his story can, by analogy, help us to understand something of Jesus' experience of incarnation. There is, however, a momentary catch. Edward is not exactly human. For that reason, this is clearly an analogy, but an interesting one. And that is why Edward is referred to as a creature rather than as a human being.

Interpreting *Edward Scissorhands*

So, what does a viewing/reading of *Edward Scissorhands* offer for an approach to Christological insights, especially for an imaginative and feeling understanding? Following the plot outline, the following points emerge:

1 With its fairy-tale opening where "once upon a time" is in a castle on a hill, way above the ordinary world, while, in the ordinary world a little girl questions her grandmother and asks her to tell a story, there is a parallel in the movie with the origins of the Gospels. These were not theological texts. Rather, they originated from the second generation of Christians asking the original disciples all about Jesus. The answers were memories, memories of stories, the wonderful impact of these stories and the beginning of the "myths"

of Jesus (in the best and biblical sense of "myth" where the story tells the truth of its subject). The way of storytelling creates an atmosphere that influences our perceptions, giving the central character a heroic status, commanding respect and awe. *Edward Scissorhands* concludes with the grandmother vouching for the truth of what she has narrated, because she was a witness and what she has seen, she has told and knows it to be true.

On the level of fairy-tale and legend, besides the obvious reference to the *Frankenstein* story, the main influence is the tale of "Beauty and the Beast." Edward is seen, at first, as a monster, a beast; he is loved by Kim, the beauty, who is self-sacrificing in allowing him to go back to his castle. Commentators have been reminded of influences from *The Hunchback of Notre Dame* and *The Phantom of the Opera*.

2 The relationship of the inventor to Edward has severe limitations as a parallel between the Father and the Son. However, as an analogy, it helps us to imagine something of the relationship. The inventor-father gives everything he has to the creature-son. He has created him, given him life, educated him (including etiquette so that he can deal with human beings with finesse), infused him with knowledge. The father-inventor lives in the son and the son manifests the inspiration and skill of the father.

One can get tangled in the language of John's Gospel exploring the relationship between the Father and the Son, their oneness, and the Son manifesting the Father. But the screenplay of *Edward Scissorhands* helps us to imagine something of this union while acknowledging that, of course, it is not like this – above all, because the Father does not, in the Christian understanding of God, die in giving life to the Son.

Another interesting fantasy example of this kind of cinema gospel parallel is found in the first 20 minutes of Richard Donner's *Superman – The Movie* (1978). Mario Puzo's screenplay is quite explicit in its use of Johannine language about the relationship between Father and Son as a way of establishing the super-human origins of Superman in Krypton and of how he will be different from human beings as he descends to earth to be one with them.

At the end of *Edward Scissorhands*, Edward, thought dead, is still alive. His memory (and spirit) lives in those he has touched and transformed. He lives in the memory of Kim who, as grandmother, continues telling the story of Edward. If the dead bones becoming enfleshed and standing up as living beings in the Old Testament book of Ezekiel, "when I open your graves and raise you from your graves, my people . . . and I shall put my spirit in you, and you will live . . ." (37:14), can prefigure the resurrection of the dead, so Edward Scissorhands's creator-father who enlivens the son, a son who receives his words from the father, and whose spirit remains with people long after he has left them, can offer some imaginative insight into the Trinity. They

illuminate the theological concepts used for trying to understand the relationship between Father, Son, and Spirit. This leads us into deeper, more religious
reflections on the movie.

3 The story of the stranger who comes into a community and transforms
their lives, sometimes with challenge and pain, a sign of contradiction which
is often misunderstood – and who then disappears is an archetypal story.
Mark Salisbury, refers to Edward as "another of Burton's archetypal outsider
figures" (Salisbury 1995: xviii).

Many of the world faiths recount this kind of tale in their tales of incarnation
of the gods. It is a popular device in literature and theatre. It has also been
popular in movies, from Terence Stamp's "angel" in Pasolini's *Teorema* to
many of Clint Eastwood's Westerns like *High Plains Drifter* and *Pale Rider* (on
which, see Chapter 5 by Robert Banks). Intervening angels have been a staple
of Hollywood for decades. Benign aliens like *E.T.* have ensured that this
archetype has value for children as well as adults (as did *Peter Pan* on whom
the character of *E.T.* is based).

So, at the invitation of Peg, the kind Avon Lady, Edward comes down to
live amongst the people. He is like ordinary people. He is also not like ordinary
people. But his presence challenges and changes their lives. Just as Jesus came
to the small and insignificant town of Nazareth ("can anything good come out
of Nazareth?" is Nathanael's skeptical question to Philip in Jn 1:47), so Edward
comes to the pretentiously simple (even kitsch) and modern American town,
Anywheresville, USA. (As did Superman in *Superman – The Movie* where he
arrived in Smallville, was found by his foster-parents, the Kents, adopted and
brought up in a hidden life until he was about 30 when he was ready to go out
into the world and work.) "Incarnation" is, then, a staple both of religious
stories and tales of popular culture.

4 While "incarnation" can be imagined, it is the nature of the incarnation
that has taxed the minds of theologians through the centuries. The phrase that
emerged from the classical disputes of the fourth and fifth centuries was
"hypostatic union." The hypostatic union meant that Jesus, the person, had
both a divine nature and a human nature – but was still the one person.
Theologians have grasped at intellectual analogies to express the humanity-
divinity union in the person of Jesus. They have adopted philosophical
frameworks, philosophical systems and language to try to express the mystery.
The faithful have accepted the mystery and try to respond to the person of
Jesus in, as the New Testament Letter to the Ephesians puts it, the breadth
and length, the height and depth, until, knowing the love of Christ, which is
beyond all knowledge, they are filled with the utter fullness of God (3:18–19).

Edward Scissorhands is a "composite" creature, not a hypostatic union, but
a creature who is like us and yet not like us – a creature who can show human
beings how to be their better selves. He has been programed by his father-

creator so that he can communicate with people. Despite his puppet-like appearance (and he has been described by reviewers as "marionette," "robot," "android," "punk doll"), he appears as a total person, different, yes, but one who has knowledge and is gifted. At one stage, the suburban women want to make him more like themselves, even trying to use makeup to change his characteristic pale features with their look of pathos. It does not work.

In puzzling over Jesus as a "composite" of the human and the divine, theologian Bernard Lonergan SJ distinguished between "knowledge" and "consciousness." Jesus, both human and divine, was gifted with divine knowledge. But how did this knowledge enter into his consciousness when he was also truly human, with human limitations of growth in understanding? Jesus had to learn in a human way, learn to express himself in human concepts and language. The profundity of the Lord's Prayer comes from a deep experience of God as Abba, an intimate term meaning "Dad"/ "Papa"/ "Poppa." But it has found human expression and vocabulary from the spiritual heritage, the Jewish scriptures that have been handed down to Jesus from Mary and Joseph.[3]

5 Director Tim Burton was quoted earlier as saying that a mask can be a device for freedom rather than for concealment. He speaks of masks as a way of expressing himself. A mask can also free people to open up much more than they would in ordinary situations. As early as the first century CE, some Christians declared that Jesus' humanity was merely a cloak or a mask, covering the real Jesus who was, in fact, divine. This was judged as heretical. But, as we listen to the Gospel stories and note how people responded to Jesus as to no other person, the idea of the freeing mask helps us to appreciate the impact of Jesus and his ability to be different and yet reach people with great freedom. Edward Scissorhands wears strange clothes, has shears for hands. Young Kevin takes him to school as a "Show and Tell" project. Edward is able to communicate, revealing sides to his listeners that they have not been aware of till then.

Jesus, seen as a prophet (with the freeing mask of the prophet) is able to preach, to tell profound parables, to heal, to raise from the dead, to hold significant encounters with a range of people, from the marginalized tax collectors and prostitutes to the officials of the land and the religious leaders and teachers. While he might caution his followers from publicizing what he is doing, he is able to show to all who can see and hear what God is really like. Chapter 15 of the New Testament Gospel of Luke, which contains the parables of the lost sheep, the lost coin, and the lost son, is introduced by the story of how the sinners crowded round Jesus. The officials complain. Luke says that Jesus reacted to these complaints, and "spoke this parable to them." In fact, he told three. Jesus, one with his father, yet human like us, tells a story of how God is like a shepherd, like a woman, like an extravagantly loving and forgiving father. Jesus, seen (and "masked") as prophet, has a freedom to say what he likes. He can challenge. He can preach. He can reveal the "good news."

6 People's response to Jesus was very mixed. Some were cautious, some were scandalized, some were fearful and begged him to leave them. Many were converted from their traditional religious way of living or non-religious living to an acknowledgement that Jesus was, at least, a prophet revealing God to the people. Their lives were transformed by their faith and they became his disciples.

The suburbanites' response to Edward was similarly mixed: first caution and fear, then curiosity and attraction. For a while, there is conversion. The story of the woman at the well in chapter 4 of the Gospel of John is one of the longest single narratives in the Gospels. It obviously offers a pattern for encounter with Jesus, the various stages of a conversion experience: a chance meeting, a practical request, hints of deeper meaning in the conversation, defensive reactions, moral righteousness (which is not warranted), a surrender to the fascinating stranger and an enthusiasm to let others know about the experience – and then being fobbed off when others encounter the stranger for themselves. It comes to mind when observing the way the women are drawn to Edward. But it is a short-lived "conversion." Human pettiness triumphs over all good intentions.

Edward has been the archetypal outsider, the stranger who is the catalyst for change and, for many, transformation. This is true of the kindly foster parents, the do-gooding mother and the laid-back father. It is true of the boy, Kevin, because Edward lets the children come to him. It is true of Kim who learns to love him. As Jn 1:12 says of Jesus, "to all who did accept him, he gave power to become children of God." Kevin's and Kim's encounters with Edward were "faith-encounters." They believed in him and were changed for the better. They took on some of Edward's qualities for their own personalities.

7 But the preceding verse in the prologue of John's Gospel (Jn 1:11) tells us that "he came to his own domain and his own people did not accept him." The incarnation stories, the stories of the archetypal stranger eventually come to their chapters about hostility and suffering and, often, death.

Jim, Kim's boyfriend, is the betrayer, even persuading Kim for some time to be part of his scheme. He is violent and rude and plans a robbery, inducing the good-natured Edward to be part of it, allowing him to be trapped by security guards with the aim of having him arrested. He would be rid of him. Jim offers Edward his mock kiss.

The fickle women turn against him. Their leader, Joyce, regards him lustfully – an episode which echoes the story of Potiphar's wife and her denunciation of the patriarch, Joseph, who refused to succumb to her seduction (Gen. 39:7–20). This story of the innocent betrayed seems to be archetypal as well. Joyce's malice spurs the women on. Esmeralda, the strange religious fanatic whom people ignored, is now listened to as she denounces Edward. Jim baits him. Edward's shears, which have been such an instrument of joy in shaping and designing, now accidentally strike Kevin and the crowd scents blood. Edward is pursued to his castle as the crowd, now a mob, want his blood. One might say he is pursued like a lamb to the slaughter. He was their servant but he is now suffering – bearing the projection of all their inadequacy and hostility (Isa. 53:6). It is not hard to hear the echoes of "Crucify him." The screenplay makes its parallels with Jesus' passion quite clear.

8 There is a final conflict. Jim pursues Edward into the castle and a struggle ensues which ends in Jim's death, a struggle between the symbol of good and the symbol of evil. Evil is overcome. It brings on its own destruction. So, good is vindicated, right is seen to be done, innocence triumphs. Kim, who has witnessed the struggle, tells the people, especially the women, to go home. She tells them that Edward is dead. His life amongst them is over. They wander silently home.

9 Edward has disappeared. He has gone back to his father's home. For the people, he is dead. But he is alive. He has gone beyond the ordinary world. Edward has no spectacular resurrection story, but it is a new life story, nonetheless.[4] Kim does not or cannot stay in Edward's castle world. She is to go back home as well. But, she knows Edward is alive – and she is to keep his memory alive. But she never sees him again.

The screenplay returns us to where the film began. Kim continues to tell Edward's story. Her granddaughter delights in hearing the story. And there is a sign of his presence. In his castle, he shapes the shrubs and hedges. But he also shapes ice sculptures, including an image of the young Kim. The ice shavings fall like snow, like grace into Kim's world – and, in her imagination, a young girl again, she dances in the snow. The telling of the story keeps Edward's spirit alive and delights those who hear it – and that includes ourselves, the audience.

Conclusion

Tim Burton and the screenplay's author Caroline Thompson would lay no claim to *Edward Scissorhands* being a theological movie let alone a theological text. However, both of them have drawn on their imaginations. They have drawn on the universal fund of archetypal stories, be they fairy-tales, legends or myths, that fascinate storytellers and story-hearers alike. These stories include the Gospel stories. Joseph Campbell, following Carl Jung in his exploration of the meanings of these stories, uses the phrase, "the hero with a thousand faces." Jesus is one of these heroes. He has become a universal figure and his life, death and resurrection have become symbols of human experience.[5]

Edward Scissorhands has many parallels with the Gospel narratives. They can be considered, at least, as literary and cinematic allusions. But, because of the meanings the skilful presentation of the parallels suggests, we can reflect in more religious vein on the movie.

We are in good company, the company of Tim Burton himself, who remarks, "I think the reason I like fairy tales so much as a form – at least my interpretation of the form – what I get out of fairy tales, folk tales, myths, are these very extreme images, very heightened, but with some foundation to them. It means something but is fairly abstract and if it's going to connect with you it will connect with you, and if it's not then it won't." And he adds something which gives some credibility to what this chapter is trying to do: "I much prefer to connect with something on a subconscious level than to intellectualize about it. I prefer to intellectualize about it slightly after the fact" (Salisbury 1995: 94).

Notes

1 Otto (1958) refers to the "holy" as *mysterium: tremendum et fascinans*, a mystery that is both awesome and frightening.

2 It is not fanciful to be linking a commercial Hollywood movie to Christology or to be using it as a source for theological understanding. A short statement made by the bishops present at the First Vatican Council, 1869–70, highlights this (though a more modern translation is desirable): "Reason, indeed, enlightened by faith, when it seeks earnestly, piously, and calmly, attains by a gift from God some understanding, and that very fruitful, of mysteries; partly from the analogy of those things which it naturally knows . . ." (Rahner 1967: 36). The other ways for fruitful insight to be achieved are from the relations the mysteries of faith bear to one another and to our final destiny. Our stories relate and dramatize "analogies" (metaphors, images, symbols) of those things which reason naturally knows.

3 Lonergan added a seriously light insight into this mystery of consciousness by remarking that while Thomas Aquinas had an extraordinary amount of philosophical and theological knowledge, he would have been hard put to make a movie of his *Summa Theologica*. He would have needed to learn the language of film which was beyond him.

4 An interesting comparison can be made with the 1967 Stuart Rosenberg movie *Cool Hand Luke*. The final six minutes of the film are also a parallel to the passion and death of Jesus. Chain-gang convict, Luke (Paul Newman), has escaped and found his way into an empty church. He talks to God, referring to him as an old man – but he finds the old man isn't listening. He is abandoned. Looking out the church window with the possibility of surrendering, he is shot and then taken to hospital

(where he dies?). But the movie does not end there. Back in the prison, his friends tell and retell the story of his death. As photos of Luke come on screen, his legend and spirit live on.

5 Storytelling has been one of the ways in which Christians and aboriginal peoples have been able to communicate. Aborigines have their mythical "dreaming" and many have been eager to learn of Christians' "Jesus Dreaming" which they can share. Asian and Pacific theologians are becoming more and more involved in this sharing of stories.

7

Redeeming Violence in the Films of Martin Scorsese

David John Graham

Introduction

The world is a violent place. The biblical comment that "(T)he earth was filled with violence" (Gen. 6:11) is as true now as when it was written. Religions and their thinkers and spokespersons (theologians) have always faced the challenge of offering a reason for it, and the question of "theodicy" (how can a loving God permit suffering?) has often engaged them. Of course, there may be no reason for it, no explanation. Violence may need no exegete to give it meaning. It has been argued that it is simply a given, a fact of life which needs no explanation, since none can be satisfactorily given for it. This is one possible answer to the problem of suffering. But it may not satisfy everyone. For some reason, people – whether religious or not – have always tried to give a rationale for pain. Christian theism, for example, has always tried to answer the problem of suffering (which is a consequence of violence), classically at least since the time of Augustine.[1] And whether or not it is a concern of thinkers and theologians, in the experience of individuals and communities, and in popular religion, it is one of the great issues for which people look for an answer. In antiquity, the classical religions into whose world Christianity was born were very concerned with suffering. Ramsay Macmullen has said that the primary purpose of ancient religions was to heal, i.e. to relieve suffering (Macmullen 1967 and 1981). Thus, at a practical level, the cults of the Roman world dealt with the pains of life, bringing their remedies and cures. The competitiveness and conflicts in this regard are well seen, for instance, in Luke's account of the growth of the church in the New Testament book of Acts (Acts 19:11–16). Of this world, Macmullen comments: "It was a real melting pot" (1981: introduction).

But as well as the suffering caused by disease and other similar causes, religions also often seek to offer explanations for suffering caused by human actions. Indeed, the two are sometimes linked, for example in the connection made between sin (human action which produces unpleasant consequences) and suffering. Any direct connection between these two things is often discussed and then rejected in the biblical tradition. For example, in the book of Job his suffering is shown to be caused by something other than his personal actions, despite the received wisdom of his friends to the contrary. Parts of the Christian gospel tradition likewise (such as Lk. 13:1–5, Jn 9:1–3) serve to break the link between human action and pain as a consequence. Yet the picture is not simple, for a link between personal morality and suffering or divine judgement does surface in other biblical traditions, such as the deuteronomic law (Deut. 28:15–29:1) and some of the Jesus tradition (e.g. Mt. 9:2, 5). The connection is not a simple one.

In this chapter, however, I do not wish to explore the subject of suffering in general, but a smaller part of that whole topic, namely the human suffering produced by the deliberate and often premeditated actions of other people: the subject of violence. Can any explanation be given for that? More specifically, is human violence simply meaningless, or can it have purpose and be "redeemed" to some higher end? In a sense, we are – like the theologians described above – playing the game of explanations. Not content simply to let things be as they are, we look for reasons and explanations for them. Be that as it may, it does seem to be a persistent human trait.

There is, however, another reason for tackling this topic in a book about theology and film. It seems, even with a cursory glance at the sorts of movies which are made and distributed, that violence is an often-recurring theme. Whether it is seen in some of the pioneer films such as Griffiths's *Intolerance*, the epic Westerns of directors like John Ford, in *film noir*, in the genre of science fiction or elsewhere, violence often plays a major role. And although there are often voices raised to complain that there is "too much gratuitous violence" either in movies or on television, could it not be that this simply reflects society and its ills? Certainly, the debate about whether violence in film reflects violence in society or causes it, will continue to be heard. Yet there was no shortage of violence long before film was invented, as our opening quotation from the Bible indicates.

There is also an act of violence at the heart of the Christian faith. Its primary symbol, the cross, is a very violent one, no matter how it is often dressed up and softened in church architecture. Because of the very nature of the cross as a violent instrument of torture and death, the early apostles encountered incredulity and scorn when trying to proclaim a message at the heart of which was a cross (Acts 26:23; 1 Cor. 1:23). Yet the "scandal" of the cross has often since been domesticated as the cross has become a religious symbol of comfort and hope, torn from its historical roots of unmentionable horror. The violence of the cross – crucifixion as a means of death, which was abhorred by Roman citizens – became the very symbol of the Christian religion. And in biblical and theological reflection, the cross has been central in Christian history. Violence has also taken a leading role in the work of religious and social anthropologists such as René Girard. Girard has made the concept of violence in religion central to his exploration of the phenomenology of religion and sacrifice (see esp. Girard 1977 and 1986).[2]

Theology, Violence, and Film

I have chosen to focus on the work of one particular director, Martin Scorsese. This will not be an exhaustive treatment of his work (on his work more generally, see e.g. Connelly 1993; Stern 1995; Thompson and Christie 1989). However, in a selective way, I want to use some of his films to explore the concept of violence, and in particular the possibility that it can have a redemptive quality. The notion of redemptive suffering is probably a familiar one; can redemptive violence be as valid?

It should perhaps be noted at the outset that Scorsese, like many other movie directors, is revisionist in his approach to filmmaking. He is a master at reworking themes which are not entirely new, but which he then recreates with fresh insight. Perhaps, indeed, there is "nothing new under the sun," and much in film (and art in general) involves the reinterpretation of older plots. This can be very creatively done, as for example when the original story is revised.

One example which Scorsese himself gives is his treatment of Jake La Motta in *Raging Bull*. He interprets the punishing which Jake receives at the hands of Sugar Ray Robinson as self-inflicted penance, a sort of seeking for atonement. He comments that, whereas Jake himself (who was a consultant for the film) explained his beating as "playing possum," in the film "Jake . . . is something else. He takes the punishment for what he feels he's done wrong" (cited in Thompson and Christie 1989: 80). This is a sort of anti-theology: unlike Christian "penal" theories of the atonement, according to which Christ takes the punishment for what humankind has done wrong (an explanation common in the sort of Calvinistic circles in which Paul Schrader, who wrote the screenplay, was brought up), we have here a reversal of that. Whether that reflects Scorsese's rewriting of Schrader (his usual practice), or as in *The Last Temptation of Christ* is Schrader's own playful interpolation, is a moot point. The concept of self-inflicted punishment however is not uncommon in Catholic theology, from some forms of ascetic monasticism to the *stigmata* (marks of Christ's suffering). Here, we have a character seeking redemption through the violence inflicted by someone else. He feels that he must pay for his own wrongdoing, and that this can be achieved through the violence of the boxing ring, as he deliberately subjects himself to punishment which goes beyond the normal bounds of the sport. The portrayal of La Motta adds a complicated twist to the biographical film of the boxer. In some ways it goes beyond the bounds of what La Motta actually wrote about his experiences in his autobiography, yet as a piece of interpretation, it is inspired.

The above example is one small illustration of the complexity of human relations and motives as they can be portrayed in film. Recently, something of a loss of innocence in Hollywood has been chronicled on the (television) screen by Scorsese himself, in a documentary series *A Century of Cinema*, first screened in Britain on Channel 4 and then made available on video. Scorsese shows how the simple American myths of directors like the early John Ford and Frank Capra become more complex, yet more realistic, as they portray characters with a perplexing mixture of vices and virtues. The simplistic distinction between the hero and the villain ("goodies and baddies") disappears under the complex reality of human nature. Violence thus becomes a powerful tool both in making revisionist statements which subvert the simplistic myths of our past, and present new, challenging parables for our present and future. The phrase "gratuitous violence," which has become something of a cliché and even jingoistic, can often be used to dismiss or criticize the portrayal of scenes in film or on television. While one would not approve of using violent scenes simply to wallow in them, clichéd responses often fail to ask what the function of the scene is. In fact, by addressing and using incidents which are all too common in society, a purpose and meaning can be found in what otherwise might appear as simply "gratuitous."

"Redeeming Violence"

The title of this chapter does have a deliberate double meaning: "redeeming" can be read as a participle, i.e. the act of bringing violence to redemption; and "redeeming" can also be read as an adjective, i.e. violence as a redemptive event itself, something which can bring about redemption. We shall now explore some of the possible ways in which some popular and semi-popular films may provide theological raw material for reflection and constructive thought in this area. The examples chosen, it has to be admitted, have no particular coherence, even though some directors and actors feature more than others; other examples might have been chosen. On the other hand, it may be said that the choice is as it is because it "works" for this argument. That is a criticism which I cannot deny. The only response I can give is that a similar attempt could be made using other film sources, and that what follows can only be judged a success or a failure on its own contents, and not on what *might* have been.

Let us consider briefly one traditional Christian theological explanation of suffering. One interpretation of the Genesis account of the Garden of Eden is to see suffering as a result of evil, and evil itself due to (human) sin. On this view, it was the disobedience of the man and the woman, the direct outcome of which was the cursing of creation and human life (Gen. 3:14–19). The Old Testament, Jewish, and Christian beliefs and practices of atonement then function to redeem humanity from sin and its effects. With a strange irony, the means of redemptive atonement in both the Jewish and Christian traditions involves an act of immense violence.[3] The system of animal sacrifice in ancient Judaism, and the figure of Christ on the cross atoning for the sins of the world, are both powerful images of redemption through violence (a fact which is fundamental in René Girard's concept of sacred or mimetic violence). The redemptive nature of the cross, in terms of Girard's model, is precisely because of its violence. In a similar way, the portrayed violence of the film can offer a scenario with hope, and not just despair.

How, then, does that sort of "sacred" violence relate to the more profane examples in the world of film or of everyday life? In a secularized world, Fritz Lang speaks for the experience of many people when he says: "Violence has become, in my opinion, a definite part in a script. It has a dramaturgical reason to be there: you see, I don't think people believe in a devil with the horns and a forked tail, and therefore they don't believe in punishment after they are dead. So my question was, for me, what are people – in what belief people [sic] – or what are people feeling . . . that is, physical pain, and physical pain comes from violence, and that I think is today the only fact which people really feel, and therefore it has become a definite part of life, and naturally also of script."[4]

Scorsese himself, heavily influenced by his directorial and genre predecessors, comments about one particular genre, that "there's no reprieve in film noir" (Scorsese 1996). And yet, influenced as he has been by *film noir* (as well as the other great traditions of film), Scorsese goes beyond the sort of bleak picture which *film noir* gives. He is supremely a reinterpreter of some of the great film traditions, and this is seen as much in his creative use of violent imagery as anywhere in his work. In this sense, he stands as one of the great revisionist directors.[5] His use of violent imagery, and his reinterpretation of that motif from previous themes in film (such as his remake of *Cape Fear*) is not merely violence without meaning. In this respect, a comparison with Quentin Tarantino's use of violent imagery might be interesting, though that lies outside our present subject. Certainly, we would disagree with Hayward's linking of the two directors' use of "seemingly gratuitous violence" when she compares Scorsese's *Taxi Driver* with Tarantino's *Reservoir Dogs* (Hayward 1996: 264). The "seemingly" in that phrase must be emphasized, for in fact Hayward acknowledges Tarantino's skilful use of even a torture scene in his film, while later acknowledging that the main character in *Taxi Driver* evolves from being a mercurial Vietnam veteran, to a vigilante hero (ibid: 410). The transformation is not accidental; although at first glance uncontrolled, the violence is in fact part of a definite strategy, both by the director and the character(s) in the film. An aspect of life which often appears without explanation is therefore given a sense of meaning, in that it has a positive outcome.[6]

Violence is also something to be rescued from, and which can provide the impulse for the demonstration of self-denying virtues. The question of justice is central in religion and in film. The central symbols of the Christian faith subvert traditional understandings of fairness. Jesus' parables portray a God who is plainly "not fair" (see e.g. Mt. 20:1–16 or Lk. 19:11–27). Many films raise acute theological and ethical questions about right and wrong, especially when the "powers that be" (rule of law, state, police, etc.) do not function to "execute wrath on the wrongdoer" (Rom. 13:4). This is a situation which Paul, for example, must have faced, yet he does not seem to address it. The "powers" are assumed to be benevolent to the law-abiding, and curb the violence and wrong-doing of others, even though the world is not like that!

In Scorsese's *Cape Fear* (1991), there is a powerful role reversal, subverting the traditional roles of hero and villain. We discover that the "criminal" (Robert De Niro) had been jailed due to his lawyer holding back evidence which might have cleared him. De Niro then returns, to bring his revenge on the lawyer and his wife. Issues of justice, then, are not cut and dried. Heroes and anti-heroes, redeemers and destroyers, become almost inseparable within the same character. The same is also true of *The Last Temptation of Christ* (on which, see the final parts of chapter 9 by William Telford in this volume).

James Monaco has said of De Niro that he is at his best when "struggling with his demons" (Monaco 1993: 152). That may also be said of the work of other actors and directors. We might compare certain films to the Jewish "wisdom" tradition (e.g. the Old Testament books of Psalms, Job, Proverbs, Ecclesiastes), in its questioning of conventional solutions to problems, especially theodicy and the problem of evil (violence). Like the sages of the wisdom tradition, many of the truly creative voices in film are liminal figures, perhaps because they attempt to push our "horizon of expectation" too far. Karney says of Scorsese's sometime screenwriter Paul Schrader, for example, that "he remains slightly outside the Hollywood mainstream" (Karney 1993: 413). Hayward also observes that often the innovative and creative directors have at times been marginalized by Hollywood (Hayward 1996: 44). The realities and nightmares of life often remain in an unresolved tension. Like the biblical figure of Job, they give no easy answers to violence.[7] And like the patriarchal narratives in the book of Genesis (chapters 12–50), which themselves show considerable "wisdom" influences (especially the Joseph novella of chapters 37–50), the principal characters often struggle with their own demons. Could the biblical characters of Jacob or Joseph, for example, be considered "heroes"? Yet it is through and in them that God works, even through their evil and scheming (Gen. 50:20). The "orthodoxy" of the comforters of Job, including Elihu and his wife, is seen to comprise hollow platitudes. Instead, traditional religious piety and explanations are abandoned in favor of the realism of the complexities of life.[8] But, as Eliade and Tillich have noted, religion is still omnipresent, albeit in a different form.

Theologically, films and their directors can be highly ambivalent figures. They often eschew the simpler way of orthodoxy which others take. In the process, they challenge convention and the domestication of the unconventional. Peter Malone's attempts to find "Christ-figures" in film works from a simple typological approach (Malone 1990). Yet life, and film, is more complex than that may suggest. His distinguishing the "Jesus" from the "Christ" type is helpful, but cannot be discussed here (see, though, Graham 1997).

We can see (some) films using violence in a creative way. Violence can be redeemed from senselessness to purpose, and can have a redemptive effect on others, both the perpetrators and recipients. It does, and must, always function like a parable, to shock and subvert our preconceptions, not for mere effect, but to change our perceptions and reactions, in particular those which many religious traditions often offer us and which leave us simply comfortable. The unsettling nature of wisdom-parable, especially in its presentation of suffering and violence, makes it a threat to orthodoxy. The way in which the more conservative traditions react to this is to canonize them, as recent scholarship has ably shown with respect to the wisdom writings (Barton 1984: ch. 7). In the same way, if the film industry and its critics were to make the once rebellious "bad boys" (and girls) become its central spokespersons, then like the process of canonization of scripture, their message would be blunted.

At this point, it would be useful to give a little background information about Scorsese and Schrader. Schrader's upbringing was, by his own account, totally aniconic: he was not allowed by his parents to watch a film until he was 17 years old, but reared in a literary environment (Thompson and Christie 1989: 53). Scorsese, in contrast, dogged by childhood asthma and in a sub-literate environment, threw himself wholesale into the delights of movie-going (Thompson and Christie 1989: 4–21). At the same time, the twin effects of a devout Catholic home and school, and the raw violence of their neighborhood of New York at that time, were making indelible marks on him which would characterize his directing career for years to come. Scorsese, growing up in New York's "Little Italy," realized quickly that the world is a dangerous place (Connelly 1993: ix; Thompson and Christie 1989: 3). Connelly, in a list of about eight of the distinctive qualities of Scorsese's films, lists "violence" as one of them; a distinguishing feature of the *auteur's* work (1993: xi). Interestingly, she does not mention their "religious" qualities in the list proper, although she does preface her remarks by saying that Scorsese shows people in their spiritual condition. In many ways, then, what we see as the end product of their filmmaking in reality reflects much of their own experience and the realities of society.

The film industry is often described as, or accused of, portraying unnecessary violence. This often comes as part of a critique, in which gratuitous violence is criticized, when film censors may be slow to allow a film's general release, and films are linked with subsequent crime, accused of inciting it: most recently, with Oliver Stone's *Natural Born Killers*. There have, however, been many previous examples, including suggestions that videos displaying violence had an impact upon the schoolboy killers of two-year-old James Bulger in Liverpool in 1993. In a much-publicized book, film critic and conservative Jewish writer Michael Medved launched a similar attack on Hollywood and its effects on "traditional values" (Medved 1992, esp. ch. 12). In many ways, the book capitalizes on the social and political interest in the "family values" of right-wing American politics. The photograph on the back cover of the paperback edition, alongside the blurb about the author, portrays him as part of the traditional family (wife and two children). Yet is the front cover's fluorescent orange, peel-off sticker, proclaiming "CAUTION Contains explicit language and descriptions" really intended as a warning in case your children pick up the book, or as an incentive to the prurient to buy it? Would anyone defend violence (or pornography) which indulges the attentions of the viewer or the reader for the warped enjoyment of it, while at the same time exploiting the victims? Yet Medved's world would be one of interminable Disney or Capra.[9] And he misses the point in another way also. There is a sense in which the religion of the movies, the cult of Hollywood, do indeed, and should, offer a challenge to traditional values, including making us rethink the religious ideals of salvation, or offering alternatives. We might even say that there is a priestly role for directors, as they offer to the mass of the people a different understanding and interpretation of reality. Certainly, in the case of Scorsese, his childhood desire to attain salvation by becoming a priest was sublimated into dispensing salvation through the cinema screen. Yet, there can often be a sort of subversive theological enterprise at work in this. The "savior"-figures are often anti-heroes, and their own vicissitudes are all too apparent, while not, however, preventing the element of hope amidst despair from being seen. Scorsese has commented that the anti-hero of *Taxi Driver*, Travis Bickle, is "spiritual," but "[I]t's the power of the spirit on the wrong road," like Charles Manson (Thompson and Christie 1989: 62). Film can therefore be revisionist in more than one sense: exploring the religious through a superficially "secular" medium, and using parable to subvert traditionalist explanations of human experience. Not that this is new: the Jewish wisdom tradition did a similar thing, and the Jesus tradition of the Christian scriptures is no less subversive.

My choice of films has been highly selective. I have used a few of those which I think "work." Other examples, it has to be admitted, might not be so convincing. Yet these examples have been enough to illustrate two main points: first, that movies and their directors can provide the film watcher with powerful religious images, at times giving important and alternative interpretations of human experience; second (to pick up the subject of this chapter), although violence can be destructive and self-destructive, it can also at times bring redemption.

Notes

1 Most of what follows will be concerned with violence, i.e. that which is deliberately perpetrated by one against another. This usually results in suffering, and is part of the "problem of evil," but of course there is much suffering – human as well as animal – which is not the result of violence.

2 See also Williams 1991; Hamerton-Kelly 1992. A more developed exploration of Girard's ideas might pay fruitful dividends in this regard, for example Hamerton-Kelly's comment that: "Violence ... is the actualization of desire's mimetic propensity as rivalry, through the process of the mediator becoming the obstacle. Violence is the whole range of this deformation of desire – from the beginning in rivalry to the climax in the killing of surrogate victims" (Hamerton-Kelly 1992: 21).

3 With respect to the Jewish faith, at least before the temple was destroyed in 70 CE. Since that time, the "day of atonement" has been marked by prayer and fasting.

4 Interviewed in Scorsese 1996. His English is rather staccato and broken.

5 The notion of Scorsese as a revisionist director is explored, for example by Connelly 1993. See also Thompson and Christie 1989; Weiss 1987; Jackson 1990 (=1992); and Stern 1995.

6 Nelmes 1996: 114. This aspect of violence is also central to Girard's work, and his interpreters such as Williams and Hamerton-Kelly.

7 Notwithstanding the issue of whether the "happy" ending of Job was not original to the text. It is interesting to compare Scorsese's *New York, New York*, which was given a second release with a happy ending, to make it a bigger box office success. Connelly remarks (1993: 67): "This version was later highly praised by critics."

8 Much in the same way that Scorsese and Schrader have left their traditional Catholic and Calvinist roots behind them; yet at the same time, their influences are seen everywhere in their work.

9 Recently, even Disney has been boycotted by the Southern Baptist Convention, because of the corporation's social welfare policies.

8

Liberation in *Awakenings*

Ian Maher

The central themes of Awakenings *– falling asleep, being turned to stone; being wakened decades later, to a world no longer one's own – have an immediate power to grip the imagination. This is the stuff that dreams, nightmares, and legends are made of – and yet it actually happened.*

(Sacks 1991: 367)

Those words of Oliver Sacks capture the essence of the remarkable events described in his book and dramatized by Penny Marshall in her 1990 film of the same name. Liberation took place in the lives of figures "turned to stone" decades earlier by the spell of a cruel virus. It also took place in the lives of all with whom they came into contact. Doctors, nurses, family, friends – none remained unaffected.

This chapter explores the theme of liberation as evoked primarily through Marshall's film. It should however be noted that it is far more than a "film of the book." The events depicted influenced its making in a profound way, with the actors themselves being deeply moved by the lives which they sought to portray. And when Lilian Tighe, the only living survivor of the patients recorded in Sacks's book, was brought to the set, dramatic representation and living reality connected in a way that affirmed the genius of the actors and the immense courage of the people who were their subjects (Sacks 1991: 377–86).

It was at Mount Carmel Hospital in New York during the 1960s where Sacks first encountered consequences of the sleeping-sickness epidemic (*encephalitis lethargica*) that swept the world in the 1920s. There he discovered people who had, to all intents and purposes, been "asleep" for years and even decades, largely oblivious to their external surroundings. They were the tip of a huge iceberg of people whose lives had been, effectively, put to sleep by the epidemic. In the 1960s there was "no major country without its complement of post-encephalitics" (Sacks 1991: xxvi).

In 1969, using a drug developed for the treatment of Parkinson's disease known as L-dopa (laevodihydroxyphenylalanine), Sacks caused an "awakening" to take place in the lives of Mount Carmel's post-encephalitic patients. His work provided unique documentary evidence for the opening of a chemical window in the lives of those patients under his care, and it attracted great interest. In the wake of a TV documentary, which used footage of Sacks' filmed record, and both radio and stage plays – including Pinter's *A Kind of Alaska* – came Marshall's film.

Robin Williams as Dr Malcolm Sayer portrays the role of Oliver Sacks; Robert de Niro is Leonard Lowe – the pseudonym used by Sacks for one of his patients – and Mount Carmel becomes Bainbridge Hospital in the Bronx. As with any cinema representation of actual events, a degree of poetic licence is taken and a somewhat sanitized picture is presented of patient symptoms and drug side-effects. Yet *Awakenings* still captures the essence of what happened at Mount Carmel over the summer of 1969. Liberation came to those connected with the events in a variety of ways, the profundity of which is exemplified in the words of the real "Leonard Lowe" in describing the impact of his own awakening:

> I feel saved . . . resurrected, re-born. I feel a sense of health amounting to Grace . . . I feel like a man in love. I have broken through the barriers which cut me off from love . . . I have been hungry and yearning all my life and now I am full. Appeased. Satisfied. I want nothing more.
>
> *(Sacks 1991: 208)*

And in his diary from the same period Sachs recorded the following words:

> If everyone felt as good as I do, nobody would think of quarrelling or wars. Nobody would think of domination or possession. They would simply enjoy themselves and each other. They would realize that Heaven was right here down on earth.
>
> *(Sacks 1991: 208)*

Liberation is a motif which runs throughout the film and is used significantly to relate to the question of what it means to be human. Essentially, liberation is concerned with overcoming all that prevents a person from becoming fully human. Both the oppressor and the oppressed need to be liberated from actions, attitudes and ideologies that are life-diminishing. This often involves radical, if not even revolutionary change in the lives of individuals, institutions and structures that are responsible for oppression.

Within the Christian religious tradition "Liberation Theology" is the term applied to the exploration of the encounter between Christian faith in practice and all that stands in the way of human beings achieving wholeness (Hennelly 1990). A politicized phrase, Liberation Theology is, however, rooted in the wider concept of salvation which J. B. Taylor describes as being concerned with "rescuing all human life from darkness and despair" (English 1994: 26).

At its heart is a belief in a God who is the prime mover in this respect and identified explicitly as such. The story of the exodus of the Israelites from slavery in Egypt is the foundational Old Testament text. In the New Testament it is through the person of Jesus Christ that the God of life, who is concerned with confronting and overcoming all that stands in the way of human freedom and wholeness, is supremely revealed (Gutierrez 1991).

From this understanding of a God who is on the side of the poor, the marginalized and the downtrodden, numerous "theologies of liberation" have evolved and they continue to develop out of the quest to discover just what it means to be human in situations of oppression (e.g. Boff 1987; Cone 1986; Sheppard 1983).

> Liberation theology, in sum, both continues and radically departs from modern theology. As a continuation, Liberation Theology represents a radical engagement of Christianity with the world, with the intent to represent human freedom and God's gratuitous activity in the questions and issues of the day. As a radically new paradigm and departure from modern theology, Liberation Theology reflects and guides a Christianity that is identified with those who suffer, that represents a freedom of transformation, and that proclaims a God whose love frees us for justice and faith.
>
> *(Chopp 1986: 153)*

Chopp thus draws attention to the step beyond modern theology – and certainly beyond classical Western theology – which Liberation Theology takes. Its proponents have been highly critical of any theology which takes a detached stance and has been scathing towards any purely academic approach (McGrath 1994: 144).

Of course, not all modern theology can be written off by liberation theologians as irrelevant at best, and a positive hindrance to issues of social justice at worst. Liberation Theology would endorse – and indeed participates in, any theological endeavor which seeks to engage with issues such as poverty, hunger and marginalization. Where it differs, and offers its greatest contribution, is in emphasizing the suffering of the poor and marginalized not as a passive compliance with suffering but as a participation in the struggle of God against oppression. Such a struggle involves a confrontation with all that lies at the root of suffering.

In contrast to the reflection followed by the action approach of much modern theology, Liberation Theology inverts the order: action comes first and then reflection, out of which comes further action. "Theology has to stop explaining the world, and start transforming it" (Bonino, in McGrath 1994:

106). True knowledge of God thus comes through commitment to the cause of those cast out to the margins and rejected by society.

In *Awakenings*, whilst Dr Sayer does not convey any overt theological stance it is arguable that an implicit theology of liberation is at work in him. This becomes apparent as the story progresses through his empathy with his patients and his willingness to take on the oppressive structures of the institution on their behalf, with little or no regard for his own personal cost (e.g. reputation, career prospects, etc.).

In an early sequence, where Dr Sayer is interviewed at Bainbridge, he tries to beat a retreat on discovering that the vacancy is for a clinical appointment rather than a research position at the chronic mental hospital. His self-perception, picked up later in the film, is one of social inadequacy. Sayer sees himself as "not very good with people." Offered the post he becomes the reluctant physician, pried away from his research laboratory and confronted for the first time since his internship with living, breathing patients. In many ways his circumstances become the trigger for the commencement of a process of liberation that has far-reaching consequences.

Yet still, for a while, he remains held captive by all the shaping influences that have created his wholly inadequate sense of who he is. Confronted, for instance, with an invitation to coffee with Nurse Eleanor Costello (Julie Kavner), Sayer declines by using the false excuse of another engagement and retreats into his world of solitary TV dinners and the study of plants. A significant point here is that Costello notices something in Sayer to which he, himself, is blind. His response to patients who have been institutionalized for many years reveals not a dispassionate researcher more at home in a laboratory, but rather a warm and caring man. Sayer's empathy with his patients in fact proves to be a vital key to unlocking the chains of resignation by which they had been held since arriving at Bainbridge.

As he explores the wards and the patient records, Sayer struggles to come to terms with the implicit acceptance by the hospital of the unchangeable nature of the quality of life for so many of its patients. Seeming to be hopelessly out of his depth, Sayer first registers that all may not be what it seems when confronted by a new arrival at the hospital. Lucy Fishman (Alice Drummond) – an immobile, apparently wheelchair-bound woman – is brought to Bainbridge following the death of her sister in whose care she had been for many years.

Sayer discovers what his fellow physicians dismiss as a reflex Lucy's ability to catch an object falling in front of her or thrown towards her. Undaunted by their cynicism, Sayer presses on to discover that various patients respond to different stimuli: for some it is a specific type of music, for others something in their visual field, for yet others the touch of another human being. Realization dawns that people who to all intents and purposes are living statues can be reached. There is a glimmer that the cruel bars by which these people are incarcerated are not immovable. The oppression of their illness is not inevitable.

Driven by a deep conviction that something is being missed, Sayer eventually identifies a common factor in a number of the Bainbridge patients. Many of those regarded by his colleagues as Sayer's "statues" had suffered from the sleeping sickness epidemic of the 1920s. With the excitement of discovering a link between the patients, comes recognition of a dreadful possibility. What if the patients were mentally "intact" but imprisoned by the ravaging effects of a virus by which they had been afflicted, in some cases, over 30 years ago?

The realization of this possibility of almost unimaginable suffering is intensified for Sayer by his conversation with Dr Peter Ingram (Max Von Sydow). Having tracked down this aged man who had been an eminent physician at the time of the epidemic, Ingram describes how the long-term damage began to manifest itself. The victims became "insubstantial as ghosts." Ingram believed that their higher mental faculties had not been spared.

His belief was not the product of any empirical scientific evidence, however, but simply because for him the alternative was unimaginable. To think otherwise was to acknowledge the immeasurable depths of suffering endured for years and decades by the victims: the suffering of healthy minds held captive in the prisons of their bodies over which they had no control, unable to communicate in any way with the outside world; a solitary confinement of the soul. Spurred on by this, Sayer intensifies his quest to break through the confinement of his post-encephalitic patients, despite the negative and some-what patronizing attitudes of his medical colleagues at Bainbridge. Their attitudes and assumptions about Sayer's "statues" were not the result of a callous approach, but rather arose from resignation. They had convinced themselves, as a consequence of both their clinical skill and years of experience in the hospital, that the people in question were beyond help. Their walls of indifference might even have been a means of protection from facing the implications of an unthinkable alternative and the feelings of helplessness that would ensue.

Maintaining the status quo of a situation that is misjudged, uncertain, or completely wrong – whether knowingly or unconsciously – is a barrier to the liberation of all the parties concerned. All are prevented from progressing towards achieving their full potential as human beings. And while it is more obvious for some than for others, the reality is that all are victims of an oppression which takes on a subtle life of its own, which is all the more insidious because of its hidden nature.

Sometimes it takes an imaginative leap, an intuitive risk, or a fresh vision to crack the shell of a rigid, hardened position. In *Awakenings* this comes through

Sayer challenging the conventional wisdom that has effectively closed the cases of the post-encephalitic patients by identifying them as beyond any hope of improvement. The scene where Sayer and Costello are coloring in squares on the floor of the patient lounge is a graphic illustration of the creative spark so often needed to ignite the liberating process. His hunch that his patient Lucy's inability to walk beyond a certain point is linked to the pattern in the tiles pays off. In the same way, Sayer just "knows" that the post-encephalitic patients are mentally alive, even though medical science has said otherwise. Tests had been run, data gathered, and conclusions drawn. The patients' condition had not changed for years. Nothing had happened to suggest that the long-standing conclusion that they were beyond reach was flawed. Sayer just "knew."

The power of Sayer's conviction is reminiscent of the account in Mark's gospel of the woman who had suffered from haemorrhaging for many years. The physicians had all given up on her but she just "knew" that if she could somehow touch the hem of Jesus' garment she would be healed. Her intuition somehow slipped the shackles of resignation, imposed upon her by the ineffectiveness of attempts to restore her to health. She reached out and touched a mystery. Various explanations might be offered of both a natural and a supernatural kind. But whether what happened was an indication of a psychosomatic illness or a divine intervention are secondary to the result. The woman was indeed liberated from her suffering (Mk 5:25–34). Sayer's "knowing" likewise goes beyond the empirical evidence. It is a leap of faith, in this case driven by the desperate need to reach his patients, who are "elsewhere."

One of the most powerful expressions of what it means to experience this sense of being "elsewhere", trapped by circumstances misunderstood and misinterpreted by others, comes in a sequence involving Sayer and Leonard Lowe. Using an Ouija board as a convenient means of providing letters to point at, Sayer holds Leonard's arm and encourages him to spell out whatever he wants to say. Very slowly, a sequence of letters emerges that initially appears to have no meaning to Sayer. But later he realizes that Leonard has provided a reference to a poem entitled *The Panther*, by the German Rainer Maria Rilke (Leishman 1964: 33). The translation from Rilke's original used in the film is as follows:

> His gaze from staring through the bars has grown so weary,
> that it can take nothing more.
> For him it is as though there were a thousand bars,
> and behind the thousand bars no world.
> As he paces in cramped circles over and over,
> his powerful strides are like a ritual dance around a centre

where a great wheel stands paralyzed.
At times the curtain of the eye lifts without a sound.
And a shape enters, slips through the tightened silence of the shoulders,
reaches the heart and dies.

In a poignant scene Sayer sits on a bench in a zoo facing the panther's cage as Rilke's words play around in his head. The animal's pacing restlessness, contained behind the bars of its cage, mirrors the physical, psychological, emotional and spiritual pain of Leonard. The bars for him are not made of steel but are forged by an alloy comprising the effects of a random virus, institutional life, and the misunderstanding of his carers. In real life Leonard, again using a letter board, stressed his identification with the poet's "panther" in the words: "This is a human zoo" (Sacks 1991: 205).

Leonard, whilst not the only post-encephalitic patient portrayed in the film, is the symbolic character through whom the consequences of a life diminished by circumstances, events and attitudes beyond his control are explored. In Leonard, the viewer glimpses both the tragedy of freedom lost and the inner yearning for liberation. Rilke's panther is a metaphor for the struggle of the human spirit to be free of all that separates it from wholeness.

From within the Christian tradition this longing for wholeness is understood as part of the human condition. It is a longing concerned not only with the removal of the physical, structural, social and emotional chains which devalue human existence, but also with a spiritual dimension. There is a deep-rooted desire for an encounter with the Divine, without which life remains unfulfilled, regardless of external circumstances. Poets, mystics, theologians have all tried to encapsulate this desire in words.

St Augustine of Hippo (354–450 CE) expresses it this way: "You awake us to delight in Your praises; for You made us for Yourself, and our hearts are restless until they find their rest in You." (Appleton 1985: 64, adapted). In other words, without the connection with God, there remains an unmet longing within the human spirit. For the Christian, the key to this encounter, the source of the "connection," is to be found in and through the person of Jesus Christ, described by St Paul as "the image of the invisible God" (Col. 1:15; see also Phil. 2:5–11). The view of what it means to be human is intricately bound up with reflecting the image of God as revealed in the person of Jesus Christ (Dyson 1983; Comblin 1990). It is an image of a caring, compassionate and suffering God.

A Christian theological perspective upon humanity as we experience it, suggests that each person has bars that prevent attainment to wholeness. Consisting of a myriad of factors, relating to culture and class, race and religion, self-absorption and spirituality, they incarcerate humanity to such an extent that it is as if the world beyond the bars did not exist. And only when they are seen as bars can the yearning for liberation take shape and form. Until then, lives are only partly lived. Sayer takes awhile to do so but gradually realizes that he, too, has his bars. It is in fact Leonard who confronts Sayer with the message of "physician heal thyself" and of his need to break out of his own emotional prison. Before the act of liberation must come the vision of liberation, something brought to Bainbridge by Sayer; something given to Sayer by Leonard.

This need for fresh vision is alluded to on numerous occasions where attention is drawn to pairs of spectacles. Sayer polishes Lucy's spectacles just prior to discovering her ability to catch them as they fall; in another scene he races through a corridor fumbling for his own spectacles only to be told by Costello that "they're on your face"; and later in the film he is sat on his bed polishing his spare sets of spectacles following an incident where a pair are broken by Leonard. At this point, faced with Leonard's rapid deterioration, it is as though Sayer is searching for a new way of seeing. He knows the cost of an institution's flawed vision to its patients and is desperate not to repeat the mistake.

Driven on by the developing empathy with Leonard and energized through the insights of Rilke's poem, Sayer eventually secures permission for the trial use of L-dopa on Leonard. The result is that Leonard eventually "wakes up," returning to a life that he involuntarily left decades earlier. For Leonard and all those around him, the effects are profound and his awakening becomes the catalyst for a whole series of awakenings. De Niro's portrayal of the sense of release experienced by Leonard as the bars of his captivity melts away is remarkable and a tribute to the actor's art of becoming his subject. So immersed in his role was De Niro, that during filming concern arose about the psychological impact upon the actor of assuming the symptoms of Leonard's condition.

With the wonderment of a child, Leonard recognizes and expresses his appreciation of all that is taken so much for granted by such a high proportion of people in comfortable Western society. Through his actions and his words, he brings home very forcefully to Sayer the realization that the bars of captivity are not made, for most people, from the consequences of physical illness but rather from their attitudes and outlook upon life. The following exchange illustrates something of the power of the awakening triggered in Sayer through his encounter with Leonard and the other post-encephalitic patients.

From Bainbridge, a rather agitated Leonard has telephoned Sayer at his home in the middle of the night desperately wanting to talk. Sayer tells Leonard to wait in his office from where the call has been made until he arrives.

SAYER: Leonard, Leonard.
(*An enthusiastic Leonard greets Sayer.*)
LEONARD: Dr Sayer, sit down, sit down.
SAYER: Why, what's wrong?
LEONARD: We've got to tell everybody, we've got to remind them, we've got to remind them how good it is.
SAYER: How good what is, Leonard?
(*Leonard picks up a newspaper and shows it to Sayer.*)
LEONARD: What does it say? It's all bad, all bad. People have forgotten what life is all about, they have forgotten what it is like to be alive, they need to be reminded. They need to be reminded of what they have, what they could lose. What I feel is the joy of life, the gift of life, the freedom of life, the wonderment of life.
(*The scene changes to the pharmacy the following morning where Sayer is talking to one of the staff.*)
SAYER: He kept saying people don't appreciate the simple things – work, play, friendship, family. He was so excited he talked till five o'clock in the morning. I don't know whether this is liberation, mania . . .
STAFF MEMBER: Or love?
SAYER: Yes. What he's saying is absolutely right, though. We don't know how to live.

This awakening in Sayer is demonstrated further when, towards the end of the film, he addresses the benefactors of Bainbridge whose generosity has enabled the L-dopa programme to take place. By this stage in the film Leonard's remarkable physical liberation had regressed and he had returned to his immobile and completely dependent state as, presumably, had the rest of those whom he had treated:

The summer was extraordinary. It was a season of rebirth and innocence, a miracle. For the patients and for us, the care-takers. But now we have to adjust to the realities of miracles. We can hide behind the veil of science and say it was the drug that failed, or that the illness itself had returned, or that the patients were unable to cope with losing decades of their lives. The reality is that we don't know what went wrong any more than we know what went right. What we do know is as the chemical window closed another awakening took place. That the human spirit is more powerful than any drug and that is what needs to be nourished. With work, play, friendship, family. These are the things that matter. This is what we have forgotten. The simplest things.

No-one involved with what took place at Bainbridge remained unaffected. The events triggered a liberating process that operated at a variety of different levels. Significant change took place which over-turned the relational dynamics of the hospital.

For Leonard, and the rest of the patients there was the short-lived experience of freedom from the imprisonment of their physical con-dition. They were able to make choices: about the food they ate; the hairstyles they wore; to read a book or smoke a cigarette. These simple things had been denied, in some cases for decades, both by the illness and the institution in which they lived.

It is hard to imagine what this release meant in psychological and emotional terms to the patients. Leonard's almost contagious joy at being able to wade into the sea fully clothed while Sayer frantically looks on, provides a glimpse. The scene dramatically portrays what Oliver Sacks seeks to convey in his description of what happened on the awakening of the real "Leonard":

> Everything filled him with delight: he was like a man who had awoken from a nightmare or a serious illness, or a man released from entomb-ment or prison, who is suddenly intoxicated with the sense and beauty of everything round him . . . He loved going out in the hospital garden: he would touch the flowers and leaves with astonished delight, and sometimes kiss them or press them to his lips.
>
> *(Sacks 1991: 208–9)*

Understandably, the film only hints at the psychological implications and ensuing trauma for the patients in coming to terms with their "loss" of so many years. Sacks' book addresses these issues in considerable depth for those seeking a more rounded picture of the events behind the film.

For the purpose of good cinema the awakening of the patients apart from Leonard is condensed into one night when they emerge from their entomb-ment. Released from their catatonia-like cocoons, bodies stretch. Arms reach out to feel the breeze from a fan and people who have been ward-mates for many years say hello to each other for the first time. The scene is charged with emotion as a form of resurrection occurs and as the patients begin to rediscover life once again through able bodies. There is a resonance here with the narrative at the end of the Gospel according to Matthew: "The tombs broke open and the bodies of many holy people who had died were raised to life." (Mt. 27:52).

The staff at Bainbridge also undergo change as a consequence of the events. Doctors, nursing staff, ancillary workers all have to reevaluate their opinions and attitudes towards the post-encephalitic patients. For years they had treated them with professional care according to established routines. But due to the long duration of their time at the hospital, the patients had become regarded as merely passive recipients of care. Their very personhood had, in some way, disappeared in the eyes of those entrusted with their care. The staff had lost sight of the humanness inherent in each one of the patients despite the awfulness of their affliction, a blindness which in itself contributed to the oppressiveness of the "caring" regime of the institution.

Consequences for all concerned with the awakening patients were immediate. The patients had become "people" again. Leonard's mother receives back her son as an articulate, walking being; nurses relate to their charges as autonomous men and women for the first time and are confronted with their individuality and specific requests; doctors who had been cynical of Sayer's work are forced to reconsider and break out of the narrowness of the conventions with which they were bound. And, of course, for Sayer a huge transformation is underway as he begins to awaken to the essential nature of relationships needed for a person to be truly human.

Despite the eventual relapse of the patients to a similar physical state as before their L-dopa medication, a transformation had taken place in the life of the carers. They would never again in the same way see "statues" but rather people trapped inside physical prisons. People who *could* be reached and who deserved their every effort.

What becomes clearly apparent in the film, is that liberation is not without cost. This is a truth arising from the fact that the essence of liberation is concerned with the casting off of that which is oppressive. The process is seldom easy, as the fuel of oppression is power which is rigidly held and exercised. Even when achieved, the maintenance of liberation also exacts a price. Liberation is a fragile flower, easily trampled by the march of self which is so often the convenient option and the very point at which it can be lost for ever. In this respect, a materialistic philosophy is in many ways as destructive to liberation as the guns and torture chambers of an oppressive regime. It is a silent, suffocating oppression that is all the more insidious due to its hidden nature. A world divided into a hugely affluent minority and a vast multitude who live in poverty is the macrocosm of what is a present reality even within the privileged minority. The drive to achieve and maintain wealth, status and power so easily becomes an insulating barrier between the sometimes unwitting oppressor and the oppressed. But it is a two-way prison wall: those on both sides need to be set free. Liberation must be experienced by both the oppressor and the oppressed if it is to be a true and lasting liberation. At that point where oppression ceases, in Christian terms the kingdom of God is made a present reality. It is a foretaste of that for which the human spirit yearns. Such longing for liberation is deep seated in the human heart. It constantly emerges to challenge the creed of the powerful which argues that might is right; it values people for who they are, not what they do; it refuses to subject morality to the evolutionary principle of the survival of the fittest.

It is therefore no coincidence that, from the perspective of Christian theology and the Christian church, the liberator *par excellence* was not the leader of a group of armed revolutionaries, but a figure marginalized by "respectable" society and then judged by it before being subjected to execution on a cross. The power of love, exemplified for Christians in the person of Christ, is the root of any act of true liberation. It is that which enables one human being to make sacrifices for the sake of another; to reach out and love the unlovable; to lay down his/her life so that someone else might live (Jn 15:13).

The hard edge of liberation is the cost to all affected by it. In *Awakenings*, this is seen in the lives of patients and carers alike. Many of the post-encephalitic patients experience first the jubilation of their new found freedom, but then the frightening realization of what their awakening means: the recognition of the "loss" of ten, 20, even 25 years of life. Partners, children, friends have died or long since left them in the care of Bainbridge hospital. They have been frozen in time only to awaken to a world that has changed almost beyond recognition from the one they knew before falling asleep.

Leonard's mother, at first overjoyed at her son's "return" grows disillusioned by his developing friendship with a young woman named Paula (Penelope Ann Miller), who visits her stroke-victim father at Bainbridge. Mrs Lowe feels pushed out and rejected despite it being the only time in Leonard's adult life that he has been *able* to even begin a friendship with a woman. The effects of his sleeping sickness have kept Leonard in chains, but the viewer is faced with the possibility that there were also other chains that needed to be released.

For Mrs Lowe herself, an awakening is required to recognize Leonard's need to be released from the exclusive bond of love in which he had been held and from which he had received her tireless care and attention. The sacrifice of a mother to love her son enough to let him go is not, however, one that Mrs Lowe is prepared or able to make – a point brought home powerfully in her appeal to the hospital authorities to end Leonard's experimental treatment.

Leonard's condition has by this stage tragically deteriorated despite Sayer's frantic efforts to reverse the decline. Mrs Lowe's appeal is quite understandable in the circumstances. But just how much of his mother's appeal is due to her own inability to cope with the pain of seeing Leonard's suffering is unclear. Leonard himself does not appear to be asked what *he* wants regarding further medication. The easiest option for Mrs Lowe is arguably an undermining of Leonard's struggle to hold on to the fleeting experience of wholeness that the L-dopa treatment has allowed him to glimpse. Mrs Lowe's love for her son arguably contributes to the loss of his liberty. Attention is clearly drawn here to the cost of liberation, though it should be noted that the real "Leonard" himself asked to be taken off the drug (Sacks 1991: 219). For Leonard and the rest of Sayer's patients the liberation of their summer awakening brought with it consequences that those who have never suffered from such an illness can only just begin to imagine. To be free for a season from the prison of their sleeping sickness aftermath, only to slip back as the medication failed, must have been a devastating experience.

Towards the end of the film, Sayer demonstrates his own awareness of this by asking Nurse Costello how right it was to "give life" only for it to be taken away. No words can comfort Sayer who is left to ponder the enigma of human suffering. But having entered into the suffering of his patients through his empathy with them, a change has taken place. Concern, compassion, love for the broken lives of the Bainbridge patients has made a difference in a situation where previously there had been no hope. There is an echo here of the Christian understanding of a God who does not remain distant or aloof from his creation but who becomes part of it (e.g. Jn 1:1–14; Phil. 2:5–11): the incarnate God became human in order not simply to know about the existence of suffering but to experience it first hand. In that sense, Sayer is very much a Christlike figure and in particular when he feels overwhelmed by the weight of human suffering.

Whatever the consequences, the experience of liberation cannot be undone and the viewer is left to ponder on what it meant to each of the patients to return once again to their helpless state. Perhaps for some it increased their hopes that a time of liberation would come again. (There were, in fact, some further brief awakenings in the lives of the real post-encephalitic patients.) Perhaps for some it provided fresh experiences to take back into their solitude as sustenance for their isolation. Perhaps for others, the flip side of the experience of being free was a more acute awareness of the oppression of their illness. There was also a cost in the lives of the rest of the residents at Bainbridge. In one scene where the post-encephalitic patients are being identified and separated from those institutionalized because of various mental conditions, the latter group is portrayed as disturbed and confused. From their perspective those being given special treatment are chosen simply on the basis of whether they can catch a ball, something which most can do themselves.

The medical reasons for this selection are far more complex and probably beyond the cognitive capabilities of many of the patients. Their *experience* is to be treated differently. As one group of patients begins to experience liberation – even at that early stage their carers' attitudes are changing – another group is feeling left out and more dehumanized than ever. Liberation for one group of patients serves to heighten another group's awareness of its very absence.

In this respect, the presence of chronic mentally disturbed patients in *Awakenings* (a dramatic invention as there was no psychiatric ward for violent patients at Sacks' Mount Carmel) helps to avoid an over-romanticizing of what took place. There is an amazing transformation in the lives of the post-encephalitic patients as well as in the lives of those around them. But it happens against the backdrop of all the rest of the work of a hospital for those with chronic mental illness.

Those affected by a range of psychoses, paranoid schizophrenia and a range of other conditions can sometimes manifest behavior that is loud, unpredictable and even violent. Communication is difficult, sometimes almost impossible. The care of such patients is extremely demanding and needs to be kept constantly under review as research moves forward. Institutionalization can seem like the easy option, and while some patients clearly require 24-hour supervision, others do not need to be kept under lock and key. Such people, sometimes for the very best intentions, are deprived of their liberty. Oppression arises not only from physical restrictions, but also results from the psychological and emotional effects of such things as prejudice and discrimination. Perhaps deliberately, whilst glossing over the unpleasant physical symptoms of real post-encephalitic patients, director Penny Marshall draws attention to the very different dynamic that arises in the presence of mentally ill patients who are not passive or pleasant. It is a necessary antidote to what could have become an unrealistic optimism in the film. Liberated attitudes come far more easily in relation to people who are easy to like. The irony, however, is that such conditional liberation is no different from qualified oppression. This point is brought home when Leonard is refused permission by the hospital authorities to go for a walk unsupervised, arguably an understandable decision at that stage of his recovery. But when Leonard is unable to cope with this decision, which effectively thwarts his plans to try and see Paula again, the liberated regime quickly reverts to its old ways. In a very heavy-handed way it confines Leonard to a ward behind bars where patients suffering from extreme mental conditions are incarcerated. It is little wonder that Leonard feels let down and betrayed by a system which opened the door ajar only to slam it tightly in his face the moment he failed to conform.

In this tragic section of the film there are echoes of the darker *One Flew Over the Cuckoo's Nest* (Milos Forman 1975). In particular, through the experience of the character of McMurphy (Jack Nicholson), the institution takes on a far more oppressive and even sinister dimension. McMurphy, a convicted criminal who is feigning mental illness, refuses to capitulate to the regime in which he finds himself and almost single-handedly takes on the institution on behalf of his fellow residents, most of whom have had their spirits crushed. Almost despite himself, McMurphy takes up the cause of those for whom the institution is a source of unreasonable oppression.

From the outset, Nicholson's McMurphy is practically the antithesis of De Niro's Leonard though, interestingly, he has been identified as a Christ-figure (Grimes in Martin and Ostwalt 1995). While linked to McMurphy's own "crucifixion" (his lobotomy by the institution) this identification also relates to the way in which he gave life to the residents around him. For a short while their zest for life was rekindled by McMurphy who, having witnessed the oppressive cruelty to his fellow residents, took up their cause. McMurphy was no saint in the conventional sense of the word, but in the sense of being someone prepared to face evil head on when those around him were powerless to defend themselves, he clearly was.

McMurphy's life ends, effectively, when the institution's treatment – a euphemism for punishment – robs him of his will to resist. He could have complied and given in but instead refused to turn his back on those he had come to know. McMurphy's actions and their consequences for him are echoes of the words of Jesus: "Greater love has no-one than this, that he lay down his life for his friends" (Jn 15:13). The struggle towards liberation, wherever and however it takes place, exacts a high price upon those involved. Sometimes it means death. But the lesson of human history is that there will always be people prepared to pay that price.

Generally speaking the characters portrayed by De Niro and Nicholson are opposites. Leonard is indebted to the institution, at least initially, whereas McMurphy recognizes its oppressive nature and challenges it; the former is compliant, the latter tries at every juncture to buck the system; one is easy for the institution's staff to like, the other is a "problem." McMurphy is seen essentially as a criminal out to deceive who needs to be controlled, whereas Leonard is seen as a tragic victim to be helped; that is, until Leonard, after living immobile in the hospital for decades, is refused his first request to experience a taste of what freedom means, in this case to simply go for a walk when *he* feels like it. His understandable fit of rage is met with totally inappropriate force and insensitivity and he is classified and incarcerated with the far more "disturbed" residents of Bainbridge in the problem wing.

It is not difficult to imagine why Leonard slides towards paranoia and feels betrayed by Sayer, or why he reaches the point of utter despair before reaching out for help. To feel the exhilaration of liberation only for it to be snatched away is a cruel act to endure, all the more so when inflicted by an institution set up for the care of those entrusted to it. Leonard, unlike McMurphy, is not lobotomized for his behavior. Instead, he is locked away with the threat hovering over him that the medication which tenuously keeps him from sliding back to his pre-awakening state will be removed. In both cases the men are powerless victims whose human dignity is abused and undermined.

The viewer is left with the unpleasant feeling that liberation is conditional upon conforming to the requirements of those who wield the power. During

Leonard's initial awakened period he is treated with the dignity and respect that befits any human being, for at that point he is "likeable." Leonard is even something of a celebrity. But as soon as he crosses the line of the institution's criteria of acceptable behaviour his freedom is curtailed. "Bad" patients are dealt with, "good" ones are cared for. Perhaps this is an over-simplification but it is one that carries at least a grain of truth in practice, and far more than a grain in emotional terms.

From this consideration of "Liberation in *Awakenings*," a number of observations can be made. Liberation happens at a range of different levels in both an individual and corporate sense. For the individual it occurs internally whenever a new perspective or novel insight finds its way through the shell of convention. To see the world through a new set of eyes can be both a humbling and an exhilarating experience. Sayer's patients certainly have an almost sacramental effect upon those who witness their awakening. Outward changes stir something deep within. Eyes are opened to realities which had not been appreciated. Leonard's disquiet, for instance, at the abundance of bad news carried in the media carries with it a power demanding attention in the context in which it is expressed. Deprived for so long of the capacity to enjoy the simple things of life, Leonard glimpses something of the wonder of the world in which we live. In the words of Gerard Manley Hopkins, "The world is charged with the grandeur of God" (Hopkins 1994).

Awakenings presents a challenge to consider how easy it is to take life for granted. The viewer is also confronted with the reality that humanness is not essentially related to a person's physical or mental capacity, nor to the ability to be a "productive" member of society. The likeable and the unpleasant, the easy and the difficult – all are equally human and deserving of the same respect and treatment. In practice this is a difficult path to follow but one which is illuminated during moments of liberation. It is certainly a path suggested by those within the Christian tradition as a practical outworking of the command of Jesus to "love your neighbour as yourself" (Mk 12:31). Those responsible for the care of the post-encephalitic patients experience a personal liberation when they see people rather than patients for the first time in years. The mundaneness of routine and the numbing effect of their thankless but vital work is lifted. Their vocation is refreshed and their attitude transformed.

For an institution or structure, liberation is experienced when individuals are seen and valued as human beings rather than as problems or as a set of presenting symptoms. In Leonard's case as the L-dopa becomes increasingly ineffective and his physical condition deteriorates, in anguish he describes himself as grotesque. He feels that he is somehow less than a person, no more than "a collection of ticks." Sayer quite genuinely refutes the description. But it is not difficult to imagine how in an institution such as Bainbridge, the staff end up seeing only the symptoms which are so demanding of their attention. This arises not from indifference or hard-heartedness. Rather, it stems from the lack of adequate resources, both personal and material, to meet the scale of such need. With such limitations, coping mechanisms become necessary which sometimes involve detachment. Pragmatic considerations result in the needs of the many preventing high levels of individual attention being given to the few or the one.

Sometimes structures and institutions become oppressive simply because of overstretched resources which result in an impersonal approach. Sometimes it is because of a complete lack of an adequate ethical or moral foundation. But whatever the cause, liberation *is* possible and does take place wherever the value and worth of each individual within the institution is recognized and accorded the dignity that each human being deserves. Once achieved, liberation can be easily lost, but the hunger for liberation will not go away.

Finally, at whatever level at which liberation takes place there is cost involved to all concerned. For those struggling towards liberation there is the experience of being on the receiving end of oppressive power and authority which by its very nature will marshal its forces to resist. For the oppressor there is the need to relinquish power, prestige and, more importantly, the attitudes which deem it acceptable to maintain a status quo by which the lives of others are diminished. The cost of liberation is always large, sometimes vast, in both human and material terms: what it purchases is immeasurable because it goes to the very heart of what it means to be human.

Thankfully, awakening moments break through in life in all sorts of unexpected places. They might only be fleeting moments or there for a season within the life of an individual or at an institutional level. Such moments cause a rethink in attitudes to take place, which may or may not have a long-lasting practical effect. But sometimes they are signposts to a better way.

9

Jesus Christ Movie Star:
The Depiction of Jesus in the Cinema

William R. Telford

Introduction

The Bible in the cinema

In referring to Jesus as a "star" (Rev. 22:16; cf. Num. 24:17), and indeed as "the bright morning star," the apocalyptic seer of the Book of Revelation may have predicted more than he intended! As we look forward to the turn of the millennium, as well as look back on a century of film, it is worth recalling the debt that the cinema owes, from its dawning, to the Bible and to Jesus, its "leading man." When we go to the movies today, we are accustomed to choosing from a wide variety of genres (the action picture, the detective story, the costume drama or "heritage" film, the gangster movie, the horror film, the Western, the sci-fi movie, the musical, the erotic thriller, the road movie, the biopic, etc.). In the primitive cinema, the number of such genres was understandably limited (Bowser 1982: 1, 3–29, cited in Musser 1993: 451). Two subjects in particular dominated the new medium, viz. the Bible and pornography, the former lending respectability to the infant art form much as the latter was bringing it into disrepute. In the early years of the twentieth century, when women screenwriters such as Gene Gauntier (*From the Manger to the Cross*, 1912) or Jeannie McPherson (*The Ten Commandments*, 1923; *The King of Kings*, 1927) were producing scripts for the growing industry (Francke 1994), movies were regarded as "a kind of pulp fiction, a form of low entertainment" (Swicord 1995: 36). The popularity as well as the profusion of religious subjects in moving pictures at this time is therefore both noteworthy and understandable. "The Holy Bible," as one critic observes, "was one of the first dramatic works adapted to the screen, simply because it presented filmmakers with material that was not only popular but dignified" (Kinnard and Davis 1992: 19). The first serious motion picture presentations at the end of the nineteenth century were based on Passion Plays (such as that performed at Oberammergau in Bavaria), "the story of Christ's sufferings from the Last Supper through his death [providing] screen practitioners with one of their most vibrant genres" (Musser 1993: 420; see also Kinnard and Davis 1992: 19–21; Ortiz 1994: 492).

The cinema, therefore, has always been interested in God and religion (Holloway 1977; Bazin 1992: 393). Films involving biblical characters or set in biblical times have been a staple of filmmaking from the very beginning (Campbell and Pitts 1981; Forshey 1992), and one of the earliest "stars" of the silent era, and one of the brightest "stars" to shine in the cinema's firmament has been Jesus of Nazareth. Before Cecil B. DeMille created his epic *The King of Kings* (1927), there had been at least 39 earlier versions of the Christ story, among them, and most notably, the aforementioned *From the Manger to the Cross* (1912) (Maltby 1990: 190). This chapter, then, will consider Jesus the movie star. While commenting on the biblical epic in general, we will focus on the Christ film in particular. After an initial discussion of the genre itself (the approaches it receives, the importance it holds, the issues it raises, the form it takes, the sources it uses, the social context it addresses, the ideology it communicates, the style it employs), we will offer a description and analysis of the characterization of Jesus in the Christ film. The problems as well as the ways of portraying Jesus will be considered. In our concluding discussion, special reference will be made to Martin Scorsese's controversial *The Last Temptation of Christ* (1988), to the objections raised against it and to the theological debate which it engenders.

The Hollywood biblical epic

Despite the scorn often directed at the Hollywood biblical epic, the genre has enjoyed considerable popularity, a high degree of commercial success, and, in its own day, much critical acclaim (Babington and Evans 1993: 5–6). When released in the late 1940s and 1950s, films such as *Samson and Delilah*, *David and Bathsheba*, *Quo Vadis?*, *The Robe*, *The Ten Commandments*, and *Ben-Hur* became top box-office hits, with *Ben-Hur*, for example , setting an unsurpassed record by gaining 11 Academy Awards (Medved 1992: 50–1). In the biblical epic, audiences were offered rich production values, high esthetic standards and sophisticated technological innovations. *The Ten Commandments* (1923), for example, was one of the first productions to demonstrate the new two-step Technicolor photography (Higashi 1994: 184) while *The Robe*, premiered at New York's Roxy in September 1953, enchanted cinemagoers (among them, a young Martin Scorsese) with the magic of Cinemascope (Thompson and Christie 1989: 117, 145). These films, too, have brought us some memorable performances (as well as a host of forgettable ones!), such as Basil Rathbone's portrayal of Pilate in *The Last Days of Pompeii* (1935) or Charles Laughton's Nero (*The Sign of the Cross*, 1932), which "if not a thing of beauty," as one critic has remarked, "is at least a joy for ever" (Butler, 1969: 30). Biblical epics have been major agents in the popularization of religion and the Bible, dramatizing, as they have done, scriptural themes of good and evil, love and hate, oppression and liberation, vengeance and forgiveness.

The features of the genre are now well known and firmly established in the popular mind, the pattern and visual style having been set by the epic's early and supreme practitioners, D. W. Griffiths (*Intolerance*, 1916) and Cecil B. DeMille (*The Ten Commandments*, 1923; *The King of Kings*, 1927). In the television documentary, *Jesus Christ Movie-Star* (Channel Four, 1992), the critic Sheila Johnston lists these features as showmanship, eroticism, vulgarity, *faux naïveté*, and picture-postcard piety (see also Aitken 1995: 1656). Johnston's less than flattering list reflects the negative light in which the biblical epic has now come to be viewed. Typical of the derision the genre often encounters is this early comment from *Time* Magazine which greeted the appearance of DeMille's *The Ten Commandments* in 1956:

> One result of all these stupendous efforts? Something roughly comparable to an eight-foot chorus girl – pretty well put together, but much too big and much too flashy. . . . What de Mille has really done is to throw sex and sand into the movie-goer's eyes for almost twice as long as anyone else has ever dared to.[1]
>
> *(Walker, 1995: 1123)*

In his autobiography, DeMille gives his own defence against such charges, claiming that, in presenting sex and violence in his epics, he had merely sought to present biblical characters in their true humanity (Hayne 1960: 364). Nevertheless, the biblical epic has repeatedly been accused of presenting two-dimensional heroes and simplistic plots ("Rome is divided as sharply as usual: naughty, gaudy Emperors, simple, ungaudy Christians, and, in between, tormented but finally clear-eyed converts"; Butler 1969: 31, of *The Robe*, 1953), and of pandering to lower instincts by offering spectacle rather than drama or spirituality. On another level, with their pietistic handling of the biblical text, they have been seen to reinforce traditional conservative teaching on the literal inerrancy of scripture (Wright, 1996).[2] Undoubtedly, many of these films evince a religious conservatism, particularly the celluloid Life of Christ, governed as it is by the restrictions imposed by its subject-matter, the Gospel narratives and the constant threat of religious censorship. Indeed, "the greatest constraint on the Hollywood Christ narrative is its requirement at least formally to accept Christ's divinity" (Babington and Evans 1993: 99).

Despite such criticisms, there is evidence of a renewed interest in the genre, and indeed of some rehabilitation of it, at least at the scholarly level (Telford 1995). Bruce Babington and Peter Evans' recent book, *Biblical Epics. Sacred Narrative in the Hollywood Cinema* (1993) treats the biblical epic with seriousness, examining with sharp insight how ethnicity, sexuality and gender as well as religion have had their effect upon the genre and exposing the banality of what passes for criticism of it. Recent reappraisals of the significance of biblical epics have stressed their championing of the place of the Judeo-Christian moral code in a world (especially that of the 1950s) in which religion was under attack, and their reinforcement of American notions of liberty and religious truth (Wright, 1996). By offering "an unconscious allegory of meanings central to American mythology" and, in particular, by "the association of the oppressing ruling class with the British, and of the oppressed but ultimately triumphant Israelites or Christians with Americans", the biblical epic "reworks the American Revolution scenario." In this respect, it has as its counterpart the Western "with its enacting of America's coming to birth as the Promised Land," both genres "symbiotically command[ing] the whole field of American cinema" (Babington and Evans 1993: 9–11, citing Wood 1975). Further, by raising questions of faith and doubt, belief and skepticism, biblical epics "also dramatize the encounter of religion and secularism in twentieth-century America" (Babington and Evans 1993: 16).

Having noted its influence, features, strengths and weaknesses, it is worth commenting briefly on the genre's history, and on the reasons for its rise, decline and fall from grace. The biblical epic may be said to have had its "garden of Eden" period in the 1920s and its "wilderness" period in the 1930s and 1940s. It recovered and enjoyed the commercial fruits of the "promised land" in the 1950s and early 1960s, only to decline thereafter. A number of reasons have been offered for its popularity, especially in the 1950s, some of which have been mentioned already (its esthetic merit, the religious subject matter, the pietistic mentality of American audiences, the sublimated lure of sex, violence and spectacle, the immediate post-war climate, the struggle against communism, the establishment of the state of Israel, etc.). A variety of factors have also been suggested for its decline, at least in the cinema (younger audiences, increasing secularism, the competition from television, significant box-office failures, escalating costs, the liberalization of censorship, etc.) (Babington and Evans 1993: 6–7). Whether it is to experience a "Parousia" or second return, is questionable but the interest shown in the 1980s in such films as Bruce Beresford's *King David* (1985), Martin Scorsese's *The Last Temptation of Christ* (1988), or Denys Arcand's *Jesus of Montreal* (1989) may indicate that its decline at least may not be considered to be terminal. As these last two examples indicate, however, the biblical film, and the filmed Life of Christ in particular, may not reappear in the form in which it has traditionally been incarnated. "Perhaps the true successors to the classic cinematic portrayals of Moses," Melanie Wright suggests, "are the big budget sensations of modern science fiction cinema" (Wright 1996). What the true successor to the cinematic portrayal of Jesus will be remains to be seen, but in a post-modern age, gritty realism, religious pluralism and the increasing march of secularism will undoubtedly be major influences.[3]

But what is the traditional form of the biblical epic? In *Biblical Epics*, Babington and Evans differentiate three sub-types of the genre: the Old Testament Epic, the Roman/Christian Epic and the Christ film.

The Old Testament epic

Within the first category are films such as *The Ten Commandments* (Cecil B. DeMille, 1923/1956), *Samson and Delilah* (Cecil B. DeMille, 1949), *David and Bathsheba* (Henry King, 1951), *The Prodigal* (Richard Thorpe, 1955), *Esther and the King* (Raoul Walsh, 1960), *The Story of Ruth* (Henry Koster, 1960), *Sodom and Gomorrah* (Robert Aldrich, 1962), and *The Bible* (John Huston, 1966). Since these have little relevance to the subject of Jesus I shall not be commenting on them

The Roman–Christian epic

The Roman-Christian epic brings us a bit closer to home. This sub-genre includes films (some already mentioned) like *Ben-Hur* (Fred Niblo, 1925/ William Wyler, 1959), *The Sign of the Cross* (Cecil B. DeMille, 1932), *The Last Days of Pompeii* (Merian C. Cooper, Ernest Schoedsack, 1935), *Quo Vadis?* (Mervin LeRoy, 1951), *The Robe* (Henry Koster, 1953), *Salome* (William Dieterle, 1953), *Demetrius and the Gladiators* (Delmer Daves, 1954), *The Silver Chalice* (Victor Saville, 1954), *The Big Fisherman* (Frank Borzage, 1959), and *Barabbas* (Richard Fleischer, 1962). With their presentation of early Christianity, although not principally its founder, and with non-biblical lead characters caught up in some way with the new religion, these films are of some interest to my theme and I shall be making some reference to them.

The Christ film

It is the third of these categories, and incidentally the least prolific of the genre where Hollywood is concerned, which shall occupy our attention in this chapter. In a manner appropriate to the subject, I shall choose twelve, in chronological order, which may be considered to be the chief commercial representatives of this sub-genre. They are as follows:

From the Manger to the Cross (Sidney Olcott, 1912)
A classic of the silent cinema, this was the first of the Christ films to be made on location in the Middle East.

The King of Kings (Cecil B. DeMille, 1927)
A major classic, this was the first full-length, silent Hollywood epic on the life of Jesus, as seen from the perspective of Mary Magdalene. It presents Mary as a rich courtesan with Judas as her lover. Its many memorable moments include Mary's riding off in her chariot to rescue her Judas from the clutches of the carpenter of Nazareth ("Harness my zebras – gift of the Nubian king!"), her subsequent exorcism by Jesus in a swirl of exiting demons, the moving giving of sight to a little blind girl and dramatic crucifixion and resurrection scenes.

Golgotha (Julien Duvivier, 1935)
Otherwise titled *Ecce Homo*, and covering only the events of Holy Week, this accomplished French production was the first sound version of the Christ film.

King of Kings (Nicholas Ray, 1961)
A remake of the DeMille version in name only, this 1960s Hollywood adaptation presents Judas and Barabbas as political revolutionaries, with Jesus as a reluctant pawn in their game. Criticized by the Catholic Legion of Decency as "theologically, historically, and scripturally inaccurate" (Kinnard and Davis 1992: 132), the film is now viewed in retrospect as better than its critics made it out to be.

The Gospel According to St Matthew (Pier Paolo Pasolini, 1964)
A low-budget, black and white, European film made by the Marxist director, Pier Paolo Pasolini and dedicated to Pope John XXIII, this unconventional adaptation of Matthew's Gospel in *cinéma verité* style had more impact on audiences than the traditional, glossy Hollywood epic, *The Greatest Story Ever Told*, which was to follow it a year later.

The Greatest Story Ever Told (George Stevens, 1965)
Perfectionism in pursuit of the Perfect, George Stevens' Christ film was the most expensive ever made. Though luminescent with its galaxy of stars, and presenting some memorable sequences (such as the raising of Lazarus as well as the crucifixion), this was a commercial failure which set the Christ film back as far as Hollywood was concerned.

Jesus Christ, Superstar (Norman Jewison, 1973)
Filmed in Israel, where young tourists reenact episodes of the life of Christ, this vibrant movie, which was based on the successful rock opera by Tim Rice and Andrew Lloyd-Webber (with a screenplay by Norman Jewison and Melvyn Bragg, and musical direction by André Previn) mixes the historical and the contemporary to good effect.

Godspell (David Greene, 1973)
Performed musically in the streets of New York, and also aimed at the youth market, this is the counter-cultural (as opposed to the Marxist) version of the Gospel of St Matthew. The film was described by its director David Greene as "a romp" (on Channel Four April 20, 1992).

Jesus of Nazareth (Franco Zeffirelli, 1977)
With a screenplay by Anthony Burgess and others (later turned into a novel
by William Barclay), this six and a half hour made-for-television movie
(screened on ITV in 1977) was the result of a promise made by its producer
Lew Grade to the Pope to do for Jesus what Grade had done for Moses in the
1975 TV-series *Moses: the Lawgiver*.
Monty Python's Life of Brian (Terry Jones, 1979)
A romp of a less tasteful kind, the Judas among the twelve and the ultimate
anti-Christ film, this perceptive, amusing and influential parody of the biblical
epic by the Monty Python team has forever tinted the lens through which the
popular imagination now views Christian origins. Here a reluctant non-biblical
lead character is caught up in the new religion to the extent of being mistaken
for the Messiah. Among the unforgettable set pieces are "What have the Romans
ever done for us?" (a lesson in imperial revisionism designed to disarm all
Zealots!) and the notorious "Always look on the bright side of life!" (the *reductio
ad absurdum* of the essence of Christian optimism – "Have a truly Good Friday!").
The Last Temptation of Christ (Martin Scorsese, 1988)
Based on Kazantzakis' novel about "the dual substance of Christ" and "the
incessant, merciless battle between the spirit and the flesh", and directed by
one of Hollywood's most distinguished filmmakers, this is one of the finest,
most religious and yet most controversial Christ films ever made.
Jesus of Montreal (Denys Arcand, 1989)
This is a French-Canadian film about actors who get drawn into a Passion
Play and whose real-life experiences, especially that of the Jesus character,
begin to reflect that of the Gospel story.

Jesus Christ Movie Star

The Christ film

Approaching the genre

The Christ film can be approached by scholars in a variety of ways. It can be
subjected to *narrative analysis* and its plot, characterization, point of view, etc.
explored, or to *esthetic analysis* which may consider its use of music, art,
locations, and settings. It can be used in *sociological analysis* and interrogated
in light of its depiction of sexuality, gender, ethnicity or religion, or in
intertextual analysis with respect to the sources by which it may have been
influenced. The Christ film is of interest to a biblical scholar like myself for a
series of reasons which I should like to comment upon briefly. In sum, these
concern the issues raised by the genre, the forms it employs, the sources it

uses, the social context it addresses, the ideology it communicates, and the style it adopts.

Issues And Importance

The Christ film raises a number of issues which tax modern critics. Chief among them have been the depiction of Jews, the depiction of women and the depiction of Jesus, the last of which concerns us here. Its supreme importance, indeed, as with the Gospels, lies in its presentation of the figure of Jesus, a subject in which there is a growing scholarly as well as popular interest (Butler 1969: 33–54; Hurley 1982; Thouart 1987; Singer 1988; Malone 1990; Kinnard and Davis 1992; Channel Four, 1992; Babington and Evans 1993: 91–168; Ortiz 1994; Aitken 1995; Halliwell 1995: 126; Telford 1995: 367–8).

Given its popularity, the Christ film is arguably the most significant medium through which popular culture this century has absorbed its knowledge of the Gospel story and formed its impression of Christianity's founder. It was Cecil B. DeMille's claim that "probably more people have been told the story of Jesus of Nazareth through *The King of Kings* than through any other single work, except the Bible itself" (Hayne 1960: 258). Although, on its first commercial release, it seems to have just managed to break even (Maltby 1990: 208), in its non-commercial form it "was one of the most viewed films of all time" (Babington and Evans 1993: 5), and one, indeed, whose image of Jesus has influenced a generation.[4] On its first release in Italy, according to Pasolini, and unlike its reception in England, *The Gospel According to St Matthew* (1964) was found to be "a disconcerting and scandalous novelty, because no one expected a Christ like that, because no one had read Matthew's Gospel." "In fact making a film about the Gospel," he also said, "meant suggesting to the Italians that they read the Gospel for the first time" (Stack 1969: 79). It is also perhaps instructive to recall, as Kenneth Wolfe points out (Wolfe 1991: 48), and as I have mentioned elsewhere (Telford 1995: 367) that at the very moment in 1977 when Don Cupitt and Peter Armstrong were airing on BBC2 their scholarly and open-ended investigation on the subject "Who was Jesus?," Sir Lew Grade's ITV epic *Jesus of Nazareth* was giving a long, firm and traditional answer to much larger audiences!

The form

The Christ film has appeared in a number of forms. Of the twelve important Christ films singled out above, it is of note that eight (viz. *From the Manger to the Cross*, 1912; *The King of Kings*, 1927; *Golgotha*, 1935; *King of Kings*, 1961; *The Gospel According to St Matthew*, 1964; *The Greatest Story Ever Told*, 1965; *Jesus of Nazareth*, 1977, and *The Last Temptation of Christ*, 1988) have conformed, in generic terms, to the classic Christ film or biopic in which the figure of Jesus is treated directly, seriously and with due respect to the original historical context. Two revitalized the Gospel story for 1970s audiences by offering it in the form of a musical (viz. *Jesus Christ Superstar*, 1973; *Godspell*, 1973), the latter presenting Jesus as a clown, a spirited icon with a previous film history familiar to fans of Bergman (*Sawdust and Tinsel* or *The Naked Night*, 1953), Fellini (*La Strada*, 1954), or of Chaplin (*The Circus*, 1928) (Holloway 1977: 121). One (*Monty Python's Life of Brian*, 1979) is a satire – a satire indeed to end all satires! – which mercilessly parodies all the conventions of the genre, and the last (*Jesus of Montreal*, 1989) is an allegory, set within a Passion Play schema, for which there have been significant cinematic precursors (cf. for example Jules Dassin's *Celui qui doit mourir* or *He Who Must Die*, 1957) (Kinnard and Davis 1992: 107–8).

Allegory, indeed, presenting us as it does with an indirect and intertextually subtle play on the Gospels, is a popular modern form for the Christ story. *Cool Hand Luke* (Stuart Rosenberg, 1967), for example, is a film about a convict on the chain gang whose indomitable and non-conformist spirit (immortalized in the extraordinary egg-eating scene) and ultimate death at the hands of the prison authorities (in a deserted chapel) inspires his fellow convicts to rise above their oppression (cf. also *Strange Cargo*, (Frank Borzage, 1940); *The Shawshank Redemption*, (Frank Darabont, 1995); Butler 1969: 156–7; Hurley 1978: 23; Hurley 1982: 68–71). Gaye Ortiz makes the point that "[m]any film heroes are in fact Christ figures, who experience the kinds of things Christ did or who personify the righteous, loving, self-sacrificing Christ" (Ortiz 1994: 495). Examples given are *Superman* (Richard Donner, 1978 and sequels), the Jack Nicholson character, McMurphy in *One Flew over the Cuckoo's Nest* (1975) (see also May and Bird 1982: 42), Clint Eastwood in *The Good, the Bad and the Ugly* (Sergio Leone, 1966), *The Outlaw Josey Wales* (Clint Eastwood, 1976) and *Pale Rider* (Clint Eastwood, 1985; on which, see chapter 5), Agnes in Ingmar Bergman's *Cries and Whispers* (1973), David Lynch's *The Elephant Man* (1980), and *The Hunchback of Notre Dame* (William Dieterle, 1939) (Ortiz 1994: 494–5). To these may also be added *Spartacus* (Stanley Kubrick, 1960; on which, see Kreitzer 1993: 21–43) where Christ is prefigured in the opening voiceover, in Spartacus' own egalitarian values and in the closing crucifixion, *On the Waterfront* (Elia Kazan, 1954), in which an ex-boxer (played by Marlon Brando) takes on the mafia who control New York's waterfront, *Serpico* (Sidney Lumet, 1973), the true story of a New York policeman whose exposure of police corruption led him to flee the country (May and Bird 1982: 42–3) and even *E.T.- the Extra-Terrestrial* (Steven Spielberg, 1982)! Again Ortiz writes:

[T]here is no way one can equate the life of Christ with the story of ET, but there are serious parallels in the story which are difficult to ignore:

ET was also a pre-existent entity, his early life was hidden from us, he came to little children, he suffered a death and resurrection and ascended to his original home. More significantly, his was a message of unconditional love, much like that seen in the crucified Christ.

(Ortiz, 1994: 494)

A variety of Christlike figures have also appeared in such films as Berthold Biertel's *The Passing of the Third Floor Back* (1935), Frank Borzage's aforementioned *Strange Cargo* (1940), John Ford's *The Fugitive* (1947), or Ingmar Bergman's *The Face* (1958) (Halliwell 1995: 126). Writing in 1982, N. P. Hurley claimed to have identified over 60 instances of these "cinematic transfigurations" of Jesus, including adaptations from the literature treated by T. Ziolkowski (Hurley 1982: 82; see also Ziolkowski 1972; Holloway 1977). As with *Strange Cargo* (1940), a number of these transfigurations present Jesus as a mysterious stranger whose presence curiously moves but also disturbs those with whom he comes in contact (cf. for example Tay Garnett's unsuccessful *Destination Unknown*, 1933 or Bryan Forbes' charming *Whistle down the Wind*, 1961; Butler 1969: 155–6; Kinnard and Davis 1992: 51–2). Here one is reminded of the story in the apocryphal Acts of John (88–9) of Jesus' perplexing appearances to James and John in the form of a child, a youth and an older man (James 1924: 251), or of the saying in the Oxyrynchus Papyri "Lift the stone, and there you will find me; split the wood, and I am there" (Grant and Freedman 1960: 45).

The sources

This reference to ancient texts prompts the question of the sources used by the directors and screenwriters responsible for the Christ film. The first and major source, of course, has been our canonical Gospels. Conflated versions of these, cited chapter and verse in the art titles (King James Version), were used by DeMille and his scenarist Jeannie McPherson in *The King of Kings* (1927), the rise of fundamentalism having made the Bible familiar to the audiences of this period (Higashi 1994: 180). The use of all four New Testament Gospels as source material, with selective borrowing, harmonization and conflation, has been a feature of the other Christ films also, with the exception of *The Gospel According to St Matthew* (1964) where that Gospel (apart from two references to Isaiah) was used alone. Borrowings, direct or indirect, from the Apocryphal Gospels, however, can also be observed. In *The King of Kings* (1927), for example, Jesus is presented, in contrast to the reticence of the canonical Gospels, as actually emerging from the tomb. This is a vault-like chamber sealed with seven seals, a detail found in the apocryphal Gospel of Peter (8:33).

A number of the Hollywood biblical epics are screen adaptations of the historical novel (e.g. *Ben-Hur*, Lew Wallace; *Quo Vadis?*, Henryk Sienkiewicz; *The Robe*, *The Big Fisherman*, Lloyd C. Douglas; *The Silver Chalice*, Thomas B. Costain; *Barabbas*, Pär Lagerkvist), the most celebrated of which is Nikos Kazantzakis' *The Last Temptation*, whose highly imaginative and provocative work of fiction formed the basis for Scorsese's film. Josephus is a favorite source for directors wishing to give their films historical verisimilitude, with information derived from the Jewish historian often being given in a voiceover in the opening sequences (as with that by Orson Welles in *King of Kings*, 1961, which depicts Pompey's entry into Jerusalem and the Temple in 63 BCE). The aspiration (if not always the achievement) to lend their films academic as well as religious respectability in the eyes of both audiences and critics has led biblical epic *auteurs* to employ a further source, viz. the results of biblical scholarship and archaeology. The desire can be seen in DeMille whose pretensions to scholarly accuracy are apparent in the promotional trailer for *The Ten Commandments* (1956) as well as in its opening sequences (Wright 1996). A similar historical concern is demonstrated by Scorsese who cites his subscription to *Biblical Archaeology Review* as a major resource for the art direction of his film, and especially for its realistic depiction of the crucifixion (Thompson and Christie 1989: 138; Babington and Evans 1993: 62). The historical tableaux in *Jesus of Montreal* (1989) are likewise based on archeological evidence and current scholarship, as too is the scene in which Arcand's Christ figure, Daniel Colombe, is crucified (Willett 1991: 14).

Social context and ideology

One of the great challenges for the filmmaker, however, is to make the Christ film both historical *and* contemporary and to bridge the gap between the first-century world and our own. *Jesus of Montreal* (1989) does this by placing the story and message of Jesus within the context of the modern mass media, especially advertising, and exploring its degrading and corrupting influences. *Jesus Christ Superstar* (1973), on the other hand, uses popular music, contemporary Israel and modern weaponry to pack its own particular punch. While DeMille did much to humanize his characters, especially with the use of medium, close-up and point-of-view camera shots (Higashi 1994: 186–7), an objective Christ, a static camera and stylized religious expressionism served to give *The King of Kings* (1927) an otherworldly aura.

In the films of the 1960s onwards, on the other hand, one notes an increasing realism (the depiction of the Virgin Mary in *The Gospel According to St Matthew*, 1964, for example, or the portrayal of Jesus' active sexuality in *The Last Temptation of Christ* 1988; Babington and Evans 1993: 108, 116). In their use of more active and intimate camera work, directors like Pasolini and

Scorsese, in particular, have created more immediacy (and less predictability) for their audiences. "Pasolini's influence over Scorsese is particularly visible," Babington and Evans suggest, "where the Italian develops counter-representations based on camera intimacy, a rough style imitating documentary (as when the camera-onlooker is blocked at the back of the crowd in Jesus's trial scene), and other devices estranging the representations of Christ from convention" (ibid.: 152). Directors also recognize that audiences come to a Christ film with centuries of Christian tradition intervening between the cinematic representation of events and the Gospels, and many indeed capitalize on this. "I did not want to reconstruct the life of Christ as it really was," claimed Pasolini in an often repeated statement, "I wanted to do the story of Christ plus two thousand years of Christian translation" (Stack 1969: 83).

The style

It is for this reason that filmmakers have drawn on a long tradition of artistic representation with respect to the biblical story. In creating their visual representations, they looked for their inspiration to the religious art and paintings of the Renaissance and to the Bible illustrations of the Victorian period based upon it, in particular those of the painter James Tissot and the engraver Gustave Doré (Kinnard and Davis 1992: 14; Babington and Evans 1993: 16, 100, 101, 118; Higashi 1994: 180, 192). As well as popularizing the already influential *Doré Bible*, DeMille incorporated, it is claimed, some 270 representations of religious paintings in *The King of Kings* (1927) and some 200 in *The Ten Commandments* (1956). Other directors were to follow this practice, a celebrated example being the frequent use of Leonardo da Vinci's famous work for the representation of the Last Supper (cf. Fred Niblo, *Ben-Hur*, 1925; Mervyn LeRoy, *Quo Vadis?*, 1951; George Stevens, *The Greatest Story Ever Told*, 1965). Painterly references abound also in Pasolini's *The Gospel According to St Matthew* (1964), Piero della Francesca being the source for the Pharisee's clothes and Byzantine painting (via Georges Rouault) the inspiration for Christ's face (Stack 1969: 84, 86). For Pasolini, as an Italian, "painting," indeed, "is the major element in the Christological tradition" (Stack 1969: 91).

But the employment of music as well as art, is another way in which the director subtly influences the audience's interpretation of what they see and hear. In *The King of Kings* (reissued in 1931 with synchronized music and sound-effects), DeMille made effective use of traditional Christian hymns played at strategic moments ("Lead Kindly Light," "Blessed are the Pure in Heart," "Abide with Me," "Nearer My God to Thee," "Jesus Christ is Risen Today," "Rock of Ages") (Babington and Evans 1993: 125). Both majestic and monumental, and virtually epitomizing the biblical epic in the popular imagination nowadays is the stirring music of Hungarian composer Miklos Rosza (*Quo Vadis?*, 1951; *Ben-Hur*, 1959; *King of Kings*, 1961). Opting for a wide selection from the Christian and classical musical tradition, Pasolini's music score gives us everything from Bach, Prokofiev and Mozart to rhythm and blues (Leadbelly), negro spirituals ("Sometimes I feel like a motherless child") and the haunting sound of the flute (played, for example, by the disciple in the boat in the otherwise risible Walking on the Water scene and at Salome's dance in Herod's court). Reference has been made to the important part played by the contemporary musical score in *Jesus Christ, Superstar* (1973) and *Godspell* (1973) but also employing electric guitars and rock percussion to far more spiritual (indeed primal) effect is the atmospheric "world music" soundtrack supplied by Peter Gabriel for Scorsese's *The Last Temptation of Christ* (1988) (Thompson and Christie 1989: 139, 142).

Where the Christ film's style is concerned, the choice of settings is another important way in which the filmmaker draws audiences into the familiar (nowadays not so familiar!) world of the Bible. Egyptian locations as well as Palestine were used for *From the Manger to the Cross* (1912). Tunisian locations have also been popular, especially the kasbah in Monastir, which has doubled for the walls of Jerusalem in many a biblical epic (cf. *Monty Python's Life of Brian*, 1979). Some directors have chosen their locations in order to reinforce, conversely, the unfamiliarity of the biblical world, or to arrest the viewer with striking images. The poor rural villages of southern Italy were chosen by Pasolini to provide the background for *The Gospel According to St Matthew* (1964) (Stack 1969: 81–2), and the grand Mesa country of Utah, with its rugged buttes, imposing desert landscapes and shades of the Western, by Stevens for *The Greatest Story Ever Told* (1965). Most of all, the exotic Moroccan locations of *The Last Temptation of Christ* (1988), along with the music, give an air of strangeness as well as spirituality to what is otherwise a familiar story (Thompson and Christie 1989: 142).

The characterization of Jesus

Problems in portraying Jesus

The predictability of the biblical story is not, however, the only problem faced by the creator of a Christ film. A number of problems confront the filmmaker, making the venture a somewhat hazardous enterprise. The first of these is the choice of the actor to play Jesus. The Hollywood star system requires well-known actors to make a film commercially viable, yet not every "star" can play Jesus. It is difficult, for example, to imagine either Arnold Schwarzenegger or Danny De Vito in the role of Christianity's founder! Stars bring with them a body of work as well as a persona which defines them in the eyes of their public. Where someone playing Jesus is concerned, there has always been a tendency for the public to be sensitive to the overlap between the actor's professional and private life. In the history of the Christ film, the leading role has therefore been played by, at times, familiar, at other times, unfamiliar actors.

Among the familiar have been H. B. Warner (*The King of Kings*, 1927), a distinguished British actor who also appeared, shortly before he died, in Cecil B. DeMille's *The Ten Commandments* (1956); Jeffrey Hunter (*King of Kings*, 1961), an American actor popular in the 1950s; Robert Powell (*Jesus of Nazareth*, 1977), a British leading man (Al Pacino and Dustin Hoffman were also considered for the part), and Willem Dafoe (*The Last Temptation of Christ*, 1988), a powerful American actor who now has an impressive body of work (*Platoon*; *Born on the Fourth of July*; *Body of Evidence*; *Mississippi Burning*). Among the unfamiliar, or relatively unfamiliar actors to play Jesus, at least at the time of the film, have been Robert Henderson-Bland (*From the Manger to the Cross*, 1912), an upper-class Englishman who later wrote two books on his experience; George Fisher (*Civilisation*, 1916); Howard Gaye (*Intolerance*, 1916); Robert le Vigan (*Golgotha* or *Ecce Homo*, 1935); Enrique Irazoqui (*The Gospel According to St Matthew*, 1964), a Spanish student who had never acted; Max von Sydow (*The Greatest Story Ever Told*, 1965), a distinguished Swedish actor but little-known outside of Europe at the time; Ted Neely (*Jesus Christ, Superstar*, 1973); Victor Garber (*Godspell*, 1973) and Lothaire Bluteau (*Jesus of Montreal*, 1989), a French-Canadian actor.

Two well-known examples demonstrate the dangers inherent in the casting process. Even though Jeffrey Hunter was older than Max von Sydow and Willem Dafoe when playing the part, by choosing a teenage idol as Jesus in *King of Kings* (1961), the film attracted the pejorative sobriquet "I was a Teenage Jesus" and tended to be dismissed. Further, while it was difficult for critics to disparage Max von Sydow's mature and accomplished central performance in *The Greatest Story Ever Told* (1965), the choice of celebrities in cameo parts (especially John Wayne's craggy centurion and his earthen affirmation, "Truly this man was the Son of God!") was distracting for audiences at the time and much criticized.

A second problem is the suitability of Jesus himself as a leading man. A central character demonstrating pacifist tendencies and a traditional asexuality (in other words, "he does not get into fights and he does not kiss anyone," (Aitken 1995: 1656)) sits uncomfortably with the cinema's predilection for sex and violence, and, especially since the 1960s, its cult of the anti-hero. As a result, screenwriters have tended to build up or develop the other Gospel characters, in particular Judas, Barabbas or Peter, allowing them to demonstrate the human passions and frailties denied to the classical Christ figure. In *King of Kings* (1961), for example, Barabbas (played by Harry Guardino in a spirited performance worthy of a younger Burt Lancaster) is presented as Jesus' *alter ego*, "the left and right hands of the same body," as the voiceover declares. Barabbas is the Messiah of war, and Jesus the Messiah of peace ("I am fire," says Barabbas to Judas, "and he is water"). Likewise Harvey Keitel's Judas in *The Last Temptation of Christ* (1988) is a strong, brave and clear-headed nationalist, arguing for a political Messiahship, with a more wimpish Jesus stating the case for an inner spirituality.

A third problem concerns the presentation of the divine as well as the human in the portrayal of Jesus. The role itself demands a great deal of any actor not to mention the director. Directorial viewpoint aside, the actor portraying Christ in any film is trapped in a maze of dramatic contradictions; he must be believably human, yet also believably divine, gentle yet forceful, charismatic yet humble. Small wonder that many otherwise good actors have fallen short attempting to interpret this complicated, prismatic role, which is as multilayered and difficult as anything in Shakespeare (Kinnard and Davis 1992: 16).

In *The King of Kings* (1927), the extraordinary steps taken by DeMille to ensure a proper attitude of reverence in respect of H. B. Warner's portrayal of Jesus are now legendary. As DeMille recorded in his autobiography:

> No one but the director spoke to H. B. Warner when he was in costume, unless it was absolutely necessary. He was veiled or transported in a closed car when he went between the set and his dressing-room or, when we were on location, his tent, where he took his meals alone.
>
> *(Hayne 1960: 256)*

As this example illustrates, earlier filmmakers, in a more religious age, and in ways that may seem rather coy to us now, were eager (for reasons of faith or to avoid controversy) to present Jesus objectively as a divine being, and to minimize the more human aspects of his character. The product of Victorian piety, their representations of him as a blond, bearded, long-haired, blue-eyed, white-robed figure, ethereal yet somewhat bland, commanding yet somewhat passive, have dominated the cinema for well over half a century.

In the more skeptical 1960s, things began to change, as the traditional depiction of Jesus' divinity, and the playing down of his humanity, became more problematic. While the theological relationship of Jesus to God, however, could be sidestepped in the allegory or satire, it could not be avoided in the classic biopic, based ultimately as it is on faith-inspired Gospel texts. Hence, although there is no specific reference in Ray's *King of Kings* (1961) to Jesus' divinity, in contrast to DeMille's earlier film, the miracles being reported for the most part rather than enacted, and the political context being more to the fore, nevertheless three miracles are shown in connection with Jesus (a paralyzed boy, a blind man and a madman), the centurion declares him to be "truly Christ" and a post-Resurrection appearance (following John's Gospel) is made to Mary Magdalene. In the contemporary period, Martin Scorsese has been the only director to tackle this problem head-on, offering us a Jesus genuinely struggling between the two sides of his nature, the human and the divine, the flesh and the spirit. It is no wonder then that this brave endeavor has excited such controversy.

This brings us to a fourth problem surrounding the making of a Christ film, namely, the ever present threat of controversy as well as the frequent exercise of censorship (Trevelyan 1973; Medved 1992; Black 1994; Aldgate 1995; Halliwell 1995). The Church has always tried to keep a proprietorial interest in the way Jesus is presented. In Britain, the depiction of Christ was banned in films following the founding of the British Board of Film Censors in 1912 and this ban was not lifted until after World War II.[5] A special licence was required for Jesus to be seen in the London screening of *The King of Kings* as late as 1928 (Babington and Evans 1993: 101), and he was edited out by the British censors from *Golgotha/Ecce Homo* (1935) which had presented French audiences with a "full-frontal" version (Channel Four 1992). In America, censorship was also exercised, although not to this extent, with the establishment in the 1920s of the Hays Office (named after its first president of whom Gene Fowler, the American writer, on behalf of many a fearful producer or actor wrote "Will Hays is my shepherd, I shall not want, He maketh me to lie down in clean postures") by the Motion Pictures Producers and Distributors of America as well as by the independent and very strict Catholic Legion of Decency founded in 1934.

Even with the liberalization of censorship in the 1960s, however, representations of Jesus continued to give offence or attract controversy. Pasolini's *The Gospel According to St Matthew* (1964) was seen as communist propaganda, and in Spain, his Christ-impersonator, Enrique Irazoqui, had to endure 15 months of hard labor in the National Service, his passport confiscated and his university career suspended for a year (Channel Four 1992). When Dennis Potter's gritty play, *Son of Man* was first shown on British television in 1969, an attempt was made by TV watchdog Mary Whitehouse to prosecute him for blasphemy. *Jesus Christ Superstar* (1973) was branded anti-Semitic in some quarters and anti-Christian in others (Channel Four 1992), and the uproar caused by *Monty Python's Life of Brian* (1979) was as fierce as it was predictable. The controversy surrounding Scorsese's *The Last Temptation of Christ* (1988) is also well documented (Cook 1988: 288; Jenkins 1988: 352–3; Leo 1988; Poland 1988; Rosenbaum 1988; Thompson and Christie 1989: xxi–vi; Medved 1992: 38–49, 207; Babington and Evans 1993: 149–50; Telford, 1995: 380–1). Paradoxically *Jesus of Montreal* (1989), although it tilts against fundamentalism, was popular in the south of the USA – to Arcand's horror (Channel Four 1992)!

Ways of portraying Jesus

In light of these problems, it is instructive to consider the various ways in which Jesus has been portrayed in the Christ film. Three specific manifestations are worthy of some comment, namely, the symbolic appearance, the guest appearance and Jesus as leading man. Where extreme reverence or censorship dictated directorial policy, various devices were employed to convey a sense of Jesus' numinous presence rather than his actual appearance. The reaction of onlookers was important, especially in the earlier films, their upward-looking faces and rapt expressions of grief or devotion becoming a stock feature of the genre (cf. *Ben-Hur*, 1925/1959; *The Robe*, 1953). A hand, both hands, his feet or even a headless trunk often signalled his presence, a famous example being the hand offering water in *Ben-Hur* ("the hand seen," in Niblo's version, "was ludicrously unlikely, being white, slim, with delicate tapering fingers, suggesting an effete fop or a woman living in idle luxury" (Butler 1969: 38)) solemnized by the awed reaction of Ben-Hur and the Roman soldier. Jesus' words are heard through the boy accompanying Peter in his interrupted exit from Rome (*Quo Vadis?*, 1951) or as a disembodied voice (Cameron Mitchell) from the cross in *The Robe* (1953).

These indeed are a common feature of the Roman–Christian epic, where the effect of Christ is made to be felt but no central representation is given. In *Quo Vadis?*, a series of flashbacks recall Jesus' call to Peter to follow him, and in *The Robe* the story of his cloak, acquired by a Roman centurion (Richard Burton) after his crucifixion, and its effects on people is explored. In *Barabbas* (1962), Jesus is seen by Anthony Quinn in a dazzling burst of sunlight, but a full view of his face is not given. At times, a subtler symbolism is employed, as, for example, in *Ben-Hur* (1959), when Jesus' blood stains the pool at the foot of the cross, and the rain turns it into ongoing rivers of water. It is even possible to suggest that, although the Christ figure is off-stage for the audience, he is in another sense present for them in the form of the hero, Judah Ben-Hur, whose life in many senses parallels that of the man who gave him "water and a heart to live" (Judah, a Jew of the same age as Jesus, with no obvious father and a mother named Miriam, or Mary, and with "softer" values than those of the imperial Messala, is humiliated and enslaved for the three years of Jesus' ministry, is vindicated, as the savior of the Roman general Arrius, returns as from the dead, vanquishes his enemy in the chariot race, through the agency of a team of four white horses, one of which is described as a "rock," and seeks the lost in the form of his mother and sister who, at the end, together with the faithful Esther, mirror the three women of the traditional Gospel story.)

Jesus has also made some memorable guest appearances in films, often in the form of visions granted to the principals. In Thomas Ince's *Civilization*

(1916), for example, the pacifist hero is possessed by the spirit of Christ (George Fisher) who inspires him to work for peace. In the closing scenes of *The Last Days of Pompeii* (Merian C. Cooper, 1935), an apparition of Jesus (played by an unbilled actor) appears before Preston Foster's blacksmith-cum-gladiator as he loses his life while saving others in the eruption of Vesuvius. A much fuller representation of Jesus was offered in D. W. Griffith's four-part *Intolerance* (1916), the New Testament segment of which featured several episodes from the life of Jesus (played impressively by Howard Gaye) such as the marriage of Cana and the woman taken in adultery, as well as the crucifixion.

It is Jesus' role as a leading man, however, which deserves most attention. After *Golgotha/Ecce Homo* (1935), a full presentation of Jesus had not been ventured until the independently produced *Day of Triumph* (Irving Pichel, John T. Coyle, 1954) where he was played by a non-professional, Robert Wilson (cf. also *I Beheld His Glory*, 1952). Before we examine his persona in the classic Christ film, two other facets of the appearance of Jesus in film should be commented upon, namely, his face and his voice.

The canonical Gospels do not tell us what Jesus looked like and so filmmakers, as already noted, have been dependent on a secondary, imagined, one might even say specious representation of Jesus in art and painting, the impetus towards which gained perceptibly after Christianity became the religion of the Roman Empire. Even then there is evidence of opposition to the very use of artistic images, the matter being resolved only at the Second Council of Nicaea in 787 (Ortiz 1994: 491). Reference has been made to the tradition (also known to Origen) that the form of Jesus altered in line with the varying perceptions of his followers (Acts of John 88–9), and this Gnostic insight can be applied in a sense to all artistic depictions. Portraits of Jesus first arose among the second-century Gnostic Carpocratians, and while Gnostics could occasionally describe him as beautiful (Acts of John 73–4; Acts of Thomas 80, 149; and James, 1924: 246, 401, 430), the influence of Isaiah 53:2–3, or even Psalms 22:7 more often led orthodox discussion to regard him as "ill-favored" or ugly (Hennecke and Schneemelcher 1963, II: 434). In the early Christian art of the catacombs, he is represented symbolically as a shepherd, and as a beardless youth, with curly blond hair and a halo, an image borrowed from the Roman sun god Apollo (Ortiz 1994: 491). This appropriation of the halo, indeed, by Christian artists, was to have such a pervasive influence that the media Journal *Variety* actually criticized one early film because it dared to show Jesus without one (Kinnard and Davis 1992: 14)! The beard, a symbol of authority, was in turn, acquired in the Byzantine period. What ultimately has come down to us, then, has been the icon of the blond, bearded, long-haired, blue-eyed, white-robed Aryan described above, an image immortalized, for example, in the misty fade-in of DeMille's *The*

King of Kings, (1927) as the little blind girl receives her sight. Although a Christ film with Jewish actors was projected (by the Danish director Carl Dreyer) (Drouzy and Jørgensen 1989: esp. 226–7), no serious film, to my knowledge, has as yet portrayed Jesus as a Jew, and with darker Semitic features, and yet such in reality would have been his appearance.

A second facet of the classic portrayal of Jesus on screen has been the language he uses and this, for the most part, has remained close to the standard text of the Gospels. Reference has been made to the selection of biblical quotations from the Authorized Version (some wrested from their original context) which were presented as captions to DeMille's audiences in his silent *The King of Kings*, (1927), and which therefore acted as the unspoken commentary on Jesus' actions. Biblical quotations likewise form the oral core of Pasolini's *The Gospel According to St Matthew* (1964), and although the language in which they are delivered is slightly antiquated, it would not have been considered strange to the average Italian (Stack 1969: 95). Actors have been able to be inventive but the written text of the Bible is still the major determinant of their scripts. While there is considerable freedom for the secondary characters, for example, in *The Greatest Story Ever Told* (1965), both Jesus and John the Baptist are given lines which are largely again taken from the King James Version. In the dramatic Raising of Lazarus scene, however, von Sydow was allowed to improvise (from passages such as Exod. 15:11; Deut. 32:39 and Ezek. 37:9) the striking prayer uttered by Jesus on this occasion (Channel Four 1992). One of the remarkable elements of *The Last Temptation of Christ* (1988) is its much more fluid use of the sacred text, presenting us with a Christ who, though he speaks in an American accent, thinks on his feet and uses language spontaneously in the cut and thrust of debate ("I've got something to tell you . . . uh . . . I'm . . . I'm sorry', he says before the parable of the Sower, ". . . but the easiest way to make myself clear is to tell you a story.") The audience is hence offered his words at a refreshing remove from the process which later crystallized such teaching into holy writ.

It is the screen personality of Jesus to which we finally turn, and confronted with such variety, let me suggest seven personae or Christ-types that the cinema has offered the moviegoers of this century. The first dominating image has been that of *the patriarchal Christ*. In earlier films the tendency was to present Jesus as a mature, majestic, ethereal, composed and essentially controlled figure. This is the Jesus of Henderson-Bland in *From the Manger to the Cross* (1912), for example, or supremely of H. B. Warner in *The King of Kings* (1927). Strong but also gentle, virile but with feminine qualities, possessing considerable "form and comeliness" yet a "man of sorrows and acquainted with grief" (Isa. 53:2–3), Warner is an avuncular Jesus with an asexual compassion for women and children. It is interesting to observe that the British actor was 50 years old when cast as Jesus. Various social, cultural and psychological influences have been suggested for this mature portrayal (Babington and Evans 1993: 22–4, 118), the relatively greater age of Victorian fathers, the tenor of Victorian religious painting and its brooding and melancholic iconography, the reflection of DeMille's own relationship with his audiences, and even the "muscular Christianity" of Bruce Barton's 1924 bestseller *The Man Nobody Knows* (Maltby 1990). None, as far as I am aware, have posited a biblical link with the Johannine tradition that Jesus was middle-aged (Jn. 8:57).

The second image is that of *the adolescent Christ*. After Warner and the removal of restrictions upon the depiction of Christ in the post-war period, the tendency among filmmakers was to present a series of more youthful Jesuses. Chief among these was Jeffrey Hunter's so-called "teenage Jesus" in *King of Kings* (1961), a figure both beautiful and idealistic, at times moody and confused, at once compassionate and self-contained. "[W]hereas in the De Mille film Jesus takes on the role of the father, Ray's Jesus is much more son than father" (Babington and Evans 1993: 133). Made by the director of *Rebel Without A Cause* (1955), and reflecting the developing youth culture, the film offers John the Baptist instead (played uncomfortably by Robert Ryan) as the patriarchal figure. Taunted by the youngest-ever Salome (Brigitte Bazlen), the older prophet is visited in prison by a Jesus come "to free him within his cell." Hunter's Jesus, for the most part, is strong, firm, gentle, showing little passion, excitability or anger, even under the threat of death. When he is beaten (his shaven armpits being momentarily glimpsed), the agonies register on Judas, who faints on seeing the cross being prepared for his friend. Here is a Christ without passion and "without sweat glands," as critics complained in commenting on the crucifixion scene (Channel Four, 1992). Even in dying, Jesus is strangely passive and controlled. "Jeffrey Hunter doesn't look as though he's been forty days in the desert, he doesn't look as if he's suffering at all and you don't feel it," comments Martin Scorsese (Thompson and Christie 1989: 131).

This leads us to the third significant Christ-type in the cinema, namely *the pacific Christ*. Jeffrey Hunter's Jesus is not only passive but pacifist. "Could simple love and brotherhood be weapons against Rome?" the film asks, as it plays Jesus and Barabbas off against each other, with the hapless Judas torn between the alternative methods of resistance they represent. In *Jesus of Nazareth* (1977), likewise, Robert Powell, in "one of the most reverent portrayals of Christ ever filmed" (Kinnard and Davis 1992: 16) presents a dignified, haunting, blue-eyed but (despite wit and perceptiveness) essentially pacific figure.

A clear antithesis, therefore, is to be found in our fourth type, *the subversive Christ* whom audiences were to encounter in Pasolini's *The Gospel according to St Matthew* (1964). Although based on a Gospel which would ordinarily lend support for a pacific Christ (Mt. 26:52), here is a conspiratorial Jesus (some even have said a Marxist Jesus) who goes around Palestine like "a revolutionary whirlwind" (Stack 1969: 95), gathering disciples, spitting out sermons and defending the poor against the priestly aristocracy. Fierce, unsmiling, ascetic, disconcerting, Irazoqui's Jesus, though still somewhat distant and detached, displays a far wider range of emotions than previous celluloid Christs, and gives to the role a refreshing urgency and vitality. The subversive Jesus was to appear again in the allegorical *Cool Hand Luke* (1967) or *Jesus of Montreal* (1989) but with his anger less in evidence. A figure who challenges the authorities and beats the system, Paul Newman's Luke is a more passive figure than Pasolini's Christ, as also is that of Lothaire Bluteau (Willett 1991). Perhaps the closest parallel in terms of drive and energy was Dennis Potter's Jesus (played to winning effect by the stocky British actor Colin Blakely) in the television play, *Son of Man* (1969). "[A] reformer, a socialist, above all a human being who 'deserved to be crucified for his sheer cheek' . . . Potter's Jesus was angry, irascible and hated the establishment of his time" (Tilby 1991: 62)

A fifth cinematic incarnation of Christ appeared a year after Pasolini's film in *The Greatest Story Ever Told* (1965). With his Byzantine look and strange, otherworldly and ascetic demeanour, Max von Sydow brought us *a mystical Christ* (with a Swedish accent) in sharp contrast to the driven figure of Pasolini. Where the Italian director's presentation is at times frenetic, that of Stevens is slow and stately. Based on John's Gospel as well as on the Synoptics, and underscored by the thoughtful and contemplative music of Alfred Newman, Stevens' film allows von Sydow's Jesus time to speak for himself, and to develop a performance which in its strength, virility and compassion equals, if not surpasses, that of H. B. Warner.

If Stevens's "Christ for the sixties" reflected the softer, more contemplative, more introspective side of the counter-culture, then *the musical Christ* of *Jesus Christ Superstar* (1973) and *Godspell* (1973) offers us its raucous exterior. These films have produced a much more animated, more energetic, more contemporary figure, with song and dance routines, a soft shoe shuffle and even the hint of a love relationship with Mary Magdalene. The singing and dancing Jesus, while not a Gospel image (although compare Matt. 11:16–19 and Luke 7:31–5), is not, of course, unknown in our ancient texts. In the Gnostic Acts of John (94–7), Jesus sings and dances with his disciples in Gethsemane (James 1924: 253–4), a passage reflected in Sydney Carter's famous 1967 song "Lord of the Dance."

In his *The Quest of the Historical Jesus* (1906), Albert Schweitzer stated (of nineteenth-century study of the life of Jesus) that it "loosed the bands by which He had been riveted for centuries to the stony rocks of ecclesiastical doctrine, and rejoiced to see life and movement coming into the figure once more"

(Schweitzer 1954: 397). This observation can be transferred to the Christ film where, since the 1960s, such vitality has become more and more apparent. In Martin Scorsese's *The Last Temptation of Christ* (1988), we have one of the most striking and complex portraits of Jesus in recent years. Here is *the human Christ* and one, it seems, with all his tortured introspection, at an opposite pole from Cecil B. DeMille's *The King of Kings* (1927). Scorsese's Jesus, like that of Kazantzakis before him, is a truly human figure grappling with the possibility and the pain of the divine. The film has been much discussed (Corliss 1988; Gallez 1989; Wolf 1989; Jackson 1990: 135–40; Muraire 1992; Babington and Evans 1993: 149–68; Telford 1995: 378–81 in addition to the literature already cited) – perhaps more than it has been seen! – and has attracted a great deal of controversy, as has already been mentioned. Three aspects of the film's treatment of Jesus in particular caused offence, and since these raise theological questions they are worth briefly commenting upon.

The first is its depiction of a sexualized Jesus with physical as well as emotional feelings of attraction for Mary Magdalene, Mary and Martha. Such criticism, however, is misguided, for it is not sex alone but *domesticity* in all its aspects which constitutes Jesus' last temptation – the enjoyment of sex, marriage and children with the women to whom he is drawn. In the words of the film critic, Pam Cook:

> The objections [to Scorsese's film] on the grounds of sex are clearly a red herring; of the two sex scenes, one shows Jesus as a non-participant observer in Mary Magdalene's brothel, followed by his refusal of her invitation to stay, while the other, in which he makes love to and impregnates Mary Magdalene during his reverie on the cross, takes place after their marriage and is directly tied to procreation. Whatever else this Jesus may be after, it is not sex.
>
> *(Cook 1988: 288)*

From a theological perspective also, there is nothing here contrary to the New Testament which presents a Jesus who "in every respect has been tempted as we are, yet without sin" (Heb. 4:15).

It is the phrase "yet without sin," however, that has led to a second condemnation of the film, namely its portrayal of a Jesus who is racked by guilt for his own sins, as well as that of others, and, prone to fear and anxiety, expresses himself a liar and a coward. While the notion of Jesus' sinlessness is found in the New Testament (cf. for example Mt. 3:13–14; Jn 8:46), it is not clear that it was of great theological concern at the earliest stage of the tradition about him. Mark, after all, lets Jesus' baptism at the hands of John "for the remission of sins" (1:5–6, 9–11) pass without comment, and has Jesus himself rebuke the rich young man for calling him good (10:17–18).

The third and most serious criticism of the film is its presentation of a "subjective," doubting Jesus who is demented and confused (an effect intensified by Scorsese's fluid, almost nervous camerawork), a weak, dithering individual who only gradually comes to see himself as the Messiah, a man struggling with his own neurotic, obsessive and masochistic tendencies and seeking to resolve these conflicts in a final act of self-destruction. "In a realistic movie he [Scorsese] tried to depict Jesus speaking with God but he ended up with a Jesus who hears voices" (Scott 1994: 197). While it would be wrong to suggest that such a portrait conforms with that of the Gospels, it is worth recalling for a moment those elements in the tradition, especially that of Mark, which present the more human, ambiguous, even contradictory face of Jesus. He is shown to be emotional (Mk 1:41, 43), distressed (Mk 14:33–4), angry (Mk 3:5), impatient (Mk 9:19), even harsh with family, opponents or disciples (Mk 3:31–5; 7:6, 27; 8:33), and thought to be mad (Mk 3:21). While advocating a pacific attitude to others (Mt. 5:33–42 par.), he nevertheless utters inflammatory words (e.g. Mt. 10:34–6), throws the money-changers out of the Temple (Mk 11:15 18 par.) and curses a fig-tree when it does not provide him with fruit (Mk 11:13–14). What makes him the Christ – for Scorsese, for Kazantzakis and arguably for the Gospels also – is his victory in this struggle of spirit over flesh, mind over matter, good over evil. In that respect, he is a salvific figure, "a prototype of the free man," a savior for a new age.

A major influence on Scorsese's film, as we have seen, was Pasolini's *The Gospel According to St Matthew*. One of the aims of Pasolini's film was to rescue the Jesus of Matthew's Gospel from centuries of religious orthodoxy and piety and to return him to the people. Scorsese's aim likewise was "to make the life of Jesus immediate and accessible to people who haven't really thought about God in a long time" (Thompson and Christie 1989: 124). It is sad, therefore, that the film has not had the audience it deserves, being shown only on British television (Channel Four), for example, as late as June, 1995.

Conclusion

In our journey through film history, we, like the three wise men, have been following a "star." We have ascertained when that star appeared, and have observed his birth in the cradle of the cinema itself. We have noted the spectacle as well as the violence with which his appearance in the biblical epic, as in the Bible story, has been associated. We have commented on the Christ film itself, on the approaches taken to it, the issues it raises, the importance it holds, the forms it has taken, the sources it has used, the social contexts it has addressed, the ideologies it has communicated, and the style it has adopted. In considering its characterization of Jesus, we have discussed the problems encountered in portraying him, and in turn the ways in which this has been done. Like the Gnostics of old, we have found a Christ who has appeared in many shapes and forms (the patriarchal Christ, the adolescent Christ, the pacific Christ, the subversive Christ, the mystical Christ, the musical Christ and the human Christ). The Christ we have found, the Jesus depicted in the cinema, has been influenced by the tradition of the evangelist, the imagination of the filmmaker and the social context of the audience. In an age which has demystified its saints, removed its icons from their pedestals, and demoted its heroes, it is fitting that the more realistic and introspective Christ of the 1990s, as brought to us by Scorsese, should share our human capacity for doubt as well as faith, for skepticism as well as hope, and that his struggle, if it is to be ours, should be seen as both real and genuine. The screen image of Jesus has varied with the shifts and currents of society itself, in line with its changing social, political and religious perspectives and values. Of the Christ of the cinema, therefore, as with the Johannine Christ, there is a sense in which it may be said that "He is in us, and we are in Him."

Notes

A version of this chapter was first delivered at the Glasgow Film Theatre as a special lecture given in connection with a "Film and Religion" Day Conference organized by the Centre for the Study of Literature and Theology, University of Glasgow (May 10, 1995). Special thanks are expressed to Dr D. Jasper and his colleagues. A further version was given as a paper at Sheffield University's Department of Biblical Studies Staff and Postgraduate Seminar, December 11, 1995. I am also grateful for the comments and suggestions received on this occasion.

1 Given the seriousness with which the subject of the Bible and film is now taken, however, it seems that the director may have had the last laugh. After large cost overruns, DeMille decided to bury, in the sands of Guadalupe, California, the Egyptian city which he had had constructed for the silent version of *The Ten Commandments* (1923), making a playful reference in his autobiography to future archeologists digging up the site (Hayne 1960: 231–2). In the interests of film history, this set has now been excavated by archeologists of the University of California (Bygrave 1991; Higashi 1994: 182, 247; Telford 1995: 366).

2 I am grateful to the author for a copy of this article in advance of its publication.

3 In this respect, one awaits with interest the projected Christ film of the controversial director, Paul Verhoeven (*Robocop*, 1987; *Total Recall*, 1990; *Basic Instinct*, 1992; *Showgirls*, 1996). Verhoeven has attended the equally controversial Jesus Seminar in America and intends to draw on its scholarly results. In private conversation, Marcus Borg has informed me that several versions of the script have now been "put by"

Seminar members for comment. The film is to be made after the completion of several current projects (Telford 1995: 367; Romney 1996).

4 In commenting upon the role of H. B. Warner who played the part of Jesus in *The King of Kings*, DeMille's now famous anecdote is worth repeating. "How perfectly he fulfilled it has never been better told than by a minister who said to him many years later: 'I saw you in *The King of Kings* when I was a child, and now, every time I speak of Jesus, it is your face I see'" (Hayne 1960: 253).

5 John Trevelyan, the British film censor, notes, for example, the following list of eliminations which operated, where religion in general was concerned, in 1931:

1 The materialized figure of Christ.
2 Irreverent quotations of religious texts.
3 Travesties of familiar Biblical quotations and well-known hymns.
4 Titles to which objection would be taken by religious organizations.
5 Travesty and mockery of religious services.
6 Holy vessels amidst incongruous surroundings, or shown used in a way which would be looked upon as desecration.
7 Comic treatment of incidents connected with death.
8 Painful insistence of realism in deathbed scenes.
9 Circumcision.
10 Themes portraying the Hereafter and Spirit World.
11 The Salvation Army shown in an unfavorable light.

(Trevelyan 1973: 40–1, 43–4)

1 Ada McGrath (Holly Hunter) and her daughter, Flora (Anna Paquin) together with the "piano on the vast beach" – symbol both of domination and liberation in *The Piano*. (Photograph courtesy of Ciby Sales Ltd.)

2 Jake La Motta (Robert De Niro) bears the marks of "redeeming violence" in *Raging Bull*. (United Artists; photograph courtesy of the Kobal Collection.)

3 Jesus (Willem Dafoe) confronted by the temptation to favor domesticity over a
different calling in *The Last Temptation of Christ*. (Universal; photograph courtesy of
the Kobal Collection.)

4 Sarah (Linda Hamilton) opts for drastic action, though with a "dulled sensitivity," in *Terminator 2: Judgment Day*. (Carolco; photograph courtesy of the Kobal Collection.)

10

The *Terminator* Movies:
Hi-Tech Holiness and the Human Condition

Gaye Ortiz and Maggie Roux

I looked on the earth, and lo, it was waste and void;
and to the heavens, and they had no light.
I looked on the mountains, and lo, they were quaking,
and all the hills moved to and fro.
I looked, and lo, there was no man,
and all the birds of the air had fled.
I looked, and lo, the fruitful land was a desert,
and all its cities were laid in ruins.

(Jer. 4:23–6)

The Terminator opens on a scene of devastation which echoes this vision from an Old Testament prophet; equally, it is a scene that could have been taken directly from Malachi, the last book in the Old Testament canon: "Surely the day is coming, it will burn like a furnace. All the arrogant and every evil-doer will be stubble and that day that is coming will set them on fire, says the Lord God Almighty. Not a root or a branch will be left to them" (Mal. 4:1–2).

The third chapter of Malachi warns of "The Day of Judgment" (recalled in the title of the sequel *Terminator II: Judgment Day*). This day of judgment was promised because although the Israelites had been rescued from exile, had had Jerusalem restored to them and had completed the rebuilding of the temple, they had lost their trust in God. Their worship was simply a matter of form and the Law was no longer revered or taken seriously.

The nation was accursed because the people made contemptible offerings to God; they were dishonest and covered themselves "with violence" (Mal. 2:16). Special condemnation is made in Malachi of the community leaders, the teachers of the law: "For the lips of the priest ought to preserve knowledge and from his mouth men should seek instruction – because he is the messenger of the Lord Almighty. But you have turned away and by your teaching have caused many to stumble" (Mal. 2:7–8).

Because of such contempt the mountains of Esau were turned into wasteland, a reminder of the earlier prophecies of Isaiah, Jeremiah, and

Ezekiel, all of whom predict the destruction of the people because they refuse to live in peace and respect for God (Isa. 34:5–15/Jer. 49:7–22/Ezek. 25:12–14, 35:1–15).

Malachi's position in the Bible links it back into the past and forward to the New Testament. The Prophets preach both warning (catastrophe arising from the wrongdoing of the people) and promise (hope in the future from one who will be born to the people): "Therefore the Lord himself will give you a sign. The virgin will be with child and will give birth to a son, and will call him Immanuel" (Isa. 7:13–15).

The imagery used by director James Cameron to introduce *The Terminator* is also the imagery of ancient biblical writers. The issues raised by the *Terminator* movies are the issues explored by Isaiah, Jeremiah and Ezekiel. How is humankind to avoid extinction, whether it be self-destruction or destruction meted out by God, unless it confronts its own evil, takes responsibility for that evil and seeks salvation?

This too is the story of the twentieth century, a time in which the speed of change has been unprecedented. In his book, *Age of Extremes: The Short Twentieth Century 1914–1991*, Eric Hobsbawm describes it as the most murderous century on record. Within that timespan, a catalog of horrors includes two World Wars and other brutal conflicts from Vietnam to Rwanda to Bosnia; the Nazi Holocaust and those of Stalin's Russia, Mao's China and Pol Pot's Cambodia; nuclear bombs dropped on Japan, and the Reagan legacy of Mutually Assured Destruction and the Star Wars programs; the growth of dangerous fundamentalisms and the terrifying prospect of nature itself in revolt against the thoughtless destruction of natural resources. In *Hopeful Imagination, Prophetic Voices in Exile* Walter Brueggemann links the challenges facing the late twentieth century to those which faced the people addressed by the biblical prophets. He draws on the traditions of Jeremiah, Ezekiel and Deutero-Isaiah to explore those challenges and the biblical promise of salvation given to Noah (Isa. 54:9–11).Do the ancient voices of prophecy and warning have any relevance today?

Perhaps the message of the *Terminator* movies is that only through understanding the value of human life will we be saved from ourselves. This essential understanding has yet to be fully grasped – the warning to us is that we cannot shirk our responsibilities as active participants in our future. The films, set in an advanced Western culture which is increasingly dependent upon technology, seems to echo Isaiah: the powerful, comfortable city of Babylon is warned that for all its magic spells and its belief in a secure, eternal existence, nevertheless "disaster will come upon you, and you will not know how to conjure it away. A calamity you cannot foresee will suddenly come upon you" (Isa. 47:11–12).

In the *Terminator* movies another Babylon – the USA, the most powerful and comfortable nation on earth – has attempted to underpin its security. Leaders and scientists (in the footsteps of the priests of Malachi) have abrogated human responsibility in their design of artificial life forms which eliminate human error in military decision making. This brings an unforeseen calamity: the machines, designed to protect humankind from itself, become super-intelligent and begin to wage war on their creators.

The pursuit of dangerous knowledge, and the possible consequences of implementing such knowledge outside of a rigorous examination of human response and responsibility, are the main concerns of the *Terminator* and *Terminator II* movies. These films fit well within the literary tradition of the novels *War of the Worlds*, *Brave New World* and *1984*; they also sit comfortably within the *Star Trek/Independence Day* genre of alien invasion movies. There is no question that the Terminator films contain excessive violence and display awesome special effects which attract audiences who are eager consumers of Hollywood action blockbusters.

As the years pass, however, it is clear that the *Terminator* films contain enduring qualities and themes which make for classic cinema. Classic cinema in turn mines deep allegorical, religious and mythological veins for its universal appeal to audiences. To undertake a theological dialog with the *Terminator* films means delving into diverse but complex concepts such as the nature of humanity; the threat or promise of technology; destiny versus free will; the future as apocalypse; and the savior/hero figure. Many of these concepts have implications affecting the others, and the authors will thus be alluding to these out of necessity.

For the purposes of this chapter, however, the *Terminator*'s cinematic nightmare of artificial life is the focus for exploring the real-life question: "How do we value what it is to be human?" This is also a question which has fascinated philosophers and theologians down the centuries. It must be approached in a qualified manner, because of the difficulty of defining what is normative, common or universal human experience. The authors take the view that the *Terminator* films can provoke thought, when placed alongside Christian biblical and theological perspectives (as well as mythological imagery), on what it means to be human.

The Box of Horrors

These following words accompany the opening scene of devastation in the 1984 film, *The Terminator*:

> The machines rose from the
> ashes of the nuclear fire.

> Their war to terminate
> mankind had raged for
> decades, but the final
> battle would not be fought
> in the future.
> It would be fought here,
> in our present:
> Tonight . . .

Set in Los Angeles, the film addresses the mission of a cyborg terminator sent from the future by a race of machine rulers to find and destroy a young waitress, Sarah Connor. She will one day give birth to the rebel human who is destined to lead a revolt against the machines. By sending a killer into the past to murder the mother of this potential savior, the machines can guarantee their bid for world domination. It is this picture of the threat of technology in general – and artificial life in particular – that sets up an exploration of the value of humanity within *The Terminator* and its 1991 sequel *Terminator II: Judgment Day*.

Today's society has moved on since Isaac Asimov formulated his famous Three Laws of Robotics in the 1950s. The First Law states that "a robot may not injure a human being or, through inaction, allow a human being to come to harm" (cited in Allen and Asimov 1993). An eminent pioneering scientist in the field of artificial intelligence, Doyne Farmer (who once referred to Mary Shelley's story as "the bugaboo of Frankenstein"), came to realize that the development of artificial life "opens a box of potential horrors worse than those that daunted Pandora." He is quoted as saying that

> It involves a threat to our species. It is easy to imagine nightmare scenarios in which cold malevolent machines, or vicious genetically engineered creatures overwhelm humanity. Once self-reproducing war machines are in place, even if we should change our minds and establish a consensus, dismantling them may become impossible – they may be literally out of our control. An escalated technological war involving the construction of artificial armies would certainly end by destroying the participants themselves and would give rise to a generation of life forms that might be even more hostile and destructive than their human ancestors.
>
> *(Levy 1992: 334)*

Levy then quotes UCLA biologist Charles Taylor who declares that as a result "artificial life violates Asimov's First Law of Robotics by its very nature" (ibid.: 335). This dilemma is pointed up in *The Terminator*, with a chilling storyline in which humankind has given over its war machine to the "machines." Such a surrender of responsibility results in the non-human taking over the decision making process completely and attempting to finally eradicate the human all together.

In *Caliban*, a collaborative work with Roger MacBride Allen published in 1993, Isaac Asimov explored the breakdown of his earlier formulation of Robotic Law. It is a story set on the planet Inferno, whose settlers fear that as robots relieve humanity of its burdens, so they will relieve humanity of its spirit, its will, its ambition. The character of Dr Fredda Leving addresses this scenario:

> What are humans for? Look around you. Consider your society. Look at the place of humans in it. We are drones, little else. There is scarcely an aspect of our lives that has not been entrusted to the care of the robots. In entrusting our tasks to them, we surrender our fate to them. So what are humans for? That is the question, the real question it all comes down to in the end. And I would submit that our current use of robots has given us a terrifying answer . . . and the true answer to that question is: not much.
>
> *(Allen and Asimov 1993: 123–4)*

The Human Response

In the *Terminator* movies human society has not yet given itself over completely into the care and control of its robotic systems; but the question facing Sarah Connor, Kyle Reese and other characters in the movie is how to avert one possible future – the future witnessed to by the cyborgs and Reese. The strong message of both movies is that "the future is not set" – humankind can make the choices required to save humanity.

It is through the character of Sarah Connor that the prophetic response required by humanity in facing the consequences of its actions is most fully explored. When we first meet her in *The Terminator* she is, in James Cameron's view, the "least likely person you can imagine on whom would be predicated the global event of a world devastated by nuclear war" (Field 1994: 87). Sarah is a 19 year-old waitress in a fast-food restaurant, whose biggest problem is a lack of attention from her boyfriend. However, from the beginning of the film we are aware of her strength and independence. Sarah Connor is challenged under the most terrifying conditions to find in herself the ability to respond in just such a way. She has first to gauge the authenticity of the fantastic story told by Kyle Reese. James Cameron describes her as no hero, "just an ordinary person who just happens to be placed in extraordinary circumstances" (ibid.:

92). She says of herself: "Are you sure you got the right person, do I look like the mother of the future? I mean, am I tough, organized? I can't even organize my own cheque book."

Sarah's response to the dramatic and violent unfolding of events is worth examination in the light of feminist biblical interpretation of the Matriarchs, the women of the Old Testament, and of their role in the formation and safekeeping of the People of God. For example, the character of Sarah, wife of Abraham, is a woman of high standing. The future is embodied in Sarah's only child Isaac. The Sarah of the Jewish myths and legends is a woman who stands for the health and wellbeing of her community (cf. Frankeil 1990).

Sarah Connor will play a parallel role in her community, as evidenced by the message she receives from her son in the future: "Thank you, Sarah, for your courage through the dark years." The reason why Kyle Reese "crosses time to meet her" is the legend of Sarah Connor herself: she "taught her son to fight, organize, prepare from when he was a kid" (Field 1994: 92).

In other words, Sarah Connor is a woman who protects the present and informs the future vision of the man who is to fight the destruction of the human race. She recognizes that present decisions will have ongoing effects on future generations. This can be seen as a female prophetic response that bonds woman to the future. She must intuit what from present action will be future consequence. Motherhood in this context stands for the active exercise of female power: Sarah's acceptance of the role of mother of a savior figure (echoing the story of another mother two thousand years ago) reminds us once again that the response of one human being can make a difference. Mary of Nazareth, in the words of the Magnificat (Lk. 1:46–55), saw the consequences of her acceptance of God's invitation stretching into the future to all generations.

Joseph Campbell, whose work on the hero figure informed Cameron's thinking for the films, identifies the hero of myth as one who answers "the call to adventure" and who "brings back (from his adventure) the means for the regeneration of his society as a whole" (Campbell 1988: epilogue). This is certainly the task which confronts Sarah, and as with many biblical heroes before her, the commission to act is questioned. She is terrified of the call – "I didn't ask for this honour, I don't want it – any of it" – but the manifestation of her heroism lies in her courageous response to extraordinary events. She is passive neither in her relationship with Kyle Reese (in which John is conceived) nor in the battle with the Terminator; indeed, she becomes Kyle's protector before he is killed.

In the follow-up *Terminator II* she is not content simply to give birth and protection to the savior, but rather to answer the challenge that "fate is not fixed." She understands her task as twofold: to conceive and birth John Connor, and to avert the very circumstances which will require him in the future to take on the savior role.

The first movie sees the transformation of the young waitress into the woman who holds the promise of the future in her womb. In *Terminator II* she has been further transformed into a warrior. It is this sequel which explores more fully the question of what is it to be human. We first must learn in *The Terminator* what it is *not* to be human – as Kyle Reese explains: "The Terminator is out there, it can't be bargained with, reasoned with, it doesn't feel pity, remorse or fear. And it absolutely will not stop – ever. Until you are dead."

We also learn that the Terminator does not feel pain, and indeed a powerful indication of the invulnerability of the Terminator comes in the opening scene. When the naked Terminator arrives from the future we see the perfection of the human form as envisaged by the ancient Greeks, further underlined as the Terminator, still naked, looks down on the city of Los Angeles as though in ownership of all he surveys. When Reese makes the same journey from the future he arrives in pain: he feels the cold, finds walking painful and his skin is badly scarred on his back.

However, those who create machines must first know what it means to be human. The Terminator is a creature covered in flesh but not made of flesh. It is obvious from his discussions with John Connor that he has no understanding of what it is to be human – why people cry, for instance, or the importance of a sense of humor. What the Terminator learns above all else is that technology has no experience of human relationships. Even though he has an impressive database of information about human behavior, relationship – a defining activity of human living – must be lived out. The machine may look human and may have an analytical function akin to human reasoning, but he lacks the essence of humanity – what some would define as soul.

The animation of a creature, so central to the discussion of artificial life, is also central to the discussion of the Incarnation in Christian theology: human life takes place in the flesh, a material being imbued with qualities such as rational thinking and tender emotion. The earlier of the two Creation stories in the Old Testament book of Genesis sets the stage for the Judeo-Christian tradition that values the union of body and soul, where "dust and breath are there in man together from the moment of creation" (Macquarrie 1982: 50). Indeed, the philosopher Kierkegaard believed that the human task is to effect a synthesis of body and soul. For Christians the worth of the physical being is derived from being part of God's creation; because it is made in God's image, therefore it is good. The importance of this goodness is evident in Christology (i.e. the study of Christ and his qualities), which places such importance not only on the fully human and fully divine nature of Christ, but also on the Christian teachings about the resurrection of the body. The essential uniqueness of human nature has been explored by theologians such as Jürgen Moltmann (1974) and Wolfhart Pannenberg (1985).[1]

In *Terminator II* the ambiguity of the human condition is explored imaginatively. The killing machine sent to destroy John is the T-1000. Its most terrifying aspect is the ability to "shapeshift." This machine can take on all the superficial attributes of humankind. How do we know under such circumstances who is human, who is not? This theme has been explored to great effect in films such as *Invasion of the Bodysnatchers* (Don Siegel, 1956), *Blade Runner* (Ridley Scott, 1982), *Starman* (John Carpenter, 1984), and *Alien* (Ridley Scott, 1979), but it also can be read in a way that taps into our own doubt about the dark side of human nature. The question about our own ability to act in an "inhuman" way brings us face to face with our potential to transgress the boundaries of acceptable human behavior. When criminals are described as "animals," is this not our way of denying our humanity in all its facets, good as well as bad? The truth is that we can sometimes be the alien, the Other, the shape-shifter.

Sarah certainly changes her shape – she was a girlish, feminine character in the first movie. When we next see her in *Terminator II* she is a muscular, lean and hard fighting machine, concentrating on maximizing her physical strength while locked in a cell in Pescadero State Mental Hospital. One reading of this change in appearance, especially when she is later dressed in battle fatigues, toting a machine gun, is that Sarah is "shifting" from feminine to masculine and from human to killing machine. Rather than seeing her in the mythological tradition of the god Proteus, who shifted shape as the unkillable, amorphous Other, we can see in Sarah a human who is bound to her form but who has honed it to its utmost physical potential. She is "strengthening her arm" and working indefatigably day and night, "girding her loins" with strength in order to fulfill her mission (quotes from Proverbs 16).

We learn that for all of John's young life Sarah has tried to ensure that he will not have to answer the call, or at least that he will not be alone in the future war. She has become a warrior employing stratagems which her son has not understood. John tells the cyborg uncomprehendingly that "she tried to blow up a computer factory – but she got shot and arrested. She's a total loser." Of course, he does not understand that her determination to build herself up both physically and mentally is a denial of human vulnerability and weakness. (Ironically the Terminator is at the same time learning vital lessons about what it means to be a human.)

What drives Sarah is a nightmare vision of annihilation, of absolute horror, and it informs everything she does and feels. But the screenplay reminds us that her vision is rooted in compassion for the "little ones": it is not the destruction of great cities or monuments to human inventiveness and power which exercises her, but the destruction of children at play. Sarah is concerned with protecting the innocent, reminding us of the biblical injunction that children should have direct access to the embodiment of the promise of the fullness of life: "Let the little children come to me, and do not hinder them, for the kingdom of God belongs to such as these" (Lk. 18:16–17).

In the mental hospital she is considered to be dangerously mad, but she keeps her sanity well protected like the wise maid of the parable Jesus told – tending the oil in her lamp in readiness for the coming of the bridegroom (Matt. 25). Sarah knows the time is at hand, that she must be ready to respond adequately. She is never guilty of a weakness often connected with women, that of passivity. The loneliness of her position is that of the one who cries in the wilderness. Sarah leads a desert existence, a hidden life. Sarah further suffers from the lack of belief in female witness. This is faced by the women of the Bible, not least in the case of Mary of Nazareth whose honour has to be defended to Joseph by an angel, and the women at the tomb of Jesus whose witness to the resurrection was subordinated to the later witness of men. The loneliness of Sarah's position is underlined by the complete lack of belief in her sanity by her son and by the medical staff at the mental hospital. The terror felt by Sarah at the way in which her testimony is not only being ignored but used against her is one of the most powerful scenes in the film. Here the less obvious signs of Sarah's heroic qualities are explored. She uses passion, deception and wile to ensure her eventual escape. These are precisely the tools used by the biblical heroines Tamar, Deborah, Judith, and Jael to ensure the survival of their people.

Sarah's own violent response recalls the violence of Judith and Jael caught also in a situation which allows no other response – a situation confronted by women today in their struggle for survival. Julia Esquivel, writing about Christian women and the struggle for justice in Central America, points out that ". . . violence or non-violence is not the question for us in Central America. It is, rather, can we live or not? We are either going to live or be exterminated. We are like the woman who has to use every means possible to save herself and her children, or be exterminated. Our people organized to use non-violent methods, and the response to all these methods has been death" (Eck and Jain 1986: 18–19).

In the hospital scene Sarah is a woman, a mother, a mental patient. She is pitted against the powers and principalities. She stands as one of the most enduring motifs of powerlessness in human experience. The women in many biblical stories have to pit themselves against just such overwhelming powers to ensure life for their children. It is all too evident that the massacre of the innocents is an enduring terror down into our own time. Sarah is an example of how the powerless defend themselves against the strong. Sarah knows the pain of loss, combat, the weight of an inhuman system, the price of human pride, and the burden of protection. She recognizes her place in the task of forming a decent future in which children will be safe.

Destiny requires a response based on free will, and it is Sarah's actions that fulfill the prophetic motto Kyle Reese brings back from the future: "The future is not set. There is no fate but what we make." As Jacques Maritain points out, the human decision to act must be based on freedom and not some divinely prepared script: "The Divine plan is not a scenario prepared in advance in which free subjects would play parts and act as performers. We must purge our thought of any idea of a play written in advance." He concludes that "in creation God takes risks and (that) free beings astonish God himself" (as quoted in Cowburn 1979: 36).

The Consequences of Vision

The growing relationship between Sarah's son John and his protective cyborg also allows the film to explore the essence of what should be valued in the human. As the cyborg spends time with the boy so it begins to learn – and we begin to reflect – on the complexity of humanity. We explore the reason for tears, the need for humor, the requirement not to kill. We learn more about John through his relationship with the cyborg: we witness the boy's inventiveness and courage, as well as the gift of friendship. We also learn more about Sarah. John understands that he was born through love and that his mother continues to be sustained by the love she shared with Reese: "In a few short hours we loved a lifetime's worth."

John's insistence, in the face of his own danger, that his mother must be rescued from the hospital points up the changing nature of the relationship between parent and child. He is growing out of the role of the son to be protected, and Sarah stands as the one who is prepared to be sacrificed on behalf of the cause. At the desert stronghold to which the trio return, John and the Terminator both begin to feel their way towards authentic human understanding, while Sarah finds new (and ironic) insights into the qualities of fatherhood. In one of the most moving scenes in the second movie she reflects that "of all the would-be fathers who came and went over the years, this thing, this machine was the only one who measured up. In an insane world, it was the sanest choice."

Sarah's determination to save her son and avert the holocaust causes her to seek out Myles Dyson, the man who is responsible for the future production of the Terminator technology. This is a man who is utterly obsessed by his work in robotics. The arm and hand of the Terminator (a legacy from the first movie's cyborg) fashion the prototype for his further inventions. It is also his God. The limbs are kept in a holy of holies secreted in the cybertronics factory. Only the high priests of science can gain admittance to the shrine.

The French writer Jacques Ellul compares human technical development with magic, in that they are both conscious attempts to control the environment in which humanity lives (Ellul 1963). Ellul sees the holy man, magician or witch-doctor performing the role of protecting society, but when we see Dyson in his home he has little thought for society, his wife and child taking second place to his work. Myles Dyson shows no interest in the ethical implications of his project. He is not an evil man, but one who is unreflective. Nothing can deflect this man from the pursuit of knowledge.

This same obsession with scientific possibilities that shows little regard for reality inhabits our world today. Rodney A. Brooks, one of the leading scientists working on artificial life systems, was once quoted as saying that his desire was

> to build completely autonomous mobile agents that co-exist in the world with humans and are seen by those humans as intelligent beings in their own right. I will call such agents Creatures. This is my intellectual motivation. I have no particular interest in demonstrating how human beings work although humans, like other animals, are interesting objects of study in this endeavor as they are successful autonomous agents. I have no particular interest in applications; it seems clear to me that if my goals can be met then the range of applications for such Creatures will be limited only by our (or their) imaginations. I have no particular interest in the philosophical implications of Creatures, although clearly there will be significant implications.
>
> *(Rodney A. Brooks, as quoted in Levy, 1992: 270)*

The science in which Myles Dyson is engaged has long been associated with the nightmare of war by robots; in 1900 the physicist Nicola Tesla, speculating on the type of machine required to dispense with men on the battlefield, understood that such a creature must be "no mere mechanical contrivance, but a machine embodying a higher principle which will enable it to perform its duties as though it had intelligence, experience, reason, judgement, a mind!" (Franklin 1988: 206).

The dangers of arrogant invention can be seen in this century's atomic genius; when Robert Oppenheimer realized the implications of his work on the atomic bomb he quoted from the *Baghavad Gita* – "I am become death, the destroyer of worlds" (on this further, see Pursell 1994). This quotation embraces the ancient understanding which Mary Shelley explored in her novel *Frankenstein*, that "dangerous is the acquirement of knowledge, and much happier that man is who believes his native town to be the world, than he who aspires to become greater than his nature will allow" (Shelley 1987: 46).[2]

Just as in Mary Shelley's story – the evil does not reside in the Creature as such, but rather in Frankenstein's determination to pursue the power of creation at all costs, with little regard for the outcome – so in *Terminator II* the scientist Dyson realizes that our constructions may, in the end, be our destruction. However, one who dares to subvert the creative power of knowledge may find himself in the position warned of in an ancient Chinese proverb: "He who rides on the tiger can no longer get off it" – the dangers of abandoning responsibility can be greater than continuing blindly. Humanity, it could be argued, loses power as it loses its self-awareness – even its recognition that such self-examination is necessary at all. When Dyson is faced with the future consequences of his research he pleads the ancient human defence – "I didn't know this would happen" – an excuse so often used against the backdrop of destroyed lives.

Dale Aukerman explores this defence of "not knowing" in *Darkening Valley – a Biblical Perspective on Nuclear War*. He cites the English historian Herbert Butterfield: "One of the greatest deficiencies of our time is the failure of the imagination or the intellect to bring home to itself the portentous character of human sin" (Aukerman 1981: 31–2). Aukerman recalls the moment in Luke's gospel where, in the "midst of the agony" of the crucifixion, Jesus said "Father forgive them they do not know what they are doing," and asks: in what ways did they not know? He understands the failure to see who Jesus was in the prophetic sense, but it is the more elemental blindness that exercises Aukerman: the blindness exposed by the lack of feeling for a fellow human being; the hardened nature of the populace to the horror of killing and torture.

This is precisely the example of humanity first encountered by the Terminator. It is in the clothes of thugs and killers – those who persecute the stranger, the weak and vulnerable – that the Terminator begins his mimicry of what it is to be human. In contrast, *Terminator II: Judgment Day* presents the Model T-1000 dressed in the clothes of the authorized authorities – the police force whose motto emblazoned on the police cars reads "To care, to protect."

In seeking to kill Dyson Sarah suffers from a dulled sensitivity – her moral vision is flawed. She sees a solution to the future apocalypse in his death, but she ignores the constraints against killing which her son John Connor has imposed upon the Terminator (who thereafter limits himself to shooting people in their legs in a recognition of some sort of ethical behavior which shapes and defines the human condition). A theological reading of Sarah's attempt to murder Dyson must be grounded in the Judeo-Christian belief that murder is wrong. The commandment against killing (Deut. 5) sets a moral limit on human actions, even in situations where the most expedient deliverance from a nightmare future would be the death of a single person.[3]

However, Sarah is presented to us as a character who has the moral background to respond when she confronts the humanity of the life she plans to destroy. When she is face to face with Dyson she is unable to go through with her plan. This is the first time that Sarah is deflected from her mission. Dyson is no monster, but a man terrified for his family.

The Transformed Creature

It is now, with the arrival of the Terminator and John at Dyson's home, that we see the connection between male and female power. Neither has the monopoly of strength or compassion. That the warrior role must be undertaken by women and that the nurturing role must be undertaken by men is the message of the scene in Dyson's house. Sarah cannot kill Dyson and so believes she has failed in her task, but John's compassion for Sarah frees her long-frozen emotions. His integrity has its root in Sarah's nurturing and her integrity is reestablished in his love.

In many myths and legends the world over, the child born to save humanity is almost always identified as male, the child born to conceive the savior is always female. There is a wholeness in this picture which is often distorted in the emphasis on the male-only redeemer role. But the two roles perhaps can be seen to make up the whole story for the human race. The child, when grown into the purpose for which he was born, must become other than the child, and the mother must become other than the parent. They must both face each other in their unique humanity. Jesus asked, "Who is my mother, Who are my brothers?" (Mt. 12:48). Sarah is both John's mother and the woman called to participate in the saving of humanity. John is both her son and the man in whom the promise of the future rests.

From this point on in *Terminator II* a reading of the two human beings – child and parent/ man and woman – as the symbols for all of us engaged in the adventure of "becoming human" is possible. If we are not yet human, we are "daily becoming so:" life for Sarah and John Connor is the process of "discovering and . . . realizing what the potentials of a human existence are" (J. G. Herder as quoted by Pannenberg 1985: 45); oddly enough, it is their encounter with a machine – a totally alien being, the Other – that helps them to find their humanity. The final sacrificial act of the film, the self-destruction of the Terminator, is born out of his reflection on the uniqueness of being human. As Sarah says hopefully, "if a machine can learn the value of human life, maybe we can too." With Sarah as a living example of transforming action, the Terminator is able to perform a truly human act – and a conscious one at that – of self-sacrifice. Jürgen Moltmann sees self-knowledge arising "at the point where man in his life is charged with something impossible by the call of God" (Moltmann 1974: 16).

The gesture of free will made by the Terminator is astonishing in its implication, namely, that the triumph of Sarah and the salvation of humanity is made dependent upon the humanizing of the cyborg. That the machine can make a thumbs-up sign – the universally human sign of victory – as Sarah lowers him into the vat which will destroy him demonstrates the complex bond of human to the Other.

Through the course of the *Terminator* films, then, the circumstances which awaken a prophetic response in Sarah are resolved in a salvific act by a machine. Christians can read the Terminator's totally selfless act as a heroic scene, resonating with the Christian belief that humanity can become, through the sacrifice of Jesus on the cross, a new creation. Jesus taught that to be truly human is to be liberated: we are allowed to make mistakes and to be frail. The danger is not in that, but rather in assuming that we can do anything. In the act of giving one's self there is a promise, in the very act of surrender, of becoming fully human:

> You are the child of man and of God, immortal
> Though doomed to die, hopeless yet fed on salvation,
> Capable of intelligence, of murder and of mercy.
> Remember your end, attend to the pricks of perfection.
> Swords in the sun; in the rain unceasing.
> But go in peace, now go forward in peace.
>   (from *Cain* by Anne Ridler, as quoted in Nicholson 1942: 38)

Notes

1 On the body/mind relationship in terms of human and artificial life, see Gelertner 1994.
2 For an analysis of the horror genre from a Jesuit perspective, and specifically of Whale's 1931 *Frankenstein*, see Blake 1991.
3 On the failure of the imagination, feeling and the "dulling of moral sensitivity" see "The Iliad, Poem of Might," in Panichas 1977.

11

Stuck in Time: *Kairos, Chronos,* and the Flesh in *Groundhog Day*

Robert Jewett

Introduction

There is an intriguing expression in the New Testament Letter of the Apostle Paul to the Galatians (Gal 6·10) that addresses the central premise of *Groundhog Day*, the story of a Pittsburgh TV weatherman by the name of Phil Connors who "gets stuck in time" (Denby 1993: 110). Connors feels caught in an endless cycle of repetition reminiscent of the despair felt by most people in Paul's time. Paul moves against the cultural stream in promising that "in its own time we shall reap a harvest if we do not give up." Here is the larger context of Paul's intriguing discussion of time and "the flesh" which has the power to sustain deadly deceptions:

> Do not be deceived, God is not mocked.
> For whatever a person sows, that he will also reap.
> For the one who sows to his own flesh will from the flesh reap corruption,
> but the one who sows to the Spirit will from the Spirit reap eternal life.
> And let us not grow weary in doing good,
> for in its own time we shall reap a harvest if we do not give up.
> So then as we have time, let us do good to all persons,
> and especially to those of the household of faith.
>
> *(Gal. 6:7–10)*

The expression *kairos idios* ("in its own time") in the final verse of this passage from Galatians implies there are moments that are appropriate, distinctive, and non-repetitive, designed by God for the harvest. Translations like the Revised Standard Version render this "in due season." In the world as God intended it, we do not go on planting a crop day after day, or cultivating and weeding day after day. For planting is followed by cultivating and nurturing and then by harvesting. Time is going somewhere because God intends it so. But Phil Connors is out in Punxsutawney, PA, for the fourth year in a row, watching the same groundhog come out of the same hole, and seeing the same people in the same celebration. He is bitter and cynical, as contemptuous of his colleagues on the camera crew as of the citizens of Punxsutawney. His orientation leads him to view the yearly celebration of the groundhog's emergence as a sign that there is really no "tomorrow." There is no "proper time," no "due season" for moving on. This throws his whole life into a tailspin. He discusses this burden with some fellows at the bar early in the film: "What would you do if you were stuck in one place, and every day was exactly the same, and nothing that you did mattered?" The guys at the bar look off into the distance for a moment and then one of them says, "That sums it up for me." Their lives also had no *kairos idios*, no "proper time" for moving on past planting and cultivating into some kind of fulfillment, into the harvest. They feel they are stuck on a treadmill for the rest of their lives. To use Paul's language, they have devoted their energies "sowing to the flesh" and now they are "reaping the corruption" of emptiness. Does *Groundhog Day* throw light on this link between time and flesh, between sowing and reaping through "doing good?" Let me begin the exploration by sketching the method I am employing in this particular exploration of film and theology.

The Method of Correlating Biblical Texts with Films

In *Saint Paul at the Movies* I laid out the idea of relating films and Biblical texts by means of an interpretive arch, which seeks analogies between ancient and modern texts and situations (Jewett 1993: 7–12).[1] One end of the arch rests in the ancient world and the other in a contemporary cultural situation reflected in a particular film. There is a conversation at each end of the arch because both the biblical writers and the filmmakers interact with their cultural situations. In the light of the historical-critical method, I understand Pauline texts in the light of their bearing on specific cultural and historical situations, and I look for modern analogies not just to what Paul wrote but also to the situations he addressed. In contrast to a tradition of abstract, dogmatic interpretation that has tended to dominate Pauline studies, I am operating on the assumption that every word of a Pauline letter is embedded in a story of a concrete community in conversation with other faith communities.

The arch between the ancient moment and the present encompasses the history of interpretation, including some of the greatest theologians in Christendom as well as the Pauline scholars of the past who reinterpreted Paul for their own cultural and historical situations. As Robert S. Corrington has suggested, we each stand in a "community of interpreters" (Corrington 1987). My work both with the Pauline texts and with contemporary films is influenced by communities of interpretation inside and outside of the academic realm. No interpreter works alone; we all negotiate the interpretive arch along cables woven by our traditions and our communities.

The contemporary end of the interpretive arch rests in my own denominational and cultural situation, which is why I avoid generalizations that claim to be universal in their scope. My primary interest is in relating Paul to the American cultural situation, which may present some limitations to the relevance of my work in an ecumenical dialog such as contained in this volume. Thus far my choice of films has been restricted to American products that have thematic and narrative similarities to a particular biblical text. Once a film is selected, it deserves and requires interpretive efforts equal to those expended on the biblical text itself. Even an amateur like myself can view a film repeatedly, study its structure and dialog, discuss it with colleagues and friends, and read reviews and articles that relate to its story and meaning. I try to devote comparable energy to exegeting the film as I do to exegeting the biblical text, although my professional training was strictly in the latter. By allowing these stories to interact, the biblical and the cinematic, new insights emerge. I look for the sparks that fly between the biblical text and the contemporary film. It is a prophetic process in which contextual truths are disclosed that throw light on contemporary situations. And like all prophetic insights within the Pauline tradition, they bear on particular moments and communities while remaining a "prophesying in part," a "seeing through a glass darkly" (1 Cor. 13:8, 12). Whether these sparks light up the present hour must be left for readers to discern and weigh.

The discipline of the interpretive arch has led me to abandon the tradition of using modern materials as mere "illustrations" of Pauline truth. To illustrate presumes that truth is already fully understood by the speaker, whereas in reality truth is itself dialectical, revealing itself to us in particular historical contexts. Thus I prefer to interweave Pauline texts with modern stories and issues, allowing each side to throw light on the other. When I select a film whose themes correlate closely with a biblical text, the modern artifact is treated with a level of respect that allows it to become a full partner in conversation with Paul the Apostle. The movie must be seen and interpreted within its cultural context if the idea of an interpretive arch is to be followed. But my impulse is prophetic rather than didactic; the creation of holistic vision does not constitute the claim of seeing timeless truth.

I need to make clear, therefore, that while each movie is treated with respect, the Pauline word is allowed to stand as *primus inter pares*. It is the "first among equals," because the inspired text of Scripture has stood the test of time by revealing ultimate truth that has gripped past and current generations with compelling power when concretized in relation to particular historical circumstances. There are ways in which great movies are also inspired. But biblical texts have sustained faith communities in circumstances both adverse and happy over several thousand years; they are formative in my own community of interpreters as well as in American culture, providing the narrative framework for many forms of contemporary entertainment, not to speak of their effect on the national consciousness and the civil religion. I come from a Wesleyan tradition that wanted to be a religion "of one book," and from a cultural tradition that viewed the Bible as the most decisive book in the world. But although the texts in the Bible deserve to be granted a measure of priority, we shall not find them to be overbearing partners in the dialog with contemporary films. Like Paul in his willingness to accommodate himself to the needs of various cultural groups (see 1 Cor. 9:19–22), I find that biblical texts when understood in the context of their original stories are flexible, adaptable and provocative in their bearing on contemporary films. In the case of *Groundhog Day*, the ancient cultural premises of Paul's treatment of time need to be laid out before the interpretive arch can be negotiated.

The Biblical Approach to Time

In the last 50 years scholars have made much of two Greek words for time found in the New Testament: *chronos* meaning linear time, from which our word "chronology" comes, and *kairos*, meaning the "appointed time" or the "time for decision" (see esp. Marsh 1952; Burns 1953; Boman 1960; Muilen-burg 1961; Cullmann 1964). The standard Greek term for cyclical time was *chronos*, with the same hour appearing each day, moving as relentlessly as Phil Connors' schedule, waking with that same six o'clock alarm every morning and going through the same routine each day (Delling 1974: 581–3; Hübner 1993: 488). Through the miracle of film, the same day is repeated over and over again like a recurrent nightmare. The weathercaster goes to the same town in Pennsylvania to a Groundhog Day celebration that happens day after day. He steps into the same pothole with icy water, has the same conversations with the same people, and celebrates the same stupid groundhog coming out of the same hole. As Jonathan Romney writes, this film "may be the purest nightmare movie Hollywood has ever produced – potentially endless rep-etition, just for its own sake" (Romney 1993). This is *chronos* in its most painful form.

The other word found in the New Testament is *kairos*, meaning significant time or fulfilled time (Delling 1965). In Jörg Baumgarten's formulation, "*chronos* designates a 'period of time' in the linear sense, while *kairos* frequently refers to 'eschatologically filled time, time for decision.'" (Baumgarten 1991). Although we do not have different words in English, we all know the difference between everyday time, when we follow our routines, and special times like birthdays or anniversaries. We remember the day we decided to marry our spouse, or when we got the new job offer, or moved into the new house. The audience of Galatians would have been even more sensitive to this set of terms than we, because the educational system was dominated by the study of rhetoric, the art of appropriate speech. They taught that there was a proper moment to say a specific thing. The ancient educational system was very concerned to train people in timeliness.

The idea of "proper time," the "time of fulfillment," plays a key role in the New Testament. Christ is the one who ushers in a new time; salvation moves believers off the treadmill. Thus Paul urges the Corinthians in 2 Cor. 6:2, "Behold, now is the acceptable time, behold now is the day of salvation." Since "at the right time Christ died for the ungodly" (Rom. 5:6) the present moment of decision is fraught with significance. The early Christians had the sense that the present time was moving quickly toward the end of the world, that the "time is shortened" (1 Cor. 7:29) in which the opportunity for conversion was present. Thus every moment was "the decisive moment" in which sides must be taken (cf. Ernst Käsemann, cited in Baumgarten 1991: 233).

The Bible teaches the significance of being responsive to time. The formulation of Ecclesiastes 3:1–8 places this in classic form:

> For everything there is a season, and time for every matter under heaven:
> a time to be born, and a time to die; a time to plant, and a time to pluck up what is planted;
> a time to kill, and a time to heal . . .; a time to embrace, and time to refrain from embracing . . .;
> a time to love, and a time to hate; a time for war, and a time for peace.

Learning to live, according to this, depends on discovering how to tell time. As Bill Murray reveals in playing the role of Phil Connors in the film, if you try to embrace when it is not the time for embracing, you are sure to get a slap in the face. He gets the same slap day after day after day. Whether the issue is planting or making war, life requires that people act in accordance with the demands of constantly changing circumstances.

Paul intensifies this usage by using *kairos*, "proper time" or "fulfilled time" to refer to the final period of history inaugurated by Christ, referring to the coming time of judgment (1 Cor. 4:5; 1 Thess. 5:1) as well as to the current moment of decision (1 Cor. 10:11). "The Pauline understanding of time culminates in the interpretation of 'the future determined by the present' and 'the present determined by the future'" (Baumgarten 1991: 233).[2] In Paul's view, the way people respond to life in the present shapes the kind of future they will have. By placing their faith in Christ, the present routine gains significance because it leads to a future called "eternal life." So from the Pauline point of view, this is what a film like *Groundhog Day* is really all about, even though the filmmakers and actors may not have fully understood these implications themselves. To live according to the flesh is to be stuck in *chronos*, to repeat the same mistakes day after day, to face the same defeat time after time. To live according to the spirit, in response to the love of Christ, is to enter the realm of *kairos*, to find fulfillment in the midst of daily routines. The trouble is, what Paul calls the "flesh" – which we might think of as willful self-centeredness – deceives people, deludes them, keeps them thinking that their attitudes and actions have no consequences. So they lock themselves in cycles of deadly repetition that lead to despair. This is why Paul issues the strong warnings that open our text, describing what we might call "The Deadly Deception of the Flesh."

The Deadly Deception of the Flesh

"Be not deceived," Paul writes, "God is not mocked. Whatever you sow, that you will also reap. The one who sows to his own flesh will from the flesh reap corruption, but the one who sows to the spirit will from the spirit reap eternal life." (Gal. 6:7–8) Paul wrote these words to Galatian Christians who were still inclined to believe that the self-centered life-style popularized by society would have no effect on their future. They had interpreted their salvation, their baptism, as a sign that their future was assured, and that therefore it no longer mattered how they behaved or thought (Jewett 1970–1; Longenecker 1990: xcix). Paul warns that such illusions will have deadly consequences (Longenecker 1990: 281). He is arguing for what we might call the principle of accountability.

Paul's idea of the flesh struggling against the spirit derived from his conviction that the old age of sin stands in conflict with the new age of Christ, and that this conflict rages inside each person at times. The flesh is the realm of self-centered pleasure, related primarily to the pleasures of public approval and honor. It leads people to think that they can gain fulfillment by manipulating others or proving their superiority by surpassing others. In the ancient as well as the contemporary world, the culture of the flesh was competitive, cut-throat, exploitative, and self-centered. The market for honor in the Greco-Roman world was extremely small, so everyone had to struggle to achieve status (Malina 1981 and 1986; Gilmore 1987; Neyrey 1990). Their behavior in the realms of religion and ethics was oriented not to intrinsic ends, for the most part, but to the goal of gaining honor. In contrast the realm of the spirit being ushered in by Christ is cooperative, caring, and non-competitive. These two realms have been in conflict ever since the time of Christ, the one leading to death and the other to life. Paul wanted the Galatians to know that if they reverted to the behavior of the flesh taught by their culture, the consequences would be disastrous. The question of whether current attitudes and behavior have future consequences is a central theme in the film, and is a central problem for current Americans and perhaps others as well. We tend to understand freedom as a kind of release from constraint. We receive signals on every side that we should just "do it," because consequences can always be fixed. Life is a comedy with happy endings if we just work the system. Phil Connors is depicted as a successful person deceived about time and its consequences, about his own life-style and its deadly future, and thus being stuck in a situation where every day is a repetition of the last; he is caught in the web of the flesh and doesn't know it. The basic illusion is discussed before the repetition of *Groundhog Day* begins. "What if there were no tomorrow?" Phil asks the guys at the bar. They reply: "That would mean there would be no consequences, no hangovers, and we could do whatever we want."

So the film depicts Phil living out this deception. Discovering that he will wake up every single morning to the same Groundhog Day, he begins to live recklessly. As Matthew Giunti observed: "At first frightened, Phil soon realizes that his time trap paradoxically affords him perfect freedom" (Giunti 1993: 430). He drives his car without worrying about wrecking it, and even causes a police car to wreck. He talks about all the things he was brought up not to do, and then does them, including robbing an armored car and driving his car on the railroad track. "I'm not going to live by their rules any more!" he proudly declares. Phil even comes to the point where he finally kidnaps the groundhog and drives over a cliff with it, dying together in the flames to escape from the cycle of *chronos*. But he just comes back the next morning to the same alarm clock at 6:00 a.m. He commits suicide in various ways, playing out the illusion of escape. But all to no avail. Richard Corliss offers a vivid description of this situation:

> . . . he is trapped in time. He wakes up the next day to discover it is still Feb. 2. The same people he saw on Groundhog Day say the same things; the same unforeseen snowstorm blows into town; Punxsutawney is Brigadoon. Phil is angry, then reckless, then depressed, then suicidal. Yet he can't die, he can't escape. He can only change.
>
> *(Corliss 1993: 61)*

One of the recent commentators on Galatians describes the underlying issue in language that could almost serve as a guide to this film. Richard Longenecker writes: "What Paul seems to have in mind here in speaking about sowing to the flesh are the libertine tendencies of his Galatian converts that he has alluded to earlier in this section: quarrelsomeness (5:15, 16), conceit (5:26), envy (5:26), living aloof from the needs of others (6:1–2; perhaps also 6:6), and pride (6:3–4). Such things not only reflect a misuse of Christian freedom (cf. 5:13) but also have disastrous results both personally and corporately, for 'destruction' is their final end." (Longenecker 1990: 281)

Each one of these features of what Paul calls "life according to the flesh" matches the way Bill Murray plays the newscaster in *Groundhog Day*. He is quarrelsome with his producer and cameraman; he is conceited; he is envious of the success of others who are able to move up in the profession and do not have to return to Punxsutawney year after year. He lives aloof from the lives of others, passing people on the streets of Punxsutawney whose troubles touch him not at all. He passes the same beggar every morning for months of repetition before he discovers this man's story. He is caught up in pride. To use Paul's language, he has been sowing to the flesh, and the film simply depicts its consequences.

Nowhere are the illusions more deadly than in the love affair Phil Connors tries to carry on with Rita (Andie MacDowell). He tries to seduce her and fails time after time, even after he contrives to fix the van so they can't leave town and learns to respond to her toast to "world peace" by saying "I'd like to say a prayer and drink to world peace." After Rita discovers that he has set her up for the romantic evening by studying her reactions, they begin to discuss what love is. In response to his statement that he loves her, Rita replies with a moral perception that seems rooted in the Pauline tradition: "You don't even know me.. Is this what love is for you?" she asks, meaning knowing how to seduce someone. "I could never love anyone like you, Phil, because you never love anyone but yourself." When Phil persists in the attempt at this false kind of love, she slaps him, again and again and again. Like many American males, Punxsutawney Phil has a difficult time figuring out the difference between genuine love and the desire to seduce someone, to manipulate and possess a partner. To use the ancient categories, it is the difference between *agape*, genuinely caring love, and *eros*, seductive love, driven by the desire to achieve pleasure by controlling others. Paul advocates the former, which is motivated by the spirit of Christ, who gave himself for others. The latter is driven by the "flesh," the desire to possess and manipulate others. The issue here is not sexual desire as such, which Paul views as a good and holy impulse (See 1 Cor. 7:7), but the tendency to subordinate others to one's own ends. "The one who sows to his own flesh will from the flesh reap corruption, but the one who sows to the spirit will from the spirit reap eternal life." (Gal. 6:8). This leads to the theme of doing good, which plays a decisive role both in *Groundhog Day* and our passage from Paul's Letter to the Galatians.

The Timely Promise of "Working for the Good of All"

Phil Connors finally gives up on the cycle of manipulation through the flesh, and begins to help other people. At first he gives the beggar a tip, then a meal, then a rescue from freezing on a bitterly cold night. He learns to run fast enough to save the life of a boy falling from an apple tree; he learns the Heimlich maneuver so he can save the life of a man choking on a bone in the restaurant; he fixes a flat tire for some vulnerable older women; he helps a squabbling couple to find a resolution. These episodes led several reviewers to refer to the Capraesque quality of *Groundhog Day*. For instance, Audrey Farolino writes: "The movie's premise is rather Kafkaesque, but its message is more Capraesque: Even if you're stuck in the same place with the same people doing the same things every day, you can find salvation of a sort through little acts of kindness and selflessness." (Farolino 1993: 31).

Although it is possible to contend that Connors "seems to become a better person more out of boredom than anything else" (Thompson 1993: 50), viewing the film through the lens of Galatians allows us to suggest that these actions indicate that Phil Connors has finally grasped the true nature of love and the need to stop playing god, which is the ultimate form of living according to the flesh. Early in the film he had snarled in response to a mildly critical comment from a co-worker, "I *make* the weather," and it becomes clear "time will be out of joint until he realizes that actually it's the weather that makes him" (Romney 1993: 34).

Later in the film, he abandons the stupid declaration to Rita, that since he keeps coming back from death, "I'm a god … I am immortal." Rita had replied with scorn, "Because you survived a car wreck?" She falls back on her 12 years in a good Catholic school to deny that Phil or anyone else can rightfully claim to be God. And it is only when he gives up this final illusion of apotheosis that he can begin, in Paul's words, "working for the good of all." The consequence is that Rita, who embodies the moral center of this film, decides that Phil is a decent human being after all, allowing a romantic, happy ending to a crazy but insightful film.

The links to Galatians are obvious. "Doing what is good" in 6:9 is "identical with the concepts of the 'fruit of the Spirit' (5:22–3) and of 'following the Spirit' (5:25; c.f. 5:16)." (Betz 1979: 281). The reference to not growing "weary" in doing good reflects Paul's fear that the enthusiasm for life in the spirit is waning, that the Galatian converts "were beginning to revert from an outgoing type of Christian faith that seeks the welfare of others to a selfish, self-contained religious stance that has little concern for others" (Longenecker 1990: 281).

The social context for this kind of "doing good" is stressed in 6:10: "Therefore, while we have time, let us do good to all, especially to those of the household of faith." The primary responsibility of these early Christians was local; most of them had very limited means and time. Their primary responsibiity was to care for the members in their small households of faith.[3] This needs to be understood within the framework of early Christian communalism and cooperation within the house and tenement churches, the small "families of faith" that marked the early church (Jewett 1994: 7–8, 73–86). This involved early Christians in seeking the good of all in good times as well as times of famine and disease, countering the despair of a cyclical life that goes nowhere. The "eternal life" of 6:8 begins now for the Galatian Christians, because Christ frees them from the treadmills of the flesh.

Conclusion

The exhortation of 6:9–10 emphasizes that each Christian group, enlivened by the spirit, has "time" to fulfill their lives. The echo of *Groundhog Day* is particularly clear in the wordplay on the word "time" (*kairos*) in verses 9 and 10 (Dunn 1993: 332). At the "proper *time*" we will reap the harvest in verse 9. "So then, as we have *time*, let us do good to all people, especially to those who belong to the household of faith." I regret that this echo of the word "time" does not show up in modern translations of the Bible, but it was clearly visible in the original Greek text, and it provides the resource to understand the deepest meaning of the film – and of the daily routines of modern life. Our times may seem to be the same day after day, stuck in *chronos*, but if we look around, there are fresh opportunities to love every day we live. New people cross our paths; new problems arise for those within the church; new challenges face us as times change in the fast moving worlds of work and social responsibility. This correlates closely with the "deeper message" of *Groundhog Day*, perceived by Richard Corliss: "It says that most folks' lives are like Phil's on Groundhog Day: a repetition, with the tiniest variations, of ritual pleasures and annoyances. Routine is the metronome marking most of our time on earth. Phil's gift is to see the routine and seize the day" (Corliss 1993: 533).

The key issue, however, in the light of Galatians is not so much seizing the day in an opportunistic manner but rather overcoming the illusions that the times and seasons can be brought under human control, that others can be mastered and seduced to suit our own rhythm and ego needs. The "life lesson, a story of self-discovery and change" (Mathews 1993: 66) of the film as well as Galatians 6 centers on the need to turn away from the illusions of the flesh. And while it remains on the fairy-story level in the film, with an undeniably amoral premise that one can "do horrible things to other people with impunity, because the next day it'll all be undone" (Romney 1993: 34), the reference in Gal. 6:8 to the spirit indicates a more serious possibility of living in the *kairos* of fulfilled time. The spirit leads the followers of Christ off the treadmill. It frees them from their culturally shaped bondage to selfish love. Thus Paul calls the Galatian Christians to discover new forms of "doing what is right" and "working for the good of all . . . while we have time." Both in the film and in Paul's mind, that is the most important indicator that someone is, in fact, unstuck in time. But to use an allusion in Matthew Giunti's review in *Christian Century*, the continued unwillingness of the American public to "roll up its sleeves and take a crack at a few of the country's enduring social problems" indicates that most of us remain stuck. And as with other cultures in the past and present, a price will inevitably be paid for such illusions.

Notes

1 Although the metaphor sounds similar, Osborne (1991) does not have the same type of dialog in mind.

2 Baumgarten (1991: 233) acknowledges that Paul's use of *kairos* has a fairly wide range of meaning, and that it sometimes overlaps with *chronos*. This is quite different from the view expressed in his earlier work. He appears to have learned from James Barr (Barr 1962), who rejected the simplistic semantics of the earlier Biblical Theology movement that assumed this theological connotation was inherent in the word *kairos* itself.

3 Hurtado (1979: 54–6) suggests in contrast that Paul may be referring to the collection that he made for the church in Jerusalem, but Dunn (1993: 33) is correct in saying this is "hardly evident from the text."

12

Moral Ambiguity and Contradiction in *Dead Poets Society*

Stephen Brie and David Torevell

Many films offer a unique opportunity for moral scrutiny and reflection. Indeed, it is unusual for any film not to deal in some way with ethical conflict or tension. This emphasis can only be satisfactorily examined with reference to the question of "meaning" in film, although it is now more customary to talk about "meanings" rather than "meaning" in film studies, since the varied and sometimes contradictory responses of an audience to a film text are one of the primary issues at stake. It is no longer possible to discover a "fixed" or unchangeable meaning to a film. This range of interpretations becomes particularly interesting when we focus on moral meanings within films and attempt to survey the kinds of ethical thinking, reactions, and evaluations a film narrative might promote. Within the context of moral theology, this is what this chapter attempts to discuss.

Moral theology or Christian ethics (we use the terms interchangeably here), is primarily concerned with two things: how to act from the right motive and how to discover what is the right action in particular situations. The basic difference between Christian ethics and other procedures and methods of moral reasoning is in the recognition that its starting point is the Christian tradition, based on the example and teaching of Jesus Christ. This chapter looks at *Dead Poets Society* through the lens of moral theology and assesses how some of the ethical dilemmas raised in the film might be interpreted. Our purpose is not to set forth a single Christian reading of the film, but rather to explore the moral ambiguities and questions the film raises for those who profess a Christian belief, together with the features of Christian theology which require attention as a result of interacting with the subject-matter of the film. Peter Weir, director of *Dead Poets Society* (1989), has argued that, in relation to his audience, "I can control what I want them to know." (McFarlane and Ryan 1981: 325). In offering contradictory readings of the film – a "preferred" reading, which positions the film as an endorsement of the individual or romantic spirit; and an "oppositional" reading, which suggests that the narrative can also be decoded as a critique of individualism and romanticism – this chapter questions the validity of Weir's claim in the process of exploring some of the moral complexities which such readings raise.

Film narrative, either intentionally or by chance, can be encoded in the production process (planning, shooting, editing), with multiple meanings. As suggested earlier, these encoded meanings will be decoded and subsequently accepted or rejected according to the viewer's sociological and ideological perspectives and level of film literacy. The viewer may also construct his/her own meaning(s) from the narrative. If these constructed meanings correspond with those intentionally encoded by the production process, they are said to support the text's "preferred" meaning/s. If the viewer's reading of the film's narrative partly supports the "preferred" meaning/s but is also partly resistive, we use the term "negotiated" reading. A reading which totally rejects the "preferred" reading is termed an "oppositional" reading.

Background to the Film

Dead Poets Society draws on several different filmic genres for its inspiration. Its academic milieu places it alongside such films as *Blackboard Jungle* (Richard Brooks, 1955), *To Sir, With Love* (James Clavell, 1966), *Dangerous Minds* (John N. Smith, 1995), and *Mr Holland's Opus* (Stephen Herek, 1995). In placing a teacher at the center of its narrative, *Dead Poets Society* also echoes *Goodbye Mr. Chips* (Sam Wood, 1939), *The Browning Version* (Anthony Asquith, 1951), and *The Prime of Miss Jean Brodie* (Ronald Neame, 1969). As a study of teenage angst, Weir's film follows, albeit at a safe distance, *The Wild One* (Laslo Benedek, 1953), *Rebel Without a Cause* (Nicholas Ray, 1955), *Running Scared* (David Hemmings, 1972), and a whole series of 1950s "juvenile delinquent" movies such as *The Delinquents* (Robert Altman, 1957), *Dangerous Youth* (Herbert Wilcox, 1958), and *Young and Wild* (William Witney, 1958).

Peter Weir was one of the main protagonists behind the Australian film industry's renaissance in the late 1970s. After studying law he moved into television production and subsequently into film. Prior to making *Dead Poets Society*, Weir had directed eight feature films. These earlier works offer clues as to the "preferred" meaning/s which may be encoded within the text of *Dead Poets Society*. The struggle of the individual against society and its institutions is a major theme linking many of Weir's narratives. In *Picnic at Hanging Rock* (1975) the repressive educational system of Appleyard College causes the same kind of problems for a group of turn-of-the-century Australian schoolgirls that Welton Academy poses for Neil and his friends in the late 1950s; *Gallipoli* (1981) investigates a different form of institutional confinement – life in the military services, and *Witness* (1985) probes the often suffocating conformity inherent within an Amish community. Thus the individualist philosophy which permeates the narrative of *Dead Poets Society* has precedents in Weir's earlier work. The origin of this philosophy may lie in the Australian's personal resistance to conformity: "I can't try to fit in with some sort of system" (Dempsey 1980: 11), and in his interest in Jungian psychology with its references to dreams and visions, all of which are in evidence within the narrative of *Dead Poets Society* (McFarlane and Ryan 1981: 325).

Although, as Giroux correctly argues, Weir has invested *Dead Poets Society* with "an aura of universality" (Giroux 1993: 42), many of the moral and ethical issues which the film confronts can be seen to grow out of and reflect specificities inherent in late 1950s American society. Keating's individualism can be seen as a reaction against a decade marked by cultural philistinism and the persecution of intellectual non-conformists. In its attempt to counterpoint the restrictive political and ideological philosophies of Eisenhower and McCarthy, *Dead Poets Society* arguably portrays a sense of the first flickerings of a new sensibility, a sensibility which would only fully ignite in the 1960s.

A Preferred Reading

The film's narrative works extremely hard in its attempt to persuade the viewer to accept Keating as a sincere, charismatic purveyor of existentialist philosophy. Why would one be tempted to question any of the motives of Mr Keating? The English teacher's extraordinary entrance follows an opening sequence which includes a montage of vignettes which reflect the cornerstones of Welton's educational philosophy – "Tradition," "Honor," "Discipline" and "Excellence." Alongside this montage, Weir presents a powerful visual metaphor, which in essence signifies the film's central theme – the freedom, or lack of freedom of the individual. For example, as the boys prepare for the first day of the new semester, the director offers a series of wide-angle shots of hundreds of birds in flight against a background of rolling countryside and expansive sky. These spacious scenes are juxtaposed with a tightly-packed shot of boys moving up and down a spiral staircase. As the boys hurry to their lessons, the camera rotates through 360 degrees to produce a shot which allows the viewer to experience their sense of claustrophobia. The atmosphere in the classrooms is equally stifling as Hager, the trigonometry teacher, sets his charges copious amounts of homework, and McAllister, the classics teacher, is seen regimenting rote learning of Latin verbs. Into this cauldron of conformity steps John Keating who immediately disorientates his students by taking them outside the confines of the classroom for what is essentially an initiation into the world of the "Free Thinker." From this point on Keating becomes the boys' spiritual leader, their "Captain," coaxing and inspiring them to take the path to self-fulfillment and to rail against the harmful, homogenizing effects of society's institutions.

Robin Williams is instrumental in extending and developing Keating's charismatic persona. No stranger to playing unconventional characters, Williams had previously portrayed the eccentric T. S. Garp in *The World According to Garp* (George Roy Hill, 1982), and the establishment-threatening Adrian Cronauer in *Good Morning, Vietnam* (Barry Levinson, 1987). As in these earlier films, Williams utilizes his considerable improvisational skills in his portrayal of John Keating, often interpreting the script in his own idiosyncratic way. Like the boys, the viewer may be captivated by Keating's rhetoric as he persuades us to "suck the marrow out of life," and to make our lives "extraordinary"; we too may emotionally bond with the teacher as he invites us to "huddle up" in order to share his wisdom; and we may share the joy experienced by Keating and his students as their triumph on the soccer field is glorified by the spirit-lifting final movement of Beethoven's "Choral Symphony."

As Giroux has argued, prior to the arrival of Keating, *Dead Poets Society* appears to present the boys as "Academic zombies living out the projections and wishes of their ... fathers" (Giroux 1993: 43). At Welton "The Law of the Father" dominates in what is essentially a patriarchal environment. Paradoxically however, none of the featured students benefits from having an understanding father in whom they can confide their innermost thoughts. Neil's father is dogmatically unbending in his attempt to control his son's life, while in contrast, Todd's father appears to be totally disinterested, the duplicated birthday present functioning as a symbolic representation of the lack of intimacy between them. Ripping pages out of textbooks and reciting poetry in caves may not appear to be excessively revolutionary behavior, yet, in the context of intensive parental and institutional pressure to conform, the boys' actions, as they strive towards realizing their own self-identities, can be seen as something more than mere tokenism.

Clearly, therefore, the "preferred" reading of the film suggests that Keating is a type of "savior" figure to those he teaches. We see a person of uncompromising commitment and enthusiasm, able to inspire in the young a view of life which sees in every moment of every day, the opportunity to live life to the full. *Carpe diem* is breathed into the very core and fiber of the students in his care. Such exhortations are not simply an appeal to the intellect, but to the whole person: heart, body, mind and spirit. Here education is concerned with developing individual potential, with the emphasis placed on encouraging personal conviction and individual choice. All the scenes which show ritual conformity, (whether in the classroom, revealing an instrumental approach towards the teaching of poetry, or comically in the school grounds, where the students are encouraged not to walk in step, but to march in their own way), persuade the viewer that student-centered learning is being put into practice. For too long Welton has produced an unfair and elitist system. Now things are about to change and the time has arrived for a truly liberal education, based on the finest ideals and values, to undercut a system which arguably perpetuates a crippling orthodoxy based on conformity and rigid discipline. Keating is to be emulated as a model teacher rather than questioned or criticized for his unorthodox teaching methods or motives.

Neil's Suicide

However, one might argue that Neil's suicide forces the viewer to reconsider such positive responses to Mr Keating. The stirrings of a negotiated or even fully oppositional reading might begin at this point in the film narrative. Tensions and conflicts could be set up in the minds of the audience. Are we, for example, to acknowledge that living with compromises within any given social context is a mature way to behave, but that such an acknowledgement sometimes demands self-sacrifice? Are we to conclude that such suicides are always meaningless and futile, rather than in any sense courageous? Should we accept that discipline and restraint are always preferable to freedom and self-expression, which might be harmful to the soul? Jewett argues that Neil "showed a fatal lack of restraint. His wildly successful performance in the play provided such a sense of his own powers that he could not bear the thought of their restraint." (Jewett 1993: 159).

It is clearly possible to argue that the suicide scene gives the overriding impression that Neil's suicide is no rash, emotional or impetuous act, but rather a predetermined and mature decision made by a person fully aware of both the motive and its consequences. Mr Keating, therefore, cannot be held responsible for Neil's death. This sense of deliberation and control is achieved primarily by the screening of a highly stylized event; the cinematic effects are achieved by the impact of a ritual action being watched, rather than by any words being spoken and heard. The dramatic power of the scene comes about primarily through the audience "seeing" the event unfold, slowly and cumulatively. Films possess this unique visual capacity. As Perkins writes: "The credibility of the movies comes from our habit of placing more trust in the evidence of our eyes, than in any other form of sense data" (Perkins 1972: 62). Often what we see wholly determines understanding and the making of meaning. (This is particularly true in Western society, which since the Enlightenment, has placed sight at the summit in the hierarchy of the senses.) The way we come to know things is often within a visual paradigm, with cognition invariably dependent upon seeing. Jenks is correct to state that "The modern world is very much a 'seen' phenomenon." (Jenks, 1995: 2).

Film is therefore crucially different from other art forms, not only in its ability to intensify our perceptions through narrative form, but through its impact of moving images, whereby the viewer is made to react to those images as he/she might to actual events themselves. The images we see in a film can influence our reading much more than the dialog we hear. A film has this means to make us feel and believe that we are eye-witnesses to actual events and actions. We may become participants, observers and readers of events and circumstances, which are often, in the normal occurence of things, unseen. This is particularly poignant in *Dead Poets Society*'s portrayal of a suicide, invariably a most private and self-preoccupied action, rarely, if ever, watched by others. The cinema becomes a privileged and a collective medium, by which the viewer/s, in the darkness of the theatre, see those things which are rarely seen outside.

Because the suicide sequence depends upon the construction of a ritual performance, it is able to carry with it a sense that things will be changed as a consequence. Ritual is never merely a performance or spectacle, but a stylized and instrumental action, able to tap those sources of our world and being which we often associate with the archaic or primitive. It has the power to transport the participant or spectator into another world, away from the mundane and everyday, to a world inhabited by the gods, the spirit, and the supernatural. As Kavanagh says of ritual, "It deals not with the abolition of ambiguity but with the dark and hidden things of God" (Kavanagh 1982: 102).

Order can be restored through acts of ritual: this is often primarily achieved by the staging of symbolic human action, movement and gesture which follow a tightly prescribed code. By insisting upon such a code, ritual performance has the ability to draw the viewers into the action and entice them into the drama. Ritual often contains a disturbing as well as a creatively restorative power; or, as Pickstock puts it when talking about the ritual dimension of liturgy: "All rituals are a declaration against indeterminacy. The chaos which the formalized and recursive nature of liturgy eschews is by implication its central concern. Every invocation betrays an absence, but it also embodies the reparation, since to call is to anticipate an answer, and to name is to bring into being." (Pickstock, 1993: 115). In *Dead Poets Society*, the suicide can be seen as an act which has a significant effect upon the world. The manner in which Weir organizes the scene implies that Neil's death releases such power. This is the ultimate means chosen by Neil, to impose order upon himself and the world in which he lives. It is no ordinary death.

It might be contended that Neil resorts to this ritualized way of doing things to communicate to those around him much more than words can ever convey. During the film, he can never find the right words to tell his father how he *really* feels. Throughout the suicide scene, Neil's body and gestures become the central symbols and metaphors to convey meaning. But if there is a message to be conveyed, it is not transparently obvious, since this would deny the mystery and ambiguity which ritual relies upon in order to be an effective agency of communication for those things which cannot be easily, precisely, or superficially said.

The suicide scene is itself a ritual performance. After highlighting the breakdown in communication between parents and son on their return from Welton, the action moves to Neil's bedroom. As the camera closes in on Neil's semi-naked body, he touches ceremoniously his nightshirt in preparation for his moment of self-sacrifice, his act of defiance which will restore his displaced sense of equilibrium. He mentally relives his performance as he lifts, in a sacred gesture, the actor's crown of victory, which he wore so triumphantly as Puck in *A Midsummer Night's Dream*. But this time he is alone at the altar which he has prepared for himself. His clothes folded neatly, he lifts the two windows of his bedroom and looks out onto a new landscape, cold, but white and pure, uncontaminated by disappointment and struggle. He breathes two deep sighs and then closes his eyes in concentrated resolve: Maurice Jarre's droning, repetitive score offers a perspective on Neil's psychological condition, and focuses attention on the impending deed. The sparse lighting reveals the turning of the door-handle, and then the feet of Neil as he descends the stairs slowly, back erect, each step formal, as if in religious procession. He enters his father's study and we are offered a point-of-view shot which closes in upon the gun with which he intends to end his life. The scene then cuts to the Perry's bedroom as they are woken by the muffled sound of gunfire. Mr Perry's awful realization of his son's death is agonizingly developed in a slow motion sequence which is heightened by Mrs Perry's hysterical off-screen wailing.

The redemptive quality of this scene is not too difficult for the viewer to experience. Throughout the episode, the dark ritual tone suggests that this death, although tragic, has much to teach the world. Here the viewer feels that he/she is witness to an act of heroic selflessness, a symbolic and cathartic event which can save the world from spiraling further into misunderstandings. In "seizing the day," Neil has shown decisively that it is possible to be true to one's self.

Therefore, even in the light of Neil's suicide, it is still feasible to suggest that Keating's philosophy and pedagogy are justified. He introduces his students to aspects of culture and ideology which allow them to change their lives: Todd masters his inferiority complex sufficiently to enable his long-suppressed voice to break free and sound a "barbaric yawp over the rooftops of the world"; Knox puts Keating's romantic esthetic into practice and wins Chris from her philistine boyfriend; and Charlie finds his true *persona* in Niwanda. When the dismissed Keating walks into the classroom in the final scene, the narrative strives to persuade us to accept a reading which supports the idea that he has contributed an important and enduring verse to the chapter of life at Welton. With the draconian Headmaster Nolan in the background, Todd stands on his desk, defiantly initiating a symbolic signaling of maintained faith in his "Captain's" philosophy. One by one the other "believers" ritualistically follow suit in a series of images of solidarity in adversity, until, of the members of the Dead Poets Society, only the "fink" Cameron remains seated. As Maurice Jarre's soundtrack reaches its climax, Keating offers a poignant "Thank you, boys" in acknowledgment of his students' symbolic gesture of support.

An Oppositional Reading

An "oppositional" reading of *Dead Poets Society* challenges the "preferred" reading discussed above. We shall now consider how this can occur. It is possible to argue that Keating simply offers "a collection of pious platitudes masquerading as a courageous stand" (Ebert 1989), and that he is little more than a secondhand oracle who fails to practice the borrowed philosophy he preaches. In common with teachers in other movies, such as Richard Dadier (Glenn Ford), who resorts to jazz as a teaching aid in *Blackboard Jungle*, and Lou Anne Johnson (Michelle Pfeiffer), who calms her disruptive students with the help of Bob Dylan's lyrics in *Dangerous Minds*, Keating borrows his "words of wisdom" from the works of others, from the poetry of Herrick, Thoreau, Whitman, and Frost. Far from being radical in his choice of writers, Keating arguably maintains a canonical curriculum. He may have "skipped the Realists," but he also chooses to ignore the radical works of contemporary writers such as Ginsberg and Kerouac. Does Keating sound his own "barbaric yawp?" Does he make his own life "extraordinary?" Maybe not. As the critic Don Shiach suggests, it is possible to imagine Keating in the 1960s "cheering from the sidelines as youth rebelled . . . working his way towards the Headmastership he is destined to fill" (Shiach 1993: 171).

Arguably Keating's philosophy is simply ethereal idealism. It can also be seen to be dangerously inappropriate for the type of student he teaches. In contrast to Dadier and Johnson who struggle to make socially disruptive individualists conform, Keating strives to turn emotionally and financially dependent students into existentialists. The featured boys represent what Doherty has termed "clean-teens" (Doherty 1988: 139), far removed from rebellious teenage icons such as Kerouac's promiscuous and irresponsible Dean Moriarty (*On The Road*); James Dean's Jim Stark (*Rebel Without A Cause*); Brando's wild biker Johnny (*The Wild One*); or even Salinger's sixteen year-old cynic Holden Caulfield (*The Catcher in the Rye*). The only acknowledgment the film makes to the burgeoning contemporary teenage music scene for example, is the aborted attempt made by Meeks and Pitts to construct a radio on which they hope to pick up Radio Free America. In a period bubbling with social, political, and cultural radicalism, Keating's romanticized esthetic appears relatively anemic. After his dismissal, the future bankers and future lawyers will remain cushioned within Welton's academic bosom, protected from the harsh realities of life outside of its middle-class confines.

The untimely death of Neil Perry undermines Keating's pedagogy. The charge that he has been scapegoated after the suicide might have some justification, and is perhaps symptomatic of the way in which establishments like Welton Academy deal with such embarrassments. But the serious, niggling questions which the suicide raises serve to expose the inherent dangers in the types of methodologies teachers like Keating adopt. This is one of the strengths of the film – to persuade the viewer by skilful manipulation of the narrative, that any decontextualized ideology, divorced from the social reality within which students like Neil and his friends live, may result in unexpected and sometimes tragic consequences.

The problem concerning the possibility of any individual becoming free from, and altering, oppressive social contexts is frequently expressed by sociologists in terms of the relationship between structure and agency. One pole in the debate – excessive voluntarism – shows little regard for the fact that we do not make history simply under the circumstances of our own choosing and that we are inevitably bound by the social context and restraints in which we live. This way of understanding social structure ignores the fact that any making of history might restructure our social context, but can never totally free reality from structure. As one college student argued in a seminar discussion, "If Keating had achieved his objectives and converted all the staff and students to his own way of thinking, his only achievement would have been to substitute one educational structure for another." New structures might well be more just, but life can never be structure-free. Conversely, the other pole – excessive determinism – simply suggests that one has little control over the circumstances of one's life and that we can do very little to alter the weight of this influence. This clearly implies an unhealthy defeatism or fatalism towards the possibility of change.

Excessive voluntarism, embodied in the figure of Keating, gives too much freedom to the agent over circumstances; excessive determinism gives too little. The problem is exacerbated in Keating's case since at times he seems to offer, in his defiance of more orthodox teaching no political or practical way forward to his students. His powers of motivation, based on the most inspirational of texts, are clear for the viewer to see, but he rarely gives any clues as to how such texts might be lived out or upheld amidst fierce criticism or opposition. His stance therefore, might be understood in terms of an esthetic means of resistance, based upon a romantic concern for self-enhancement, and rooted in a belief in the freedom of the individual, without regard to any corresponding transformation of the social world in which that individual lives. As Giroux states: "Keating ... eschews any notion of resistance which calls into question how operations of power work to promote human suffering, and social injustice, and exploitation" (Giroux 1993: 44).

Clear lines of demarcation between Neil's death and the death of a martyr are, however, easily drawn. For the martyr, death is not the aim. A martyr does not will his/her own death, but is prepared to die for the truth, if it should come to that. The Christian religion has consistently condemned suicide as a rejection of the sanctity of the gift of life and as an affront to the love of self and neighbor. Reiterating Saint Thomas Aquinas' view that it is God's decision not ours when we should die, contemporary Roman Catholic teaching states: "Suicide contradicts the natural inclination of the human being to preserve and perpetuate his life. It is gravely contrary to the just love of self. It likewise offends love of neighbour. We are stewards, not owners of the life God has entrusted to us. It is not ours to dispose of" (*Catechism of the Catholic Church* 1994: 491). For those who have sympathy with such views, it is difficult to accept that Neil's death was in any sense necessary to change the world. (God never wills that one takes one's own life.)

A convincing reading of the event might suggest that Neil lacked both self-knowledge and knowledge of the world. The "dramatic" suicide was nothing more than a desperate act of overwhelming frustration at not being able to pursue the career he had set his heart on. Jewett writes that "It was a desperate expression of his power to resist, even with his father's means. It was the ultimate perversion of "seizing the day" (Jewett 1993: 159). Could it ever be argued that the only way out was death? The inability of a father to see reason and respond to the needs of a son is no justification for such an act of violence upon the self. Here the immaturity of the adolescent who cannot get his own way is revealed. Following a similar pattern, Charlie, in an earlier scene, had stood up in assembly and stated that a call from God had been received, and that it was now time for girls to be admitted into Welton. As the camera focuses on the other students' reactions, the viewer is led to believe that it is only the impetuous hotheads like Charlie who are susceptible to such melodramatic demands for fairness.

As the narrative progresses others also indulge in similar attention-seeking acts. Neil's folly is to have more devastating results than the humiliating beating imposed upon Charlie by the Headmaster, but both are born of the same immature struggle to confront the injustices of the world which limit and crush the individual spirit. In Neil's case, the act of defiance is based upon a more dangerous blurring of the worlds of illusion and of reality. His "performance" is the last romantic staging of a personal play which ends, like all tragedy, in the death of the hero. Neil is incapable of separating art from life. Death for this "actor" is the gateway to purity, but the consequences of such a yearning stem from a romantic imagination dangerously cultivated by Keating. What kind of Romanticism does Neil's decision to commit suicide ultimately rest upon? The viewer becomes increasingly aware of an educational philosophy which appears to encourage such futile gestures. Any sense of power to change the world is given up, not released by such actions as those of Neil and Charlie. To see them as more than this is to tempt ourselves as viewers into similar self-deception. The Keatings of this world show no regard for teaching skills which might help students to change those things which do harm to the spirit. In the world Neil inhabits, clearly such skills and competencies are essential.

Although *Dead Poets Society* demonstrates how one adolescent deals so tragically with personal disappointment and frustration, there are hints during the film that Neil initially attempts to deal positively with his situation. For example, the scene where he goes to Keating's room to tell him his father has demanded that he quit the play is one moment in the narrative when the viewer senses that there might be the possibility of solving the dilemma in a conciliatory way. But again, the viewer becomes unsure whether Keating is offering sound advice or whether he is simply leading Neil into further turmoil. (Earlier, Keating had told his students that, "there is a great need in all of us to be accepted, but you must trust what is unique or different about yourself, even if it is at odds or unpopular.") During the counseling scene he draws on those metaphors of the theatre which he knows will appeal to the aspiring actor. He tells him to stop "playing the part of the dutiful son": he must go to his father and tell him that acting is not a passing whim, but a conviction and a passion. Keating denies Neil's claim that he is trapped, and that in any case, if his father will not listen to him, it doesn't matter, since he will soon be out of school and then he can do "anything he wants." Neil must demonstrate to his father who he *really* is, that he has a passion for acting, and that any continued pretense is only "acting a part."

As attempts fail to convince his father, we see Neil's disappointment turn from frustration to hopeless resignation, and finally, to despair. There appears to be no way back. Neil turns away from, rather than towards the world: the result is psychological isolation. This condition is familiar to contributors to the history of Christian theology. For Saint Augustine of Hippo, such a predicament entails a state of sin, since this tortuous turning in on oneself, involving an angst of introspection, prevents the self from being open to others and to God. He writes, "the will which turns from the unchangeable and common good and turns to its own private good or to anything exterior or inferior, sins" (cited in Hodgson and King 1985: 18). For Kierkegaard, too, sin is this kind of frustrated despair: "Sin is : before God in despair not to will to be oneself, or before God in despair to will to be oneself," a view which effectively highlights the crucial point that sin is not the turbulence of flesh and blood but is the spirit's consent to it (cited in Hodgson and King 1985: 191–2). This "giving in" sums up Neil's tragedy, for his consent to the turbulence of the flesh meant that he could discover no answer to his problem except his own death.

Such an "oppositional" reading of *Dead Poets Society* might also suggest that the emotionally charged closing scenes, far from presenting an accurate reflection of the meaning/s constructed by the narrative as a whole, are the result of Hollywood's insatiable demand that closure should induce a "feel-good" factor. It can be argued that Jarre's score and the boys' show of emotion in these final moments counterpoint rather than support the film's "preferred" meaning/s, and therefore actually argue for the victory of society over the individual. The realities are that Keating has lost his teaching post and is forced to revert to a "discourse of politeness" (Giroux 1993: 47), Neil is a teenage suicide statistic, and Evans Pritchard PhD will soon find his way back onto the curriculum. Such a reading might argue that the film actively reinforces the status quo by illustrating the dangers of nonconformity, and the impossibility of resisting what Norman Mailer has termed "the totalitarian tissues of American society" (Mailer 1957).

Conclusion

Dead Poets Society can be seen as both an endorsement of individualism and the romantic spirit, and as a critique of the dangers inherent in such a philosophy. In offering "preferred" and "oppositional" readings we hope to have highlighted some of the ways in which a filmic text can be both ambiguous and contradictory and perhaps cast some doubt over the validity of Weir's claim that, in relation to his audience, "I can control what I want them to know" (McFarlane and Ryan 1981: 325). We have shown that the film raises serious and problematic ethical questions for Christians in respect of how to understand suicide. Is Neil's suicide an act of heroism which draws attention to the injustices of the world and through which others might learn, or is it simply a misguided act of folly, selfish to the extreme? Similarly, it is never easy for the viewer to discern whether Keating was exercising extraordinary Christian courage in his adoption of the radical methods he employed with his pupils, or whether, in truth, he was largely motivated by a wrongheaded and proud determination to shock. The "right action" to take in such schools as Welton Academy is never given a clear-cut answer in *Dead Poets Society*. For example, it might be argued that Mr Keating always tried to behave according to the principles of Christian love, or *agape*, and that this is shown most vividly in his insistence that pupils must be given opportunities and advice to achieve their full potential. Christian *agape* always demands that one tries to work for the good of the other person without reserve or distinction, unconditionally. Barclay writes that *agape* is "an undefeatable attitude of goodwill . . . an attitude of goodwill to others no matter what they are like" (Barclay 1971: 40). In a similar way, the exhortation to "seize the day" could be said to reflect a distinctively biblical emphasis about living life to the full, rooted in an embrace, not a denial, of the God-given goodness of creation. In Mr Keating's concern that his pupils relish the sweetness of every moment, some Christian viewers might recognize a strongly New Testament emphasis. For example, the Johannine theme, "I came that they may have life, and have it abundantly" (Jn 10:10) and the Matthean emphasis in the Sermon on the Mount about not worrying about tomorrow (Mt. 6:34) point to obvious overlaps with Mr Keating's approach to and philosophy of life. Similarly, in his pupils' responsive endeavours to free themselves from any oppressive external constraints, they may be said to reflect a biblical understanding of human personhood since, having been made in the image of their creator, they become determined to pursue lives of dignity, truthfulness and freedom (Gen. 1:27).

However, although the radical demands of love underpin Christian notions of moral motivation and action, no easy or uncontested answers to the most appropriate ways of behaving in specific situations have ever been given by Christians. Those trying to act out of Christian love still require gifts of discernment and insight in order that their actions may reflect those of Christ in the new and challenging circumstances in which they and others find themselves. Therefore, love which is superficially formed and simply content to "mean well" is often claimed to be irresponsible, unhelpful and potentially dangerous. For example, Preston suggests that this ability to reflect on the possible consequences of certain types of action is one of the most important elements in developing an approach to Christian living. He comments: "Some of the worst sins against love have been perpetrated by those who 'meant well'" (Preston 1994: 98). This point is well taken in relation to our consideration of the "Christian" nature of Mr Keating's action. Even if we sense that throughout the film his motivation is pure, there is always a feeling too that his well-meaning exhortations are somewhat immature and his judgments not always wise. Mr.Keating might well have believed that what he was advocating to his pupils had the potential to change their lives forever and for the good, but his lack of discernment and incapacity to foresee the possible consequences of his "philosophy" might betray a significant lack of spiritual depth or awareness for some Christian viewers.

There are other important ethical issues raised by the film for the Christian viewer, which cannot be gone into here. The insights drawn from the "oppositional reading" certainly inform the way in which Christian theology's own self-criticism in the West has been conducted of late. The debate about the relationship between structure and agency is found in discussions about "structural sin" within Liberation Theology. Concern centers around the interrelationship between asocial, atomistic or individualistic definitions of sin on the one hand, and social or institutional definitions on the other. Often the debate focuses on the tension between unjust structures of power and individual culpability or complicity in such structures. The social, political and collective dimensions of sin began to be emphasized in order to resist merely private or individual notions. For Gutierrez, for example, it is important to emphasize that sin has a collective form, often embedded in unjust structures and organizations. Christian salvation – and the understanding of the human being implicit within that – can never be separated off from concern about economic, political and social liberation. In contrast to Keating's apparent naïveté about the power and influence of social structures, liberation theologians attempt to identify the sources and presences of such "institutionalized" sin, with a view to liberating people from its effects.

As we have said, the film gives neither a clear-cut answer to any such questions, nor, therefore, a simple "Christian" message. The film's inherent ambivalence and tension should not, however, disappoint us. For its strength and success surely reside in its portrayal of ethical ambiguity and contradiction.

13

Between Eden and Armageddon: Institutions, Individuals, and Identification in *The Mission, The Name of the Rose*, and *Priest*

Vaughan Roberts

Introduction

This chapter will explore issues arising from *The Mission*, *The Name of the Rose*, and *Priest* through the language of Eden and Armageddon, both of which have a significant place within the overtly religious and wider cultural context of Western filmmaking. I shall begin by briefly outlining the plots of the three films and then, in the next section, sketch out how a number of motifs from the biblical books of Genesis and Revelation emerge in those movies. In addition, I aim to examine how these films set out the tensions between individuals and institutions (in this case, the Church) in the light of some current thinking on identity, roles, and scripts within organizations.

Résumé of the plots

The Mission *(1985)*

The film explores an historical incident in the colonial past of Spain and Portugal and the role of the Church in the European conquest of South America. The central characters are Fr Gabriel (Jeremy Irons) a Jesuit missionary and Rodrigo Mendoza (Robert De Niro) a mercenary and slave-trader. Initially the two are in conflict over the native Guarani Indians whom Fr Gabriel seeks to convert and Mendoza to enslave, but after Mendoza kills his own brother over Carlotta (Cherie Lunghi) Fr Gabriel challenges him to demonstrate penance by helping him and other Jesuits to build a mission above the waterfalls, in the heart of the Guarani's territory, thus protecting them from slave-traders. Mendoza also becomes part of the Jesuit order.

These missions are drawn into both the Church's political intrigues in
Europe, where it is attempting a balancing act between the Spanish and
Portuguese, and the wider difficulties of the Jesuit Order within the politics
of the Church. The Pope has sent an emissary, Altamirano (Ray McAnally) to
report on the matter. For the sake of the Church's interests he decides that
the missions should be closed and the Jesuits withdrawn which would allow
the slave-trade to expand. The colonialists burn the missions and massacre
both the Indians and priests and the climax of the film explores the responses
of Fr Gabriel and Mendoza to this inevitable outcome – with Fr Gabriel
staying true to his vision of his calling as a priest and Mendoza being true to
his nature as a fighter and organizing violent resistance among the Guarani.
Both fail to prevent the slaughter and die in the process.

The Name of the Rose *(1985)*

Of the three movies discussed here *The Name of the Rose* is the only one based
on a novel (Eco 1983). The story of the same name, written by the Italian
academic and semiotician Umberto Eco, operates at one level as an example of
the "whodunnit" genre. Yet it also has been perceived as an historical novel as
well as a contemporary social commentary. These different readings are
maintained to some degree in the film but it works most overtly as a
whodunnit. This is clear from the outset when we discover a Franciscan
monk, Bro. William of Baskerville (Sean Connery), arriving at an unnamed
monastery with his assistant Adso of Melk (Christian Slater) for a major
ecclesiastical debate about whether Jesus and his disciples owned their clothes.
However, the Abbot (Michael Lonsdale) asks Bro. William to investigate the
mysterious death of one of the monks.

Bro. William quickly concludes that this was an act of suicide but further
deaths follow and the conference on poverty is overtaken by an inquisition
into heresy led by the Jesuit Bernard Gui (F. Murray Abraham). Increasingly,
Bro. William's investigation is focused on the library but, to start with, it
is difficult to tell whether this is because of his character's obsession with
books or because it holds the key to the murders. It emerges that the
monastery has what is probably the sole surviving copy of the second book of
Aristotle's poetics – a book about humor. The person responsible for the
deaths of the monks is the monastery's librarian the venerable Jorge, who
believes that humor is weakness and that laughter frees people from proper
fear of God. The film ends with a solution to the conundrum of who is the
murderer and why but, like *The Mission*, it also ends with chaos and fire as the
monastery, the library and the last copy of Aristotle's book is engulfed by
flames.

Priest *(1994)*

This story opens by setting up the tension between the individual and the institution with the dramatic scene of an older priest taking the large crucifix from his church and running it through the window of his bishop's study. The subsequent plot takes up this theme of disillusionment with the Church through the different approaches of a young priest, Fr Greg Pilkington (Linus Roache) and an experienced parish priest, Fr Matthew Thomas (Tom Wilkinson). At one level the film can be seen as a generic story contrasting the accommodation between ideals and reality made by those in an organization for some time with the idealism of the newcomer, but *Priest* could also be viewed as portraying the contemporary tension between an older generation of priests influenced by the Second Vatican Council and Liberation Theology and a younger more conservative body of clergy which has emerged under the present Pope.

The relationship between the two priests and their tensions with the Church are developed through two subplots. The first is the child abuse taking place within one of the church families, which the daughter (Lisa Unsworth) hesitatingly mentions to Fr Greg during a confession. The second is Fr Greg's understanding of his own homosexuality, which develops as he falls in love with Graham whom he meets in a bar. Both issues are framed as matters of conflict between institutional obligations (the secrecy of the confessional and the vow of celibacy) and Fr Greg's personal calling to care for the abused daughter and to freely love Graham. The film is brought to something of a resolution in a dramatic confrontation at a mass including an exchange of biblical "proof" texts on the question of homosexuality and a reconciliation between Fr Greg and Lisa.

Common Themes

Eden and Creation

When the woman saw that the fruit of the tree was good for food and pleasing to the eye, and also desirable for gaining wisdom, she took some and ate it. She also gave some to her husband, who was with her, and he ate. Then the eyes of both of them were opened.

(Gen. 3:6–7a)

The creation stories in Genesis are a complex set of narratives which mix human sexuality, the search for knowledge and the politics of gender in a fashion that remains intriguing and controversial. This could be due to the fact that, over time, one aspect of the Eden myth has tended to be the focus of most of the debate – i.e. the easy equation of sin and sexuality by some Christian traditions. So much so, it is possible to lose sight of some of the other elements which make up the story – such as the desire for wisdom and knowledge, and the motif of lost innocence. It is striking that these three elements from the Eden narratives (the loss of innocence, the quest for knowledge and sexuality) play a key part in *The Mission*, *The Name of the Rose* and *Priest* while the idea of sin is played down.

I shall start by examining the notion of the search for knowledge. This is probably most overt in *The Name of the Rose* where Bro. William places great store by the process of reason and much of the plot is centered directly or indirectly on the monastery's repository of knowledge, the library. Bro. William's search for Aristotle's lost work eventually takes precedence over the debate about poverty and the lives of those who are to be burnt for heresy. However, the story is not just about the quest for objective knowledge; Bro. William's personal story is important too and, as the film unfolds, we discover more about his life and how he has changed over the years. It is William's companion Adso who draws much of this information out of him and he also appears to play the part of student to the older Franciscan's role of mentor.

This subjective quest for the self and the task of mentor in this process is also crucial to *The Mission* and *Priest* where the personal struggles of Rodrigo Mendoza and Fr Greg Pilkington form a key part of the plot and where the characters of Fr Gabriel and Fr Matthew Thomas have the roles of teachers to the new initiates. However, it would be wrong to see these two films as solely about the *personal* pursuit of knowledge since in both we are encouraged to reflect about wider, social implications. For instance, in *The Mission* questions are raised about the "civilizing" aspects of European education on the Guarani Indians, while in *Priest* we are invited to reflect on the implications of Fr Greg's quest for inner knowledge of himself on his parish and the Church as a whole. Linked to the first Eden motif (the quest for knowledge) is that of the second: sexuality. This has already been noted as one of the subplots to *Priest* and Fr Greg's search for self-knowledge cannot be divorced from his exploration of his sexuality. Curiously, as watchers of the film we are given no history to this aspect of his life and yet there are indications that such a history exists. Fr Greg seems to know what he's doing when he takes off his clerical collar and puts on his leather jacket as he prepares to go out to a gay club. He knows where the club is and does not spend time having to search around for it. There is nothing to suggest that this is the first time he might have realized that he is gay. When he returns to his room he puts his collar back on and reassumes his role as a priest but it is clear that his sexuality is separate from the part that he plays in the Church and the community (Goffman 1959).

For Fr Greg the search for self-knowledge and the search for his sexuality are in conflict; however, for Adso, in *The Name of the Rose*, the connection is more positive. His encounter with the unnamed girl in the kitchen is in contrast with the images of repressed sexuality in the monastery. It is clear that the girl is required to exchange sexual favors for food with one or more of the monks and yet her relationship to Adso seems to be of a different nature. Yet, the question still arises: does their intercourse arise out the fact that she has been led to believe that this is what men expect of her, or from an independent act of self giving? The encounter with Adso as he is leaving at the end of the film suggests the latter and it is made explicit in his final commentary, that of all the encounters he had in the monastery (including those with his mentor, Bro. William) it was the one with the girl which had the most lasting impact upon him. If this meeting awakened Adso to a new aspect of experience then sex produces a different kind of awakening in *The Mission*. It is Carlotta's intimate relationship with his brother while he is away capturing slaves which acts as the catalyst for Rodrigo's act of vengeance and it is his remorse over the killing that eventually leads him back into the jungle, this time as a Jesuit. Human sexuality is shown once again as playing an important part in the process of self-knowledge and it is also a factor in the third element: loss of innocence.

I have commented on how several of the characters in these three films are portrayed as showing a certain naïveté – Fr Gabriel in his trust of the inquiry into the mission settlements; Adso in his questions to his master; Fr Greg in his reactions to the realities of parish life; Bro. William in his almost childlike enthusiasm for books. All come away from their celluloid encounters changed people. For them nothing was ever the same again and their worlds (if they survived) would be forever seen through the lenses of that experience. Even though Fr Gabriel and Rodrigo Mendoza were murdered by the slave traders the film ends with a note that the struggle goes on to this day and that there are still priests who take the side of the Indians. Perhaps the most poignant moment in *The Mission* comes at the end when the few Guarani children who have survived return naked into the jungle leaving behind all the trappings of the Europeans with the exception of a musical instrument – in a return to innocence. These connections with the Eden story – the quest for knowledge, the significance of human sexuality and the motif of lost innocence – all play a key part in plot and character development, but the shape of these three films also emerges through the conflict between individuals and institutions, and it is to that aspect of the drama we now turn.

Institutions, individuals, and identification

In her discussion of the nature of the Church Gillian Evans has noted a widespread identification in some parts of contemporary Western culture between institutions and repression (Evans 1994: 12). The Church represented in each case is the Roman Catholic Church but I would argue (speaking personally out of my Anglican context) that the characters, their stories and the organizational tensions can stand for the Church in its widest sense as well. Furthermore, it is significant that in these films the corporate, repressive aspect of the Church is represented by one individual – a white, male authority figure. Significantly, the three films all share in the portrayal of hierarchical oppression within and without the institution of the Church. Thus, in *The Mission* it is both the Indians and the Jesuits who suffer at the hands of the Pope's emissary, Altamirano; in *The Name of the Rose*, it is the local poor and the Franciscans who are tyrannized; while in *Priest* it is the bishop who is domineering and arrogant towards those who obstruct his career.

A key symbol for this repression is the Church's attitude towards wealth, which can be represented much more tangibly on film than can, for instance, the more abstract concept of power. I have already mentioned that the reason for Bro. William being at the monastery was for a debate about whether Jesus and his disciples owned their clothes. If the answer to that is no, then the obvious next question is: Why then has the Church amassed all its wealth? This subplot is supported by the contrast between the opulent clothes of the prelates and the simple dress of the Franciscans; by the well-fed stomachs of the monks and the poverty of those who scavenge from the monastic community and by the inquisition into the heresy of the Dolcinites and their lifestyle of penitence and poverty. Similar features are to be found in *The Mission*. The rich clothes of the Pope's emissary and the slave-traders contrast sharply with those of the Jesuits, while the simplicity of the wooden mission dwellings is very different to the stone houses and churches of the Europeans. The same is true of *Priest*, although it is more understated. The bishop's attachment to the finer things of life are shown through a brief shot of an antique ink stand on his desk and, when the bishop wishes to show his displeasure with Fr Matthew, he takes away one of the priest's few "luxuries" a dilapidated Mini Metro car. Although the word hypocrisy is not mentioned in any of the three films – it is there by implication. This tension between the corruption of the Church and the idealism of the individual is fundamental to the three plots and we must examine it in more detail.

Time and again in *The Mission, The Name of the Rose* and *Priest* we see the Church making demands on characters which they find difficult or impossible to accept. For Fr Gabriel and Rodrigo Mendoza it is the relinquishing of their mission and the abandonment of the Guarani Indians to the slave trading colonialists. For Bro. William of Baskerville it is a different kind of abandonment. He clearly feels that he is being asked to give up the way of reason and logical argument in the face of irrationality and superstition. This idea is underlined further by the censorship of Aristotle's work on humor by the librarian, the venerable Jorge. The pressure on Fr Greg Pilkington is in reconciling his sexuality, particularly his homosexuality, with the official teaching of the Church. A similar problem exists in a heterosexual context for Fr Matthew Thomas but Fr Greg also has to cope with a wider social stigma as well. This motif of male homosexuality is also a sub-plot in *The Name of the Rose* and lies behind the first death that Bro. William is asked to investigate. The area of conflict between the individual and institutional is heightened in each case by the Church's hypocrisy over the issue of wealth. However, if we look behind this dramatic construct it seems to me that these two elements from the three plots reflect much wider aspects of our contemporary culture.

First, the centrality of individualism in Western society is well documented (e.g. MacIntyre 1981; Milbank 1990; Gunton 1993) but what has received less comment is the way in which the model of the individual human being has also become the model for understanding collective human organizations (Brunsson and Olsen 1993). In this respect "hypocrisy" (i.e. the meeting of competing demands from inconsistent environments) is seen in an individualistic way and organizations are judged, like a person, on whether they have remained true to their ideals. Thus, just as individual hypocrisy occurs when a person fails to remain true to his or her own ideals, so organizational hypocrisy is perceived when an institution acts in different or even conflicting ways. While this makes for good drama and clear characterization, particularly in the case of the Pope's emissary in *The Mission*, one of the roles that organizations can be called upon to perform is to hold together or reconcile such conflicting ideals; hence, the popularity in current organizational literature for numerous diverse models (eg Morgan 1986; Mintzberg 1989) or polarities marking out a spectrum of opinion (Brunsson 1989; Hampden-Turner 1990). Yet, while these images allow competing convictions to be held together in the world of organizations they do not make good cinema which, as a number of commentators have noted, has been encouraged by the ideology of individualism (Metz 1982, Turner 1993). This is reinforced by the function of the camera which acts as the eyes of the individual viewer. It is striking that in all three films "heroic" individuals are cast against "compromised" individuals who represent hypocritical organizations (the pope's emissary, Bernard Gui and the bishop).

The spectator's identification with the camera plays an important part in the second factor on which I want to comment in this section – the concept of "role." Identification is a key element in film theory (Lapsley and Westlake 1988; Easthope 1993). In their discussion of *American Graffiti* Lapsley and Westlake argue that the movie is, like many realist texts, concerned with the question of identity regarding the central character (Curt Henderson) and, furthermore, the identification with this character by the spectator plays a crucial role in the film:

The resolution, therefore, of the question of Curt's identity is also the production of a spectator position, one of knowledge and outside of contradiction. The spectator is seemingly outside the process and therefore can imagine him or herself as completely grasping the process.

(Lapsley and Westlake 1988: 174)

Interestingly, the three films under discussion all revolve around pairs of characters and, in particular their *justification* of their role or their *search* for a role to play. Spectators are given a choice of identification in this process. It is not my aim to address the issue of female identification in these films, although I do recognize that with six male lead characters there are questions that can be raised regarding the place of women in all three films. Thus I shall confine my discussion to issues of identification in the area already defined – around the tension between individuals and institutions. In each film one of the male characters in the pair has arrived at an, albeit sometimes uncomfortable, accommodation with the Church (Fr Gabriel, Bro. William and Fr Matthew). They are put in a mentor role over the other character (Rodrigo Mendoza, Adso of Melk, Fr Greg) who are all learning the "script" for their part of the organization or culture which, in turn, means that the process of identification is taking place at a number of levels (Mangham 1995). To start with a spectator may identify with one or other of the two *roles* (mentor/student) or with the *relationship* or with the *wider tension* between the characters and the institution.

Curiously, while some people writing about cinema have criticized it for attempting to mimic the real world, others dealing with the "real" world have been keen to take up images drawn from the "fictional" world of theatre and film. Thus, the metaphors of role and script have been used to explore human social and organizational interaction. Role has been described as "A central unit of analysis in sociology and social psychology. It refers to the duties, obligations and expectation which accompany a particular position" (Sims, Fineman and Gabriel 1993: 289). The idea of a script in a group context, meanwhile, refers to: "meaning-making processes within organizations . . . routinized responses [which] . . . facilitate the interpretation of information, actions and expectations" (Mangham 1995: 493, 495).

This suggests that the traditional distinction between "reality" and "fiction" is too easily drawn as well as pointing to the deeper problems of identification underlying *The Mission*, *The Name of the Rose*, and *Priest*. All of them seem to reflect the dysfunction in our late twentieth-century Western culture between individuals and institutions, in this case the Church. The conflict between personal lives and communal expectations is a conflict of identification, roles and scripts. There are many "parts" to play and many "film-sets" on which to play them, even in one pluralistic organization such as the Church. The dysfunctions and tensions that Rodrigo, Adso and Fr Greg face are very real in the Church but they also work as a metaphor for the issues that confront us all in learning roles and scripts in society.

Armageddon and telos

Of the three films *The Name of the Rose* is most overt with its references to Armageddon and other motifs from the Book of Revelation but these particular movies, and others, can be seen in a wider teleological framework, patterñ of ideals or ultimate human fulfilment (Horton and Mendus 1994). However, *telos* is not just about human goals, there is an important chronological element as well. In his discussion of *Blade Runner* and *Wings of Desire*, David Harvey suggests these two movies highlight the fact that in our culture "there is a crisis of representation of space and time" (Harvey 1989: 322). A crucial component of this crisis appears to be the central characters' detachment from any sense of past or history. Such a view seems to link up to MacIntyre's analysis of our detached post-Enlightenment condition (MacIntyre 1981) and the need to discover a renewed understanding of the human *telos*. In other words, a vision of our history is fundamental to our vision of the future, while an understanding of our future is vital to our actions in the present. Thus, MacIntyre believes the past should be regarded "neither as mere prologue nor as something to be struggled against, but as that from which we learn if we are to identify and move towards our *telos* more adequately" (MacIntyre 1990: 79). Harvey is critical of how *Wings of Desire* and, to a lesser extent, *Blade Runner* resolve themselves through romanticism. Neither film, he argues: "has the power to overturn established ways of seeing or transcend the conflictual conditions of the moment" (Harvey 1989: 322).

There is common ground here with the ending of *Priest* in which those members of the congregation who cannot accept Fr Greg are asked to leave the parish before the service begins then, as the worship progresses, the gay cleric and the abused daughter embrace during the administration of communion and the film closes. The perceptions of some within the institution about gay men has not been "overturned," the dissatisfied members of the congregation have merely left that church. Reconciliation is discovered at a personal, rather than communal, level and the future is portrayed in terms of the oppressed embracing and supporting each other rather than being embraced and supported by society at large. Furthermore, there is no sense in which the past has been reclaimed or retold. The Church remains an institution of oppression and the figure of Jesus on the cross is frequently used as a focus for that view. There is no perception from the characters in this film that Jesus himself can be seen as someone on the margins of his society and religious establishment (Borg 1987; Dunn 1991; Meier 1991).

In this respect, *The Mission* and *The Name of the Rose* do attempt to retell and reappropriate the past. Although the latter film never escapes its literary origins and even in its motion picture version keeps the role of the narrator (Adso of Melk) to provide its framework, it does attempt to forge a link with the flow of history. *The Mission* too, while retaining a firm grip on its realist pretensions, also clearly establishes similar connections. It is framed by the words: "The historical events represented in this story are true, and occurred around the borderlands of Argentina, Paraguay and Brazil in the year 1750."

The movie finishes with a caption about the ongoing struggle of the Native Indians and the priests:

> The Indians of South America are still engaged in a struggle to defend their land and their culture. Many of the priests who, inspired by faith and love, continue to support the rights of the Indians for justice, do so with their lives.
>   The light shines in the darkness and the darkness has not overcome it.
>
> *John Chapter 1, verse 5*

Thus the past is re-appropriated and the narrative is not left rootless, although there may be questions about using uncritically the stereotype of an intimate connection between Christianity and colonialism.

Priest ends with strong echoes of the heavenly *telos* presented in the Book of Revelation, symbolizing an ultimate goal. In Revelation, after the tribulations of the end times, the community of the Lamb (the eucharistic community) are embraced by God's love and gathered in worship wearing symbolic white robes (Rev. 7). At the end of *Priest*, after many trials, the abused daughter and the abused priest embrace in love at mass in a similar eucharistic context (the community of the Lamb) – a parallel that is underscored by the white vestments of the clergy. By contrast, *The Mission* and *The Name of the Rose* bear more than a passing resemblance to that alternative *telos* envisaged by Revelation – the violent and cataclysmic end to space and time. There is a hint of this fiery and violent ending in the myth of the lost innocence where Adam and Eve are prevented from ever returning to the Garden of Eden by the presence of an angel with a flaming sword (Gen. 3:23–4). The "apocalyptic" ending is clearly conscious in *The Name of the Rose* because, as we noted earlier, Eco based his novel on the seven plagues of Revelation 15 (Eco 1985) but the similarity with the way in which *The Mission* concludes is striking. It is tempting to note one of the main concerns in the West at the time these two films were made was the destruction of society through nuclear conflict, whereas *Priest* was made in a very different cultural environment with great fear over the destruction of lives through AIDS. I am conscious of Lapsley and Westlake's strictures against "the illusion of contradiction resolved" (Lapsley and Westlake 1988: 155) and Harvey's censure of romantic endings but nevertheless a further (partial) resolution of the tensions between the individual and institution is suggested independently by all three films. It is most overt in *The Name of the Rose* where there is a discussion between Bro. William and the venerable Jorge over the question of humor. The librarian believes that it would be a recipe for chaos if humanity was permitted to laugh at everything and that: "Laughter kills fear and without fear there can be no faith. . . ."

Laughter plays a small but crucial role in the other two films as well. Fr Greg is sent away from the parish for a period of readjustment with an austere priest who will only speak Latin to him and clearly regards him with loathing. There is a moment of conspiracy between Fr Matthew and Fr Greg when they use laughter to cement their bond as friends and priests, while at the same time seeing off any fear of this priest and, I suspect, the bishop and the institutional Church. In this respect Jorge was right. Humor has a complex place within groups relating to testing social phenomena like taboos, shared trust and conformity (Sims, Fineman and Gabriel 1993: 158–68). Jorge is right in seeing that laughter and fear are intimately related and that the former can kill the latter. However, it is also true that laughter can bring fear to the surface.

In *The Mission*, after discovering that Carlotta loves his brother instead of himself, Rodrigo storms back out into the street and picks an argument with a bystander who was laughing at something unrelated but who Rodrigo, in his state of mind, thinks is laughing at him. His brother chases him and says that Rodrigo's argument is with him and not with this stranger. The ensuing duel and killing is crucial to moving the plot forward. None of these three films could be remotely described as comedies and yet laughter plays an important point in each of them. If the romantic view of Armageddon, or the human *telos*, is a loving embrace and the radical vision is the destruction of existing order – is it the cynic who is left to laugh at our fragile efforts to reconcile our personal values and our communal lives?

Conclusion

I have argued that *The Mission, The Name of the Rose,* and *Priest* dramatically explore a number of aspects of the human condition: our quest for a teleological frame of reference, our communal search for meaningful roles and scripts and the double-edged nature of the human desire for knowledge with its concomitant loss of childlike innocence. In addition, I have suggested that there are various overt or subtle cross-references to the myths of Eden and

Armageddon in the Jewish and Christian traditions. The three films all have a distinct moment of closure which returns the focus to individuals. For the first two it is a concluding word from the narrators (the pope's emissary and Adso), while for *Priest* it is the hug for Fr Greg and Lisa in the context of the mass. I have touched on the importance of individuality in movies as a genre, even in representing organizations. Perhaps one of their functions in modern, or even postmodern, society is in providing tragic and comedic narrative for us to explore our identities and roles. As Umberto Eco points out in his observations about *The Name of the Rose*:

> a novel has nothing to do with words in the first instance. Writing a novel is a cosmological matter, like the story told by Genesis (we all have to choose our role models, as Woody Allen puts it).
>
> *(Eco 1985: 20)*

The same (individualistic) God-like perspective may also be reflected in both the process of making a film and, indeed, the creative act of watching it.

14

The Spirituality of *Shirley Valentine*

Clive Marsh

Introduction

In this chapter, the film *Shirley Valentine* will be used as a means of access to a discussion about Christian understanding of the "Holy Spirit." In Christian theology the "Holy Spirit" is understood as the third person of the Trinity i.e. the third way in which God is understood to be God, in addition to God's being called "Father" and "Son." There must always remain, in Christian understanding, a sense in which God is mysteriously beyond the grasp of human thought and human experience. But "the trinity" is the most developed way, conceptually speaking, in which Christians speak of the reality of God. God understood as trinity means God as always *beyond*, *alongside*, and *within* the created order. Christian understanding of God does not, however, relate these three dimensions (of God's being beyond, alongside, and within creation) directly to the so-called three "persons" of the trinity (Father, Son, and Spirit). For God is held to be always three-dimensional, even when a single "person" of the trinity is being considered. Nevertheless, a discussion of God as Spirit readily introduces an exploration of God's being *within* the created order and within human beings. Consideration of God the Spirit, in other words, is one approach to grasping the three-dimensional nature of God. Our discussion of the film *Shirley Valentine* focuses, then, – by virtue of the film's own subject-matter – upon the way in which the Spirit of God interweaves with the inner life of human beings. Through consideration of the mysterious workings of the human spirit, we are led to probe Christian understanding of the Spirit of God at work at the heart of what Christians call "creation."

Examining the Film

Shirley Valentine is a "woman of spirit." Though wavering and initially uncertain as to whether to join her friend Jane on a trip to Greece, she has the guts to go. Jane leaves Shirley to fend for herself for the first part of the holiday, but Shirley finds her feet, comforted by her speaking to the rock on the beach – an echo of her talking to the kitchen-wall at home. She confronts herself, "finds herself" again, being able to reassess, in middle-age, where the last 20 years have gone. She reviews her life, the loss of her youthful vigor, and the relative loss of a carefree approach to life which she and Joe, her husband, had enjoyed. She ponders what Joe has become. In allowing herself to be seduced by Costas, she retains control of herself to the extent that she finds her freedom again – this is what she wants. She also loses control in the sense that she rediscovers the positive dimension of "letting go" of herself.

Shirley Valentine can be read in a number of ways. It is a study of middle-age, especially of the reappraisals of married life which many middle-aged married people are compelled by changing circumstances to conduct. It is an exploration of a woman's experience of self-discovery, written by a man (Willy Russell, writer of both original stage-play and the film's screenplay), and directed by a man (Lewis Gilbert). It is a gentle comedy, the kind which a major network can put out on evening prime-time TV without causing great offense, guaranteeing good TV ratings. Though it struggles through a tension between form and content to declare how seriously it wishes to be taken, the film nevertheless raises some key issues about human living. In particular, it addresses questions, and offers tentative answers, about the spiritual resources which human beings require, and reveal themselves as possessing or receiving, in order to be able to handle seemingly ordinary, but demanding, issues of human interrelationship.

The basic contours for a discussion of the role of the spirit of God in human life which this film offers will first be sketched, before being explored in more depth in due course. Three aspects can be highlighted. First, *the fact of Shirley praying* should not go unnoticed. When about to leave for Greece, in the midst of her own reservations about the consequences of her actions – shared before God – she utters a genuine intercessory prayer:

> God. God, I know . . . I'm bein' cruel, an' I know I'll have to pay for it, when I get back. And I don't mind payin' for it then. But just . . . just do me a favour, God, an' don't make me pay for it durin' the two weeks. Keep everyone safe. Please.

More prominent, though less obviously prayer, are Shirley's conversations with the wall and the rock. These are, at the very least, necessary externalizations of herself, or means of self-examination. They may be negatively construed as cries for a relationship which she generally does not enjoy with other human beings at this point in her life. But they are aspects of the relationship with herself, which Shirley needs to rediscover, which merit closer scrutiny. More positively, they may be construed as a form of "therapeutic meditation" (Brummer 1984: ch. 2), although further examination will be needed to establish whether they can indeed be called "prayer."

Second, Shirley's *quest for freedom* can be examined from the perspective of the experience of God as Spirit. Much is made in the film of Shirley's loss of freedom since the days when she was Shirley Bradshaw. Either marriage itself has inevitably proved restrictive, or Shirley has allowed marriage to stifle her. The title song of the film ("The Girl Who Used To Be Me") announces from the outset the theme of flying as freedom; flying away to Greece, yet also rising above her present situation in order to examine it. The film begins to consider the implications of her actions (going to Greece, becoming involved with Costas) and thus prevents her flight becoming a form of sheer escapism. It does not go far in this direction. But in delivering an ambiguous ending – it is not clear that all things will be well and that Shirley and Joe will even be reunited (i.e. the quest for freedom is not simple) – the film's treatment of the subject provides resource-material for a careful examination of the nature of human freedom. Above all, the film poses the question of the origin and nature of the resources (e.g. the power of personal reflection and self-analysis, inner strength) upon which this quest for freedom is based.

Third, the *quest for relationship* which unites the first two theological aspects highlighted – Shirley's prayer and her quest for freedom – should also be considered. It is not wholly clear that Shirley wants Joe any more. She is unlikely to leave him. She will make do. But she longs for him to be more the fun-loving Joe she knew when they first met. Her reflection on their early relationship borders on the nostalgic, yet expresses a present need in her too: she has lost a fun-loving side to her. Her relationship with Jane is more of a release, a safe place where she can be more herself. That relationship mirrors earlier "nights out with the girls." But Jane's fickleness only emphasizes Shirley's aloneness. Shirley's contact with her daughter (Millandra) and daughter's friend (Sharron-Louise), though representing on Shirley's part a further attempt to recreate a lost past, only emphasizes the cultural and age gap between them. Shirley lacks satisfying relationships in a number of directions. However self-seeking his own motivation may have been, Costas fills the gap and enables Shirley to have an immediate (sexual) need met, in a way which spurs on her general reassessment of who she is both as an individual and in relation to others.

These three features in the film provide, then, a basis for a dialog with Christian theology about a contemporary understanding of spirit. The fact that Christian theology would unavoidably address issues of prayer, freedom and relationship in its discussion of the presence and action of the Spirit of God in contemporary human life makes the film a useful discussion-partner.

Exploring Christian Theology

Willy Russell is not, of course, presenting Shirley Valentine as someone who consciously offers a theological interpretation of what is happening to her. Nor does he give any clue that he himself would offer such a reading. Even the moment of explicit prayer in the film may be considered as no more than a figure of speech, or a defensive reaction to which an easy psychological explanation can be offered. At one level, Willy Russell has simply written a sensitive, compelling story, drawing, no doubt, on his experience as a hairdresser, as a result of which he would have gained immense insights into the lives of his women clients. No other defense than the actual conversation we shall conduct between the film and Christian theology (here, specifically, pneumatology: the study of spirit) will be offered here for the legitimacy of such a reading of the film. Nor will it be argued that this is the only possible reading of the film. It clearly is not. The conversation with Christian pneumatology is simply one possible reading of the film. If what Christians claim of God in relation to the Spirit is true, however, then the Spirit of God must not be evident only in so-called "religious experiences." The film itself invites the dialog, given what Christian theology says about the workings of God as Spirit. The very possibility of the dialog between the film and Christian theology, then, supports the legitimacy of the enterprise. In Christian understanding, talk of the spirit is a means of talking about the being and action of God in precisely the areas which can be drawn from the film *Shirley Valentine*. Reference to Christian tradition – biblical and beyond – readily supplies exploration of the spirit of God in terms which illuminate our reading of the film. Christian theology can thus bring these understandings to the film, and then in turn receive back resource material from the film to aid its own interpretation, be that through the film's denial of Christian insight, confirmation, or radical questioning.

We begin by addressing Shirley's praying. In the words of the Apostle Paul: ". . . the Spirit helps us in our weakness; for we do not know how to pray as we ought, but that very Spirit intercedes with sighs too deep for words" (Rom. 8:26). This insight of Paul's is used by some Christians to support the practice of glossolalia ("speaking in tongues"). Whether or not such a use is legitimate, Paul is clearly here locating the work of the spirit of God in the depth of human experience in such a way that God supports the flagging spirit, and brings to voice the human cry, be it for release from oppression or for restoration of lost relationship. This illuminates well Shirley's "cry from the heart" in her feelings of uncertainty about going to Greece (wanting to do it, yet knowing there'll be negative reactions later), and in her intercession for her family. Perhaps neither she nor Russell can say where such a cry of the spirit comes from. But Paul's insight suggests that deep in the human soul/spirit the divine spirit is at work. In that partnership at depth, the spirit of God helps people to pray. Shirley herself experiences what the Ulanovs call prayer as "primary speech" (Ulanov, A. and B. 1985: ch. 1; see also for example Hughes 1985: ch. 4). Their words issue a challenge to those who may feel skeptical about viewing Shirley as one who prays:

> Prayer is not just primary speech, image-laden and without sound. It is also ordinary human talk that addresses an other in familiar conversation about familiar things. Critics of prayer accuse those who pray of narcissistic withdrawal, of merely communing with their own wishes and fantasies, hiding from the tough problems and insoluble conflicts of the world.
>
> Such critics must begin to pray. Then they will see how different the actual experience of prayer is from their reduction of it.
>
> *(Ulanov, A. and B. 1985: 8)*

Her "prayer," however, as we have seen, takes on other forms than petition (praying for herself) or intercession (praying for others). Her talking to the wall and to the rock is not strictly conversation, for neither object talks back. But is prayer always (or ever?) conversation in Christian understanding? Christians may stress that prayer is about a two-way relationship: "we talk to God, God talks to us." But the word "talk" in the second clause of that rather easy slogan is arguably less concrete than its use in the first, if not indeed wholly metaphorical. The sanity of people who "literally" hear the voice of God is often, rightly, brought into question. Perhaps, then, reading Shirley's talk to the wall and to the rock as prayer is far from illegitimate. Indeed, Christian understanding of contemplative prayer may well provide a clue to what Shirley is doing.

Jürgen Moltmann writes:

> There are many definitions of meditation and contemplation, and many distinctions have been made between the two. For my own practical purposes I would interpret meditation as the loving, suffering and participating knowledge of something; and contemplation as the reflective awareness of one's own self in this meditation. In meditation, people

submerge themselves in the object of their meditation. They are wholly
"absorbed" in it and "forget themselves." The object is submerged in
them. In contemplation, they recollect themselves. They come back to
themselves after they had gone out of themselves and forgotten themselves ... there is no meditation without contemplation, and no
contemplation without meditation. But if we want to understand the
two, it is useful to make this distinction.

(Moltmann 1992: 202–3)

The appropriateness of Moltmann's words for our enquiry – taken, significantly, from a book exploring the doctrine of the spirit – are plain. Shirley
relates to the wall and the rock in such a way that she gets outside of herself
in order to examine who she is. She then returns understanding herself better.
There may well be psychologically explicable factors of comfort and security
at work here. This does not alter a human need for possessing a healthy
relationship to oneself in order to begin to understand oneself. The question
then is what form this relationship to self takes, and what support it requires.

The "object" of Shirley's meditation and contemplation is not, of course,
the wall or the rock. In the same way as an icon, though itself worthy of
veneration, is not the ultimate focus of devotion, the wall and rock are means
through which Shirley attains a degree of self-understanding. The true object
of her meditation and contemplation is the desire for relationship, or an as yet
unknown other to whom Shirley wishes to relate. In no sense does she appear
to think of this "unknown other" as God. At issue, though, is whether the
source of her desire for relationship, and the spiritual empowerment of Shirley
to move beyond her conversations with wall and rock to express herself and to
find more whole and authentic relationships, are not best understood and
described as the divine work of the spirit.

Shirley's unwitting practice of prayer thus links directly to her desire for
relationship. The promotion of relationship is itself consistently seen throughout Christian tradition as the work of the spirit of God (Baelz 1982: ch. 2). In
a recent work of Christian systematic theology, for example, Stanley Grenz
locates himself firmly in the Western Augustinian tradition which understands
the Spirit to be the relationship between Father and Son within the Trinitarian
nature of God (Grenz 1994, for example 91, 93, 108, 138, 149, 486–8).
Questions have been raised about whether such an understanding renders the
Spirit a weak third person of the trinity. But there is no avoiding the need and
desire on the part of Christians in both the East and West to clarify the work
of God as community-creator in terms of God's work as Spirit. The work of
the Spirit is the work of God to constitute relationship between human beings
and between human beings and God. As the Spirit who inspires prayer, the
Spirit of God in turn inspires people to relate to other human beings and in

that way celebrate their God-given capacity for relationship (Hughes 1985: 28–9). In the same way, then, as Christian theology links prayer with the formation and fostering of relationship, so also Shirley's prayer (to the wall and the rock) is "answered" in the courage she can show to reassess herself in her aloneness and strike out on a new path of relationship.

Finally in this section, we must reflect further upon the spirit as the spirit of freedom. Again, it is no coincidence that the Christian tradition has explored the notion of freedom (expressed more recently, and with different nuances, as "liberation") in terms of the work of God as Spirit (Moltmann 1992: ch. V). The Spirit in Christian theology has symbolized release and free expression in individual experience and in corporate worship, building upon insights which reverberate through the Bible (e.g. I Sam. 19:19–24, Jn 8:31–6, 14:25–7 and 15:26; I Cor. 12; II Cor. 3:17). This has frequently led to the opposite of what the Apostle Paul was struggling to emphasize to the Corinthian Church. Instead of the unity which was needed as the expression of oneness in Christ, the strangeness of the Spirit's effects upon believers often seemed to cause disunity. Nevertheless, such an emphasis is crucial within an understanding of the Spirit as the Spirit of God. The strange spirit which is God at work freeing people from what restricts and oppresses them will not be bound by human institutions, not even the Church, necessary though such institutions may be (see for example Doctrine Commission 1991: 85–91). God questions the rationality of human enterprise and the desire for order and control through the work of the Spirit in human affairs. Shirley can only experience her own release through the costly (and irrational) risk-taking of her flight to Greece and the challenge to the institutional structure of her own marriage through her brief encounter with Costas. Whether the specifics of her actions can be said to be "the will of God" is open to question. But the work of the Spirit, as the spirit of freedom, nevertheless presses her to break out of her present situation, as a direct result of her prayer and quest for relationship. On this understanding, the Spirit as the spirit of freedom is none other than the redemptive spirit of Christ, who rescues (saves) people from what constrains and crushes them (Welker 1994, 108–24, who also draws out fully the moral and political dimensions of the Spirit's liberation). This theme of liberation/redemption is dwelt on more fully elsewhere in this volume (e.g in chapters 4, 5, 7, and 8). It is often a dominant theme in films (*One Flew Over the Cuckoo's Nest*, *The Shawshank Redemption*) and frequently dealt with more darkly. In approaching *Shirley Valentine* from a pneumatological perspective, however, and drawing attention to the link between spiritual presence and liberation, we are also suggesting where explorations of other films, whose focus is redemption/liberation, might usefully lead.

Questioning Christian Theology

We have now brought from the Christian tradition some insights which deepen our understanding of possible theological themes which can be drawn from the film *Shirley Valentine*, as outlined in our initial sketch. The next step must be to invite the film to respond to our proposals. Our question, again, is not whether such a reading of the film is possible. Much more constructively, we must ask: granted that ours is a possible reading, what has the film got to teach Christian theology, in relation to the insights we have brought?

The first and most obvious challenge of the film relates to the content of the object of Shirley's praying. It may be disputed whether Shirley's talking to the wall or the rock is prayer in any sense at all. Christian theology could refuse to enter into dialog on the grounds that the link is unfounded. But if it is granted that Shirley's practice in this regard is at least having the *function* of prayer, then the question as to the nature of the object to which/whom Shirley speaks arises. To express the matter in contemporary fashion: is God "really there," working in a way Shirley herself does not explicitly recognize, responding to Shirley's need, or desire, to step outside of herself in her talk to the rock or the wall? God is thus seen to be spiritually present within Shirley's experience, but unbeknown to her, working to facilitate her self-understanding and ability to relate. Or does the conclusion that Shirley is praying – when we realize that there is nothing there but the wall or the rock – merely highlight that God is not "really there"? God may thus be necessary for human beings – as a fictional figure, a human construct, a psychological prop – but does not "exist" as such.

Shirley Valentine presents in stark form, in the context of ordinary, daily human life, the debate between realists and non-realists in contemporary Christian theology in the West. Realists hold that God is really there. Non-realists hold that there is no reality to which the label "God" can be given, but that God is a fictional construct. (On all this, see Ward 1982 v Cupitt 1980; Harries 1994 v Freeman 1993; Thiselton 1995.) Both groups, however, are theistic in the sense that both hold a belief in God, or a commitment to the idea/concept of God, is necessary for human well-being. Shirley Valentine's practice of praying could thus be read in one of three ways. First it could be read as a psychological need which would no longer be necessary as and when her relationships were on the road to restoration. This would be a reductionist reading. Shirley's talking to the wall and the rock is explicable psychologically in terms of something she currently lacks. It represents something else only temporarily. Second, it could be seen as the prayer of a non-realist, who could be persuaded that her talk to the wall or rock was very much part of being human and that she would no doubt continue the practice even when her relationships improved. Such a practice means, then, that whether she talks to the rock, wall or to God is really no different in *function*, even though the meaning of the term "God" – now understood as a human concept – would not be without significance. This practice could thus be equated with "talking to oneself," a practice deemed psychologically important in order that one enjoys a relationship with oneself. Third, it could be the prayer of a realist who has yet to discover that she is already participating in a practice of prayer she does not yet fully comprehend, one which requires a conviction that God as Spirit works in and through such human experience. Such a reading would require much greater attention as to what/who the God is to which/whom she is praying. Shirley's practice is thus recognized as fundamentally human, and she would benefit more fully from exploring the depth of her practice.

All these readings are possible. The film offers no reflection upon what Shirley is doing, even whilst presenting Shirley herself in the midst of deep self-questioning. From such an angle of approach, the first reading presents itself as thus the most plausible. This would, however, be an unsatisfactory reading. For Shirley Valentine, even if in some way psychologically deficient through her "praying," is certainly a representative figure. And such a universal deficiency would thus merely raise other issues pertinent to Christian theology (e.g. universal sinfulness, the notion that all human beings are flawed or incomplete in some way). In short, a reductionist reading far from dispenses with the question of a theological reading either of the film or the basic human experiences which it portrays. Some form of theistic reading of the film therefore offers itself as likely in so far as Shirley, whilst acknowledging a gap in her life, seems not to consider her need to "talk to herself" as anything especially unusual. Nor is she presented as in any way especially unusual for so doing. Indeed, though Joe's talking to the same kitchen wall later in the film may be considered as symptomatic of his own lost relationship, it may equally be regarded as a necessary step in his own development of a relation to self which then propels him towards a new, more whole stage in his life.

Which reading of Shirley's practice is to be adopted, however, if the reductionist reading is rejected? Shirley probably does believe in the God she prays to, as a result of her own residual Liverpudlian Christianity. This does not, of course, establish the existence of the God she believes in. Nor is a link immediately forged with her meditative practice. It does, however, for the viewer give a context to the relation to self which her talking to the wall and the rock expresses, and which we see developing throughout the film through her practice of "prayer." Even if Shirley's practice is classed as no more than "therapeutic meditation," if we follow Brummer's analysis, such meditation nevertheless presupposes "certain metaphysical beliefs about the existence and nature of God and his agency in the world" (Brummer 1984: 28). Again this far from establishes the existence and presence of such a God. But the dialog between the film and theology sharpens a viewer's insight into the link between human psychological well-being, meditative practice, interrelationship and metaphysical conviction. Even if metaphysical convictions may be open to deconstruction by non-realist means, the function of metaphysical statements remains indisputable.

A second challenge of the film to Christian theology is brought by the staggering ordinariness of Shirley as a character and the subject-matter of the film. Where she lives, her routine, the favors she undertakes for others (feeding a neighbor's dog), her "out-of-character" fling (a standard trip to Greece, a holiday romance) are all very ordinary indeed. These are not obvious candidates to be read as "spiritual experiences." For that very reason, however, the film offers a sharp challenge to Christian theology. It is precisely in examination of the Spirit that Christian theology has frequently focused attention upon the spectacular, the miraculous, the supernatural. There are good grounds for this. We referred earlier to the Spirit's strangeness or irrationality (Schweizer 1980: 10–14; Moltmann 1992: ch. IX). The New Testament (the Gospel of Luke and the Book of Acts especially) links the Spirit with miracles (Schweizer 1980: 57–65). The damaging consequence of construing the Spirit's strangeness as a separate (spiritual) experience, however, is a sharp separation of "religious experience" from "normal" or "daily" life (see Davies 1973, a book which, if written fresh today, would no doubt include more reference to the doctrine of the Spirit).

Working out an understanding of Spirit in dialog with such a film as *Shirley Valentine* prevents the sharp separation of the religious from the everyday. However, unlike some approaches to theology from the recent past which would simply see Shirley's experience as complete in itself, to which a theological interpretation would add nothing substantial, the approach I am adopting here acknowledges Shirley's pilgrimage through the film as genuinely an encounter with and exploration of God as Spirit. Reading her experience in this way therefore would add to and enhance her experience of fully human, ordinary life and not merely reinterpret it with different words (Welker 1994, 258–64). In saying this I also reveal that I clearly favor a realist reading of the film. A non-realist reading is not ruled out, but how Shirley's experience is being understood, and how it is to be referred to (i.e. not as an "encounter") would need to change.

Shirley's experience thus remains ordinary. But her experience discloses an evident distinction between her own spirit and an "other" to whom she relates in internal conversation. In this way, she embodies the possibility of others seeing how ordinary life is suffused with the Divine spirit in very specific concrete ways. The challenge to Christian theology and practice is to work much more with this insight into the relation between the divine and the human in the human spirit, rather than to dwell more keenly upon the spectacular in exploration of the work of the Spirit of God.

Questioning the Film

Before turning finally to what the dialog between the film and Christian theology produces as far as a Christian pneumatology is concerned, it is worth turning back to the film directly once more. For we can now pose questions of the film itself, informed by the theological discussion. We will admittedly be influenced by factors which lead us to conclude that the film could have been different in order to address more clearly our purposes; i.e. in order to give us more material to work on a pneumatology, the film should have done x or y. Such an approach would clearly be unfair. Nevertheless, our discussion does highlight one or two problems with the film as a film which are worth mentioning.

The first difficulty is the absence of attention to the potential emotional, let alone moral, complexity of Shirley's adulterous encounter with Costas. Admittedly, the film ends at precisely the point where such a question would most forcibly arise – with the appearance of Joe in Greece. Whilst acknowledging that what was happening to Shirley during her stay in Greece was of crucial significance, the film does not condone her action as though a holiday fling would solve anyone's mid-life crisis. But it does allow its relatively lighthearted tone to mirror Shirley's happy-go-lucky approach to life. In the process, in order to maintain its light-hearted feel, it leaves so much unexplored (above all the clash between Shirley's courage, self-assertion and rediscovered confidence on the one hand, and her guilt and uncertainty on the other – not just about her time with Costas, but about the whole Greek adventure). Strick (1989, 346) accurately refers to such gaps as "chasms of unexplored implication."

This first difficulty relates to a second, already mentioned briefly earlier. The tension between form and content in the film is so great, that its seriousness, and the even profound insights it contains at times are in danger of being wholly lost in the overall levity of its tone. The importance of the film's subject-matter, and the sensitivity and thoughtfulness with which Russell handles this, become downplayed. The film is made, of course, to entertain rather than inform or provoke. However, despite its levity, it does operate at a deeper level. The superficial impression that a holiday fling might do someone a power of good – which can be recognized as largely a fantasy on a first and only viewing – conflicts with the undoubted impact that the film has had on people who viewed it one or more times and were led to reassess their own situations. Because it is not simply a comedy (and its open ending highlights the fact) a yet more searching treatment of what was going on inside Shirley is called for. This would, naturally, serve the purposes of this essay. But such an expansion of the film is called for less by a theological reading of the film *per se* and more by the ambiguous messages communicated by the film as a whole. The ending is unsatisfactory for a "good night's entertainment," but most apt for a film about which one is meant to think, reflect and discuss until deep into the night. The film presents itself, however, as much more of the former.

Reformulating Christian Theology

Neither of these objections, major though they may be, should detract from the fact that this film can stimulate theological discussion very well indeed. Its "levity" relates directly to its popularity: it has gained a mass audience. If work has to be done to enable theological discussion to follow, then so be it. It at least has the potential to begin many such discussions. It does not deliver to Christian theology readily packaged answers to theology's questions. Nor does it simply illustrate a presupposed pneumatology. We saw in the central section that it embodies key late twentieth-century challenges to any contemporary understanding of the Spirit. In conclusion, then, it is appropriate to summarize where the dialog has taken us.

First, *Shirley Valentine* compels contemporary Christian theology to conceive of the Spirit of God only in terms of *the concrete spirit*. Rather than being contradictory, this juxtaposition of concreteness and spirit reminds Christianity of the incarnational basis of its understanding of the Spirit of God. This was referred to in chapter 2 as Christian theology's "christological concentration." This does not mean that Christianity focuses only on the figure of Jesus of Nazareth. Rather, it channels its understanding of God through the life, practice, death and resurrection of Jesus of Nazareth, in working out within concrete human history what is consistent and continuous with that life. Any understanding of spirit which seeks to side step messy materiality is simply not Christian. Christian theology is not a materialist ideology in the sense that it believes all its ideas to be reducible to, or determined by, sociopolitical, economic or biological factors. But as "the most materialist of religions" it will entertain no understanding of spirit which fails to interpret the ordinary experience of human beings. The Spirit of God does not lift people out of their lives. It transforms their understanding and experience of it.

Second, *Shirley Valentine* reminds Christian theology that a pneumatology which fails to link experience and exploration of the Spirit in the life of the human individual with *human inter-relationship* will be inadequate. The Spirit is God who enables people to relate to each other, and to relate well, in a way that they prosper and flourish in their mutuality. *Shirley Valentine* is all about the breaking free from stifling relationships not necessarily to begin wholly new ones, but with the intent of transforming existing relationships. The role of the Spirit in *Shirley Valentine* can be seen within Shirley Valentine herself. But it is inaccurate for Christian theology to interpret her experience as an inner experience alone. Nor would it be accurate to locate the work of the Spirit in her as an individual as temporally prior. The Spirit is at work in the life of Shirley Valentine before, during and beyond her mid-life crisis; and within her and between her and those close to her. Her "praying" is in part possible because she had already glimpsed the potential of authentic relationships, relationships she felt she had lost. There is thus a constant interplay between dependence and interdependence in her own experience of Spirit.

Finally, it is important to link the very exercise undertaken here – using a film to explore the Spirit – with the content of the theological theme being explored. The use of Shirley Valentine in this way reminds Christian theology that a Christian pneumatology cannot be any other than a *public pneumatology*. In other words: no Christian understanding of the Spirit of God is adequate which fails to see God's Spirit at work in human experience generally, in a way which enables God to speak to the Church from potentially unlikely sources. I choose my words carefully. I do not speak of "general human experience," as there may not be such a thing. Nor, as I have stated earlier, do I imply that Christian theology has nothing distinctive to offer in the context of explorations of human experience. Christian theology is needed to interpret in a specific way for humanity a particular reading of God's Spirit in action. Christian theology is thus the tense result of the multiple dialogs which occur inside and outside of the Church (see ch. 2 above). Where this public dimension is denied, then Christian theology has become ghettoized. In short, and with specific relation to the subject-matter of this chapter, where the Spirit of God is seen as the possession of the church alone, then the Church has lost the Spirit. The Church only gains its fleeting grasp of the Spirit when it both examines its own understanding past and present, and keeps its conversation alive with the wider world in all its variety and complexity. From that wider conversation, as well as from its reformulation of its own tradition, it learns more about the God whom it seeks to grasp, disclose and portray.

Shirley Valentine is no theologian. She may be felt to be, at best, someone of implicit, or perhaps residual, faith, hailing as she does from that most religious of cities, Liverpool. Be that as it may, the film about her is a rich resource for a contemporary understanding of God as Spirit.

15

Did You Say "Grace"?: Eating in Community in *Babette's Feast*

Clive Marsh

Contemporary Christian theology faces a challenge in the huge shopping malls built in, or outside, cities influenced by Westernized culture. Clusters of friends and family groups share a tray of burgers and drinks and plunge french fries into ketchup dips before a huge backdrop of multiple video screens. The shared meal is a snatched meal, caught quickly (at its worst: "customers are requested not to stay longer than 20 minutes at a table") between two stages of a shopping excursion, or prior to a visit to the multiplex, at which popcorn will be dispensed as if this were a secular eucharist.

> Concessions aren't reduced tickets for senior citizens and students. Concessions are popcorn, Coke, hot dogs, ice-cream. They're the heart of the multiplex business ... The concessions stand runs right round the gleaming central tower ... The tower is to the foyer what the altar is to a cathedral.
>
> *(Butler 1994, 18)*

Obvious theological responses suggest themselves. The analysis of sociologists delivers a stage on which the theologian can perform: theological and moral critique of consumerism and sermons against the distortion of religious ritual could readily slip from the tongue. Yet communal eating – even if rapid – is perhaps inevitably better than eating alone. And if burgers have become the only food which contemporary Western families (families structured in many kinds of different ways) or groups of friends – especially the young – find the opportunity to share together, then perhaps they even become our spiritual food. Nevertheless, Christian theology might still want to say something about the speed and the meaning (or missed meaning) of the meal.

There have been a number of recent films about food. *Tampopo* (Juzo Itami, 1986), *The Cook, The Thief, His Wife and Her Lover* (Peter Greenaway, 1989), *Like Water For Chocolate* (Alfonso Arau, 1992), and *Eat Drink Man Woman*

(Ang Lee, 1994) are four of the most prominent to have been shown widely to critical acclaim in the West over the last decade. All films link the theme of food in some way with sex, death, power or spirituality. A fifth, *Babette's Feast* (Gabriel Axel, 1987) has similar preoccupations, though the religious element is more evident throughout than in many food films. This film will become for us a discussion partner in the exploration of the spiritual significance of the communal sharing of food in the contemporary West.

We begin with a short summary of the film's content. Key aspects of the film which invite the ensuing discussion will then be drawn out. An exposition of Christian understandings of the term "sacrament" and "Holy Communion" (viz. Mass, Eucharist, Lord's Supper, Breaking of Bread) then follow, built upon by a comparison between the interpretation of the film's presentation of the "Feast" and the meaning and significance of the communion meal in Christian practice and thought. A reconsideration of contemporary practices of communal eating in the West concludes the chapter. The interaction between the film's subject-matter and Christianity's central symbolic meal thus enables the eating habits of contemporary Westerners to be examined from a "sacramental perspective." This chapter therefore addresses such questions as: how do we eat today? who do we eat with? what significance do we attach to eating? what do our eating habits tell us about what we think and believe? what is a sacrament? what sense is to be made, if any, of the notion of "sacramental eating"?

Babette's Feast is based on a short story by Isak Dinesen (Karen Blixen) first published in 1950, though not appearing in book form until 1958 (Thurman 1984, 366–7; Dinesen 1986). Gabriel Axel's 1987 film version is a close rendering of the text of the story. It took Axel fourteen years to fulfil his ambition to film the story (Forbes 1988: 106). But the result is something of a minor masterpiece, even "occasionally surpassing its source ... [i]n its succinct visualisation" (Combs 1988: 75). *Babette's Feast* won the Oscar for best foreign-language film for 1987 and was widely well-reviewed (e.g. Combs 1988; Pulleine 1988).

The film tells in an unassuming and humorous way the story of a Parisian chef who flees the events in 1870s Paris during the Franco-Prussian War of 1870–1 and ends up in Denmark (Norway in the original story) begging for help from two elderly sisters who run a small, sectarian, ascetic religious community there. The chef, Babette, stays with them many years, falling in with their ascetic practices, relearning her own trade in a much more frugal form so as not to offend, and gradually becoming accepted by the small community. By chance, she wins a large amount of money through her only link with her Parisian past – a lottery ticket still in her possession – and she offers to cook a meal for the community with her winnings. After initial reluctance, the sisters permit Babette to provide the meal, wholly unaware that she will in fact expend all of her winnings on the lavish spread. The meal is initially an embarrassment to the sisters and a cause of guilt on the community's part. But the impact of the meal is such that the community rediscovers both a sense of joy and its lost communal dimension.

The focus of the story and the film, which provides the works with their common title, is the feast itself. In the film version, this is a 20-minute sequence near the end of the 100-minute film in which the unfolding of the meal's impact is treated in beautiful cinematic detail. Much of the sequence depends less on dialog than on close attention to facial expression, eye-movement, and gesture. The film records the shift from the community's initial resolve to think nothing of the food, and to avoid talking about it, through their unavoidable enjoyment of food, drink and general conviviality, to a new found enjoyment of each other, via a process of healing and reconciliation of the wounds of scarred relationships between them. Only the surprise guest – the outsider – General Loewenhielm, who happens to be staying with his aunt when the meal takes place, is not privy to the pact of "not mentioning the food." He is there to enjoy it, appreciates its quality, understands its significance and can both interpret it for the community and express the liberation that he, too, has found through being temporarily part of the community's life.

Theological interpretation of the film could begin at a number of points. I have written up elsewhere the results of using the film in an extended (two-day) exercize in the context of theological education (Marsh 1993). Within that experiment, in addition to the stimulus provided by the film for reflection on the meaning of communion, many other topics were taken up: faith and the arts, leadership in the church, the question of how churches grow, and the church in wider society. The extent to which Babette may be considered a "Christ-figure," relevant to our own enquiry here but not a theme which can be developed in any detail, also invites consideration. For the purpose of our immediate study I must simply focus on features of the film which contribute to a dialog about the meaning of communion. Four features present themselves, most of which derive directly from the film's portrayal of the meal itself, and which invite comparison with aspects of Christian celebration of communion.

First, it is striking that there are elements of both confession and absolution present during the meal. Mirroring part of the necessary process of preparation for the receipt of communion bread and wine in Christian liturgies, one brother owns up to having cheated another in the past (see e.g. *Lutheran Book of Worship* 1978: 56, 77, 98; ASB 1980: 120–1 or 126–7, 186–7; URC 1989: 6–7 and 24–5). This, in turn, draws out honesty in the other brother. Forgiveness and reconciliation result from the exchange. It is a development of the Dinesen story, yet Axel has wholly appropriately caught the intention of the text.

Second, word and sacrament are found together, mutually complementing
each other. The meal comprises not merely bread and wine (yet, as will
become clear, it can be considered "sacramental" nevertheless). The General,
however, provides both an interpretative commentary upon the meal as well
as a sermon. The words he speaks alongside each course have a similar
function to a communion liturgy. His declarations to the gathered community
of the identity of the food and drink placed before them (Amontillado . . .
genuine turtle soup . . . Blinis Demidoff . . . Veuve Cliquot 1860) attempt to
open the eyes of the community to what they are actually eating and drinking.
His speech takes on the role of an accompanying sermon, which incorporates
experience of his own, reflected upon in the light of his contact with the
community itself, and issuing in a clarification of what he has discovered both
about himself, but also about life more generally. In this way, the General's
role is similar to that of a priest: interpreting the symbolic elements and
relating life-experience to them for the community's benefit. As a result, the
food is not eaten "unworthily." The concern which the Apostle Paul had
expressed about some celebrations of the communion meal in the early
Christian community in Corinth (I Cor. 11:27), as a consequence of which the
need to harness appropriate interpretation with symbolic eating was seen to be
necessary in the Christian liturgical tradition, does not apply here. The people
are enabled to understand, even if in quite a different way from a communion
meal as such, the significance of what they eat.

Third, much attention is given to the responsibility of the community to
summon up a collective memory of their founder. This feature forges a
complex link with the Christian practice of communion. Communion, of
course, rests on a collective memory of Jesus Christ's life, death and
resurrection, Christianity's unintentional "founder." Most Christian denomi-
nations do, however, have secondary founders (e.g the Lutherans have Luther,
the Methodists have Wesley, the Salvation Army has William Booth). Rather
than note their recollections as being directly about their immediate founder,
who himself was a follower of Jesus Christ, we should observe that they
function as a community narrative. The community members are telling their
own faith story in recollecting their founder and their own dealings with him
(Hopewell 1988).

Babette and the General never meet. Yet it is the General who is Babette's
representative nevertheless. He alone is able to draw upon an appropriate
memory in a way which interprets the food enjoyed at the meal for the
community. He is physically present for them. Babette remains hidden. She is
the provider of the meal: the one who has expended all her wealth (all she
has), and the one who creates the meal. As viewers, we are privy to the
industry behind the scenes, and witnesses to her exhaustion and satisfaction at
the end of the meal: she has given of herself as well as her wealth. She has

been able to be who and what she is: an artist. We are invited by the film, then, to explore – fourth – the scale of Babette's self-sacrificial act, which she has nevertheless undertaken in one sense *for herself*.

What, then, is the value of bringing such features of the film alongside Christian theological understanding of communion as a sacramental meal? First we must explore further the term "sacrament" itself. Then we must enter more fully into the meaning of communion.

Avery Dulles defines a sacrament in the following way:

> A sacrament is, in the first place, a sign of grace. A sign could be a mere pointer to something that is absent, but a sacrament is a "full sign," a sign of something really present ... Beyond this, a sacrament is an efficacious sign; the sign itself produces or intensifies that of which it is a sign ... the sacraments contain the grace they signify, and confer the grace they contain.
>
> *(Dulles 1976: 61)*

Strictly referring to two practices in Protestant traditions (baptism and eucharist), and seven in Catholic and Orthodox traditions (baptism, eucharist, confirmation or chrismation, anointing, penance, holy orders and marriage), a sacrament is an act or event in which the particular action of God is held to be guaranteed. God *is* really present; God's grace really is imparted in sacramental acts. This is not to deny that the grace of God may come to people in other ways or at other times (in a sacrament-like kind of way). But sacraments are focal points of God's presence and gracious action. They are, then, not just signs, or even just symbols. They mediate that to which they refer (namely, the grace of God).

A celebration of communion, then, in the Christian tradition, is a place where the presence of God and the availability of the grace of God are *guaranteed*. This guaranteed availability is not due to any particular standing of any minister or priest. It is not due to any particular procedure or the result of any appropriate following of set ritual. Christian churches/denominations differ widely in their communion practices, and this is evidenced in different understandings of the importance of procedure and appropriate personnel. But in no Christian tradition is the availability of the grace of God *dependent* upon human practice.

In Christian tradition, then, a celebration of communion is a symbolic shared meal which enables people to participate in the presence of a loving, gracious God. The symbolic elements of bread and wine define precisely what kind of God Christians believe God to be. The bread and wine relate to the self-giving of God as evidenced in the self-giving of Jesus of Nazareth, whom Christians call Christ. The bread and wine relate to the body and blood of

Jesus the Christ, the expenditure of whose life Christians claim to be an action in which God's own self was somehow being given. Communion recalls that past event, but also celebrates the present of a God who continues to operate in a Christ-like way. Participation in communion in the present, then, signals a preparednes's on the part of Christians to participate in the action of such a self-giving God.

In Christian understanding, however, the death of Jesus is regarded as a "sacrifice to end all sacrifices." This was a feature of the understanding of the death of Jesus found in the New Testament Letter to the Hebrews (see for example Heb. 7:27, 9:14, 9:25f, 10:10–18). Christian faith and thought was modifying sacrificial practice within the Jewish tradition from which Christianity emerged. But without attention to Judaism (and not only as a "past" religion) Christianity will not rightly be understood. It is therefore necessary at the very least to understand something of Jewish sacrificial tradition in order to read communion aright.

Joseph Martos identifies three types of sacrificial offerings over against which communion should be compared: gift offerings, shared offerings and sin offerings. Gift offerings "acknowledged dependence on a transcendent reality for the things (people) possessed and enjoyed" (Martos 1981: 235–6). Shared offerings noted the need for union with a transcendent reality for right living (Martos 1981: 236), whilst sin offerings acknowledged "past disregard of the transcendent reality" and "disobedience of the transcendent order" (ibid.). Martos notes the regulations for such practices in the Hebrew Bible, in Deuteronomy 26, Leviticus 3 and 16, and Exodus 24. Martos's summary is helpful, especially in so far as it simplifies a complex set of data about diverse practice (see, for example Rattray 1985 for one of many further ways of reading the material). We cannot enter here into the many questions often associated with the link between sacrificial practice and the Christian practice of holy communion (is the very notion of a need for sacrifice inappropriate when thinking of a loving God? what are we to make of the notion that God provided the sacrifice? does the continued practice of communion suggest a need for further sacrifice, despite some Christian protestations to the contrary?). We must, however, note the link and make use of it in our interpretation, for it is crucial in assisting our reading of *Babette's Feast*.

In Christian readings of the communion, the self-offering of Jesus the Christ is seen first and foremost as a sin offering. On a Christian reading, of course, Jesus' death thus understood in no way suggests that he was offering his life in death as a sin offering for his own sin. In early Christian readings, his death was quickly interpreted as a death on others' behalf, Jesus Christ receiving the penalty due to others for their sin (see, for example Rom. 3:23–6, 5:6–9). Whatever may be the appropriateness of such a reading (from historical, theological or moral points of view), the important legacy for our own purpose is that the communion meal becomes a corporate context for the identification of wrongdoing and for the giving and receiving of forgiveness.

A communion celebration is, however, also identifiable in terms of a gift offering and a shared offering. For as long as bread has been broken and eaten and wine poured and shared amongst Christian groups, thanksgiving has been offered for the work of God as undertaken in Jesus Christ. Furthermore, lest it become a thanksgiving offering too related to a past event, the sense of the continued presence of a living God – the need for union stressed by a shared offering – has been a feature of communion practice. Though heavily spiritualizing the sacrificial tradition, Christianity nevertheless appropriated the religious elements contained in sacrificial practice within its own worship. It is in its central symbolic meal, the communion, where so many of those features are to be found in Christian ritual.

Most dimensions of the sacrificial tradition attend, of course, to the vertical axis: the relationship between the human and the divine. Sacrifice in the context of worship could, however, never be a vertical affair only. Horizontal relations are always also in view. Public worship can never be merely private practice: a matter between the believer and his/her god. Shared offerings highlight this feature of worship directly. The two dimensions are also neatly preserved in the ambiguity of the word "communion" itself. Communion is always and at once communion with God and communion between partici-pants. The two dimensions cannot be separated. With all this in mind, it is appropriate to turn back to the film.

Babette's feast is an ordinary, but special, thanksgiving meal. There could be no better way of describing the appropriateness of an interpretation of the meal in eucharistic terms. "Eucharist," one of the five possible names for communion, means "thanksgiving." If many Protestants would later resist a sacrificial reading of the communion (lest the communion be seen as an unnecessary, and thus blasphemously impossible, re-sacrifice of Christ), nevertheless the practice of offering a sacrifice of praise and thanksgiving would be supported. A celebration of communion is a eucharist: a thanksgiving for the work of God in Christ. If such thankful joy is absent from communion, then an entire dimension has been lost. Babette's meal is a thank-offering: for her life, her very survival, her art, her being welcomed. It is not clear that she is giving thanks to God. But there is an inner need to give thanks, as strong an urge as her need to be artistic with food. Babette's feast is thus clearly comprehensible in terms of a gift-offering. The theological twist which is introduced by Dinesen into the task of interpreting the meal is that it is the French ("*Papiste?*") outsider, of unclear theological persuasion, who seems more evidently to show gratitude for "the things (people) possessed and enjoyed" than the religious community whose theology should more logically lead to their expressing such gratitude.

What, though, are we to make of that most powerful of understandings of sacrifice in relation to the communion meal – the sin-offering – in bringing it alongside Babette's feast? Clearly it would be quite wrong to seek for too neat allegorical allusions in either text or film. *Cailles en sarcophage*, the serving of which conclusively reveals to the General the identity of the chef of the meal, may well symbolize the close link between food and death (Hill 1992: 148). Perhaps to seek a link with an Exodus motif – though inviting – would be to go too far (Exod. 16:13). But the notion of Babette giving of herself in a manner which liberates the community she serves at least suggests at a general level a reading of the meal as sacrificial, and eucharistic, even in this third sense. It is the community's sin – their estrangement from each other, their gradual disintegration, their loss of relationship, their loss of common purpose – which renders their members in need of fresh salvation. It is not clear whether it was Babette's intent to provide this. We do know that Babette cooked the meal *for her*. She was who she was and could do no other. It was her free choice to expend all she had on the meal. She was benefitting. The community benefitted too.

The parallels with the understanding of Jesus Christ in relation to the Christian community, and in Christian celebration of communion, are obvious, even if they are not a perfect match. Jesus is understood to have given his own life for the salvation of the world. The church represents the community of those who have recognized and participate in this salvation. Jesus' self-giving was not just a task he had to do. He gave his whole self. He did this, in Christian understanding, because of who he was: God's ultimate messenger (Messiah), representing directly, in some sense, God's own self. The communion is thus the meal of those who continually reappropriate that act of God's self-giving in Jesus Christ. Christians thus do not just speak of a past event. They celebrate a living presence. But they celebrate that living presence always mindful of sin and its consequences in and beyond their own community. They do, however, celebrate with joy and thankfulness and seek to work hard at good relations with other Christians and with all. That at least, is how a communion can be understood if all three understandings of sacrifice are taken together.

Babette, of course, does not give up her life. In some ways she has already given up one life, the life she left in France. But in terms of the story of *Babette's Feast*, her very existence apart, she does give all she has. Unlike the emphasis upon Babette the artist, Christian tradition has been reluctant to focus upon what Jesus the Christ undertakes *for himself*. Yet at least in modern tradition, which since the so-called "Quest of the Historical Jesus" has stressed much more the humanity of Jesus Christ, there has been attention to the human will of Jesus. If Jesus did not do what he did for himself, it has been suggested, then his activity for others is less comprehensible and authentic (see, for example Ritschl 1902, 474–7). Despite these words of defense, it would, however, be wrong to suggest that the parallel is neat at all points.

On the basis of identifying the meal as a kind of sin–offering, however, it can also be interpreted as a shared offering. The community has need to rediscover right living and is enabled to through the meal. The members "know" that they are dependent upon God, but they are not living according to their theological knowledge. They are not living in the light of the gracious activity of the God they believe in. The self-giving of Babette, as itself an act of thanksgiving, liberates the community from its self-preoccupation, and reminds them of the one who forgives beyond measure, and on whom they depend for all their own right living.

The meal thus contains all the ingredients of a communion meal in Christian understanding. The meal can be understood in the light of the Jewish sacrificial tradition, Christ can be seen to be represented by Babette, the priest by the General, and the consequences of participation are evident in the members of the community who partake of the meal. But so what? What is the value of working through such an extended analogy? Those suspicious of too heavy a theological reading of the film, or the meal, may quickly wish to say: "but it's still just a meal, even if it is quite a special one, with a pleasing effect upon those who enjoy it." Indeed it is, and Gabriel Axel himself begs for caution: "It's a fairy tale, and if you try to over-explain it, you destroy it . . . The moment you start to dissect the film it becomes symbolic, and I resist that" (Forbes 1988: 106).

These words are, however, those of an artist wishing the artistic product to stand in its own right, in its irreducibility. Axel cannot deny to others the right (and the need) to interpret his art. And indeed, Axel himself offers crucial insights of his own: "it's Babette's meal and her art which liberates their minds and gives them all the strength to be themselves . . . Karen Blixen says that spirituality and sensuality go together" (ibid. 107).

We may be justified, though, in considering not just the spirituality of food, but also the full ramifications of their *corporate* eating in the context of the religious community's own life and their sense of their own narrative history. It is along this track, I suggest, that a most fruitful interpretation of *Babette's Feast* as a form of communion can be found, one which, in turn, leads to a demand to reconsider not only Christian communion practice, but also contemporary communal eating habits.

Communion is a sacrament and thus a "means of grace." It is a holy act because the presence and action of God is acknowledged within it. But it loses its ordinariness at great cost. The ambiguity of the "Last Supper" in the life of Jesus, from which Christian faith and practice derives its understanding and elements of its ritual, requires attention to such ordinariness. Jesus' last meal with his disciples before his arrest, trial and crucifixion was probably a Jewish Passover meal (see the Gospels of Matthew 26:17–35, Mark 14:12–31 and Luke 22:7–38). It had symbolic meaning within Jewish tradition but was given – either by Jesus or, soon after, by his immediate followers – a fresh symbolic meaning. But it remained a "real meal." So much Christian practice in past and present overlooks this. The "ordinariness" of the meal has been reflected in Christian tradition less through the scale and context of the eating than in its regularity. Those who have participated in communion often have respected its lingering mystery, but stressed their need for regular receipt of symbolic bread and wine (or just bread). It is to be taken in like water and air. It is that essential. Those Christians who have participated less frequently (sometimes as infrequently as once a quarter or once a year) have done so through a keen sense of their own unworthiness and their need to prepare for receiving. A profound irony lies in the fact that in recent times in the West, communicants of a more catholic persuasion (who possess a stronger sense of the sacrament's mysterious depth) have received more regularly; whilst those standing in some branch or other of the protesting tradition (where the sacrament has sometimes become no more than a mere sign) have received communion less. One wonders which tradition has maintained communion's "ordinariness" the more.

The relative loss of the meal's original ordinariness in Christian tradition does, however, beg questions about how the communion's horizontal dimension has been maintained in Christian practice. Above all it has been spiritualized. The communal dimension is preserved in the emphasis attached to the communion as the family meal of the "Body of Christ," the Church. The church meets for its family meal, knowing that its members are spiritually bound together by the Spirit of God. But such relations, being preeminently spiritual, need not necessarily be good human relations, of course. Christian traditions (Methodism?) or particular Christian churches (in the evangelical tradition? in close-knit communities? in small churches?) which have specifically worked at, and sometimes succeeded, in fostering good human relations amongst members have often, in practice, *displaced* their attention to "fellowship" (good human interrelationship) away from their celebration of communion into other departments of church life: house groups, cell groups, social events. One might have expected a central, symbolic meal not merely to symbolize the unity (despite difference) of the members of a Christian community, but actually to encourage it. In this sense, the decline of the significance of the communal meal in *Babette's Feast*, prior to Babette's self-sacrificial meal, is all the more striking. Something needed to happen to reintroduce fuller human interrelationship into the context of the meal itself for communal and individual well-being to be restored. In sacrificial terms, the full scope of the meal as a shared offering was being insufficiently explored.

Babette's feast remained a "real meal," however, even though it was clearly a special one. It transformed the life of the community not through itself being transformed into a symbol, but remaining an authentic meal with a symbolic function. It functioned sacramentally by turning the routine into a channel of grace without ceasing to be an occasion when the religious community were actually fed and watered.

These observations suggest ways in which contemporary Christian thought and practice may be open to challenge: the communion has lost a sense of the ordinariness of the original meal, or has frequently displaced the human interrelationships which feature as part of a "real meal." More space would be needed to develop these points further. But we must not, in any case, press the precise identification of *Babette's Feast* as a communion meal too far. Neither Dinesen nor Axel explicitly presents the meal as a communion celebration. Our enquiry has simply noted the striking nature of the possible links and pursued them as far as they will go. However, we need only recognize a sacramental element to the meal for the parallel to be persuasive and instructive. After all, not all Christians recognize a need for sacraments (the Salvation Army and the Society of Friends see no need for them). For some Christians, the whole world is sacramental. This cannot mean that all that is, or all that happens, is equally able to make available the grace of God. But it does mean that no firm rules can be laid down about how and where the grace of God may be disclosed. For Christians who stand in a tradition which celebrates sacraments (two or seven), the sacraments thus become focal points which guide understanding of who God is, and the way in which God can be said to speak and act, and what kind of presence and action can be expected through the whole of life.

Emerging from the specific linking of features of Babette's feast with Christian thought about and practice of communion, though, we are left at least with the possibility of identifying a sacramental quality to human meals. If sacraments take up ordinary elements and see how their use may enable divine reality to become evident in the midst of ordinary human life, then both the story and the film press for consideration of the community's missed meaning in their usual shared eating habits. Perhaps they had become too frugal for their own good. They were not enjoying the fruits of the created order at all, and needed to be shocked into appreciating its richness. They would not be able to continue eating in the style to which Babette had introduced them (if only on economic grounds!). But through their special meal they had more than glimpsed something new and fresh which would affect their future gatherings. Similarly, participation in human life with a sacramental awareness does not mean actually seeing God in all things. Human beings cannot, after all, bear that much (divine) reality. But the community would no doubt meet rather differently when it met again to eat. Their bread and fish meals – their constant recreations of the meals of the original Jesus community (Crossan 1994, 170–81) – would take on a new quality.

If the film creates a challenge to Christian thinking about its own central symbolic (and sacramental) meal, and invites a broader consideration of the meaning of sacrament, then the conversation it invites Christian theology to conduct with it also issues in a challenge to the hasty, public (or private/ privatized) eating habits of individualized Westerners. Perhaps eating is more sacred an activity than much of our contemporary habits suggest. We eat to live, and not *vice versa*. But the question of what we live *for* remains to be asked. The practice of eating raises so many profound issues: whether to eat animals, how much to eat, how lavishly to eat, how much to spend on food, whether to eat alone, who to eat with, how much time to spend on such a seemingly functional activity. *Babette's Feast* sharpens our engagement with such questions. And in its quiet, quaint, modest way it urges us to think about what we eat, where our food is from, who has prepared it, who we share it with (and why). And it confronts us with the possibility that the sharing of food in company, when time and care is devoted to the task of preparing and eating it, is a prime moment of divine disclosure in the contemporary world which one can only call "sacramental." At a time when so many cultural analysts speak of fragmented Western culture, when Western churches may too easily have bought into an over-individualized culture, and "sacrament" is hardly an everyday word, *Babette's Feast* provides a powerful challenge to a lack of corporate grace at the meal table. This is no "dinner party theology," for dinner parties are often places of gross avoidance of the issues between people which Babette's feast sacramentally disclosed and dealt with. But it is a proposal for greater openness to the possibility of the word of "grace" being spoken wherever two or three are gathered together to share food. *Babette's Feast* is, in my view, misunderstood even in its own textual and filmic terms when not interpreted in the light of the Christian sacramental tradition. The community enjoys a good meal. But it is not "just a meal." In its special ordinariness, so much more occurs. This is to be celebrated. It is also worth grasping not for the sake of analysis alone, but for the purpose of narration and repetition. Dinesen and Axel might well feel, to adopt a colloquialism, that we are making a meal of their story here. We are on the point, perhaps, of making more of the tale than either ever meant us to. But people have always said that about the Last Supper.

5 Phil Connors (Bill Murray) "sows to the flesh" in being stuck in time in *Groundhog Day*. (Columbia/Tri-Star; photograph courtesy of the Kobal Collection).

6 Noble fostering of the romantic spirit, or irresponsible pedagogy?: the moral dilemma created by Mr Keating (Robin Williams) in *Dead Poets Society*. (Touchstone Pictures; photograph courtesy of the Kobal Collection.)

7 The food gets to work on the unsuspecting guests, who resolve not even to mention it, in *Babette's Feast*. (Betzer-Panorama/Danish Film Institute; photograph courtesy of the Kobal Collection.)

8 George Bailey (James Stewart) and Mary Hatch (Donna Reed) enjoy the "feelgood factor" and live an abundant life in *It's a Wonderful Life*. (RKO; photograph courtesy of the Kobal Collection.)

16

Optimism, Hope, and Feelgood Movies: The Capra Connection

Stephen Brown

Daring to put in a good word for optimism, hope, and feelgood movies can, these days, feel like doing a stand-up routine at a funeral directors' convention. In the aftermath of two World Wars, the Jewish Holocaust, the development of nuclear weapons and mass starvation one can understand why optimism may have had a thin time of it. There is now a significant number of people so outraged at the seemingly unremitting pain of the universe for whom the idea of optimism is not only inappropriate but a shockingly insensitive response. The cinema has been a mass media barometer and chronicler of this century's most desperate hours. From at least as early as 1916 (an episode in D. W. Griffiths's *Intolerance*) films have remoulded our imaginations, addressing the epic issues and leading us into the grime that the world puts us through. But there have also been directors who have lifted our eyes to the stars. And when that happens one thing is certain. Whilst this genre is not his monopoly, sooner or later a connection is made with Frank Capra. Born in 1897, Capra's career began in the silent era and, following the advent of sound, enjoyed a string of successes before and after World War II. He continued making films, though less frequently, up to the 1960s. Capra died in 1991.

His output has become synonymous with feelgood movies, not least for the whimsical comedy present in many of them. Rather than offering theoretical *a priori* speculation about the meaning of life, human experience is the starting point from which Capra seeks to explore existence. Also, his work abounds in optimism. This is chiefly the result of his championship of ordinary people in their efforts to triumph over powerful forces. Capra's hope is more related to a sense of God as the ultimate in our lives, giving us a view of "The End" to which we are beckoned.

It is my perception that elements like feeling good, optimism, and hope have some correspondence to theological terms such as glory, the Kingdom of God, and eschatology. There is inevitably some overlap from one term to another. Of the three, glory is probably the word in most general use. Yet it is difficult to define. The arts help us experience what we cannot adequately put into words. Glory tells "of the majesty and self-giving of God and of man's response to God in adoration and in fellowship, in worship and in life" (Ramsey 1983: 176). In the course of sharing in that glory we ourselves move towards being glorified. Capra's view is not unlike that of the Letter to the Romans (8:19–25): we will feel good about life as we come to realize that the creation longs for the time when the glory of God shall be revealed to us. The Kingdom of God is a term often treated within the broader subject of eschatology (c.f Macquarrie 1970, Richardson and Bowden 1983). But this is not always so. Barth, for example, distinguishes the two. It is useful for our purposes to give separate consideration to the Kingdom of God. This is because of its connotations of being already here (Mt. 12:28 etc.) or imminent (Mt. 3:2) or within us (Lk. 17:21) as well as a state of being that is at the end of and beyond time. In this context God's reign, even if hidden, has begun. Capra's optimism depicts a world ultimately under the reign of a good God, though by the time of *It's A Wonderful Life* (1946) that is a heavily qualified scenario.

Not to have heard the word "eschatology" before is not the end of the world. It may well be the least accessible of the three theological terms in use here. Eschatology relates to the so-called "Last Things" – death, judgment, heaven and hell. Since the word's first appearance in 1844 it has come to deal with rather more than the hereafter. It is an examination of the effect of the End – our end and purpose – on all that happens now. This perspective of a creator who is also our destiny, leading us on to new worlds and new ways of being, resonates with Capra who finds such hope when his characters at last begin to see and hence rejoice in their true status. What seems like despair in (*Meet John Doe* (1941) and *Mr Smith Goes to Washington* (1939), for example) is but the prelude to hope. Of all Capra's films *It's A Wonderful Life* best combines a sense of feeling good with an understanding of glory; an optimism that has the Kingdom of God clearly in its sights; and a hope based on a Christian eschatology. *It's A Wonderful Life*, generally regarded as Capra's masterpiece, spawned a host of films with allied themes. The following year *The Bishop's Wife* (Henry Koster, 1947) starred Cary Grant as a roller-skating angel. The first version of *Miracle on 34th Street* (also made in 1947 by George Seaton) tried to cash in on Capra's whimsy and fantasy. At regular intervals since then there have been films made with reference to *It's A Wonderful Life*.

Feelgood Movies and the Glory of God

To those pained by films that dare to send us away happy, Frank Capra seems to be asking what is so bad about feeling good. Forty years after making *It's A*

Wonderful Life Capra quoted Fra Giovanni with approval: "The gloom of the world is but a shadow. Behind it, yet within reach, is joy. There is a radiance and glory in the darkness, could we but see, and to see we have only to look. I beseech you to look!" (Basinger 1986: ix). It was the magic of all existence that Capra wanted to capture on the screen. He clearly believed in a graced nature, one that is within reach. Natural theology makes the assumption that some knowledge of God is self-apparent. It can be "read off" from the world through its beauty and extraordinariness. It does not have to be revealed to us. It is there for any reasoning person to infer. Critics of natural theology say that in a century of great horrors we cannot, on the evidence of our own eyes, see the presence of God's loving activity. It has to be made known to us. The great films have been one of the means whereby people have been led beyond the surface appearance of things. Capra's natural theology is qualified. George Bailey (who is "not a praying man") is without any absolute knowledge of his place in the universe. He is dutiful but resentful and hopeless. He needs the aid of revelation (Clarence and all his works) to respond in praise. George mainly fails to see that he has a wonderful life, bank debt and all. He cannot discern on his own the goodness of God. It requires the sending of an angel to make clear to him that "the universe is unfolding as it should. Therefore be at peace with God" (Walker 1975: 3).

One of this century's great theological exponents of God's glory has been Hans Urs von Balthasar (1905–88), a Swiss Roman Catholic. Drawing heavily on the early Church Fathers, he espoused an approach which believes that there is nowhere lacking in God's grace. Our task is to look for beauty because the natural tendency of God's being is to take form, to become incarnate, to display splendor. Clarence is sent to invite us to *see* by looking properly at our world and feeling good about it.

Less than two years after *It's A Wonderful Life* was premiered the anonymous poem *Desiderata* was published. Parts of it are now as often to be found on a poster or an advert as in a book. Both the poem and *It's A Wonderful Life* reflect those aspects of the American Dream to do with the feeling that you can go out and find happiness. *Desiderata* enjoins its readers to

> Go placidly amid the noise and haste . . . for the world is full of trickery. But let this not blind you to what virtue there is; many persons strive for high ideals, and everywhere life is full of heroism . . . Neither be cynical about love; for in the face of aridity and disenchantment, it is as perennial as the grass . . . You are a child of the universe no less than the trees and the stars; you have a right to be here . . . With all its sham, drudgery and broken dreams, it is still a beautiful world.
>
> *(Walker 1975: 2–3)*

Desiderata and Capra's film are twin aspects of an outlook that expects to discover and thank God "for everything that is natural, which is infinite, which is Yes" (cummings 1989: 76). *It's A Wonderful Life* opens with snow descending beautifully over Bedford Falls. On the soundtrack intercessions are being offered for George. The camera pans upward to the heavens and in the infinity of space the stars look gently down. Capra depicts it as a benign but not indifferent universe. (The existentialist author, Albert Camus, once described it as being both.) In *It's A Wonderful Life* the heavens are not only telling the *glory* of God, they also speak of the *love* of God. Clarence is heaven's response to George's plight.

Desiderata and *It's A Wonderful Life* both hold a renewed sense of the faith of the Pilgrim Fathers. America, or in this case post-war America, is a New World in which to delight. There is a fresh start to be made and the hardship of former times is not to blind us to this possibility. It was a spirituality that succored its younger generation, among whom would be the parents of Steven Spielberg. *Close Encounters of the Third Kind* (1977, Special Edition 1980) is one of the most beautiful films ever made. Steven Spielberg wanted the scene when the spaceships land to be a "cathedral of light." Fra Giovanni's words find resonance here too. Most people in *Close Encounters of the Third Kind* fail to see that the world is charged with a grandeur other than of a human kind. It takes a special kind of person to discern this. The little boy, Gary, does. So do Roy (Richard Dreyfuss) and others who are drawn to Devil's Tower, Wyoming where the aliens communicate through light and music and gesture something of the glory of the creation. Steven Spielberg's creatures (to reach their apotheosis in *E.T.: the Extra-Terrestrial,* 1982) are not hostile but reflect a world that is very good. In *It's A Wonderful Life* George takes some time to reach a similar conclusion. This slow dawning of the spiritual truth is a perennial theme of movies. In *Groundhog Day* (1993) a world-weary weather forecaster Phil Connors (Bill Murray) first exploits the world into which he has been allowed to enter. Bill Murray all but pulls off his Capra-esque awakening to the belief that life is wonderful. It starts snowing again when his redemption is completed in a declaration of love to the girl he adores. In *It's A Wonderful Life* the snow starts again once George really wants to live.

All these films imply that if we stay long enough and look hard enough we will see a radiance and glory in the darkness, could we but see, and to see we have only to look. The revelations of divine purpose that all these films offer their main characters are both a privilege and a responsibility. They all have an experience of ecstasy. Ecstasy (from the Greek: *ec-stasis*) is the movement of something from its proper place to another. Theologically it is God going forth from what (s)he is (divine) into what (s)he is not (human). In *It's A Wonderful Life* the divine is above the earth and visits it in emergency. A more orthodox Christian understanding is that the divine is with us (i.e. immanent) as well as transcendent. In the human being, ecstasy is a state of rapture where the soul, liberated from the body, contemplates divine things. George experiences a liberation from his earthly existence and is given a divine perspective. In his case it is to demonstrate how terrible life would be without him.

Optimism and the Kingdom of God

For those unable to suspend disbelief, a dangling thread of doubt about feelgood movies remains. If we can only feel good where angels, unidentified flying objects or time warps are involved it may be that we are getting by on "cheap grace" (Bonhoeffer 1948: 37). Feelgood differs from escapist fantasy. Hollywood often gets described as "The Dream Factory" even though many feelgood movies do not deal with elements of questionable existence such as UFOs and angels. That does not make them immune to the charge of being unrealistic for whilst what is presented is possible it is considered unlikely. Realism is philosophically a problematic notion but in general thought means that which has an objective existence. Postmodernism is just one of the more recent movements in a long line to question and qualify "realism" in some way. There is suspicion of meta-narratives which appeal to scientific rationalist conclusions or the absolutes of a religious faith. Culturally these have often been oppressive of individuals, failing to value the role of difference, particularity, creativity and interpretation that each person brings to bear on "truth." Film narrative almost invariably centers on particular individuals, rather than mass movements. Through the protagonists we learn of *their* truth but empathize with it and extrapolate a truth for ourselves. Theology would want to claim that one particular story – that of God in Christ – is open enough for all of us to find ourselves, each in our own way, within its magic and be reconciled to one another through it.

Realism and truth

Feelgood movies echo the cry of Blanche DuBois in *A Streetcar Named Desire*. "I don't want realism. I'll tell you what I want. Magic!" (Williams 1949: 100). This is not as escapist as it may sound. Jean Renoir, talking of American films after having just seen a musical, said there was no realism in them: "No realism, but something much better, great truth" (Truffaut 1982: 157). The great truth Renoir speaks of relates not just to how life is currently ordered. It is a recall to the fundamental issues of how we live and die. The makers of the 1990 smash hit *Pretty Woman* readily acknowledged its origins in "Cinderexpletive deleted-ella." That such a story has endured many centuries and has appeared in various cultural guises gives testimony to its potency. *Pretty Woman* manages to present to us an idea that has been depicted time after time. The great truth here is that "there is nothing love cannot face" (1 Cor. 13:7) even if one is a prostitute (Julia Roberts) and the other a millionaire (Richard Gere). Furthermore, good fortune comes to one who has been unfairly treated. But we already know the basic story-line. This partly explains why we feel so good. We are meant to be optimistic.

A working definition of optimism, even if not expressed in inclusive language, runs as follows: "a way of thinking and living which affirms on the one hand the capacity of man to improve himself and the whole human condition, and on the other hand, claims that ultimate reality, being under the control of good rather than evil, supports, if not guarantees this improvement" (Kegley 1967: 237). A high value is placed on human achievements and aspirations and on culture and civilized attitudes in the Christian tradition, stemming from an emphasis on human experience of God rather than theoretical speculation.

In Capra's films, this optimism about human achievement often takes on a communal shape. God-fearing small town communities looking out for one another are often contrasted with the cut and thrust of big city life. Bedford Falls is presented as a model of how a community could operate. It is an optimistic paradigm of the Kingdom of God, of how things could be. As such we can usefully entertain, interpret and criticize the model of community life in our attempts to discover the rule of God in our own lives. In *It's A Wonderful Life* the Martini family are Italian immigrants living in one of Potter's slums. The Martinis come to have a home of their own through the collective endeavors of the building and loan company. George Bailey is later rescued by a bevy of loving friends which seems to represent the whole community apart from Potter. Such films are in revolt against an understanding that this life has to be a vale of tears whereby souls are made for the next. All shall be well and all manner of things shall be well in *this* life.

A modified belief in social improvement

Capra's cause was often cited as "the common man." He told a research student "I didn't think he was common. I thought he was a hell of a guy. I thought he was the hope of the world" (Shindler 1973: 131). Capra was not one to heed Samuel Goldwyn's dictum that if you want to send a message use Western Union. In the legacy that Capra has left us there are several precursors of the *Pretty Woman* kind of fable. In *Lady for a Day* (1933) he had already put down a marker for the lowly and meek. It was to become a leitmotif of much of his subsequent work, including a 1961 remake called *Pocketful of Miracles*. In *Mr Deeds Goes To Town* (1936), *Mr Smith Goes to Washington* (1939) and *Meet John Doe* (1941) it is the power of one unintimidated person against corporate cynicism that ultimately which wins the day. More recent literature has debunked some of Capra's real-life commitment to the ordinary individual, but at least in his films it is an unmistakable strand. The belief of these films is that wrongs, if exposed, will be righted. The prospects of such total victory, however, become bleaker with the years.

Perhaps Capra's direct experience of World War II dented his optimism. A start was made on *It's A Wonderful Life* less than 12 months after the war ended. It could be said that Capra came face to face in those war years with the stubborn, perplexing and disheartening endurance of evil. Social change, by itself, would not bring about the Kingdom of God. Capra moved more towards one of America's leading theologians, Reinhold Niebuhr (1892–1971). Niebuhr was an early opponent of theologies and philosophies that took insufficient note of human imperfectibility (see for example Brown 1986; Rasmussen 1989). He argued that the flawed nature of human beings reduces the efficacy of all attempts at moral and social advance. Capra, in the 1930s, would have been out of sympathy with Niebuhr. Films such as *Mr Deeds Goes to Town* and *Mr Smith Goes to Washington* have extraordinary endings. The hard facts of structural sinfulness are skilfully depicted by Capra only to be jettisoned in the last reel by an unlikely upbeat ending. They neatly illustrate Niebuhr's case against the weakness of liberal notions. Liberal theology, Niebuhr felt, took insufficient heed of the corporate dimension of sinfulness. The vested interests of power bases – the subject of many Capra films – are unlikely to be transformed, this side of heaven, by "moral man in an immoral society" (the title of a 1932 book by Niebuhr). Institutions and nations are shaped by power rather than persons, even if those power bases do change to accommodate emerging ideologies. That is not to say we should give up trying to usher in the Kingdom. The cross and resurrection are God's affirmation that reconciliation and salvation are to be initiated here and now. Capra's answer had been that if enough moral people arose then they would form a power structure capable of converting immoral society. In *It's A Wonderful Life* such transformations have come to be viewed as tentative and temporary. The crowd demanding their money back when there is a run on the bank is illustrative of the immensity of the task. "We've got to stick together," implores George. Most of them do. People start getting decent houses. Potter's self-aggrandizement is often thwarted. The town rallies round the war effort. Much bravery is shown by those called up. Whatever may divide a community is counterbalanced for Capra by his discernment of common values that hold it together. Yet some things do not change and there are reversals of fortune

too. Potter is not defeated. George, on a dark reading of the text, fails to
discover his true self or actualize his potential or participate in shaping
structures. The majority of people remain tied to an ideology that represses
them. Potter is accurate in calling them "suckers." They have bought into a
slimmed-down version of the American Dream that affords them a limited
amount of freedom in return for doing jobs they may not much like and
receiving bills they can barely settle for commodities they questionably do not
need.

Frank Darabont directs *The Shawshank Redemption* (1995) with the same
kind of ardour that says the human spirit cannot, or need not, be quenched. It
is particularly reminiscent of early Capra. C. H. Dodd, an influential British
theologian, was arguing round about the same time that the Kingdom of God
was at least in part already here in power – "The Kingdom of God has come
close to you:" Luke 10:9 (Dodd 1936). Dodd's "realized eschatology" recalls
the early church's sense that whoever has accepted God's rule has "tasted the
powers of the age to come" (Heb. 6:5). The belief is that those who accept
this have been given the power to become children of God with its attendant
liberation from human convention. Dodd's case for a partially realized
Kingdom may have been overstated as the shadow of Nazi tyranny fell over
the world. Yet Dodd usefully reminds us that power to become children of
God (who begin living the life of the new age) is on offer to each succeeding
generation. In as much as people rise to its challenge, so is the Kingdom of
God realized on earth as it is in heaven. In *The Shawshank Redemption* Tim
Robbins plays such a subject of God's new kingdom. Andy Dufresne is a man
convicted of a murder. Over the years of imprisonment we see him hold on to
his integrity. George Bailey's prison may have no bars but he feels as trapped.
Andy becomes, like George, a pillar of his small community. Despite a corrupt
environment (prison officers on the make) he finds quiet ways of championing
the needs of fellow prisoners. It is a triumphant moment when after years of
steady progress he makes his escape. The "Redemption" of the title refers to
the change in others as well as himself. Even if the jailbreak had not succeeded,
the same could be said of Andy; as Clarence says in *It's A Wonderful Life:*
"Strange, isn't it? Each man's life touches so many other lives, and when he
isn't around he leaves an awful hole, doesn't he?" Andy literally leaves an
awful hole, the one by which he escapes. More than that, there is a sense of
loss felt by those left behind. His friend Red is near-suicidal when he himself
is finally paroled. Cut adrift from his fellow inmates and, at that point, unable
to trace Andy his life becomes one big hole. Redemption for Red occurs when
he is reunited with Andy. Because Andy has now informed the police of the
specific corruption of the prison staff there is a change of staff (and possibly
conditions) at Shawshank State Prison. Again we have a scenario of one
individual making the difference. A blow for the Kingdom of God has been

struck. By the time of *It's A Wonderful Life* this was for Capra the only way in which he believed structural improvement could occur: by every practical, individual step taken. George Bailey's father, earlier in the picture, says "I feel that in a small way we are doing something important. Satisfying a fundamental urge. It's deep in the race for a man to want his own roof and walls and fireplace, and we are helping him to get those things in our shabby little office."

Withdrawal and flight increasingly become the stock-in-trade of Capra heroes who once so courageously defeated opponents. George Bailey does not even leave his small town. The Kingdom theology implied is paradoxical in that it is both already here but has not yet arrived. Capra holds these notions in somewhat uneasy tension. God's reign holds sway over those who have so far acknowledged it. George by the end of *It's A Wonderful Life* has acknowledged it (the "already" element of the paradox). Potter has yet to learn to live within the Kingdom of God (the "not yet" element). It takes the language of poetry to express the paradoxical nature of the Kingdom:

> It's a long way off but inside it
> There are quite different things going on:
> Festivals at which the poor man
> Is king and the consumptive is
> Healed . . .
>
> *(Thomas 1983: 35)*

Reinhold Niebuhr saw all these small victories and fragile alliances as a first step towards the Kingdom of God. It is within such a faith system that Capra's optimism belongs. It can be criticized as revisionist. George has to adjust his attitudes to fit with the facts of his existence – and to be glad about it! To quote St John of the Cross: "I am not made or unmade by the world but by my attitude to it." That is to begin living the life of the Kingdom. That is Capra's ideological position. Viktor Frankl, a Nazi concentration camp survivor and psychotherapist, in attempting to explain how hope can inform the most nightmarish of situations quotes Nietzsche: he who has a *why* to live for can bear almost any *how*.

Hope and Eschatology

As a spiritual virtue hope differs from optimism and its belief that people will improve. Hope would not be destroyed if there were no human improvement. Nor are hope and feeling good always linked. Hope can at times be more than a passing feeling, one that "springs eternal in the human breast" (Pope 1965:

184). Many directors successfully maintain a credible hope amidst human suffering. Few can do it with as light a touch as Capra.

Theologically, hope is ultimately for future fulfillment in God. In Christian terms the resurrection is that contradiction of hopelessness. It is God's promise for a transformed future. Therefore a lived-out response to that promise is a sign of such hope. In film, as in all storytelling, the dramatic turning point often comes when such a future hope provides the hero with the necessary energy to face and conquer some adversity. It may be an act of faith: "Hope that is seen is not hope" (Rom. 8:24). Hope is therefore linked with what is known in theology as eschatology; the End of everything. Eschatology is the study of Last Things such as heaven, hell, death and judgement. George Bailey only really begins to know who he is in the great scheme of things when given a privileged, if painful, disclosure by a messenger from heaven.

Tillich: the search for lost identity

The theology of Paul Tillich is useful to our understanding of George Bailey. Drawing on existentialism and depth psychology, Tillich argued that human beings are separated from the "ground of being" (Tillich's term for God); from themselves; from others. Our estrangement leads to anxiety and sadness that we cannot see beyond this world. George Bailey's self-denial displays symptoms of this spiritual ambiguity. His selfhood feels diminished, not realized, by forgoing travel. The lighting and camera work are especially apt at displaying this sense of loneliness. George's shadowed, distorted face moves into close-up as he hears that his late father's company will be allowed to continue if he gives up his plans to move. That isolation is physically displayed at the railway station when he hears that his brother has married. The rest of the welcoming party move away and George is left in frame. Later that night, after the homecoming party, a lonely George is pictured in the middle of the town's main street.

Parry (Robin Williams) and Jack (Jeff Bridges) in Terry Gilliam's *The Fisher King* (1991) are, respectively, through trauma and guilt out of touch with their own personhood. Ray (Kevin Costner) in *Field of Dreams* (1989) is haunted by never having really known his father. The hope, for Tillich, is seen as the spirit in us being driven into actualizing our potential. As we search for "New Being" – Tillich argues that Christ is the one who has broken down the estrangement between us and God – what we are and what we have the potential to become is bridged. Culture is the milieu in which this divine activity occurs. The theological struggle from alienation to self-transcendence is perpetual, with many battles lost. Hope lies in believing we are never ultimately overwhelmed. It is through George's doubt that glory comes.

Through his acknowledgement of human lack ("Lord, I'm not a praying man
. . . I'm at the end of my rope.") God is disclosed. George Bailey goes off the
rails because his whole life has been building up to this moment, reminding
us of Milton's phrase in *Paradise Lost* where in Book 3 God has made Adam
"Sufficient to have stood, though free to fall." In *The Fisher King* Jack just
wishes he "could pay the fine and go home" but his continued suffering brings
him to the aid of Parry and this becomes the touchstone for his own salvation.
Parry, who is steeped in the traditions of the Holy Grail, is like the wounded,
dying Fisher King. He has through witnessing his wife's murder gone mad
and eventually goes into a coma from which Jack releases him. In Robert
Zemeckis's 1994 film *Forrest Gump*, whilst Forrest experiences loss – his
mother, Bubba his friend, and Jenny the object of his desires – he never seems
to grow in spirit. As such the theology of Tillich does not satisfactorily
converge with this innocent who traverses the world but emotionally never
leaves home. Perhaps Tillich would argue that Forrest fails to emerge from
"false consciousness" to move to the next stage of true being. Or is it that he
has always been called "stupid" and his sense of lack is always before him?
"How blest are those who know their need of God; the kingdom of Heaven is
theirs" (Mt. 5:3). Forrest represents that category of people who are already
within the Kingdom and whose presence among the rest of us is an
encouragement to catch up. Jenny, his lifelong friend, fruitlessly tries many
paths to salvation. Forrest seems to possess what Thomas Hardy described as
"Some blessed Hope whereof he knew and I was unaware" (Gardner 1973:
758). Capra and Zemeckis are stronger than Tillich in celebrating life as it is
"with all its sham, drudgery and broken dreams." George comes to see what
Forrest already knows. "You've got to do your best with what God gave you,"
says Forrest at one point. In Balthasar's view, God came not just as a teacher
(to tell us what is true) nor as a redeemer (to make us good) but as a revealer
of divine love, glory and beauty. Forrest is one on whom the message is not
lost. After finally getting married to Jenny he remarks of a sunrise: "I couldn't
tell where heaven stopped and the world began."

Someone to watch over me

George Bailey, in Paul Tillich's terminology, has neither Spiritual Presence
nor Spiritual Community at this point. George has yet to be grasped by the
impact of the ultimate, unconditional divine Spirit on his spirit. Nor has he
quite realized the support to be derived from a Spiritual Community. George's
own circle of friends and relatives become such a Spiritual Community when
they mysteriously gather to uphold him and protect him from financial ruin.
We are not alone on earth nor in heaven. His brother toasts him as the richest

man in town. Clarence ethereally leaves him a copy of *Tom Sawyer* inscribed "Dear George:- Remember *no* man is a *failure* if he has *friends*. Thanks for the wings! Love Clarence." In *Field of Dreams* Ray makes the baseball park and, as the voice promised, "he will come." The ghost of "Shoeless Joe" Jackson is a representation of Ray's father. Baseball stands as a metaphor of eternal values. Its rules and size of pitch have never changed. These converge with the counter-culture of Ray and his wife, who met on campus at Berkeley in the 1960s. In coming face to face with the baseball legend (the Spiritual Presence), Ray sees himself as meeting his own father. He is at last, through this gift of his father from eternity, able to gain access to the lost son inside the man. The baseball players become, in Tillich's model, the Spiritual Community representing the company of heaven.

George Bailey's spiritual progress is in the other direction. There has been much that is childlike about his behavior, as with Forrest Gump. The Christmas setting of *It's A Wonderful Life* is a major visual clue. Childishness drives George's dreams. His father never really listens to him. Peter asks George, as if for the first time, what his plans are. This is on the eve of going to college after four years in the building and loan company! When as a boy he needs his father's *immediate* advice about Gower's poisonous prescription Peter sends him away. Yet George models himself on the father who has never heeded him. He remains locked in an immature dependence on him. George, having undergone the hell of his nightmare experience, comes home as a man having put away childish things. He joins the others in the carol "Hark the Herald Angels Sing" with its words "Born to raise the sons of earth. Born to give them second birth." George does not want to be born again because he sees the sense of conforming. It is because he wants now to have New Being, to be a person. He wants now to throw his lot in with the Spiritual Community of Bedford Falls rather than time-serve them whilst yearning to be elsewhere.

The End

The Fisher King is a rare modern film. At its conclusion "The End" is blazoned on the screen as the buildings behind Central Park, New York City, light up. *It's A Wonderful Life* concludes with the same two words against a background of bells ringing; the trademark of Liberty Films. The other films treated here do not use these words, indicative of today's more tentative and fragmentary understandings of how life will proceed after the credits have rolled. There is unashamed hope in *The Fisher King* as in *It's A Wonderful Life*. It is the end of Parry's pain and denial of a terrible tragedy and the end of Jack's self-punishment over the deaths of innocent people in a restaurant. Their respective nightmares are over. In *It's A Wonderful Life*, when George Bailey's nightmare is over, Potter remains unpunished but we can see how hollow his victory is. He is a "warped, frustrated old man." Jesus repeatedly says of the hypocrites that they have their reward already (Mt. 6:2, 6, 16). Potter likewise already has his reward, the only one he is ever likely to get. Much good may it do him, the film seems to imply.

That strong sense of unresolved guilt in *The Fisher King* is more directly addressed in *It's A Wonderful Life*. Clarence writes on the flyleaf of the book he leaves for George that no man is a failure if he has friends. There is a gap of 45 years between the making of these two films. In the first the assurance of divine intervention and forgiveness remains intact. If an angel tells you something then you have been told! In the latter film these old certainties have gone. No longer can it be taken on trust that the filmmakers and audiences share (if they ever did) the same theological assumptions that "God's in his heaven and all's right with the world" (Browning 1940: 171). Or that happy-ever-after endings are credible. (Were they ever more than a hope, even in Capra's day?) Nevertheless, in the end, *The Fisher King* so works with its characters' nightmares that a benison falls on each. Ransomed, healed, restored, forgiven, they find their way home. They are assured of God's presence and, through Parry's Little People, a Spiritual Community.

Happy endings and hopeful narratives

The question remains as to whether there is a *happy* ending to any of the films we have examined. *Field of Dreams* contains a satisfying resolution. The film ends with lines of automobiles driving towards the field. People are curious about, even hungry for, a spiritual experience. *Forrest Gump* ends, as it begins, with a feather floating in a seemingly random fashion. At the start of the film it comes to rest at Forrest's feet. He picks it up and puts in a book in his briefcase. At the end the feather floats off again on its travels. There is frequent reference in the film to destiny. "Life's a box of chocolates," says Forrest more than once, "you never know what you're going to get." The inference could be that life is ruled by blind, chaotic circumstances. Forrest again and again finds himself thrust into the center of America's historic moments. Through clever computer work we see him meeting Presidents and rock stars, bringing influence to bear on some of them. Like Capra's hero, his life touches so many other lives. Forrest's encounters suggest that there is no such thing as accidents. Life is held together by one who watches over us. At the end Forrest puzzles over whether we have a destiny: "Or are we just floating about accidental-like on a breeze? Maybe it's both." At this point the feather floats off again. It is as if the film, as distinct from Forrest, puts its emphasis on the sheer randomness of life. Both *It's A Wonderful Life* and

Forrest Gump illuminate our understanding of destiny but ultimately destiny only makes sense within the greater frame of the whole of Being. The Shorter Catechism of the Anglican Church asks: "What is the true end of man?," to which the answer given is, "To glorify God and enjoy him forever." I understand this to be a corporate purpose, not confined to certain individuals (or one gender) such as George or Forrest.

By way of a summary of Capra's theological position it would be hard to better Jürgen Moltmann. Moltmann (1967) suggests that it is a wonderful life because it is a promising life. If the cross identifies itself with our present human condition then the resurrection is God's promise of a future transformation. Capra's resignation to the slowness, even impossibility, of love and peace is matched in *It's A Wonderful Life* by a growing acceptance of this end of all time perspective. The whole film has been shot from this heavenly point of view; the angelic throng bending near the earth to touch their harps of gold. Humans cannot effect their own transformation by themselves. This present life can only be wonderful if we believe in God's promise through the risen Christ to be with us to the end of time, working with us. The use of the seasonal Christmas carol in the final scene of *It's A Wonderful Life* (already referred to) acts as a seal of that guarantee. In the examples of more recent films we have examined there appear to be modern filmmakers who agree with Frank Capra that glory, the Kingdom of God and eschatology are concepts worth serious attention. With Capra they seem to suggest that life is not a totally meaningless and random existence if looked at from the point of view of the end. In that context feeling good, optimistic and hopeful can continue to have an intellectual respectability among filmmakers.

Part Three

17

On Systematizing the Unsystematic: A Response

David Jasper

I recently had occasion to fly across the Atlantic. The plane was equipped with individual televisions positioned in the back of the seats in front, each screen about four inches across. Although I was traveling in what is respectfully described as "economy class," we were offered the choice of six channels for the duration of the eight-hour flight with a menu of cartoons, feature films and sport. Like many of my fellow passengers I spent some time flicking in a desultory fashion between channels, catching snatches of Bruce Willis posturing in torn shirt designed to show his ample muscles, an actress posturing in a dress designed to show her ample bosom, and miniscule monsters rampaging around a tiny Jurassic Park. From time to time, like animals in some ghastly scientific experiment, trapped in our cramped seats, we were fed with food packaged in little plastic containers. A small child sitting next to me sat for the whole of the flight utterly absorbed in his own world of cartoon characters, his eyes rarely diverted from the little square of screen, isolated in the individual world of his headphones and utterly oblivious to the world around him, all bizarrely suspended in an artificial atmosphere five miles above the surface of the ocean.

The experience of watching a movie in a plane highlights the escapist quality which characterizes popular Hollywood cinema. It is there to help us through the tedium of inactivity, and is supremely an art of illusion. Whatever "happens" is entirely inside one's head, and is fragilely dependent on the vicissitudes of international "box office" success. From its very inception, Hollywood has revolved around money and profit, as a tinsel world in which the stars are paid enormous sums of money, and all too often fall from their dizzy heights as dramatically as they climb to fame. Hugely systematic as a commercial enterprise and oblivious of the human waste which it casts in its wake, the popular cinema nevertheless trades in the myths of the "unsystematic" – the maverick hero, the individual who defeats the corrupt corporation, the ugly duckling who becomes the beautiful princess. All, however, are ultimately conformists. Even the myths of religion are drawn into the cinema's affirmation of simple, basic values which we would like to think lie at the heart of our culture, in spite of everything that appears to the contrary. The Christian gospel becomes the greatest story ever told, and we discover that it is, in fact, the story of mid-1960s America, celebrating the rugged landscapes of the American West in a panoply of "guest appearances" by the major Hollywood stars of the day. This greatest story, in George Stevens's 1965 film version of it, proved to be far too long for the attention span of the commercial cinema audience and was cut from an initial four hours and twenty minutes to a mere three hours and ten minutes, and had been told much better 12 years earlier by the same director in the *bona fide* "Western" *Shane*. Alan Ladd in buckskin was a more acceptable savior for the cinema audience than the rather unctuous Jesus of Max Von Sydow.

Like theology, Hollywood thrives on systematization and is caught in its toils. Just as theologians look to philosophy and continually reinvent religion within the context of changing understandings of our world and its society, so the cinema assures us that, in spite of all our fears to the contrary, things will work out and the story can still be told. Because in our apparently (perhaps necesssarily) indestructible hope in the possibility in our society of what Jürgen Habermas calls "communicative action," the authority of the sacred and the authority of the normative continually reassert themselves against the apparent aberrations of corrupt principalities, powers and corporations; in the films discussed in this volume the shadow of theology is ever present in stories which would never be conceived of in themselves as theological or even religious. But, ironically, it takes the institutional powers of the Church and the corporations of Hollywood studios to remind us of this. And just as theology has been struggling for years to come to terms with the desystematiz- ing insights of the "postmodern condition," so none of the commercial films here discussed ventures far into the deconstructive insights of postmodernism, with its sense of the failure of narrative and its undermining of reference. Such things are left to the few who haunt the art-house cinemas rather than the multitudes who finance the blockbusters or hang upon the platitudes of the Oscar ceremonies.

That is the negative side of the story. Neither systematic theology, nor popular cinema are all bad. They are simply dangerous and powerful instruments when used in the wrong hands. Even the most cursory glance at the Christian tradition will indicate the dangers of theology which becomes too closely identified with institutional power and vested interests, and the need for continual reformations through individuals like Martin Luther (looking back to the fragile figure of Jesus himself). Ironically, perhaps, the cinema has repeatedly focused upon just such singular figures in films as different as *The Mission*, the *Terminator* movies, or even *Babette's Feast*, in its seeming celebration of freedom and the individual human values of love, mutual responsibility and laughter. For the illusion must be maintained that however corrupt our world, *we* as viewers are ultimately better than that, and that we are not one of the amorphous crowd sustaining the power of the prevailing system. There is always a balance to be maintained between freedom and necessity, between order and spontaneity. Within the illusion, which may, perhaps, be some form of vision, the necessity of freedom must be sustained.

Paul Tillich describes the task of systematic theology as being to explain the contents of the Christian faith in a methodological reflection which is necessarily abstracted from the cognitive work in which one actually engages. As far as he is concerned, the primary, though not the only source, for Christian theology is the Bible. It is certainly not insignificant that few of the films discussed in this book are directly drawn from biblical material though it may have many indirect allusions to it. There is, certainly, a vigorous Hollywood tradition of filming biblical stories, though on the whole these have illustrated either particular religious or ideological readings of the Bible or, as we have seen in the case of Stevens's *The Greatest Story Ever Told*, they have promulgated a view of modern American society sanctioned by biblical reference. On the other hand, almost all the films mentioned are seen as somehow relating to the gospel story through "Christ-figures," through themes of redemption and liberation, or images of apocalypse. Generally speaking there is a nervousness about such references, indicated by a repeated disclaimer that there is, of course, no *overt* theology in *Edward Scissorhands* or *Shirley Valentine*. Viewers not inclined to impose such readings on these films might be justifiably skeptical or even affronted by the suggestion that religion is being inflicted on them indirectly. On the other hand, it could be argued that this is a justifiable "theology by negotiation" which consciously accepts the tentative relationship between religion and culture, existing as a dialog in which culture – following H. Richard Niebuhr and Jakob Burkhardt – is understood as non-authoritarian in character, with a spontaneity in all social discourse as an expression of a spiritual and moral life. Commercial cinema within society, therefore, should not be trying to do the work of theology (hence the unease associated with specifically "biblical" films), but, though itself born of an institution which works within a powerful and self-perpetuating system, should still somehow purport to dramatize, honestly or dishonestly, those spontaneous freedoms which lie – or ought to lie – at the heart of a living culture.

Thus we see how almost all of the films which are the particular concern of this volume draw upon strong mythical themes, usually realized through a commentary on contemporary life. In a sense, like all myths and fairy tales, they mimic theology though without theology's claims for methodological

order and reflection. As with all good stories, unless one responds to them
with feeling and empathy they fail to work at all, nor do they require the
intellectual assent which theology finally demands. Indeed, in the case of the
Terminator movies it is the relentless series of powerful images which sustains
the viewer's response and which are the vehicle for the possible reading
offered in the essay in this book. Certainly the theme of these films is a
powerful one, all the more so as it is embedded in fears deep within our own
culture, but one suspects that the commercial success of the *Terminator* movies
is more closely related to their extraordinary special effects and their ability to
frighten than to any specific response to their "message." This is not to deny,
however, that the mythological quality of the narrative is enduring and even
profound. It is actually the basic simplicity of the movies which makes them
so successful. As in all enduring legends, the issues and plot are simple and
primitive. Their strength is apparent when read against biblical texts from
Jeremiah, Malachi and the apocalyptic tradition, for the films are capacious,
largely empty containers which readily accept readings against the Bible and
theology, allowing us to recognize both that our condition is universal, and to
believe that the story of victory against all the odds is not just a childish
dream, but has a precedent in the greatest story ever told.

In other words, I would hesitate a little before I give assent to the claim
that the issues raised by the *Terminator* movies are the issues explored by
Isaiah, Jeremiah and Ezekiel. From the writings of the Hebrew prophets arises
an enduring tradition of theological reflection which is intrinsic to the texts
themselves. These are books which burn with a fire of religious passion and
the issues explored in them cannot be disentangled from that passion. The
same cannot be said of James Cameron's movies which, the stage having been
set so that the viewer is in no doubt what to think, then deny the need to
think any further and invite us on a roller coaster that depends upon
Cameron's undeniable directorial ability to keep the action going at a terrific
speed. Precisely for the reason that he does not quite manage this in the
second film – *Terminator 2: Judgment Day* – which tries to be just a bit too
clever for its own good, this film lacks the raw mythic power of the original.

Of course the images, particularly of a futuristic Los Angeles torn by war
and destruction, relate to biblical passages like Jeremiah 4:23–6. But I do not
think that for this reason they necessarily prompt theological reflection, for in
the end they are just good entertainment within both myth and an environment
(the cinema) that is ultimately reassuring and safe. As long as Sarah Connor is
around we know that humanity will defeat the machine nightmare. What is
more frightening than the echoes from the Bible is the intrinsic, unconscious
consumption by the film of the paying viewer. In our age of mechanical
reproduction terrible machines do stalk our society and govern our lives with
images that precede the real, inverting its causal and logical order – and those

machines are television and cinema screens. As we celebrate the victory of the cyborg and Sarah Connor over the T1000 we are as much victims of the compulsion to watch the simulacra on the screen as the citizens of 2029 are victims of the murderous robots. I think again of the child in the transatlantic jet literally imprisoned by the tiny screen and the images in his head for eight hours.

For Tillich, as we have seen, the primary source of systematic theology is the Bible, which, though itself a series of exercizes in interpretation, provides many of the most powerful and enduring mythic patterns and figures in our cultures. This is not exclusively so, since Christian theology has also drawn, perhaps less overtly, upon other mythological traditions, and our literature and art is saturated in postfigurative patterns and characters from a huge and eclectic range of mythical sources. Many of these frequently become fused or intertwined – the figures of Jesus and Dionysus for example, or patterns and narratives which derive spontaneously from various traditions. At the same time parallels in film, literature or art with patterns or figures in the Bible may be formal not ideological, in the sense that a character who is prefigured by the life of Jesus may be utterly remote from the Jesus of the gospels and Christian tradition – a madman, an opportunist, or many other things. It is necessary, therefore, to be very careful when claiming that a character in a film may be described as a "Christ-figure," or suggesting that a Christology may be read into, or reflected in, a pattern of events.

In the case of Tim Burton's *Edward Scissorhands* the argument for a cinema gospel parallel is, on the surface, tempting but ultimately a distraction from what is really a rather slight modern fairy story that draws on a range of mythic antecedents from *Frankenstein* and *Peter Pan* to 'Beauty and the Beast'. Edward, more than most of us because of the peculiar nature of his "creation," is an uneasy combination of the creative and gentle with the destructive. Indeed the very source of his creativity, his scissors/hands, is also the source of his destructiveness (which is also a self-destructiveness, as he keeps on cutting himself), and his ultimate defect. Burton's obsession with masks which grant a "certain weird freedom," protects the character of Edward from the necessity of being either fully coherent or substantial. What he offers in this film is a motif which allows him to scratch (literally!) the surface of modern American suburbia, play with a trivial love story and revisualize a classic fairy story set in the castle, with a degree of light humor. Any intertextuality with the Bible serves to underline more the universal nature of the biblical texts rather than develop our understanding of them in a modern context.

The popular cinema is well adapted to portraying myth and legend in settings with which the contemporary viewer can immediately identify. Literature has always performed this function, but the powerful immediacy of the screen image and its ability to absorb its viewer more readily, and often more cheaply and less demandingly, than a book can its reader, grants it a dangerous accessibility to the most enduring patterns and stories in our mythic traditions. Consciously or unconsciously, the Bible lies at the heart of those eclectic traditions, an anxious influence which does not necessarily bring with it the theological tradition within which the books of the Bible are read as Holy Writ. Indeed, it may be the case that the images of Scripture are often dramatically more powerful in art than this tradition can tolerate, which is why the art of the Bible has always maintained an awkward relationship with the theological faith from which it first grew.

Although, as we have seen, both Christian theology and popular cinema sustain a deep suspicion of postmodernity and its discontinuities, film has nevertheless tended to celebrate its secularism with insights which recognize a shift from past illusions of faith and tradition, even where these insights appear to coincide with the grand illusions of the biblical tradition. Thus, the endless films in our time with an apocalyptic theme pick up on a religious form which is particularly relevant at a time which is conscious of its potential for self-destruction. Where it seems to me the cinema comes closest to stimulating theological reflection, however, is not by its themes or specific motifs (directors, with the occasional exception like Martin Scorsese are theologically illiterate, nor should they be expected to be otherwise) but by its very form and nature. That is, films like *Apocalypse Now* are precisely examples of what they set out to portray – a literal hell for director and actor, involving the viewer in a demonic celebration of war whose impact is far more powerful than any story told. What is so chilling about such films is that there is literally nothing outside the text for the viewer trapped in front of the screen.

So, we have moved beyond an exploration of themes, motifs and familiar narrative patterns. In some ways, one of the most "theological" films discussed in this volume is *The Piano*, not because it *is* "theology" or concerned at all with God, but because, as an intertextual reading with Mark's Gospel demonstrates, its exploration of power, will, freedom, language and silence, exercized upon the audience literally as well as through narrative and story (the film is an intensely uncomfortable voyeuristic experience), provokes the possibility of a theological thinking which the film itself neither has nor necessarily demands. It does, however, give rise to a possible hermeneutic strategy which links it with a work like Mark's Gospel. And just as that Gospel is deeply disturbing and, arguably, inconclusive, so the film leaves us without proper resolution, though formally some kind of restoration has taken place.

Films, like most art, are often most interesting to the theological enterprise when they are being least theological. This claim, of course, needs some qualification. When a film which is concerned with a particular issue in contemporary experience – AIDS, for example – begins to use the language and images of traditional religion, one becomes suspicious and parallels quickly tend to become caricature or pastiche. On the other hand, attempts to "see God" in the everyday course of life tend, like all religious overstatements, rapidly to become tedious, trite, or unctuous. But where, as in Jane Campion's film, real issues of human interrelationships are explored – such issues as cannot be unraveled by mere human bravery or ingenuity (neither, that is, by Arnold Schwarzenegger nor Monsieur Poirot), then we are led to the question of whether theology might indeed have a place in our discussion and our interpretation.

I have left to this relatively late stage in my discussion a more detailed look at both *Shane* (1953) and the Western films of Clint Eastwood since they seem to me to be almost as close as anything (with the exception of Scorsese's work, to which I will come in a moment) to "theology" on film. Although *Shane* has not stood the test of time as well as many critics seem to think, it is, rather self-consciously, one of the great Westerns, inhabiting America's great indigenous myth with artistic ease. It works so much better than Stevens's later life of Christ because it is precisely more honest – instead of claiming that the Holy Land is really the American West, it portrays that epic landscape in its own colors and with its own mystery and story. That story, it is true, is simple and moralistic, undeviating in its imagery and utterly without irony, but precisely for those reasons it allows its images to work as myth powerfully and directly upon the audience. As a drama of salvation in the "holy land" of the American West it fulfils the viewer's fantasies without disturbing the longings which underpin them. In the darkened cinema (or living room), the film offers an undemanding and voyeuristic, non-liturgical hope of redemption, the specific fulfilment of a generalized dream.

For these reasons *Shane* is a great Western, while Eastwood's *Pale Rider*, though flawed, moves beyond the myth in a disturbing vision which is a more self-conscious and less narcissistic intertext with Scripture, broken open in the initial quotation from and commentary on the twenty-third psalm in which its promises and assurances cannot be accepted – until the appearance of the Preacher fulfils the desires and petitions of the prospectors and their children in ways which they fear and fail to understand. Eastwood's character, honed on the figure of the Man with No Name of his earlier spaghetti Westerns, is darkly complex, working on a number of levels, and crawls inside Western stereotypes only to deconstruct them. The classic lone outsider, he is both "systematic" in his reference, and utterly unsystematic to the point of incoherence. As in most of Eastwood's Westerns the film has a dark and subversive comic quality which works against the myth of the film, and yet at the same time sustains it at a level which is far more immediate to the audience. But it is precisely the different levels at which the Preacher works, none of them made quite coherent with the others, which prevents us from reading the film (as we read *Shane*) simply against theological language or motif. In the phrase which occurs on a number of occasions in this book, we do not merely revisit theology seen "through the lens" of Eastwood's films, though, through biblical quotation and implication, theology is never far away, but always disturbed, and uprooted by the violence of the Preacher. He is everyone's ideal of the lone Western hero, but his coming does not merely set things right.

In Eastwood's movies, and perhaps even more in Scorsese's, as David Graham points out, life and film are more complex than simple religious readings would allow, and their violence may be redemptive (or perhaps cathartic) but at the same time feeds upon the intrinsic voyeurism of the cinema and its ability to access our darker natures with almost no cost – or at least, apparently so. Because film is a solitary and finally undemanding medium (neither of which characteristics apply to the live theatre), it offers the viewer a position of mastery and extraordinarily intimate access to human experience and emotion. At a recent conference on film and persecution, I was struck by the audience's initial fascination and growing horror as it watched the film about the making of Francis Ford Coppola's *Apocalypse Now*, in which actors and director were drawn into the insanity of the film itself, and there was no distinction to be made between film and "reality" in a real apocalypse of disintegration and cruelty. It was truly a moment of insight into the heart of darkness *in* film itself.

At this point (as in religious experience) when one starts back into a terrible recognition of what we are doing as viewers and recognizes that we *are* responsible and can bear this no longer, perhaps theology as a systematic activity is again called for. The difficulty for films made to make money within the entertainment industry is that by drawing back from the excess within which, unbearably, morality and re-vision begins again, they repeatedly offer shocking scenes which *ought* to be unwatchable, but must be sanitized to satisfy the peculiar sensitivities of the censors. One example of this is the repeated rape of the prostitute Tralala in Ulrich Edel's film of Hubert Selby Jr's book *Last Exit to Brooklyn* (1989), which, in the original book, is brilliant and finally unreadable, but in the film is turned into a bizarre moment of tenderness that is, ultimately, far more shocking. How does one watch the unwatchable – portray the terrible moment of Mark 15:34 – when theology becomes absolutely necessary?

When Just Jaecken's *Emmanuelle* (1974) was released in Britain it was advertized, by no less a homely figure than genteel TV presenter Katie Boyle, as "the film that makes you feel good without feeling bad." The cinema in this instance offers us, in other words, soft pornography without the shame. Alone in near-darkness the viewer is allowed to shed communal, moral responsibility and is free to "feel good" about mildly erotic (though highly exploitative) images of sexuality. Ultimately the same morality is true of such serious commercial films as *Schindler's List* or even *Groundhog Day*. If the theologian Jürgen Moltmann is right when he suggests that Christianity is the religion not of the hope of the optimist but of the hope of the hopeless, then commercial cinema is ill equipped to explore this kind of hope. The "Jesus" film (with the extraordinary exception of Pasolini's art-house *The Gospel According to St Matthew*) struggles to be serious and, with profound irony, is subverted by the far more serious comedy of *Monty Python's Life of Brian* (1979), which leaves theology out of it and endlessly exposes what we do with theology and institutional religion as a means of self-justification. In the mainstream of Hollywood cinema perhaps only Martin Scorsese sustains a consistently "theological" possibility, by continually deflecting the aspirations and anticipations of the viewer in complex visions which both confuse and prompt attempts at systematization out of the threat of chaos. Most of Scorsese's films offer essentially simple stories as vehicles for intricate and multilayered explorations of motivations and relationships. Often self-consciously referential they avoid the narcissistic indulgence in cinema such as is found in the highly amoral films of Quentin Tarantino. Scorsese is in many respects reminiscent of the writers of the gospels – a teller of a simple story with a driven and often ambiguous central character embedded in a tradition, and with a defined point of view (which is the invitation to the theologian) frequently erupting into violence and confusion.

The violence of redemption in Scorsese's films is never unambiguous and never offered cheaply. *The Last Temptation of Christ* (1988) was bound to offend (just as was Kazantzakis's original novel), because, offered as a Hollywood film in the tradition of Nicholas Ray and George Stevens, the film transgresses the demands of its audience, asking too much of them in a medium whose power is effective in as much as, demanding nothing of the viewer, it seems to offer the viewer the power to understand without the need seriously to think or change. In a curious way, Kazantzakis's *film*, though not his Jesus, is most deeply Christocentric precisely because it demands too much, and is inevitably sacrificed on the altar of commercially constructed "good taste."

Conclusion

This concluding chapter has been deliberately critical of much of the writing which precedes it in this book. In being so, it is aware that the reader may return defensively and with a degree of relief to discussions of specific films which encourage us to effect some coherence between them and biblical or systematic theology, spirituality, liturgy, or broader themes like liberation and the human condition. I would not wish to deny the effectiveness and power of films such as *Babette's Feast* or the *Terminator* movies. They may, indeed, contribute significantly to a proper revitalizing of the religious imagination in a time when the power of the word and the accessibility of theology are arguably less than in almost any other period. But where popular art, as in the church frescoes and miracle plays of the late Middle Ages in Europe, has made a serious contribution to theological reflection, it has done so successfully because it has been two-edged, ironic, difficult and ambiguous. The danger of Hollywood cinema lies in its deliberate and commercial habit of absorbing all vision into its own, offering the viewer a commodity which can be consumed without fear of significant change or disturbance. Such is true of most of the films discussed here, even (or perhaps especially) when they feed upon violent images.

Thus, the USA absorbs the Holy Land and produces the biblical epic. *Shane* is at least more honest, being an indigenous myth, while *Pale Rider* or *Unforgiven* begin to deconstruct the myth though remaining within the esthetic conventions and accepted narrative and character norms of the industry. Theology, whether within the Judeo–Christian tradition or otherwise, emerges from more problematic and disturbing material than Hollywood dare show. Such complex and arresting images, as in the gospels themselves, will move beyond the tolerable towards a Passion which is far more than simply, at best, illustrative or derivatively productive of "Christ-images" or fleeting moments of reprieve within the general comfortable slumber of a religious tradition. Perhaps the task of the cinema is finally impossible – overcoming and exorcizing the morbidity of its own voyeurism by asking the viewer, as sole final moral arbiter, to watch the unwatchable without allowing any escape into a rhetoric which confuses the "real" with sanitized and permitted images on the screen. For from such an aporetic position – one which attempts to think the unthinkable and know the unknowable *as* unthinkable and unknowable – theology has always and alone emerged.

The cinema is, by its very nature, a house of illusions. From the little screens on the transatlantic jet, film is in the business of taking us out of our world for an hour or two under the delusion that we are totally in control. (We can choose which channel to watch, and even turn the set off; or can we?) We must, therefore, be perpetually watchful that the illusions of the screen do not also include the illusion of theology in a mere celluloid simulacrum of redemption and salvation. Theology needs its own illusions in order to do its work. But those who undertake it usually believe that redemption and salvation are more than words, and far from illusory.

18

Theology Beyond the Modern and the Postmodern: A Future Agenda for Theology and Film

Clive Marsh and Gaye Ortiz

Introduction

We acknowledged at the start of this book that it is both a good and a bad time to be publishing such a work. We noted the changing character of Christian theology, given the challenge of postmodernism to all "metanarratives" and all claims to universality. As theology cannot but be keenly interested in both, such a challenge at the very least questions the implied unity and comprehensive reach of Christian theology. But it does much more. It undermines a basic premise upon which so much of the discussion which has gone on in the realm of "theology and film" has been conducted. It requires that such discussions be undertaken with much greater self-consciousness as to their cultural embeddedness than ever before. If films, for example, can be said to be about "life," they cannot be about "life in general." Even claims that they describe or address the so-called "human condition" must be open to question. If the term "human condition" remains meaningful at all, it would appear, then it cannot be as a term which of itself defines any particular way in which humans are human.

But if postmodernism issues a major challenge to traditions of discussion in "theology and film" – as it undoubtedly does – then theology returns the compliment. In order to address the nature of the challenge in reverse, we must note the way in which contemporary Christian theology is reacting to the postmodern mood. We noted one possible reaction (i.e. acceptance and absorption into theology of postmodern insights) in the introductory chapter to this book. In now acknowledging that Christian theology – in a variety of forms – is unlikely to accept uncritically an indifferent, limitless plurality, or to assent to the signing of the death warrant of metanarratives, we must consider two further movements in contemporary Christian theology.

The two to be considered may be called "the new conservatism" and "postliberalism." "New conservatism" relates to the now well-documented assertiveness of the so-called "New Right" in Western Christianity (see for example the work of Bruce 1995, and 1996: ch. 6). Such an approach in effect bemoans the decline of "Christendom," mourning the loss of the impact of Christianity upon Western, cultural values. The public role of Christian theology must therefore be to reassert "traditional values" in prophetic manner, thereby reclaiming Christianity's proclamatory voice in Western society. In the midst of this process, somewhat ironically, allies for the cause are enlisted from a variety of places (see for example David Graham's mention of Medved in ch. 7). This trend in Western Christianity must by definition be suspicious of the cinema, because of its espousal of secular values. It can welcome particular films, but only those which evidently provide good, wholesome "family viewing." But we can see that, as a result, there is always much more to its supposedly religious agenda than meets the eye. And it must be accepted that support of film which provides "family viewing" may, in fact, be tantamount to baptizing a whole set of values which may not fit together neatly with Christianity (a state of affairs which is often left ill-explored).

The second form of theology to be considered is often termed "postliberalism," though it is far from a unified movement (see for example Placher 1989). Postliberalism is more sophisticated and thoughtful than new conservatism, but no less committed to the rediscovery of what may be called "distinctively Christian" beliefs and ideas in contemporary public discussion. In response to postmodernism's commendation of flux and fluidity, this form of Christian theology acknowledges the need to ask questions as to what constitutes Christian identity: you have to have some idea of what constitutes "Christianity" so that you have something to work with. But this does not necessarily mean that all beliefs and doctrines are neatly prescribed and clear-cut. Postliberalism's concern is clearly driven by an intent to reassess Christianity's (and religion's) role in the rediscovery of human community in the West. This has led, in particular, to a widespread rediscovery and re-exploration of the doctrine of the trinity ("the distinctively Christian understanding of God"). Implicit in this softer of the two forms of Christian counter-assertion to a radical version of postmodernism is the notion that identity is a communal affair, that religion is necessary for that identity, and that human society is weakened (ultimately destroyed?) where neither community nor religion is cherished.

Postliberalism has gone a long way, then, to accepting the postmodern challenge to universals, in acknowledging that Christianity is but one religion amongst many, and only ever exists in particular forms. Where postliberals often differ from each other, however, is in determining what is to be done with this insight into Christianity's inevitable particularity. Are religious communities so wholly distinct that their worldviews cannot be compared (as implied by Lindbeck 1984; see discussion in Marshall 1990)? In accepting that truth is always particular, can there be no appeal to experience in search of "the truly human"? By being *post*liberalist, this position critiques Christian liberalism's apparent stress, on the one hand, on the human individual, and, on the other, on the supposedly universal concept of the "human condition." In theory at least, postliberalism can welcome discussion in "theology and film". But unlike liberalism, out of which so much discussion in theology and film has emerged, posliberalism emphasizes more the complexity of, and the critical edge implicit within, the conversations between diverse and particular Christian theologies and films. Theologies and films must both be viewed more radically as culturally-embedded products containing conscious and sub-conscious codes and mythologies.

Attentive readers will have noted already that there is a strong affinity between the three directions of contemporary theology now sketched (post-modern theology – as outlined in the Introduction to this book; new conservative theology; postliberalism) and the three possible ways of constru-ing the relationship between Christian theology and culture, as presented in chapter 2:

- theology against culture   (new conservatism)
- theology immersed in culture   (postmodern theology)
- theology in critical dialog with culture   (postliberalism).

The linking is far from neat. Many forms of postliberalism, for example, would feel uneasy that such a critical conversation with culture can be had in the way suggested in chapter 2 (on which, see Kamitsuka 1996 v Lints 1993). Be that as it may, the affinity noted has value. For it enables us to pinpoint tendencies in contemporary Christian theology in the West in relation to each tendency's understanding of the link (or not) between theology and culture. It is on this basis that a judgment as to the potential value of film for theology will be reached.

It is in the midst of this maelstrom of theological debate, then, that this book tries to find a place. The natural ally of the "theology and film" discussions of recent years has undoubtedly been theological liberalism. Such a liberal approach had seemed to fit into the "theology immersed in culture" approach: theology could be "read off" from film perhaps a little too easily. Those engaged in the theology/film debate – many of the contributors to this book included – may, however, be unhappy to be labelled postmodernist without further ado, even though postmodern theology attends closely to theology's immersion in culture. Most would accept that a critical conversation of some sort is going on between Christian theology and film. So what is the future for theology and film discussions in the light of our mapping exercize

(in the Introduction and throughout Part One), and in the light of the actual
critical conversations (Part Two)?

As a final contribution to that debate, prompted by David Jasper's critique,
in this final chapter we reinterpret the book's contents in relation to the
question of theology and film's agenda for the foreseeable future. In our view,
there are four themes which emerge clearly from the book:

- Systems past and future
- The return of the universal
- Popular film and the question of a "popular theology"
- Theology in and out of church.

After examining these four themes briefly, we shall pose the question of what
a "postliberal theology of film" might look like.

Systems Past and Future

"Systematic theology" – the ordered structuring of Christian theology's topics
or themes – is not supposed to have a present. "Systems" are held to belong
to the past. They are impositions and marks of a totalitarian tendency. As
Gabriel Fackre has shown, however, systematic theologies galore have
appeared in recent years (Fackre 1993 and 1995). This feature of the
contemporary theological scene may well be due to hordes of middle-aged
male academics wanting to make their mark in the history of Christian
theology before retiring from their teaching posts, or at least due to their not
heeding feminist questioning about the very wisdom of constructing "systems"
at all. Be that as it may, women systematicians are admittedly thin on the
ground (though see now Carmody 1995 and the tellingly collaborative volume:
LaCugna 1993).

Questioning of Christianity's, and Christian theology's, systematic character
is important for, and throughout, this book. Film simply will not deliver a
systematic theology. If theological discussion of film is to address the topics or
themes which have traditionally been considered under the heading of
"systematic theology," then it can only be as a result of sifting, sorting and
shaping the results of the conversations (though for a preference for the term
"constructive" over "systematic" theology for such an undertaking, see for
example Hodgson 1994, esp. 35–41). To some extent this "systematizing" has
gone on: we signalled at the outset that different themes would, in practice,
be dealt with during Part Two. But the ordering is an imposed order. The
central, critical question is only whether this ordering distorts or is disrespect-
ful to the films being interpreted. In our view, this book has not been guilty of

such distortion precisely because the discussion entered into, through engagement with any particular film (e.g. via "negotiation" – Marsh; "intertextuality"
– Rhoads and Roberts; or use of an "interpretive arch" – Jewett), derives
from, and relates to, the relevant film's subject-matter in every case.

But what is the value of "systematizing" at all? Why not just let the films
speak, not only about the themes picked up in this book, but about others too?
(Let's hear it – in other words – for Babette as "Christ-figure" as well as for
the Feast as a sort of communion.) The value of systematizing is two-fold.
First, it points out the "gaps." This does not means that a predetermined set
of conclusions have to be reached by dialog between theology and film. Rather,
knowledge of the customary themes of systematic theology presents a range of
topics, encompassing the widest possible range of human experience (and
human experience of the divine). Film may be able to stimulate and participate
in discussions on all expected topics. On the other hand, it may prove limited
– for example through its proverbial attention to the "human interest" angle –
in what it can deliver through its dialog with theology. Or it may reveal
emphases or preoccupations (e.g. with "Christ-figures") which distort any
resulting theological insights.

Second, the systematizing *process* is worth noting, to show the way in which
reflective theology is necessarily abstract, and at one or two stages removed
from concrete expression or encounter. In other words, film, like life
experience, works with the gut first. This gut-level response is then *part of*
the resulting theology, even if the necessary reflective process seems to
distance a theological turn-of-phrase from the immediacy of the linking of
experience and insight. The resulting theology need not, of course, be any less
real than the event which gave it birth. But it needs noting for what it is:
reflection. The test of any (abstract, analytical, systematic, constructive,
reflective) Christian theological statement is not the level of its abstraction.
Three questions are best asked of any theological statement:

● Does it offer a creative and truthful interpretation of the concrete
   experience and encounter from which it came?
● Does it provide a means of linking – even critically – with identifiable
   Christian tradition?
● Does it inform future Christian practice and thought?

If these questions are answered affirmatively, then the explorative process has
been – and will continue to be – worth the effort.

The Return of the Universal

Like any other discipline in the humanities, theology can no longer make
ready assumptions about the inherent meaningfulness of the term "the human
condition." Discussions within the realm of theology and film which appeal to
films' exploration of the "human situation" or "life issues" must therefore be
more carefully constructed than they often have been in the past. Dialogs
between theology and film must now be acknowledged to be conversations
between particular (culturally embedded) formulations of an aspect, or aspects,
of Christian theology and particular (implicitly or explicitly encoded) understandings of the same theological topic, even if presented in non- or even anti-
theological terms in filmic form. The task of carrying out such a conversation
is yet more complex and sophisticated than we have been able to conduct in
this book. It is this critical conversation which David Jasper clearly longs for.
Our goal was always modest and introductory. But Jasper is right to push the
conversations on a stage further.

It is not, however, a wisdom which can end up being cynical of any film
being interpreted. If this were so, then filmic integrity would be lost, and the
moral credibility of the dialog denied. Jasper is not, however, calling for a
cynical approach in asking for a properly critical theology. But nor is he wholly
affirming postmodernism in appealing to it to make his deconstructive case.
Nor, again, is he being merely moralistic in wanting the dialog between
theology and film to deliver something useful for contemporary thought and
practice. There is, though, an undoubted moral seriousness about his critique
which reflects an impatience with the lack of an overall cutting edge in the
dialogs conducted in Part Two of this book. The theological core to his
critique is at least akin to that levelled by postliberalism against Western
Christianity's liberal past. Jasper would doubtless not own the "postliberal"
tag as such, certainly not in the form espoused, for example, by John Milbank
(as, for example, in Milbank 1990). This does not matter very much. His
critique reminds all those trying to contribute to the theology/film debate to
be sharper in the critical dimension of their theology even whilst taking film
seriously.

The moral intensity of Jasper, however, merely reiterates a point made
earlier: there is something about the "Enlightenment, liberal, modernism" –
in large part now rightly rejected – which must not be lost sight of. Interest in
"the human condition," "the human situation" or "the human being generally"
presents a false universal, against which an emphasis upon particularity offers
appropriate protest. And yet despite the tragically ironic consequences of such
universal interest in the human being (such that the individual human being
has become an object of idol-worship), as Vernon White has recently shown

quite clearly, it would be unwise to join the bandwagon of rejecting such a tradition in blanket fashion (White 1996). From an orthodox, Christian theological perspective, then, White feels able to argue strongly for a necessarily dialectical understanding of the human person (individual and corporate), claiming that such an understanding has to be grounded ontologically in the trinitarian being of God. Such a conclusion will not be accepted by all who wish to own the label Christian, let alone all readers. But his proposal at least provides an example of how contemporary theology is seeking to address the legacy of the Enlightenment: acknowledging the postmodern critique, but not accepting it wholesale. From a Christian perspective, whether following White directly or not, attention to the human inevitably entails recourse to the theological – in both particularity and universality.

Popular Film and the Question of a "Popular Theology"

Theology may well have to deal with the ordinary, the mundane; but in trying to do its work in dialog with film, does it deal with the banal, the trivial? It is interesting to observe this as a thread of concern throughout the book. David Browne observed that film and film study have often been received as trivializing exercizes. David Graham revised a view of seeing God in everything in terms of God being capable of being experienced through anything, though he noted that the search for Christ-figures may tell us very little. Marsh sought to fashion a theology of ordinariness, though Jasper observed that seeing God in the everyday can end up being a "tedious, trite or unctuous" claim. Linking theology and film may thus merely compound a concern that the subject-matter of theology (God!) may either be being lost sight of altogether, or at least devalued.

An immediate counter to this claim from within Christian theology itself is, of course, possible. Vexing though it may be to work out in practice, Christian formulations of the so-called "doctrine of incarnation," which press for attention to God's enfleshment in human form, invite theological reflection upon the mundane. The commitment to belief that God can be found in human form (however that belief may be understood and expressed) cannot be confined solely to a belief about the first-century figure of Jesus of Nazareth, and remain a Christian belief, no matter how much Christians may differ as to the nature of the claim in relation to Jesus. Contemporary Christian theology is committed to examining what it means for God to be found in human form today. In the contemporary climate it may be necessary to make maximum use of that rather anthropomorphic approach to the doctrine of God in order to formulate an understanding of God at all. The very credibility of

God language – what has "God" got to do with human life? – is at stake here. Such an approach is also consistent with a broader notion of incarnation which sees God present throughout creation.

This "incarnational defence" of our undertaking is an important one but cannot rest unopposed. In a helpful study, Sarah Coakley has shown that at least six distinct understandings of incarnation can be seen to be operative within Christian theology, one of which amounts to saying very little about what difference the claim for God incarnate actually makes, meaning merely "the profound implication of God in the whole breadth and range of human development" (Coakley 1988: 104). As Coakley notes, it is only when the claim of incarnation is linked with some sort of understanding of how Jesus of Nazareth helps Christians to make sense of God that the relatively "weak" (even if profound) understanding of incarnation just cited can actually become fruitful. Interestingly, Vernon White reads Coakley's first definition as amounting to a "trivial generality" (White 1996: 124), echoing the fear that has sounded throughout this book. If an incarnational strategy is to be used to defend a theology of the ordinary, then, it needs refining further if it is to be persuasive.

It is at this point that we must look at the juxtaposition of, and tensions between, a number of features of the book in the light of Jasper's critique. The first is the evident feature that few of the films studied in Part Two may be regarded as "art-house" films. With the possible exception of *Babette's Feast*, all of the films considered may be called "popular films" – hence our use of the term "movies" in the book's sub-title. We have thus provided ideal material for our potential critics within theology, by choosing films which may be called "low" rather than "high" culture. We have, however, also sought to show that theology can – and must – work with such popular resource material (thereby echoing the strategy of Ostwalt and Martin 1995). A second point derives from David Jasper's implication that there are certain kinds of films which will more readily lend themselves to theological interpretation, more so, indeed, than the ones considered. Whilst agreeing with the first part of the implied claim, our disagreement about the second is likely to focus upon how broad the net can be spread in search of theologically useful material. Perhaps theology has less of a choice of the materials with which it must work, in order to be culturally comprehensible (we resist the word "relevant" as theology's potentially critical edge is then blunted), than it once had. Theology *has* to work with some new materials, as well as old ones, in order to complete its task.

This discussion relates, however, to a third point: the postmodern climate within which we all work in the West. Postmodernism is playing an important role in challenging dominant trends in culture and scholarship, and in pressing for the revaluing of past traditions. In the process, it has needed to relativize in order that revaluation takes place. Revaluation has often entailed a simple equalizing of value, and a failure to acknowledge, for example, why a classic in art or literature has been called such. But this has immense dangers, not least in playing down the need for traditions of interpretation and the adequate recognition of the communal contexts within which traditions are reworked (see for example O'Neill 1995; Eagleton 1996).

There is a sense, though, in which the way theology is being done in this book affirms the postmodernist strategy of asking questions of dominant traditions. In the interests of the future forms and content of Christian theology – and those who participate in it – all contributors deem it essential that film be considered. But they would clearly argue differently as to which films (and what kind of films) might prove profitable for theological discussion, and also on whether/how universals such as "God," "the human condition" or "religious experience" are to be discussed in relation to film. In this, we are all caught up in our own debate.

The bottom line is that an incarnational defense is possible: God, in Christian perspective, is tangled up with the ordinary, the mundane, the seemingly trivial, in a way which is worthy of close examination. Playing the incarnational defense in relation to the theology and film debate, in a postmodernist climate, means that it cannot easily be presupposed which conversations with which films may deliver useful theological material. But incarnation is not pantheism. God is to be distinguishable from the everyday whilst being acknowledged to be firmly in the midst of it, in the same way that Jesus Christ is a "sacrament" (see ch. 15 above): as an admittedly heavily interpreted figure, "Jesus" functions as a decisive clue to what God is like and where God can be found.

For this incarnational defense to work, two things are required: a clear theological identity (which Christian theology must bring to a film, though that identity will never be uniform); and an expectation of mutual critique. This identity will inevitably be related to what Christianity makes of the figure of Jesus of Nazareth. But it will not be wholly consumed by it. The nagging reference to a historical figure does, however, preserve the rootedness of Christian thought and practice in both past and present. As a result, Christianity maintains a firm commitment to understanding God as being entangled in the world's history.

Giving attention to popular film does run the risk of producing a theology of the trivial, rather than an accessible theology. But at its best, it is a challenge to theological elitism. Challenges to First World elitism have come in a variety of forms from outside the First World (e.g. Latin American Liberation Theology and South African Black Theology), and have emerged in a number of forms from within (e.g. feminist theology, North American Black Theology, theology from the city). Theology undertaken in dialog with film offers a further, different kind of, challenge, overlapping with some of the existing forms of questioning. It would be quite wrong to imply that this voice derives primarily from communities who are oppressed or suffering. But how is this challenge to theology, then, to be understood? It is at this point that we must pay attention to its location.

Theology In and Out of Church

"Missiology" is the technical term for the study of the interface between church and world. It has often been supposed, in theoretical terms, that theologians do their work in the church, and then they (or others, e.g. priests, missioners, evangelists, preachers, or whatever) pass on the contents of theology to those around. In this way, the church has done – and does – its missionary work. Alongside this simplified picture, of course, it has always also been known that theology does not actually work like that. Theologians are always present in both church and world, and their theology reflects this. There must without doubt be a necessary theoretical distinction to be drawn between church and world ("church" relating to a concern to ask questions about Christian identity and particularity in the midst of diverse discussions). But to separate the two as sharply as it is often supposed can be, distorts both the task of Christianity's self-understanding and self-presentation, and the task of theological construction itself.

Theology and film discussions are inevitably located on the borderlands of the church (e.g. in pizza parlors, as suggested in this book's introduction). That should not also mean that they be located on the borderlands of theological construction. To push the inadequate spatial imagery a stage further: the tools of theological construction (i.e. a range of Christian theological resources and methods, with experience of a diversity of living communities who use these resources and methods, and a critical mind) are taken to where film begins to stimulate theology-like discussion, and put into effect. Theology is done where the interaction happens. We may choose to call such activity "missiology" rather than "theology proper," largely because it happens outside the church. But the denotation is misleading, not least because it implies that the so-called "missiological" context is where theology is presented, not constructed. The critical dialogs which theology and film debate actually generates, however, suggest a more complex reality.

Missiology is undoubtedly an unhelpful word. It carries too many negative connotations within it. Perhaps talking of the "public forum of theology" would be better. And, indeed, the public character of theology has received much attention – in diverse ways! – on both sides of the Atlantic in the last decade or so (see Tracy 1981; Thiemann 1991; Ford 1992; Montefiore (ed.)

1992). But the link with the theological discipline of missiology is important nevertheless, precisely because it is in this realm where much helpful work (often overlooked by those engaged in constructive theology, and until recently frequently crowded out of theology syllabi) has been undertaken regarding the interaction between theology and culture/s (e.g. Thomas 1995).

Towards a Critical, Postliberal Theology of Film?

We have been arguing in this book for attention to a constructive and affirming critique of the liberal tradition as the theological background against which a proposal for the next step of Christian theology's engagement with film should be understood. The future, for want of a better term, must in some sense be postliberal (particular, but not wholly negating attention to the universal; dialectical, but retaining keen interest in identifiable Christian identity). Our own project has been exploratory and experimental, and we acknowledge our collective debt openly to the prior work of some of our own contributors (e.g. Jewett and Malone), to pacesetters in the field (e.g. Hurley) and to others who approach a similar subject-matter from a rather different perspective (e.g, May, Martin and Ostwalt, Miles). We trust that we have stimulated readers to be critical, but also to have ventured their own theologically creative endeavors in dialog with film. Such a reaction is to be expected more from the already theologically-inclined. Without such engagement, we suggest, important public discussion about the credibility and comprehension of the topics which theology has traditionally handled will simply not be had, let alone heard.

We would like to think, though, that the not-so-theologically inclined will have been stimulated too. If philosophical or more broadly ideological, rather than explicitly theological, dialog with film has suggested itself, then so be it: important discussion in relation to human wellbeing, praxis and communal life, will at least have been fostered. And if either kind of discussion results, then we have every reason to believe in the practical importance of deep-pan, and not just thin-crust, theology.

Annotated Bibliography

The following bibliography contains all written and videotaped material referred to throughout the book, together with selected other useful material, often related to films not considered in this volume. Notes are interspersed throughout the bibliography, to indicate especially helpful texts.

Adams, D. and Apostolos-Cappadona, D. 1987: *Art As Religious Studies* (New York: Crossroad).

Adams, R. H. 1964: "How warm is the cold, how light the darkness" *Christian Century* (Sept. 16), 1144–45. An essay on the work of Bergman.

Agan, P. 1993: *Robert De Niro: The Man, the Myth, the Movies* (Robert Hale).

Aitken, T. 1995: "The Greatest Story – Never Told" *The Tablet* (Dec. 23/30), 1656–8.

Aldgate, A. 1995: *Censorship and the Permissive Society. British Cinema and Theatre, 1955–1965* (Oxford: Clarendon Press).

Alexander, J. F. 1993: "And That's That: Sin, Salvation, and Woody Allen" *Other Side* 29 (Jan.–Feb.), 53–5. Compares *Husbands and Wives* with *Enchanted April*.

Allen, R. M. and Asimov, I. 1993: *Caliban* (Millenium Orion Books).

Alvarado, M. and Thompson, J. O. 1990: *The Media Reader* (British Film Institute). Excellent general "media studies" text which locates film within other media.

Anderson, J. C. and Moore, S. (eds) 1992: *Mark and Method: New Approaches in Biblical Studies* (Fortress).

Andrew, D. 1976: *The Major Film Theories: An Introduction* (New York: Oxford University Press). Concentrates on theorists (Munsterberg, Arnheim, Eisenstein, the Russian Formalists, Kracauer, Bazin, Metz, and Mitry).

Apostolos-Cappadona, D. 1984: *Art, Creativity and the Sacred: An Anthology in Religion and Art* (New York: Crossroad).

Appleton, G. 1985: *The Oxford Book of Prayer* (Oxford University Press).

(ASB) 1980: *Alternative Service Book* (Oxford University Press and Mowbray).

Aukerman, D. 1981: *Darkening Valley: A Biblical Perspective on Nuclear War* (Seabury Press).

Babington, B. and Evans. P. W. 1993: *Biblical Epics. Sacred Narrative in the Hollywood Cinema* (Manchester University Press/St Martin's Press).

Baelz, P. 1982: *Does God Answer Prayer?* (Darton, Longman and Todd).

Balthasar, H. U. von 1975: *Elucidations*, tr. J. Riches (SPCK).

Barclay, W. 1971: *Ethics in a Permissive Society* (Fontana).

Barr, J. 1962: *Biblical Words for Time* (Allenson/ SCM Press).

Barth, K. 1957: *Church Dogmatics II/1* (T & T Clark).

——1958: *Church Dogmatics IV/2* (T & T Clark).

——1968: *The Epistle to the Romans*, tr. E. C. Hoskyns (Oxford University Press).

——1986: *Wolfgang Amadeus Mozart* (Eerdmans).

Barthes, R. 1972: *Mythologies (Paladin)*.

Barton, J. 1984: *Reading the Old Testament* (Darton, Longman and Todd).

Basinger, J. 1986: *The* It's A Wonderful Life *Book*. (Wesleyan University).

——1994: *A Woman's View: How Hollywood Spoke to Women 1930–1960* (Chatto & Windus).

Baudrillard, J. 1988: *The Evil Demon of Images* (Power Institute of Fine Arts).

Baumgarten, J. 1991: Entry on *"kairos,"* in H. Balz and G. Schneider *Exegetical Dictionary of the New Testament Vol. 2* (T & T Clark).

Bazalgette, C. and Buckingham D. 1995: *In Front of the Children: Screen Entertainment and Young Audiences* (Bristol Film Institute).

Bazin, A. 1992: "Cinema and Theology" *The South Atlantic Quarterly* 91(2), 393–408.

Beck, R. 1996: *Non-Violent Story: Narrative Conflict Resolution in the Gospel of Mark* (Orbis).

Becker, E. 1985: *Denial of Death* (Free Press).

——1975: *Escape From Evil* (Free Press).

Bedouelle, G. 1986: "Film and the Mystery of the Person" *Communio* 13 (Spring), 84–94.

——1985: *Du spiritual dans le cinéma* (Cerf).

Bentley, P. 1990: "Funerals, Frigidity and Fanaticism: The Representation of Religion in Australian Feature Films" *St Mark's Review* 142 (Winter), 12–15.

Berger, A. A. 1991: *Media Analysis Techniques* (Sage). A basic and useful "primer" which identifies and illustrates key approaches to media analysis.

Berkhof, H. 1989: *Two Hundred Years of Theology* (Eerdmans).

Betz, H. D. 1979: *Galatians* (Hermeneia).

Bingham, J. 1972: *Courage to Change: An Introduction to the Life and Thought of Reinhold Niebuhr* (University Press of America).

Black, G. D. 1994: *Hollywood Censored. Morality Codes, Catholics, and the Movies* (Cambridge University Press).

Blake, R. A. 1991: *Screening America: Reflections on Five Classic Films* (Paulist).

Boff, L. 1987: *Jesus Christ Liberator* (SPCK = Orbis 1978).

Boman, T. 1960: *Hebrew Thought Compared with Greek* (SCM Press).

Bonhoeffer, D. 1948: *The Cost of Discipleship*, tr. R. H. Fuller (SCM Press).

Bordwell, D. 1985: *Narration in the Fiction Film* (Methuen). A "classic" text on film narrativity, which complements and expands on the ideas presented in "Film Art".

——1989: *Making Meaning: Inference and Rhetoric in the Interpretation of Cinema* (Harvard University Press).

——and Carroll, N. 1996: *Post Theory: Reconstructing Film Studies* (University of

Wisconsin). A critique of psychoanalytic and structuralist approaches to film which argues persuasively for cognitivism.

——and Thompson, K. 1993: *Film Art*, 4th edn (McGrawHill). Particularly good on "narrativity" and film form. Lucid and accessible.

Borg, M. J. 1987: *Jesus: A New Vision – Spirit, Culture, and The Life of Discipleship* (HarperCollins).

Bowser, E. 1982: "Preparation for Brighton: The American Contribution" in R. Holman (ed.) *Cinema 1900–1906* (*Fédération Internationale des Archives du Film*), 3–29.

Boyd, M. 1957: "Theology and the Movies" *Theology Today* 14/3, 359–73.

Bremer, D. and Myers, C. 1994: "The Flutter of History: Wim Wenders' Film View of Angels in Our Midst" *Sojourners* 23 (July) 42–5. Considers *Wings of Desire* and *Faraway So Close*.

Bridge, D. 1995: "Back to the Cinema: Theology Reflects on the Arts" *Epworth Review* 22 (Jan.), 39–44.

British Universities Film and Video Council 1995: *Film and Television in Education* (Blueprint).

Brode, D. 1993: *The Films of Robert De Niro* (Virgin).

Brown, R. McA. 1986: *The Essential Reinhold Niebuhr: Selected Essays and Addresses* (Yale University Press).

Browning, D. S. 1987: *Religious Thought and the Modern Psychologies: A Critical Conversation in the Theology of Culture* (Fortress).

Browning, R. 1940: *Poetical Works of Robert Browning* (Oxford University Press).

Bruce, S. 1995: *Religion in Modern Britain* (Oxford University Press).

——1996: *Religion in the Modern World: From Cathedrals to Cults* (Oxford University Press).

Brueggemann, W. 1986: *Hopeful Imagination: Prophetic Voices in Exile* (SCM Press).

——1993: *Texts Under Negotiation. The Bible and Postmodern Imagination* (Augsburg Fortress/SCM Press).

Brummer, V. 1984: *What Are We Doing When We Pray?* (SCM Press).

Brunsson, N. 1989: *The Organization of Hypocrisy: Talk, Decisions and Actions in Organizations* (Wiley).

——and Olsen, J. P. 1993: *The Reforming Organization* (Routledge).

Burns, A. L. 1953: "Two Words for 'Time' in the New Testament" *Australian Biblical Review* 3, 7–22.

Burrows, E. (ed.) 1995: *British Cinema Source Book* (British Film Institute).

Butler, I. 1969: *Religion in the Cinema* (A. S. Barnes & Co.).

Butler, R. 1994: "A Night at the Pictures in 1994," in *Independent on Sunday* (Dec. 16), 18–19.

Bygrave, M. 1991: "My name is Cecil, King of Kings" *Sunday Telegraph* (Feb. 3), 13.

Cameron, J. 1991: Terminator II: Judgment Day – Film Production Notes (Carolco Productions).

Campbell, J. 1988: *Hero with a Thousand Faces* (Princeton University Press).

Campbell, R. H. and Pitts, M. R. 1981: *The Bible on Film: A Checklist, 1897–1980* (Scarecrow).

Camus, A. 1982: *The Outsider*, tr. J. Lavedo (Penguin).

Capra, F. 1971: *The Name Above the Title* (Macmillan).

Carmody, D. L. 1995: *Christian Feminist Theology: A Constructive Interpretation* (Blackwell).

Carney, R. 1971: *American Vision: The Films of Frank Capra* (Cambridge University Press).

Carr, W. 1990: *Ministry and the Media* (SPCK).

Carroll, N. 1996: *Theorizing the Moving Image* (Cambridge University Press). A collection of 28 essays from a philosophical perspective.

Carter, S. 1990: "Avatars of the Turtles" *Journal of Popular Film and Television* 18, 94–102.

(Catechism) 1994: *Catechism of the Catholic Church* (Geoffrey Chapman).

Channel Four Television, 1992: *Jesus Christ Movie-Star* (TV documentary; April 20).

Chopp, R. S. 1986: *The Praxis of Suffering: An Interpretation of Liberation and Political Theologies* (Orbis).

Clayton, J. P. 1980: *The Concept of Correlation: Paul Tillich and the Possibility of a Mediating Theology* (De Gruyter).

Coakley, S. 1988: *Christ Without Absolutes: A Study of the Christology of Ernst Troeltsch* (Clarendon Press).

Coates, P. 1994: *At the Intersection of High and Mass Culture* (Cambridge University Press).

Cobb, K. 1995: "Reconsidering the Status of Popular Culture in Tillich's Theology of Culture", in *Journal of the American Academy of Religion* 63, 53–84.

Collins J., Radner, H. and Preacher Collins, A. 1993: *Film Theory Goes to the Movies* (Routledge/American Film Institute). A lively and interesting application of theory to mainstream cinema, including essays on *Thelma and Louise*, *The Silence of the Lambs* and *Boyz N The Hood*.

Comblin, J. 1990: *Being Human: A Christian Anthropology* (Burns & Oates).

Combs, R. 1988: "*Babettes Gaestebud (Babette's Feast)*" *Monthly Film Bulletin* 55, 74–75.

Commins, G. 1987: "Woody Allen's Theological Imagination" *Theology Today* 44 (July), 235–49.

Comstock, W. R. 1975: "Myth and Contemporary Cinema" *Journal of the American Academy of Religion* 43, 598–600.

Cone, J. 1986: *For My People* (Orbis).

Connelly, M. K. 1993: *Martin Scorsese: An Analysis of His Feature Films, with a Filmography of His Entire Directorial Career* (McFarland).

Connor, S. 1989: *Postmodernist Culture: An Introduction to Theories of the Contemporary* (Blackwell).

Cook, D. 1991: *A History of Narrative Film* (Norton). Comprehensive history of world cinema with examples of detailed analysis.

Cook, P. (ed.) 1985: *The Cinema Book* (British Film Institute). A key book which identifies and describes critical approaches to cinema and provides an important sourcebook for film studies students.

——1988: Review of M. Scorsese's "The Last Temptation of Christ" *Monthly Film Bulletin* 55, 287–8.

——and Dodd, P. (eds) 1993: *Women and Film: A "Sight and Sound" Reader* (Scarlet Press).

Cooper, J. C. and Skrade, C. (eds.) 1970: *Celluloid and Symbols* (Fortress). Written from the perspective of "secular theology, this collection builds on an existential, analytic approach.

Corliss, R. 1988: "A Critic's Contrarian View" *Time* (Aug. 15), 44.

——1993: Review of *Groundhog Day*, in *Time* (Feb. 15), 61.

Cormack, M. J. 1994: *Ideology and Cinematography in Hollywood* (St Martin's).

Corrington, R. S. 1987: *The Community of Interpreters: On the Hermeneutics of Nature and the Bible in the American Philosophical Tradition* (Mercer).

Cowburn, J. 1979: *Shadows and the Dark: The Problems of Suffering and Evil* (SCM Press).

Creekmur, C. R. and Alexander, D. 1995: *Out in Culture: Gay, Lesbian and Other Queer Essays on Popular Culture* (Duke University Press).

Cross, F. L., (ed.) 1957: *The Oxford Dictionary of the Christian Church* (Oxford University Press).

Crossan, J. D. 1975: *The Dark Interval: Toward a Theology of Story* (Argus; revised 1988, Polebridge Press).

——1994: *Jesus: A Revolutionary Biography* (HarperSanFrancisco).

Cullmann, O. 1964: *Christ and Time: The Primitive Christian Conception of Time and History* (Westminster/ SCM Press).

cummings, e. e. 1989: "I thank you, God, for this most amazing day," from *Selected Poems 1923–1958* (Faber & Faber).

Cuneen, J. 1993: "Film and the Sacred" *Cross Currents* 43 (Spring), 92–104.

Cupitt, D. 1980: *Taking Leave of God* (SCM Press).

Dahlber, B. 1964: "The Bergman Trilogy" *Christianity and Crisis* 6 (July), 135–9.

Davies, J. G. 1973: *Every Day God: Encountering the Holy in World and Worship* (SCM Press).

Davies, P. R. 1995: *Whose Bible Is It Anyway?* (Sheffield Academic Press).

Delling, G. 1965: Entry on *"kairos ktl"* *Theological Dictionary of the New Testament* 3, 459–65.

——1974: Entry on *"chronos"* *Theological Dictionary of the New Testament* 9, 581–93

Dempsey, M. 1980: "Inexplicable Feelings: An Interview with Peter Weir" *Film Quarterly* 33 (4), 2–11.

Denby, D. 1993: Review of *Groundhog Day*, in *New York* (Mar. 1), 110.

Denzin, N. K. 1991: *Images of Postmodern Society* (Sage). A stimulating account of postmodernism applied to a range of media forms by an important author in this field.

Dewey, J. 1994: "The Gospel of Mark" in E. S. Fiorenza (ed.) *Searching the Scriptures*, Vol. 2: *A Feminist Commentary* (Crossroad) 470–509.

Dillenberger, John 1987: *A Theology of Artistic Sensibilities* (SCM Press). Focused more on theological engagement with the fine arts, though still very useful. Contains two chapters drawing out the significance of the interaction for theological method and education.

Dinesen, I. (Karen Blixen) 1986: "Babette's Feast" in *Anecdotes of Destiny* (Penguin), 21–68.

Doctrine Commission 1991: *We Believe in the Holy Spirit* A report by The Doctrine Commission of the General Synod of the Church of England (Church House Publishing).

Dodd, C. H. 1936: *The Apostolic Preaching and its Development* (Hodder & Stoughton).

Doherty, T. 1988: *Teenagers And Teenpics: The Juvenilization of American Movies in the 1950s* (Unwin Hyman).

Dostoyevsky, F. 1970: *The Idiot*, tr. D. Magarshack (Penguin).

Drouzy, M. and Jørgensen, L. N. (eds) 1989: *Letters About The Jesus Film. 16 Years of Correspondence between Carl Th. Dreyer and Blevins Davis* (University of Copenhagen).

Dubin, S. C. 1992: *Arresting Images: Impolitic Art and Uncivil Actions* (Routledge).

Dulles, A. 1976: *Models of the Church* (Gill and Macmillan; 2nd edn 1987).

Dunn, J. D. G. 1991: *The Partings of the Ways: Between Christianity and Judaism and their Significance for the Character of Christianity* (SCM Press/Trinity Press International).

——1993: *The Epistle to the Galatians* Black's New Testament Commentary (Black/ Hendrickson).

Dyer, R. 1990: *Now You See It: Studies on Lesbian and Gay Film* (Routledge).

——1992: *Only Entertainment* (Routledge). One of a series of lucid books by the same author dealing with gay issues and themes in cinema, this one grapples with the intellectual interrogation of "entertainment" and the notion of "camp."

Dyson, A. O. 1983: Entry on "Anthropology, Christian" in A. Richardson and J. Bowden (eds) *A New Dictionary of Christian Theology* (SCM Press), 23–7.

Eagleton, T. 1996: *The Illusions of Postmodernism* (Blackwell).

Easthope, A. 1993: *Contemporary Film Theory* (Longman). Provides useful accounts on psychoanalytic approaches to film, including fetishism, ideology and subjectivity, gender and the gaze.

Ebel, H. 1978: "The New Theology: *Star Trek, Star Wars, Close Encounters*, and the Crisis of Pseudorationality" *The Journal of Psychohistory* 5, 487–98.

Ebert, R. 1989: "Review of *Dead Poets Society*" reproduced in *Cinemania '95* (Microsoft).

Eck, D. and Jain, D. 1986: *Speaking of Faith* (The Women's Press).

Eco, U. 1983: *The Name of the Rose* (Secker & Warburg).

——1985: *Reflections on* The Name of the Rose (Secker & Warburg).

Edwards, O. C. Jr 1990: "Exempla V" *Anglican Theological Review* 72 (Winter), 89–94. Considers *Places in the Heart* and *Babette's Feast*.

Eliade, M. 1961: *The Sacred and the Profane* (Harper – Row).

Eliot, T. S. 1944: *Four Quartets* (Faber).

Ellis, J. 1992: *Visible Fictions: Cinema, Television, Video* revised edn (Routledge). Provides a lucid and thought provoking overview of media fictions.

Ellul, J. 1963: *Technological Society* (Cape).

English, D. (ed.) 1994: *Windows on Salvation* (Darton, Longman and Todd).

Evans, G. R. 1994: *The Church and the Churches: Toward an Ecumenical Ecclesiology* (Cambridge University Press).

Fackre, G. 1993: "The Surge in Systematics: A Commentary on Current Works" *Journal of Religion* 73, 223–37.

——1995: "The Revival of Systematic Theology: An Overview" *Interpretation* 49, 229–41.

Farolino, A. 1993: Review of *Groundhog Day*, in *New York Post* (Feb. 12), 31.

Ferlita, E. and May J. 1976: *Film Odyssey: The Art of Film as Search for Meaning* (Paulist Press). The authors approach film through the Judeo-Christian theme of fundamental hope.

Field, S. 1994: *Four Screenplays* (Dell).

Fiorenza, E. S. 1983: *In Memory of Her: A Feminist Theological Reconstruction of Early Christianity* (Crossroad).

Fiske, J. 1989: *Understanding Popular Culture* (Routledge).

——1990: *Introduction to Communication Studies* (Routledge). Very useful introduction to structuralism and semiotics.

Folsom, J. K. 1970: "*Shane* and *Hud*: Two Stories in Search of a Medium" *Western Humanities Review*, 24 (4), 359–72.

Forbes, J. 1988: "Axel's Feast" in *Sight and Sound* (Spring issue), 106–7.

Ford, D. F. 1992: *A Long Rumour of Wisdom: Redescribing Theology* (Cambridge University Press).

Forshey, G. E. 1978: "The Apocalyptic Mood in Contemporary Films" *explor* 4, 28–38.

——1980: "Popular Religion, Film and the American Psyche" *Christian Century* 97 (Apr. 30), 489–93.

——1992: *American Religious and Biblical Spectaculars* (Praeger).

Fox, M. (ed.) 1987: *Hildegard of Bingen's Book of Divine Works with Letters and Songs* (Bear and Company).

Francke, L. 1994: *Script Girls: Women Screenwriters in Hollywood* (British Film Institute).

Frank, V. 1994: *Man's Search for Meaning* (Pocket Books).

Frankeil, T. 1990: *The Voice of Sarah: Feminine Spirituality and Traditional Judaism* (HarperCollins).

Franklin, H. B. 1988: *War Stars: The Superweapon and the American Imagination* (Oxford University Press).

Freedberg, D. 1989: *The Power of Images: Studies in the History and Theory of Response* (Chicago University Press).

Freeland, C. A. and Wartenberg T. E. (eds) 1995: *Philosophy and Film* (Routledge). Attempts to do for philosophy what this present volume undertakes for theology. Includes essays on *Sea of Love*, *Casablanca* and *Ghost*, *White Palace*, and *Europa Europa*, together with theoretical pieces and studies of specific themes and film directors.

Freeman, A. 1993: *God In Us: The Case for Christian Humanism* (SCM Press).

Friedman, L. 1993: British Cinema and Thatcherism (UCL Press). A useful account of British "national cinema" which includes "the religion of the marketplace" and accounts of filmmakers and independent production.

Fuller, P. 1990: *Images of God: The Consolations of Lost Illusions* (The Hogarth Press).

Fuller, R. 1968: "2001: A Space Odyssey" *Theology Today* 25/1, 277–80.

Gadamer, H.-G. 1979: *Truth and Method* 2nd edn (Sheed and Ward).

Gallafont, E. 1994: *Clint Eastwood: Filmmaker and Star* (Continuum).

Gallagher, S. 1989: "Searching for God in Popular Culture: The Last Crusade, The Final Frontier and The Abyss" *Radix* 19/2, 22, 26.

Gallez, J. P. 1989: "The Christ of Scorsese or Vulnerability Transformed. Religion and Film" *Temps Modernes* 44 (514), 35–46.

Gardner, H. (ed.) 1973: *New Oxford Book of English Verse* (Oxford University Press).

Gelertner, D. 1994: *The Muse in the Machine: Computers and Creative Thought* (Fourth Estate).

Gerber, L. E. 1993: "The Virtuous Terrorist: Stanley Hauerwas and *The Crying Game*" *Cross Currents* 43 (Summer), 230–4.

Gershwin, I. 1992: "Someone To Watch Over Me," in *Fascinating Rhythm: the Collaboration of George and Ira Gershwin* (D. Rosenberg: Lime Tree).

Giannetti, L. 1990: *Understanding Movies* 5th edn (Prentice Hall).

Gibson, A. 1969: *The Silence of God: Creative Response to the Films of Ingmar Bergman* (Harper & Row). Gibson offers a "theoesthetic" response to Bergman, as a dialog with modern atheism.

Gilmore, D. G. (ed.) 1987: *Honor and Shame and the Unity of the Mediterranean* (American Anthropological Association).

Girard, R. 1977: *Violence and the Sacred* (Johns Hopkins University Press).

——1986: *The Scapegoat* (Johns Hopkins University Press).

Giroux, H. A. 1993: "Reclaiming the Social: Pedagogy, Resistance, and Politics in Celluloid Culture" in Collins, J., Radner, H. and Collins, A. P. (eds) *Film Theory Goes to the Movies* (Routledge), 37–55.

Giunti, M. 1993: "Bill Murray grows up?" *Christian Century*, 110 (Apr. 21), 430.

Glazter, R. and Raburn, J. (eds) 1971: *Frank Capra: The Man and His Films* (Ann Arbor).

Goethals, G. T. 1990: *The Electronic Golden Calf: Images, Religion, and the Making of Meaning* (Cowley).

Goffman, E. 1959: *The Presentation of Self in Everyday Life* (Penguin).

Graham, D. 1997: "Images of Christ in Recent Film," in Porter, S., Hayes, M. and Tombs, D. (eds) *Images of Christ: Ancient and Modern* (Sheffield Academic Press).

Grant, R. M. and Freedman, D. N. 1960: *The Secret Sayings of Jesus* (Collins).

Gray, E. D. 1981: *Green Paradise Lost* 2nd edn (Roundtable).

Green, C. (ed.) 1990: *Karl Barth: Theologian of Freedom* (Collins; now T & T Clark/ Fortress).

Greenberg, H. 1994: Review of *The Piano*, in *Film Quarterly* Vol. 47, No. 3 (Spring), 46–50.

Grenier, R. 1991: "Hollywood's Holy Grail" *Commentary* 92 (Nov.), 50–3. Considers *The Fisher King* and *Barton Fink*.

Grenz, S. 1994: *Theology for the Community of God* (Broadman & Holman/Paternoster).

Guerif, F. 1986: *Clint Eastwood: The Man and his Films* (St Martin's Press).

Gunton, C. 1993: *The One, the Three and the Many: God, Creation and the Culture of Modernity* (Cambridge University Press).

Gutierrez, G. 1991: *The God of Life* (SCM Press).

Halliwell, L. 1995: Entry on "Censorship" in J. Walker (ed.) *Halliwell's Filmgoer's Companion* (HarperCollins) 118–19.

——1995: Entry on "Christ" in J. Walker (ed.) *Halliwell's Filmgoer's Companion*, (HarperCollins), 126.

Hamerton-Kelly, R. G. 1992: *Sacred Violence: Paul's Hermeneutic of the Cross* (Augsburg Fortress).

Hamilton, W. 1993: *A Quest for the Post-Historical Jesus* (SCM Press).

Hampden-Turner, C. 1990: *Charting the Corporate Mind: From Dilemma To Strategy* (Blackwell).

Harpole, C. (ed.) 1994: *History of American Cinema* (Charles Scribner).

Harries, R. 1994: *The Real God* (Mowbray).

Harvey, D. 1989: *The Condition of Postmodernity: An Enquiry into the Origins of Cultural Change* (Blackwell).

Hatt, H. 1990: "The Dialogue of Theology with Film" *Encounter* 51 (Spring), 103–23.

——1992: Relating to the Indigenous Culture: Theology and Film in Dialogue" *Arts: The Arts in Religious and Theological Studies* 4 (Summer), 15–17. Discusses *Johnny Belinda*.

——1993: "Recovering the Myth of the Orphan and Renewing the World of the Family" *Encounter* 54 (Spring), 119–42. Considers *Regarding Henry* and *Grand Canyon*.

Hayne, D. (ed.) 1960: *The Autobiography of Cecil B. DeMille* (W. H. Allen).

Hayward, P and Wollen T. 1993: *Future Visions* (British Film Institute).

Hayward, S. 1996: *Key Concepts in Cinema Studies* (Routledge).

Hein, D. 1986: "Interpretations of the Divine Presence in History" *Saint Luke's Journal of Theology* 29 (Mar.), 107–16. The topic is discussed with reference to *Raiders of the Lost Ark*.

Hennecke, E. and Schneemelcher, W. eds. 1963: *New Testament Apocrypha* (SCM Press).

Hennelly, A. T. (ed.) 1990: *Liberation Theology: A Documentary History* (Orbis).

Hick, J. 1983: *The Second Christianity* (SCM Press).

——1989: *An Interpretation of Religion* (Macmillan).

Higashi, S. 1994: *Cecil B. DeMille and American Culture. The Silent Era* (University of California Press).

Hill, G. 1992: *Illuminating Shadows: The Mythic Power of Film* (Shambala).

Hillier, J. 1993: *The New Hollywood* (Studio Vista). A useful account of contemporary Hollywood practice, with chapters on black filmmakers, women filmmakers and independent production.

Hobsbawm, E. 1994: *Age of Extremes: The Short Twentieth Century 1914–1991* (Michael Joseph).

Hodgson, P. C. 1994: *Winds of the Spirit* (SCM Press). A difficult, but rewarding, piece of constructive theology which deals with all of Christian theology's main themes, taking full account of the contexts and crises within which theology is done in the West today.

Hodgson, P. and King, R. (eds) 1985: *Readings in Christian Theology* (Fortress/SPCK).

A useful reader, containing primary texts from 2000 years of Christian thought, grouped in chapters addressing Christian theology's main themes (God, Christ, church etc.).

Holloway, R. 1977: *Beyond the Image: Approaches to the Religious Dimension in the Cinema* (World Council of Churches). An ambitious, wide-ranging and important early study, focusing on the religious in film, though also addressing (in a chapter misleadingly entitled "A Theology of the Cinema") interconnections between the history of film and the history of Christian theology. A final chapter considers "The Filmmaker as Biblical Theologian." There is a useful, though inevitably dated, bibliography.

Hopewell, J. F. 1988: *Congregation: Stories and Structures* (SCM Press = Fortress 1987).

Hopkins, G. M. 1994: *The Works of Gerard Manley Hopkins* (Wordsworth).

Horstman, J. E. 1992a: "Haunted by a Violent God" *Other Side* 28 (Mar.-Apr.), 38–40. A treatment of the work of Paul Schrader and Martin Scorsese.

——1992b: "Hollywood's Heavenly Headache" *Other Side* 28 (May-June), 32–4.

Horton, J. and Mendus, S. (eds) 1994: *After MacIntyre: Critical Perspectives on the Work of Alasdair MacIntyre* (Polity Press).

Hostetter, R. 1985: "A Controversial 'Witness'" *Christian Century* 102 (Apr. 10), 341–2.

Hübner, H. 1993: Entry on "*chronos*," in H. Balz and G. Schneider *Exegetical Dictionary of the New Testament Vol. 3* (T & T Clark).

Hughes, G. 1985: *God of Surprises* (Darton, Longman and Todd).

Hurley, N. P. 1970: *Theology Through Film* (Harper & Row). A seminal text now overtaken in some of its theological assumptions and in choice of films, but remaining valuable for its persuasive recognition of the value of film for theological education. Starts from the assumption that movies are for the masses what theology is for an elite.

——1978: *The Reel Revolution. A Film Primer on Liberation* (Orbis).

——1982: "Cinematic Transformations of Jesus," in J. R. May and M. S. Bird (eds) *Religion in Film* (University of Tennessee Press), 61–78.

Hurtado, L. W. 1979: "The Jerusalem Collection and the Book of Galatians" *Journal for the Study of the New Testament*, 5, 46–62.

Jackson, K. (ed.) 1990: *Schrader on Schrader and Other Writings* (Faber & Faber; reprinted 1992).

James, M. R. 1924: *The Apocryphal New Testament* (Clarendon Press).

Jasper, D. 1993: *Rhetoric, Power and Community: An Exercise in Reserve* (Macmillan).

——1994: "Living in the Reel World: The Bible in Film" *Modern Believing* 35/1, 29–37.

Jauss, H. 1970: "Literary History as a Challenge to Literary Theory," in *New Literary History* 2, 7–37, reprinted in T. Bahti tr. *Toward an Aesthetic of Reception* (Harvester Press 1982, 3–45).

Jenkins, D. 1983: Entry on "Culture" in *A New Dictionary of Christian Theology* A. Richardson and J. Bowden (eds) (SCM Press), 137–41.

Jenkins, D. E. 1984: *The Glory of Man* (SCM Press).

Jenkins, S. 1988: "From the Pit of Hell: the Making of 'The Last Temptation of Christ'" *Monthly Film Bulletin* 55, 352–3.

Jenks, C. (ed.) 1995: *Visual Culture* (Routledge).

Jewett, R. 1970–1: "The Agitators and the Galatian Congregation" *New Testament Studies* 17, 198–212.

——1993: *Saint Paul At the Movies: The Apostle's Dialogue with American Culture* (Westminster/John Knox). A key contribution to the ongoing discussion about, and use of, biblical resonances in film. Explores the contemporary theological significance of these resonances in search of a way in which the insights of the Apostle Paul may be heard today. Treats 11 films, including *Star Wars*, *Amadeus*, *Tender Mercies*, *Tootsie* and *Ordinary People*.

——1994: *Paul the Apostle to America: Cultural Trends and Pauline Scholarship* (Westminster/John Knox).

John of the Cross, St 1953: *The Complete Works of St John of the Cross* vols 1–3, revised edn, tr. E. A. Peers (Burns Oates and Washbourne).

Jowett, G and Linton, J. M. 1980: *Movies as Mass Communication* (Sage Publications).

Kahle, R. and Lee, R. E. A. 1971: *Popcorn and Parables* (Augsburg).

Kamitsuka, D.1996: "The Justification of Religious Belief in the Pluralistic Public Realm: Another Look at Postliberal Apologetics" *Journal of Religion* 76, 588–606.

Kaplan, A. E. 1990: *Psychoanalysis and Cinema* (Routledge).

Karney, R. 1993: *Who's Who in Hollywood* (Bloomsbury).

Kavanagh, A. 1982: *Elements of Rite* (The Liturgical Press).

Kazantzakis, N. 1991: *The Last Temptation* (Faber & Faber; original E. T. Bruno Cassirer 1961).

Kegley, C. W. 1967: Entry on "Optimism," in J. Macquarrie (ed.) *A Dictionary of Christian Ethics* (SCM Press; reprinted in J. Macquarrie and J. F. Childress (eds) *A New Dictionary of Christian Ethics* (SCM Press 1986: 438–9).

Kelly, A. 1974: "The Word and the Story" *Compass Theology Review* 2, 27.

Kelsey, D. 1989: "Paul Tillich", in *The Modern Theologians* vol. 1 (ed.) D. Ford (Blackwell), 134–51.

Kerouac, J. 1957: *On the Road* (Viking Press).

Kerry, H.T and Myers, L. 1976: "*One Flew Over the Cuckoo's Nest*: A Psycho-Symbolic Review" *Theology Today* 33/3, 285–90.

Kesey, K. 1988: *One Flew Over the Cuckoo's Nest* (Picador; original edn 1962).

Kinnard, R. and Davis, T. 1992: *Divine Images: A History of Jesus on the Screen* (Citadel).

Kleinbaum, N. H. 1989: *Dead Poets Society* (Bantam Books).

Kraps, J. M. 1985: "The Gospel According to Eastwood" *Christian Century* 102 (Aug. 14), 740.

Kreitzer, L. J. 1993: *The New Testament in Fiction and Film: On Reversing the Hermeneutical Flow* (JSOT). Explores the way in which films may help us see new things in biblical texts ("reversing the hermeneutical flow"). Deals with *Spartacus*, *Ben-Hur*, *Barabbas*, *Dr Jekyll and Mr Hyde*, and *The Trial*.

——1994: *The Old Testament in Fiction and Film: On Reversing the Hermeneutical Flow* (Sheffield Academic Press). Considers *The Ten Commandments*, *Moby Dick*, *East of Eden* , *Frankenstein*, and *A Farewell to Arms*.

Kreiziger, F. A. 1982: *Apocalypse and Science Fiction: A Dialectic of Religious and Secular Soteriologies* (Scholars Press).

Kuhn, A. 1990: *Alien Zone: Cultural Theory and Contemporary Science Fiction Cinema* (Verso).

LaCugna, C. M. (ed.) 1993: *Freeing Theology* (Harper Collins/T & T Clark).

Lapsley, R. and Westlake, M. 1988: *Film Theory: An Introduction* (Manchester University Press/ St Martin's Press).

Lauder, R. E. 1989: *God, Death, Art and Love: The Philosophical Vision of Ingmar Bergman* (Paulist Press).

Leibrecht, W. 1984: Entry on "Paul Tillich," in *A Handbook of Christian Theologians* M. E. Marty and D. G. Peerman (eds) (Lutterworth/Abingdon Press), 485–500.

Leishman, J. B. (ed.) 1964: *Rainer Maria Rilke: Selected Poems* (Penguin).

Leo, J. 1988: "A Holy Furor" *Time* (Aug. 15), 42–4.

Lerner, M. 1994: "*Forrest Gump*, The Christian Right, and the Deprivation of Meaning" *Tikkun* 9 (Sept.–Oct.), 5–8.

Levy, S. 1992: *Artificial Life – The Quest for a New Creation* (Cape).

Lewis, C. S. 1993: *The Screwtape Letters* (Fount; original edn 1942).

Lindbeck, G. A. 1984: *The Nature of Doctrine* (Westminster Press/SPCK).

Lints, R. 1993: "The Postpositivist Choice: Tracy or Lindbeck?" *Journal of the American Academy of Religion* 61, 655–77.

Lonergan, B. S. J. 1964: *De Verbo Incarnato* (3rd edn; Gregorian University Press).

Longenecker, R. 1990: *Galatians* Word Biblical Commentary 41 (Word).

Loretan, M. 1988: "'*Schwarzer Engel am weissen Himmel der Lagunenstadt': zur blasphemischen Provokation von M.Scorseses Film* 'The Last Temptation of Christ'" *Reformatio* 37 (Dec.), 435–44.

——1993: "*Sein-können geht vor sollen: Interpretation der Dekalog-Filme Kieslowskis als ästhetische Modelle moralischer, existenzieller und religiöser Erfahrungen*" in W. Lesch and M.Loretan (eds) *Das Gewicht der Gebote und die Möglichkeiten der Kunst* (Editions Universitaires), 103–30.

(Lutheran) 1978: *Lutheran Book of Worship* (Augsburg Publishing House and LCA Board of Publication).

McBride, J. 1996: *Frank Capra: The Catastrophe of Success* (Faber).

MacDonald, A. 1991: *Films in Close-Up* (Inter-Varsity Press).

McFarlane, B. and Ryan, T. 1981: "Peter Weir: Towards the Center" *Cinema Papers* 34 (Sept./Oct.), 323–9.

McGrath, A. E. 1993: *The Renewal of Anglicanism* (SPCK).

——1994: *Christian Theology: An Introduction* (Blackwell; now in 2nd edn. 1996). Probably the best single-volume introduction to Christian theology available. In three parts, considers the history, sources and methods, and content of Christian theology. The material in part three (chapters 7 to 16) would supplement well, for those new to the subject, the theological aspects of the studies in part two of this book.

MacIntyre, A. 1981: *After Virtue: a study in moral theory* (Duckworth).

——1990: *Three Rival Versions of Moral Enquiry: Encyclopaedia, Genealogy and Tradition* (Duckworth).

Macmullen, R.: 1967: *Enemies of the Roman Order* (Cambridge University Press).

——1981: *Paganism in the Roman Empire* (Yale University Press).

Macquarrie, J. 1970: *Principles of Christian Theology* (SCM Press).

——1982: *In Search of Humanity* (SCM Press).

——1987: "Baptism, confirmation, eucharist," in *Signs of Faith, Hope and Love: The Christian Sacraments Today*, J. Greenhalgh and E. Russell (eds) (St Mary's Bourne Street) 57–70.

Mailer, N. 1957: *The White Negro* (City Lights Books).

Malina, B. 1981: The New Testament World: Insights from Cultural Anthropology (Knox/ SCM Press).

——1986: *Christian Origins and Cultural Anthropology: Practical Models for Biblical Interpretation* (Knox 1986).

Malone, P. 1971: *The Film* (Chevalier Press).

——1990: *Movie Christs and Antichrists* (Crossroad; = Parish Ministry 1988).

——1996: "Christ figures and Jesus figures of the 90s," in May, J. R. (ed.) *New Image of Religious Film* (Sheed and Ward).

Maltby, R. 1990: "*The King of Kings* and the Czar of All the Rushes: the Propriety of the Christ Story" *Screen*, 31 (2), 188–213.

——and Craven, R. 1995: *Hollywood Cinema* (Blackwell). Very good general introduction and overview, with a useful chapter on critical approaches.

Mangham, I. L. 1995: "Scripts, Talk and Double Talk" *Management Learning* 26 (4), 493–511.

Marsden, M. T. 1984a: "The Making of *Shane*: A Story for all Media," in James C. Work (ed.) *Shane: The Critical Edition* (University of Nebraska Press), 338–53.

——1984b: "Savior in the Saddle: The Sagebrush Testament," in James C. Work (ed.), op. cit., 393–404.

Marsh, C. 1993: "A Feast of Learning: On Using Film in Theological Education" *British Journal of Theological Education* 5/2 (Winter 1992/93), 33–43.

——1996: "Letting the World be the World" (with a response by Francis Watson) *Reviews in Religion and Theology*, 3, 1996/2, 76–81.

——1997: "Can Anything Good Come Out of Hollywood?: Film as a Challenge to Theological Method," in *Film and Religion* D. Graham (ed.) (St Mungo Press).

Marsh, J. 1952: *The Fulness of Time* (Nisbet).

Marshall, B. D. (ed.) 1990: *Theology and Dialogue: Essays in Conversation with George Lindbeck* (University of Notre Dame Press).

Martin, J. and Ostwalt, C. E. 1994: *Screening the Sacred: Myth, Ritual, and Religion in Popular American Film* (Westview Press). Important collection of essays considering a variety of films from theological, mythological and ideological perspectives. Links with this present work in its desire to attend to popular film. *Psycho, Blood Simple, Ironweed, Platoon, Star Wars, Alien*, and *Rocky* feature amongst the specific films considered.

Martin, T. M. 1981: *Images and the Imageless: a Study in Religious Consciousness and Film* (Bucknell University Press). The first study to treat film and theology from within a framework of the philosophy of religion. Martin argues that humans need stories to make sense of life, and considers the role of filmic stories in the development of religious consciousness.

Martos, J. 1981: *Doors to the Sacred* (SCM Press).

Mathews, J. 1993: review of *Groundhog Day*, in *Newsday* (Feb. 12), 66.

Mathews, T. D. 1994: *Censored* (Chatto & Windus).

May, J. R. 1982: "Visual Story and the Religious Intention of Film," in J. R. May & M. Bird *Religion in Film* (University of Tennessee Press), 23–43.

——(ed.) 1992: *Image and Likeness: Religious Visions in American Film Classics* (Paulist). Comprises 15 detailed studies of films by various authors, including Wall on *2001: A Space Odyssey*, Hurley on *On the Waterfront*, and Apostolos-Cappadona on *Ben-Hur*. Other films covered include *High Noon*, *The Wizard of Oz*, *Casablanca*, and *One Flew Over the Cuckoo's Nest*. The book concludes with shorter treatments of a further 20 films, including *East of Eden*, *Midnight Cowboy*, *Close Encounters of the Third Kind*, and *Hannah and her Sisters*.

——(ed.) 1996 *New Image of Religious Film* (Sheed and Ward).

——and Bird, M. S. (eds) 1982: *Religion in Film* (University of Tennessee Press). Collection of studies in three parts, covering methods, themes and directors. May, Hurley and William Parrill offer a number of contributions. Section III includes short studies of Altman, Bergman, Coppola, Hitchcock and Kubrick, amongst others.

Medved, M. 1992: *Hollywood vs. America. Popular Culture and the War on Traditional Values* (HarperCollins/Zondervan).

Meier, J. P. 1991: *A Marginal Jew: Rethinking the Historical Jesus*: vol.1 (Doubleday).

Metz, C. 1982: *Psychoanalysis and the Cinema: the Imaginary Signifier* (Macmillan).

Milbank, J. 1990: *Theology and Social Theory: Beyond Secular Reason* (Blackwell).

Miles, M. R. 1985: *Image as Insight: Visual Understanding in Western Christianity and Secular Culture* (Beacon). Focuses upon fine art, but argues strongly for a broader vision of how the visual (including the popular visual) and the religious interrelate.

——1995: "Fashioning the Self" *Christian Century* 112 (Mar. 8), 273–5. Deals with Robert Altman's *Ready-to-Wear*.

——1996: *Seeing and Believing: Religion and Values in the Movies* (Beacon). A most useful study, following a cultural studies approach, focusing upon the treatment of religious themes and figures, and on race, gender, sexuality and class in contemporary movies. Like this present work, acknowledges the shift of focus from churches and synagogues to the movie theater as the place where "congregations" meet to consider issues and values. This work is highly critical of some of the values which Hollywood espouses. Deals with 15 films in some detail, including *The Last Temptation of Christ*, *Jesus of Montreal*, *The Mission*, *Romero*, *The Handmaid's Tale*, *The Long Walk Home*, *Thelma and Louise*, *The Piano*, and *Jungle Fever*.

Milne, T. (ed.) 1993: *Time Out Film Guide* 3rd edn. (Penguin Books).

Milton, J. 1990: *The Complete Poetry of John Milton*, revised edn (Anchor).

Mintzberg, H. 1989: *Mintzberg on Management: Inside our Strange World of Organiz-ations* (The Free Press).

Moltmann, J, 1967: *Theology of Hope*, tr. J. W. Leitch (SCM Press).

——1974: *Man* (SPCK).

——1992: *The Spirit of Life* (SCM Press).

Monaco, J. 1981: *How to Read a Film* (Oxford University Press).

——1993: *The Virgin International Encyclopedia of Film* (Virgin).

Montefiore, H. (ed.) 1992: *The Gospel and Contemporary Culture* (Mowbray).

Moore, P. C. 1988: "The Last Temptation of Christ" *Crux* (December), 11–14.

Morgan, G. 1986: *Images of Organization* (Sage).

Morgan, J. 1995: *The Film Researcher's Handbook* (Blueprint).

Muilenburg, J. 1961: "The Biblical View of Time" *Harvard Theological Review* 54, 225–71.

Mulvey, L. 1989: *Visual and Other Pleasures* (Macmillan).

Muraire, A. 1992: "The 'Last Temptation of Christ' and the Scandal surrounding the Scorsese Film in the United States" *Revue française d'études americaines* 52, 187–98.

Musser, C. 1993: "Passions and the passion play: Theatre, film and religion in America,1880–1900" *Film History* 5 (4), 419–56.

Myers, C. 1988: *Binding the Strong Man: A Political Reading of Mark's Story of Jesus* (Orbis).

——et al 1996: *Say to this Mountain: Mark's Story of Discipleship* (Orbis).

Nelmes, J. 1996: *An introduction to Film Studies* (Routledge). A useful general book, with definitions of key terms and case studies.

Nelson, J. W. 1976: *Your God is Alive and Well and Appearing in Popular Culture* (Westminster).

Nelson-Pallmeyer, J. 1992: *Brave New World: Must We Pledge Allegiance?* (Orbis).

Neve, B. 1992: *Film and Politics in America* (Routledge).

Neyrey, J. H. 1990: *Paul in Other Words: A Cultural Reading of His Letters* (Westminster/John Knox).

Niebuhr, H. R. 1951: *Christ and Culture* (Harper and Brothers).

O'Brien, T. 1988: "Hope in the Movies" *Religion and Intellectual Life* 5 (Winter), 109–18. Considers *Thérèse, Chariots of Fire, Mephisto,* and *Amadeus.*

——1990: *The Screening of America* (Crossroad).

O'Neill, J. 1995: *The Poverty of Postmodernism* (Routledge).

Orr, J. 1993: *Cinema and Modernity* (Polity Press).

Ortiz, G. 1994: "Jesus at the Movies: Cinematic Representation of the Christ-Figure" *The Month,* (December), 491–7.

Osborne, G. R. 1991: *The Hermeneutical Spiral: A Comprehensive Introduction to Biblical Interpretation* (Inter-Varsity Press).

Otto, R. 1958: *The Idea of the Holy* (Oxford University Press).

Panichas, A. 1977: *The Simone Weil Reader* (David McKay).

Pannenberg, W. 1985: *Anthropology in Theological Perspective* (T & T Clark).

Peavy, C. D. 1974: "The Secularized Christ in Contemporary Cinema" *Journal of Popular Film and Television* 3/2, 137–55.

Peck, R. A. (ed.) 1993: "Myth, Religious Typology and Recent Cinema" *Christianity and Literature* 42 (Spring), 391–478.

Perkins, V. F. 1972: *Film As Film* (Penguin).

Phelps, G. A. 1979: "The Populist Films of Frank Capra" *Journal of American Studies* 13, 377–92.

Phy, A. S. (ed.) 1985: *The Bible and Popular Culture in America* (Fortress/Scholars Press).

Pickstock, C. 1993: "Liturgy and Language: The Sacred Polis," in P. Bradshaw and B. Spinks (eds) *Liturgy in Dialogue* (SPCK).

Placher, W. 1989: "Postliberal Theology," in D. F. Ford (ed.) *The Modern Theologians Vol.II* (Blackwell), 115–28. A useful introduction within an essential guide to modern and postmodern Christian theologies (now in an expanded one-volume edition).

Plaskow, J. 1980: *Sex, Sin and Grace: Women's Experience and the Theologies of Reinhold Niebuhr and Paul Tillich* (University Press of America).

Poague, L. 1975: *The Cinema of Frank Capra* (Tantivy).

——1994: *Another Frank Capra* (Cambridge University Press).

Poland, L. W. 1988: *The Last Temptation of Hollywood* (Mastermedia International).

Pope, A. 1965: *Collected Poems* (J. M. Dent and Sons).

Preston, R. 1994: *Confusions in Christian Social Ethics* (SCM Press).

Propp, V. 1975: *The Morphology of the Folk Tale* (University of Texas Press).

Pulleine, T. 1988: "Babette's Feast" *Films and Filming* (Feb.), 28–9.

Pursell, C. 1994: *White Heat: People and Technology* (BBC Books).

Pyle, F. 1993: "Making Cyborgs, Making Humans: Of Terminators and Bladerunners," in Collins J., Radner, H. and Preacher Collins, A. *Film Theory Goes to the Movies* (Routledge/American Film Institute).

Rafferty, T. 1992: "Mud" *New Yorker* 67 (December 2), 156–9. Considers *Cape Fear* as Christian allegory.

Rahner, K., SJ 1967: *The Teaching of the Catholic Church as Contained in her Documents* (Alba House).

Ramsey, A. M. 1983: Entry on "glory," in *A Dictionary of Christian Spirituality* G. S. Wakefield (ed.) (SCM Press), 175–6.

Rappoport, A. R. 1987: *Ancient Israel: Myths and Legends* (Mystic Press).

Rasmussen, L. (ed.) 1989: *Reinhold Niebuhr: Theologian of Public Life* (Collins).

Rattray, S. 1985: Entry on "worship," in *Harper's Bible Dictionary* P. J. Achtemeier (ed.) (Harper and Row), 1143–7, esp. 1143–4.

Rhoads D. and Michie, D. 1982: *Mark as Story: An Introduction to the Narrative of a Gospel* (Fortress).

Richardson, A. and Bowden, J. (eds) 1983: *A New Dictionary of Christian Theology* (SCM Press).

Riches, J, (ed.) 1986: *The Analogy of Beauty: The Theology of Hans Urs von Balthasar* (T & T Clark).

Ridler, A. 1942: "Cain," in N. Nicholson (ed.) *Anthology of Religious Verse* (Pelican), 38.

Ritschl, A. B. 1902: *The Christian Doctrine of Justification and Reconciliation* (2nd edn T & T Clark; English tr. of German 3rd edn of 1888).

Romney, J. 1993: Review of *Groundhog Day,* in *New Statesman and Society* (May 7), 34–5.

——1996: "A Basic Instinct to Shock" (interview with Paul Verhoeven on his latest film *Showgirls*) *Guardian* (Jan. 6), 27.

Rose, B. 1977: "It's A Wonderful Life: The Last Stand of the Capra Hero" *Journal of Popular Film* 6, 156–66.

Rosenbaum, J. 1988: "Raging Messiah. The Last Temptation of Christ" *Sight and Sound* 57, 281–2.

Ross, A. 1989: *No Respect: Intellectuals and Popular Culture* (Routledge).

Roth, W. and Thienhaus B. (eds) 1989: *Film und Theologie: Diskussion, Kontroversen, Analysen* (Steinkopf).

Ruether, R. R. 1992: *Gaia and God: An Ecofeminist Theology of Earth Healing* (HarperCollins).

Rushdie, S. 1988: *The Satanic Verses* (Viking Penguin edn 1989).

Russell, W. 1989: *Shirley Valentine and One for the Road* (Methuen).

Russell-Jones, I. 1992: "Cady's Cross and the Cross of Christ" *Journal for Preachers* 15/3, 34–6. Discusses *Cape Fear*.

Sacks, O. 1991: *Awakenings* (Picador).

Salinger, J. D. 1951: *The Catcher in the Rye* (Hamish Hamilton).

Salisbury, M. (ed.) 1995: *Burton on Burton* (Faber & Faber).

Schaefer, J. 1949: *Shane* (Houghton Mifflin).

Schein, H. 1984: "The Olympian Cowboy," in James C. Work (ed.) *Shane: The Critical Edition* (University of Nebraska Press), 405–17.

Schrader, P. 1972: *Transcendental Style in Film: Ozu, Bresson, Dreyer* (University of California Press).

Schweitzer, A. 1954: *The Quest of the Historical Jesus* (SCM Press).

Schweizer, E. 1980: *The Holy Spirit* (Fortress = 1981 SCM Press).

Scorsese, M. 1996: *The Century of Film: A Personal Journey* (Connoisseur Video).

Scott, B. B. 1994: *Hollywood Dreams and Biblical Stories* (Augsburg Fortress). Incorporates treatments of a wide range of films into thematic chapters.

Shelley, M. 1987: *Frankenstein or the Modern Prometheus* (Marshall Cavendish).

Sheppard, D. 1983: *Bias to the Poor* (Hodder & Stoughton).

Shiach, D. 1993: *The Films of Peter Weir* (Letts & Co.).

Shindler, C. 1973: *Hollywood During the Great Depression 1929–1941* (University of Cambridge, unpublished thesis).

Silke, J. R. and Henstell, B. (eds) (undated): *Frank Capra: One Man-One Film*. Discussion no. 3. American Film Institute.

Silverman, K. 1991: "Male Subjectivity and Celestial Suture: It's A Wonderful Life" *Framework* 14, 16–22.

Sims, D., Fineman, S. and Gabriel, Y. 1993: *Organizing and Organizations: An Introduction* (Sage).

Singer, M. 1988: "Portrayals of Christ on Film" *Film Comment*, 24 (5), 44–9.

Smith, P. 1993: *Clint Eastwood: A Cultural Production* (University of Minnesota Press).

Smoodin, E. 1994: *Disney Discourse* (Routledge).

Stacey, J. 1993: *Star Gazing: Hollywood Cinema and Female Spectatorship* (Routledge).

Stack, O. (ed.) 1969: *Pasolini on Pasolini: Interviews with Oswald Stack*. The Cinema One Series, 11 (Thames and Hudson).

Stam, R., Burgoyne, R. and Flitterman-Lewis, S. 1992: *New Vocabularies in Film Semiotics* (Routledge).

Stassen, G. H. et al. 1996: *Authentic Transformation: a New Vision of Christ and Culture* (Abingdon).

Stern, L. 1995: *The Scorsese Connection* (British Film Institute).

Strick, P. 1989: Review of *Shirley Valentine*, in *Monthly Film Bulletin* 56, 345–6.

Strinarti, D. 1995: *An Introduction to Theories of Popular Culture* (Routledge). A well-received guide to the main contemporary, competing theories of popular culture (Frankfurt School, Structuralist, Marxist, Feminist and Postmodernist).

Strug, C. 1995: "Apocalypse Now What? Apocalyptic Themes in Modern Movies" *Word and World* 15 (Spring) 159–65.

Sweet, L. 1991; Review of *Awakenings*, in *Monthly Film Bulletin* 58, 72–3.

Swicord, R. 1995: "Review of L. Francke, *Script Girls: Women Screenwriters in Hollywood*" *Sight and Sound* 5 (2), 36–7.

Swidler, L. et al. 1990: *Death or Dialogue?: From the Age of Monologue to the Age of Dialogue* (SCM Press/Trinity Press International).

Sykes, S. W. 1984: *The Identity of Christianity* (SPCK).

Tarantino, Q. 1994a: *Reservoir Dogs* (Faber & Faber).

——1994b: *Pulp Fiction: Three Stories . . . About One Story . . .* (Faber & Faber).

Taylor, J. R. 1987: Review of *The It's A Wonderful Life Book*, in *Films and Filming* 396, 43–4.

Taylor, M. C. and Saarinen, E. 1994: *Imagologies: Media Philosophy* (Routledge).

Telford, W. R. 1995: "The New Testament in Fiction and Film: A Biblical Scholar's Perspective," in J. G. Davies, G. Harvey and W. Watson (eds)., *Words Remembered, Texts Renewed. Essays in Honour of J. F. A. Sawyer* (Sheffield Academic Press) 360–94.

Thiel, J. 1994: *Nonfoundationalism* (Fortress).

Thiemann, R. 1991: *Constructing a Public Theology: The Church in a Pluralistic Age* (Westminster/ John Knox).

Thiselton, A. 1992: *New Horizons in Hermeneutics* (HarperCollins).

——1995: *Interpreting God and the Postmodern Self* (T & T Clark).

Thomas N. (ed.) 1995: *Readings in World Mission* (Orbis/SPCK).

Thomas, R. S. 1983: "The Kingdom," in *Later Poems: A Selection* (Papermac).

Thompson, B. 1993: Review of *Groundhog Day*, in *Sight and Sound* (May), 50.

Thompson, D. and Christie, I. (eds) 1989: *Scorsese on Scorsese* (Faber).

Thouart, D. 1987: "Film Portrayals of New Testament Figures (Jesus, Judas, Barabbas, Mary, Pontius Pilate)" *Historia* (484), 109–13.

Thurman, J. 1984: *Isak Dinesen: The Life of Karen Blixen* (Penguin).

Tilby, A. 1991: "The Bible and Television," in D. Cohn-Sherbok (ed.) *Using the Bible Today* (Bellew Publishing Company) 38–46.

Tillich, P. 1951: *Systematic Theology* vol.1 (Chicago University Press = SCM Press 1953).

——1957: *Systematic Theology* vol. 2 (Chicago University Press/SCM Press).

——1963: *Systematic Theology* vol. 3 (Chicago University Press = SCM Press 1964).

——1989: *On Art and Architecture* (Crossroad).

Tracy, D. 1981: *The Analogical Imagination* (SCM Press). A difficult, but rewarding, treatment of Christian theology's interaction with its "three publics:" church, academy and society.

Traube, E. G. 1992: *Dreaming Identities: Class, Gender and Generation in 1980's Hollywood Movies* (Westview Press).

Trevelyan, J. 1973: *What the Censor Saw* (Michael Joseph).

Truffaut, F. 1982: *The Films in my Life*, tr. L. Mayhew (Allen Lane).

Turner, G. 1993: *Film as Social Practice* 2nd edn (Routledge). A good general introduction.

Ulanov, A and Ulanov, B. 1975: *Religion and the Unconscious* (Westminster).

——1985: *Prayer as Primary Speech* (SCM Press = John Knox Press 1982).

(United Reformed Church) 1989: *Service Book: The United Reformed Church in the United Kingdom* (Oxford University Press).

Vardy, P. 1987: "The Theology of Star Wars" *Month* 20/1, 14–18.

Vogel, S. 1993: "The Silence of the Lambs" *Stimulus: The New Zealand Journal of Christian Thought and Practice* 1 (Nov.), 18–21.

Walker, G. T. 1975: *Go Placidly Amid the Noise and Haste: Meditations on the "Desiderata"* (Bethany).

Walker, J. (ed.) 1995: *Halliwell's Film Guide* (HarperCollins).

Wall, J. M. 1971: *Church and Cinema: a Way of Viewing Film* (Eerdmans 1971). Based on a distinction between plot-driven "discursive, and artistic "presentational" films, Wall seeks the director's vision of reality as a mode of revelation.

——1985: George Stevens: a Film Journey, *Christian Century* 102 (July 17–24), 684–85.

——1991a: "Confessing Without Repenting" *Christian Century* 108 (Jan. 16), 35–6. Considers *The Godfather Part III, To Sleep With Anger, Dances with Wolves*, and *Alice*.

——1991b: "The Unexpected World of Barton Fink" *Christian Century* 108 (Oct. 2), 868–9.

——1991c: "In the Streets with Martin Scorsese" *Christian Century* 108 (Nov. 20–7), 1083–4.

——1993: "Widening Experience: Seeing Through Film" *Christian Century* 110 (Oct. 20), 1003–4.

Walsh, J. 1996: *Introduction to Contemporary Cinema* (UCL Press).

Ward, K. 1982: *Holding Fast to God* (SPCK).

Warren, M. 1992: *Communications and Cultural Analysis: A Religious View* (Bergin & Garvey).

Warshow, R. 1974: "Movie Chronicle: The Westerner," in Jack Nachbar (ed.) *Focus on the Western* (Prentice-Hall), 45–56.

Watson, F. 1994: *Text, Church and World* (T & T Clark/Eerdmans).

Weiss, M. 1987: *Martin Scorsese: A Guide to References and Resources* (G. K. Hall).

Welker, M. 1994: *God the Spirit* (Fortress).

Wheale, N. (ed.) 1995: *The Postmodern Arts* (Routledge). Contains a useful series of introductory chapters exploring the features of postmodernism with respect to the arts. Includes a chapter by the editor on *Blade Runner*, often regarded as the quintessential postmodern film.

White, J. 1994: "Death of the British Sunday," in *Independent* (Dec. 19), 17.

White, V. 1996: *Paying Attention to People* (SPCK).

Wilkes, K. 1969: *Religion and Technology* (Oxford Religious Education Press).

Willett, M. E. 1991: "Jesus the Subversive: *Jesus of Montreal* and Recent Studies of the Historical Jesus" *Centerquest Adult Resource* VII (July), 13–20.

Williams, D. S. 1986: "The Color Purple: What Was Missed?" *Christianity and Crisis* 46 (July 14), 230–2.

Williams, J. G. 1991: *The Bible, Violence, and the Sacred: Liberation From the Myth of Sanctioned Violence* (Harper San Francisco).

Williams, R. 1987: "The nature of a sacrament," in *Signs of Faith, Hope and Love: The Christian Sacraments Today* J.Greenhalgh and E.Russell (eds) (St Mary's Bourne Street), 32–44.

Williams, T. 1949: *A Street Car Named Desire* with *The Glass Menagerie* (Penguin).

Wink, W. 1980: *Transforming Bible Study* (Abingdon/SCM Press).

Winnert, D. 1993: *"Radio Times" Film and Video Guide* (Hodder & Stoughton).

Wolf, S. 1989: *Martin Scorsese's Film Die letzte Versuchung Christi. Dokumentation/ Analyse von Zuschriften an FBW und FSK* (Filmbewertungsstelle Wiesbaden (FBW); Spitzenorganisation der Filmwirtschaft e.V).

Wolfe, K. 1991: "The Bible and Broadcasting," in D. Cohn-Sherbok (ed.) *Using the Bible Today,* (Bellew Publishing Company), 47–67.

Wollen, T. and Hayward, P. 1993: *Future Visions: New Technologies of the Screen* (British Film Institute).

Wood, M. 1975: *America in the Movies* (Basic Books).

Wood, R. 1976: *Personal Views: Explorations in Film* (Gordon Fraser). A book which bridges a "watershed" in British film theory and includes chapters "In Defence of Art" and on realism and ideology.

——1981: "Ideology, Genre, Auteur" *Film Comment* 13, 46–51.

Wood, R. C. 1994: "The Tears of Things" *Christian Century* 111 (Feb. 23), 200–2. Discusses *Shadowlands*.

Woolf, C. 1987: *Frank Capra: A Guide to References and Resources* (Hall).

Work, J. C. (ed.) 1984: *Shane: The Critical Edition* (University of Nebraska Press).

Wright, M. 1996: "Moses at the Movies: Ninety Years of the Bible and Film" *Modern Believing* 37/1, 46–54.

Wright, W. 1975: *Six Guns and Society: A Structural Study of the Western* (University of California Press).

Ziolkowski, T. 1972: *Fictional Transfigurations of Jesus* (Princeton University Press).

Index of Biblical References

Film Index

General Index